CW00486198

Internationales Jahrbuch des Deutschen Idealismus

International Yearbook of German Idealism

Internationales Jahrbuch des Deutschen Idealismus
International Yearbook of German Idealism

15 · 2017

Psychologie
Psychology

Herausgegeben von/*edited by*
Dina Emundts (Berlin) und/*and* Sally Sedgwick (Boston)

Redaktion/*Associate editors*
Jaroslaw Bledowski und/*and* Anne Mone Sahnwaldt

Begründet von/*founded by*
Karl Ameriks (Notre Dame) und/*and* Jürgen Stolzenberg (Halle/S.)

Fortgeführt von/*continued by*
Fred Rush (Notre Dame), 2008–2014, mit/*with* Jürgen Stolzenberg (Halle/S.)

DE GRUYTER

ISBN 978-3-11-067364-7
e-ISBN (PDF) 978-3-11-067369-2
e-ISBN (EPUB) 978-3-11-067376-0
ISSN 1613-0472

Library of Congress Control Number: 2019948947

Bibliografische Information der Deutschen Nationalbibliothek
Die Deutsche Nationalbibliothek verzeichnet diese Publikation in der Deutschen
Nationalbibliografie; detaillierte bibliografische Daten sind im Internet
über http://dnb.dnb.de abrufbar.

www.degruyter.com

Inhalt

I. Beiträge/Essays

II. Rezensionen/Reviews

III. Anhang/Appendix

Vorwort

Der Band 15 des *Internationalen Jahrbuchs des Deutschen Idealismus* ist dem Thema *Psychologie* gewidmet. Wir freuen uns, dass wir herausragende Autorinnen und Autoren gefunden haben und danken ihnen herzlich für ihre Beiträge. Außerdem danken wir den Rezensenten für ihre Rezensionen. Unser Dank gilt außerdem auch diesmal Jaroslaw Bledowski und Anne Mone Sahnwaldt für die kompetente redaktionelle Betreuung des Bandes.

Band 15 wird der letzte Band des *Internationalen Jahrbuchs des Deutschen Idealismus* sein, da der Verlag aus unterschiedlichen Gründen dessen Erscheinen einstellt. Wir danken an dieser Stelle noch einmal allen, die an der Entwicklung des Jahrbuchs unter unserer Herausgeberschaft seit 2012 maßgeblich beteiligt waren; dazu gehörten Karl Ameriks, Gertrud Grünkorn, Rolf-Peter Horstmann, Fred Rush und Jürgen Stolzenberg. Wir danken außerdem Christoph Schirmer und Serena Pirrotta dafür, dass sie bei allen Schwierigkeiten Ansprechpartner waren und wir trotz aller Differenzen gute Gespräche führen konnten.

Dina Emundts (Berlin) und Sally Sedgwick (Boston)

https://doi.org/10.1515/9783110673692-001

Preface

Volume 15 of the *International Yearbook of German Idealism* is dedicated to the theme of psychology. We are pleased to include papers in the volume from outstanding authors and reviewers, and we thank them for their contributions. Jaroslaw Bledowski and Anne Mone Sahnwaldt were once again indispensable in helping us prepare the volume for publication. We are grateful to them for their reliably adept editorial assistance.

De Gruyter has decided to cease publication of the *Yearbook,* and this will be its final volume. We are indebted to all those who have assisted us in the production of these volumes since we took over as co-editors in 2012. Most especially, we wish to thank Karl Ameriks, Gertrud Grünkorn, Rolf-Peter Horstmann, Fred Rush and Jürgen Stolzenberg for their guidance and support. In recent years, our De Gruyter contacts Christoph Schimer and Serena Pirrotta have been helpful in responding to our queries and in discussing various – and sometimes difficult – publication matters with us. We owe them our thanks as well.

Dina Emundts (Berlin) und Sally Sedgwick (Boston)

https://doi.org/10.1515/9783110673692-002

Einleitung

Das Thema des vorliegenden Bandes ist *Psychologie*. Wir haben dieses Thema gewählt, weil wir den Eindruck haben, dass im Bereich der Klassischen Deutschen Philosophie im Moment viel zur Psychologie geforscht wird und neue Perspektiven erschlossen werden. Dies liegt vielleicht daran, dass die Klassische Deutsche Philosophie Fragen in der Erkenntnistheorie und Metaphysik behandelt, die man heute eher der Psychologie und Philosophie des Geistes zuordnen würde und die in der zeitgenössischen Philosophie viel Interesse hervorrufen. Zu nennen sind hier Fragen zu den Themen Einbildungskraft und Bewusstsein und zur Rolle von Gefühlen und zum Verhältnis von Geist und Körper. Das Interesse an den Theorien der Klassischen Deutschen Philosophie im Zusammenhang mit derartigen Fragen und Themen hat möglicherweise auch noch andere Gründe. So steht man in der gegenwärtigen Philosophie Vermögenstheorien wieder aufgeschlossener gegenüber als dies lange der Fall war. Dies befördert erfreulicherweise auch eine konstruktivere Auseinandersetzung mit Kants Psychologie der Vermögen. Weiterhin gründet das Interesse an der Psychologie dieser Zeit sicherlich darin, dass sich aufgrund der auf allgemeine Strukturen ausgerichteten Erkenntnistheorien immer wieder aktuell die Frage stellt, wie das Individuum oder der „subjektive Geist" und also auch wie psychologische und anthropologische Faktoren in Erkenntniskonzeptionen berücksichtigt sind und werden können.

' Das Spektrum dieses Bandes ist trotz der Zentrierung auf das Thema Psychologie breit angelegt, denn die Aufsätze sind mit einem je eigenen Zugang zu dem Thema ausgestattet. In diesem Band versammeln sich Beiträge, die die psychologischen Theorien eines Philosophen oder eines Werkes herausgearbeitet haben, solche, die eher einem besonderen Aspekt der Psychologie eines Philosophen nachgehen, und Beiträge, die sich mit der Psychologiekonzeption in der Zeit des Deutschen Idealismus, also von verschiedenen Philosophen oder in der größeren Entwicklungslinie, beschäftigen.

Unsere Erwartungen an die Aktualität des Themas haben die versammelten Aufsätze dabei auf das beste und in vielfältiger Weise bestätigt. So wird in diesem Band aus verschiedenen Richtungen thematisiert, welche Rolle der Körper spielt, wie Leidenschaften und Gefühle einzuordnen und inwiefern die jeweiligen Theorien naturalistisch sind. Zudem tritt Patricia Kitcher dafür ein, die Vermögenspsychologie bei Kant ernst zu nehmen. Gary Hatfield gelingt es, bei Kant eine Bedeutung von „subjektiv" aufzuzeigen, die für das Begriffsverständnis und für die Entwicklung der Psychologie im neunzehnten Jahrhundert von großer Bedeutung ist. Sowohl Johannes-Georg Schülein als auch Jeffrey Reid suchen in

https://doi.org/10.1515/9783110673692-003

der Klassischen Deutschen Philosophie Verbindungen zu Freud bzw. der Psychoanalyse. Dies sind nur Beispiele, die durch alle Beiträge dieses Bandes ergänzt werden können. Um dies in einer Gesamtübersicht darstellen zu können, werden die Aufsätze im Folgenden kurz vorgestellt.

Die Sammlung wird durch einen Aufsatz von Dieter Sturma eröffnet. Dieser eignet sich als Auftakt besonders gut, da er es sich zur Aufgabe macht, eine Darstellung und Einschätzung des Verhältnisses der Psychologie von Kant, Fichte, Schelling und Hegel zur gegenwärtigen Psychologie zu geben. Sturma beginnt mit der Feststellung, dass die gegenwärtige Psychologie die Beiträge der Deutschen Idealisten zum Selbst nicht wirklich zur Kenntnis nehme und daher deren Potential auch nicht ausschöpfen könne. Er lenkt unsere Aufmerksamkeit dann auf für das Thema wichtige Gemeinsamkeiten von Fichte, Schelling und Hegel mit Kant: Diese Philosophen stimmen mit Kants Kritik an der rationalen Psychologie überein, dass viele von deren Behauptungen unwissenschaftlich sind. Sie stimmen aber mit Kant auch darin überein, dass man die rationale Psychologie nicht durch einen reduktiven Naturalismus überwinden sollte. Bei Fichte wird Kants „Ich denke" eine fundamentale praktische Tätigkeit, die unser Bewusstsein und Leben ermöglicht. Für Schelling sind rationale Strukturen in der Natur realisiert, und Natur ist zugleich wiederum die Bedingung für Geist; Selbstbewusstsein hat selbst eine Naturgeschichte. Auch Hegel denkt die Seele als natürlich determiniert, aber nicht als ganz aus Natur entstehend. Wie Sturma zeigen kann, stellt Hegel hier fundamentale Fragen zum Verhältnis von Geist und Natur. Er führt damit auf für heutige Diskussionen relevante Weise vor Augen, wie man die Seele naturalistisch bestimmen kann, ohne reduktionistisch sein zu müssen.

Zu Kant sind drei Aufsätze versammelt. Es geht in ihnen erstens um das Verständnis von Kants Vermögenspsychologie, zweitens um die Möglichkeit empirischer Psychologie und drittens um Fragen zur Entwicklung des Begriffs des Subjektiven, der für die Psychologie eine zentrale Rolle spielt.

Der Beitrag von Patricia Kitcher „Kant's Moral Psychology in the Fact of Reason" beschäftigt sich mit der Bedeutung der Vermögenspsychologie für Kants Moralphilosophie. Kitcher argumentiert gegen drei Gründe, die gängiger Weise dafür angeführt werden, dass bei Kant Vermögenspsychologie keine große Rolle spielen könne. Erstens nehmen einige Forscherinnen und Forscher, die die Vermögenstheorie zurückweisen, an, dass Kant behaupten muss, dass die psychologische Erklärung von freien Handlungen nicht möglich sei, weil er behauptet, dass Freiheit nicht erklärbar sei. Zweitens gibt es andere, die hervorheben, dass Kants praktischer Beweis der Realität der Freiheit darauf beruhe, dass man den Standpunkt der ersten und nicht der dritten Person einnehme und dass dieser Beweis auf diese Weise nicht zu einer wirklich wissenschaftlichen Psychologie gehören könne. Der dritte Grund hängt damit zusammen, dass Kant versichert, dass seine Untersuchungen der Moral unabhängig von denen zur menschlichen Natur erfolgen. Demgegenüber bestreitet Kitcher, dass man durch solche Überlegungen begründen könne, dass Kant ein Gegner der Vermögenspsychologie sei. Sie zeigt vielmehr auf, wie die Vermögenspsychologie für die Möglichkeit der Moralität verantwortlich ist. Auf diese Weise gibt sie uns auch ein neues Verständnis von Kants praktischem Beweis der realen Möglichkeit der Moralität.

Der Fokus des Beitrags von Katharina Kraus „Rethinking the Relationship between Empirical Psychology and Transcendental Philosophy in Kant" liegt auf Kants empirischer Psychologie und ihrem Verhältnis zur Transzendentalphilosophie. Kraus beschäftigt sich besonders mit der Unterscheidung zwischen innerem Sinn und empirischem Wissen von unseren inneren Erfahrungen. Sie buchstabiert aus, was die Rolle der Begriffe sowie der Grundsätze und Ideen ist, um empirisches Wissen und empirische Psychologie zu ermöglichen. Ihr zufolge ist Kant zu der Behauptung verpflichtet, dass wir weder empirisches Wissen von uns selbst noch wissenschaftliche empirische Psychologie haben könnten, wenn wir nicht die Idee der Seele als einen apriorischen Begriff der reinen Vernunft hätten. Die Möglichkeit der Psychologie wird also durch den Appendix der Dialektik der *Kritik der reinen Vernunft* geklärt. So gibt Kraus auch ein einschlägiges Beispiel dafür, dass den Vernunftideen für unser Wissen eine zentrale Rolle zukommt.

Gary Hatfield setzt sich in seinem Aufsatz „Modern Meanings of Subjectivity: Philosophical, Psychological, Physiological" mit den Bedeutungen von „Objektivität" und „Subjektivität" in ihrem Wandel auseinander. Er geht hierbei von den prominenten Thesen aus, die Lorraine Daston und Peter Galison entwickelt haben. Eine dieser Thesen lautet, dass im neunzehnten Jahrhundert der Begriff „Subjektivität" die Bedeutung erhalte, dass subjektiv ist, was für jedes Subjekt anders sein könne. Hatfield setzt dieser These und der entsprechenden Darstellung der Geschichte eine überzeugende Alternative entgegen. Hierfür zeigt er zunächst, dass unter *Subjektivität* nicht nur dies verstanden wurde, sondern zeitgleich und sogar fundierender war die Bedeutung von *subjektabhängig*, was gleichzeitig zulässt, dass das Subjektive zwischen Individuen nicht variiert, sondern konstant ist. Dies wird mit Blick auf Descartes und Locke, vor allem aber bei Kant gründlich belegt. Kant kennt zwei Bedeutungen von *subjektiv*: erstens die, bei der angenommen wird, dass für jedes Subjekt das Subjektive verschieden ist; zweitens die, bei der angenommen wird, dass die Subjekte das Subjektive teilen. Weiterhin zeigt Hatfield, dass diese Differenzierung des Begriffs auch von späteren Philosophen aufgenommen wurde. Die letzten beiden Teile widmen sich der Entwicklung der Begriffe *subjektiv* und *objektiv* bei Goethe auf der einen und in der Psychologie des neunzehnten Jahrhunderts auf der anderen Seite.

Einem Thema der Psychologie in der Philosophie Fichtes geht der Beitrag von Manja Kisner nach. Fichte spielt aber ferner auch in den Texten von Reid und Sturma eine wichtige Rolle. Kisner untersucht in „Fichte's Moral Psychology of Drives and Feelings and its Influence on Schopenhauer's Metaphysics of the Will" den Einfluss von Fichte auf Schopenhauer in Hinblick auf die jeweilige Moralpsychologie. Sie analysiert dafür Fichtes *System der Sittenlehre* und Schopenhauers *Welt als Wille und Vorstellung*. Der erste Teil des Aufsatzes widmet sich der Konzeption des unmittelbaren Wissens von uns selbst. Obwohl Fichte und Schopenhauer sowohl Objektwissen als auch eine besondere Art des „Wissen von sich" kennen, unterscheiden sich die beiden Konzeptionen sehr voneinander. Dies insbesondere dadurch, dass Schopenhauer dem Leib eine andere Rolle zuschreibt als Fichte. Im zweiten Teil des Aufsatzes werden die jeweiligen Konzeptionen von Gefühlen einer genaueren Analyse unterzogen. Hier spielt jetzt auch für Fichte der Leib eine besondere Rolle, denn die erste Erfahrung des Selbstwissens ist durch leibliche Erfahrung von Gefühlen gegeben. Auch bei Schopenhauer spielen Gefühle eine bedeutende Rolle, die der bei Fichte durchaus ähnlich ist. Für beide sind diese Gefühle Gefühle der Begrenzung, die die Bedingungen dafür bilden, dass dieser Begrenzung entkommen werden kann. Deutlich wird durch Kisners Ausführungen auch, dass beide Philosophen psychologische Konzepte wie Gefühle und Leibempfindung in ihre Philosophie systematisch integrieren.

Zu Hegel und Psychologie sind in diesem Band vier Beiträge zu finden. Der Aufsatz von Willem deVries spürt naturalistische Tendenzen bei Hegel auf. Die zwei folgenden Beiträge von Andreja Novakovic und Julia Peters beschäftigen sich mit Themen, die man klassischer Weise der Philosophie der Psychologie und Anthropologie zuordnen würde: mit dem Thema der Leidenschaften und ihrer Beherrschung und mit dem Thema der Rolle des Körpers. Im Beitrag von Georg Sans geht es um die Rolle der Psychologie für Hegels Religionsphilosophie.

Willem deVries arbeitet in „The Space of Intelligence" den interessanten Tatbestand heraus, dass Hegel oft räumliche Metaphern nutzt, um Phänomene des Geistigen zu charakterisieren. Dies ist, so deVries, kommentierungsbedürftig, weil für Hegel Objekte im Raum nur äußerlich und unwesentlich verbunden sind; Raum ist frei von Subjektivität und Geist. DeVries stellt dann heraus, dass Hegel räumliche Metaphern besonders dann benutzt, wenn es darum geht, das mechanische Gedächtnis zu beschreiben. Wie der Raum, so ist mechanisches Gedächtnis durch eine Art „gleichgültiger Leere" ausgezeichnet. Durch diese wird Denken und Bedeutung aber ermöglicht. Wie wir äußere Objekte und ihre kausalen Beziehungen im Raum lokalisieren können, so können wir auch nur mithilfe des natürlichen mechanischen Gedächtnisses höhere Formen von Subjektivität oder Geistigkeit erreichen. DeVries möchte durch diese originellen

Beobachtungen und Deutungen aufzeigen, dass sich in Hegels Philosophie des Geistes deutlich naturalistische Gedankengänge finden lassen.

Andreja Novakovic beschäftigt sich in ihrem Beitrag „Hegel on Passion in History" mit der Frage, was bei Hegel „Leidenschaft" bedeutet und welche Rolle sie in Hegels Philosophie der Geschichte spielt. Diese Frage führt Novakovic zu psychologischen Fragen: Sie entwickelt Hegels Auffassung von der Struktur unserer Motivationen und von unserem Bezug zu Gegenständen, wenn wir Interesse am Gegenstand haben (was Hegel mit dem Ausdruck „die Sache" ausdrückt). Auf dieser Grundlage kann Novakovic die Bedeutung von Leidenschaft klären, nach der ihr zufolge ein besonderes Verhältnis von Allgemeinem und Partikulärem gemeint ist. In diesem Sinne ist, so die These Novakovics, Hegels Behauptung zu verstehen, dass Leidenschaft ein Ausdruck der Vernunft ist. Novakovic kann außerdem vor diesem Hintergrund sehr gut erhellen, was Hegels Verständnis historischer Individuen ist. Auf diese Weise kann der Beitrag auch zeigen, dass psychologische Fragen zur Klärung der Geschichtsphilosophie aufschlussreich sind.

Julia Peters widmet sich dem Thema des Körpers bei Hegel. Sie argumentiert in ihrem Aufsatz „Hegel and Goethe on the Symbolism of Color" dafür, dass der Körper einer Person für Hegel viel mehr ist als ein Instrument, das von der Person (oder anderen) benutzt werden kann. Unsere Beziehung zu unserem Körper ist, so Hegel nach Peters, viel inniger als das. Der Körper ist nämlich die unmittelbare Existenz des Ichs und der Freiheit. Peters expliziert ihre Thesen zum Verhältnis von Personen zu ihrem Körper bei Hegel durch eine Interpretation von Hegels Thesen zur Sinnlichkeit, genauer zur visuellen Sinnlichkeit. Da Hegel in dieser Auffassung maßgeblich von Goethe beeinflusst war, behandelt Peters hier neben Hegel auch Goethe. Die These lautet, dass wir in der visuellen Sinnlichkeit ein Beispiel dafür sehen können, wie unser Körper Zustände unserer Seele konstituiert. Unsere Körper bestimmen unsere Sinne, und dabei bewirken sie den Inhalt unserer Empfindungen und also auch den Inhalt unserer mentalen Zustände. In der Sinnlichkeit gibt es nach Peters daher das, was man als leibliche Form des Geistes bezeichnen kann, und man kann visuelle Sinnlichkeit nach Peters sogar als eine Form leiblichen Selbstbewusstseins ansehen.

Georg Sans konzentriert sich in seinem Beitrag „Hegels Psychologie der Religion" auf die Frage, inwiefern für das Verständnis von Hegels Religionsphilosophie seine Auffassung von Psychologie in den Blick genommen werden sollte. Auf diese Weise zeigt er auf, welche Bedeutung der Psychologie bei Hegel für andere Bereiche zukommt. Zunächst diskutiert er die Frage, welche Idee der Gliederung der Religionsphilosophie zugrunde liegt, und zeigt, dass man bei der Beantwortung dieser Frage die Philosophie des subjektiven Geistes berücksichtigen muss. Im Weiteren werden die einzelnen Teile der Religionsphilosophie

einer genauen Betrachtung unterzogen. Zunächst geht es um den Vorstellungscharakter der Religion, dann um das religiöse Gefühl und schließlich um den
Kultus. In diesem Zusammenhang wird besonders herausgestellt, dass es innerhalb der Religionsphilosophie auch einen praktischen Teil gibt.

Mit dem Thema Psychologie bei Schelling beschäftigen sich Johannes-Georg
Schülein und Daniel Whistler. Johannes-Georg Schülein entwickelt in seinem
Aufsatz „„Der Geist ist nicht das Höchste'. Schellings Psychologie in den *Stuttgarter Privatvorlesungen* von 1810" Schellings Theorie menschlicher Psyche in
den Stuttgarter Privatvorlesungen. Diese Theorie zeichnet sich dadurch aus, dass
Schelling in ihr sowohl die These der Fragilität der Rationalität vertritt als auch
meint, der Mensch könne in seiner Psyche und Rationalität durch Gott stabili-
siert werden. Schülein deckt zunächst einige von Schellings metaphysischen
Grundthesen zur Struktur der Wirklichkeit auf, um aus ihnen Grundprinzipien
für Schellings Psychologie zu gewinnen. Die Psychologie wird dann in ihren
Grundzügen entwickelt und hierbei werden Schellings Überlegungen zu Pathologien und Gesundheit einbezogen. Der immer wieder gezogene Vergleich zu
Freud dient unter anderem der Herausarbeitung des Charakters von Schellings
Konzeption, die einerseits das Irrationale einbezieht und dadurch für die Moderne anschlussfähig ist, dies aber andererseits in einer wenig „modernen" Weise
macht, nämlich so, dass sie eine Überwindung des Irrationalen durch das Göttliche denkt. Anschließend nimmt Schülein seine Behauptung, dass Schellings
Thesen voraussetzen, dass wir nur durch ein göttliches Prinzip gesund sein
können, zum Anlass für einen Ausblick auf einen erhellenden Vergleich mit Hegels Konzeption des Geistes und dessen Überlegungen zu Pathologien und Gesundheit.

Daniel Whistler analysiert in „Schelling's Politics of Sympathy: Reflections
on *Clara* and Related Texts" die Bedeutung der psychologischen Konzeption der
Sympathie in einigen von Schellings Schriften des Zeitraums 1804–1815. Er kann
erhellend zeigen, dass für Schellings Philosophie dieser Zeit Sympathie insgesamt
von großer Bedeutung ist. Weiterhin wird deutlich, dass Schelling diesen Sym-
pathiegedanken mit einer populistischen Auffassung von Philosophie verbindet.
Philosophie ist damit gerade kein Gegenstand von Bildung, sondern Ausdruck
einer gemeinsamen Tätigkeit, in der man sympathetisch miteinander verbunden
ist. Whistler setzt dieser Idee eines gemeinsamen Philosophierens kontrastierend
die Kantische Idee der Philosophie als einem Medium trockener Prosa entgegen.

Der den Band abschließende Beitrag von Jeffrey Reid schlägt die Brücke zur
Frühromantik und zur weiteren Entwicklung der Psychologie im neunzehnten
und zwanzigsten Jahrhundert. Reid wendet sich in seiner Abhandlung „Friedrich
Schlegel and Romantic Psychology: The Fragmentary Self as Ironic System – 'By
their fruits ye shall know them'" der Rolle der Psychologie bei Schlegel zu. Zu-

nächst kontrastiert er die mechanische und materialistische Psychologie der Aufklärung mit der der deutschen Romantik, welche Geist als etwas aufgefasst hat, das essentiell intersubjektiv, selbst-schöpfend und selbst-setzend ist. Er beschäftigt sich dann intensiv mit Schlegels Texten aus der Athenaeum-Periode. Diese dienen hier als ein Beispiel für die Psychologie der Romantik. Wir können nach Reid den Charakter von Schlegels Psychologie und deren zentralen Begriffen wie *Witz* und *Ironie* nur verstehen, wenn wir den Einfluss von Fichtes Konzept der Subjektivität und den der Naturwissenschaften des achtzehnten Jahrhunderts berücksichtigen. Besonders wichtig ist hier die Entwicklung des Galvanismus in der Chemie und des Vitalismus in der Medizin. Am Ende stellt Reid die Verbindung zur modernen Psychoanalyse her, zu der die Romantische Psychologie hingeführt habe. Damit endet auch dieser Beitrag mit der These, dass die nachkantische Philosophie eine Vorbereitung oder Einleitung der weiteren Entwicklung der Psychologie im neunzehnten und zwanzigsten Jahrhundert darstellt.

Introduction

The theme of volume 15 of the *Yearbook* is psychology. We chose this topic, because it is our impression that much exciting work is currently being done in this area by scholars of German idealism. It now seems to be widely appreciated that classical German philosophy was preoccupied with the kind of problems in epistemology and metaphysics that we would today classify as belonging to the philosophy of psychology or mind (*Geist*), problems that are stimulating much exciting contemporary discussion. It is increasingly recognized that the German idealists sought answers to questions about the nature of the imagination and consciousness, the philosophical significance of feelings, and the relation between mind and body. But the current interest of scholars of classical German philosophy in these and related matters may have further explanations, as well. In general, contemporary philosophy is exhibiting greater openness to discussions of the various faculties than has long been the case. Fortunately, this has awakened constructive reconsideration, for instance, of Kant's psychology of the faculties. The present interest of scholars of German idealism in the area of psychology may also be traced to a curiosity about how psychological and anthropological factors pertaining to the individual subject (or "subjective spirit") are and can be accommodated within our theories of knowledge.

Psychology is the central theme of this volume, but we interpret that theme broadly and have commissioned papers that address a wide range of topics from various perspectives and points of departure. Some of the essays focus on the psychological assumptions of a single philosopher or single work; others cast their net more widely and look for patterns in approaches to psychology in the era of German idealism in general.

The papers collected here confirm our belief in the contemporary relevance of our theme, and they do so in diverse and compelling ways. Some of our authors explore perspectives on the implications, for psychology, of the body; others consider questions about how we should best classify passions and feelings; others ask whether a particular psychological theory should or should not be considered "naturalist". Patricia Kitcher urges that, even today, Kant's faculty psychology deserves to be taken seriously. Gary Hatfield draws attention to the tremendous importance of the Kantian conception of the "subjective" for the development of nineteenth century psychology. Both Johannes-Georg Schülein and Jeffrey Reid look for connections between classical German philosophy and Freud (or psychoanalysis). These are just a few examples of the breadth of topics covered in this volume. In what follows, we offer brief synopses of each of the twelve papers.

https://doi.org/10.1515/9783110673692-004

Our collection opens with an essay by Dieter Sturma who gives us an informative overview of the psychologies of Kant, Fichte, Schelling and Hegel, and considers the relevance of their views for contemporary approaches to psychology. In "Philosophy of Psychology in German Idealism", Sturma contends that contemporary philosophy of mind could benefit from a better appreciation of the contributions of the German idealists, and he highlights some of those contributions in his essay. We learn from Sturma that Fichte, Schelling and Hegel endorse Kant's skeptical view of the unscientific claims of speculative rational psychology. They follow Kant, in addition, in not trading rational psychology for reductive naturalism or positivism. On Sturma's representation, Fichte transforms the Kantian logical subject or "I think" into the fundamentally practical activity that makes possible our consciousness and even our life. In the case of Schelling, rational structures are present in nature itself, even though nature is at the same time a condition of mind and even though self-consciousness has a natural history. For Hegel, the soul is naturally determined but does not wholly arise out of nature. Sturma furthermore suggests that Hegel's non-eliminativist approach has much to offer contemporary philosophy of mind.

We have included three essays on Kant. The first sets out to illuminate the nature of Kant's faculty psychology; the second concerns Kant's account of the possibility of empirical psychology; the third poses questions about the development of a concept that is of central importance for psychology, namely that of the subjective.

In "Kant's Moral Psychology in the Fact of Reason", Patricia Kitcher challenges three reasons commonly given for supposing that faculty psychology plays no significant role in Kant's view of morality. First, some suppose that since Kant insists that our freedom is inexplicable, he must also be committed to the thesis that a psychological explanation of free action is impossible. Second, others point out that since Kant's practical proof of the reality of freedom depends upon adopting a first-person rather than a third-person perspective, his proof cannot belong to a properly scientific psychology. The third objection is a response to Kant's insistence that his moral philosophy is independent from a study of human nature. In response to these objections, Kitcher clarifies the significance of Kant's faculty psychology for his moral philosophy. She argues that his faculty psychology is central to his effort to establish the very possibility of morality, and she gives us a novel interpretation of Kant's practical demonstration of the real possibility of morality.

The focus of Katharina Kraus's essay is Kant's empirical psychology (as laid out primarily in his *Anthropology*) and its relation to his transcendental philosophy. In "Rethinking the Relationship between Empirical Psychology and Transcendental Philosophy in Kant", Kraus considers the Kantian distinction between inner sense and the empirical cognition of our inner experiences. She lays out Kant's arguments for the role of concepts of the understanding as well as principles and ideas of reason in making empirical cognition and empirical psychology possible. On her reading, Kant is committed to the assumption that we would have neither empirical cognition of ourselves nor a science of empirical psychology without an *a priori* concept of pure reason, namely the idea of the soul. Kraus explains Kant's account of the possibility of psychology by relying on the Appendix to the Dialectic in his first *Critique*. She urges us to appreciate the role Kant assigns ideas of reason as necessary conditions of our knowledge.

In his essay "Modern Meanings of Subjectivity: Philosophical, Psychological, Physiological", Gary Hatfield challenges the history of the concepts "objectivity" and "subjectivity" recently defended by Lorraine Daston und Peter Galison. Hatfield charges that the latter are mistaken in maintaining that the concept "subjectivity" in the nineteenth century was invariably associated with traits that distinguish subjects from one another. Hatfield rests his alternative interpretation on texts of Descartes, Locke and especially Kant. He points out that, for Kant, "subjectivity" can be used to imply variability among subjects, but it can also be associated with traits that all subjects necessarily possess. According to Hatfield, this latter Kantian conception of subjectivity gets taken up by later philosophers. In the final sections of his paper, Hatfield explores developments in the concepts of subject and object in Goethe and in nineteenth century psychology.

With Manja Kisner's paper, we turn to the topic of psychology in Fichte's philosophy. (Fichte features prominently in the contributions of Reid und Sturma as well.) In "Fichte's Moral Psychology of Drives and Feelings and its Influence on Schopenhauer's Metaphysics of the Will", Kisner examines the impact of Fichte's psychology (in his *System of Ethics*) on Schopenhauer's moral psychology in *The World as Will and Representation*. She dedicates the first part of her essay to the conception of immediate knowledge. Although Fichte and Schopenhauer both distinguish an immediate knowledge of self from our knowledge of objects, they characterize this distinction differently. They differ, for example, in the precise role they assign the body. In the second part of her paper, Kisner subjects their respective conceptions of human feeling to careful analysis. We learn about the special role Fichte associates with the body, since in his view our first experience of self-knowledge is given through the bodily experience of feelings. Kisner points out that feelings have an important role to play in Schopenhauer's psychology as well. For both philosophers, feeling is a limitation or determination of ourselves, and it is through feeling that we experience our limitations – our finitude. It is through feeling, as well, that we become aware of our drive to overcome limitation. In Kisner's view, both philosophers thus systematically integrate psychological concepts into their philosophies, such as the concepts of feeling and bodily sensation.

Four of our authors direct their attention to Hegel's psychology. Willem DeVries detects naturalistic tendencies in Hegel's psychology. Andreja Novakovic und Julia Peters consider themes in Hegel that classically belong to the philosophy of psychology and anthropology, themes such as the role of the passions and our mastery of them, and the psychological effects of our bodies. The essay by Georg Sans examines the role of psychology in Hegel's philosophy of religion.

In "The Space of Intelligence", Willem deVries highlights the fact that Hegel often uses spatial metaphors to describe mind or Spirit. As deVries points out, this is odd given that Hegel holds that objects in space are related purely contingently and externally, and that space is devoid of subjectivity or Spirit. De Vries notes that Hegel uses spatial metaphors to describe mechanical memory in particular. Mechanical memory is a means by which the production of thought and meaning are possible, and it is like space in that it can also be described as in some respect an indifferent emptiness. Just as we can only locate outer objects and their causal connections in nature's empty space, so we can only achieve higher forms of subjectivity or Spirit with the help of our natural capacity for mechanical memory. A larger aim of deVries's essay is to draw our attention to "deeply naturalistic threads" in Hegel's philosophy.

Andreja Novakovic considers the meaning of passion in Hegel and its role in his philosophy of history. In "Hegel on Passion in History", she highlights some of Hegel's central psychological commitments, for example, his view of the structure of our motivations and of our relation to the objects in which we take a special interest (when we concern ourselves with what he refers to as the "matter at hand" [*die Sache*]). Novakovic clarifies the meaning of passion in Hegel, which on her reading implies a particular relationship between the universal and the particular. She furthermore defends the thesis that passion for Hegel is an expression of reason. She furthermore uses her account of Hegelian passion to illuminate his account of the historical individual. In doing so, she demonstrates how Hegel's psychology can also help us better understand his philosophy of history.

Julia Peters explores the theme of the body in Hegel. In her paper "Hegel and Goethe on the Symbolism of Color", she suggests that Hegel considers a person's body to be more than an instrument for the use of that person or other persons. According to Peters, Hegel wants to convince us that the relation between our bodies and our persons is more intimate than that. A person's body, on Hegel's account, is the immediate existence of the 'I' and of freedom. Peters suggests that we can discover Hegel's argument for the intimate connection between our bodies and our freedom in his treatment of the nature of sensation. In sensation, we encounter what Peters describes as a bodily form of Spirit. Her discussion focusses, in particular, on Hegel's theory of visual sensation (heavily influenced by Goethe). It is her thesis that Hegel considered visual sensation to itself be a form of bodily self-consciousness. Our bodies determine our sensations; in doing so, they affect the content of our sensations and thus also the content of our mental states. We can therefore discover in Hegel's account of sensation an example of how our bodies partly constitute the state of our souls.

In his paper "Hegel's Psychology of Religion", Georg Sans considers the relevance of Hegel's psychology for our understanding of his philosophy of religion. Sans sets out to thereby demonstrate the importance of Hegel's psychology for other parts of the Hegelian philosophical system. He begins with an inquiry into the idea of structure that serves as the basis of Hegel's philosophy of religion, and argues that we can only answer this question if we take Hegel's philosophy of subjective spirit into consideration. Sans furthermore takes a close look at the individual parts of Hegel's philosophy of religion. He considers Hegel's treatment of the representational resources and content of religion, the role of religious feeling, and finally the phenomenon of the cult. In this connection, Sans places particular emphasis on the practical part of Hegel's philosophy of religion.

Schelling's psychology is the focus of the contributions of Johannes-Georg Schülein and Daniel Whistler. In his paper "'Der Geist ist nicht das Höchste'. Schellings Psychologie in den *Stuttgarter Privatvorlesungen* von 1810", Schülein considers the theory of the human psyche that Schelling spells out in these lectures. Schülein suggests that Schelling defends a thesis about the fragility of rationality in the lectures, and implies as well that a human being achieves psychic stability and well-being only through God. Schülein exposes some of Schelling's basic metaphysical assumptions about the structure of reality in order to establish that these principles lie at the basis of Schelling's psychology. He specifies features of Schelling's psychology and draws out the way in Schelling's reflections on pathology and health are integral to it. Schülein's frequent comparisons of Schelling to Freud allow him to highlight certain features of the Schellingian position. It is a position that, on the one hand, incorporates reference to the irrational (and thus builds a bridge to modernity), and on the other is perhaps somewhat less modern in that it conceives of the overcoming of the irrational as possible through God.

Daniel Whistler's contribution, "Schelling's Politics of Sympathy: Reflections on *Clara* and Related Texts", offers an analysis of the meaning of the psychological conception of sympathy in some of Schelling's writings from 1804–1815. Whistler illuminates the way in which sympathy is of great significance for Schelling's philosophy during this period. Whistler furthermore proposes that Schelling associates his own conception of sympathy with a popular conception of philosophy. Schelling considers philosophy to be not so much an object of education as an expression of a common activity, an activity in which persons are sympathetically united. Whistler contrasts this idea of a common philosophizing with the Kantian idea of philosophy as a medium for dry prose.

The final contribution of this volume forges a bridge to early Romanticism and the further development of psychology in the nineteenth and twentieth centuries. In "Friedrich Schlegel and Romantic Psychology: The Fragmentary Self as Ironic System – 'By their fruits ye shall know them'", Jeffrey Reid gives us a discussion of the psychology of Friedrich Schlegel. Reid contrasts the mechanical and materialistic psychology of the Enlightenment with that of German Romanticism, which on his account considered mind or spirit to be essentially intersubjective and self-creative or self-positing. Reid is especially concerned to suggest that the literary fragments of Schlegel's *Athenaeum* period writings (1797– 1800) are paradigmatic expressions of Romantic psychology. He argues, in addition, that we can only properly understand the nature of Schlegel's psychology and the role he assigns to concepts such as wit (*Witz*) and irony (*Ironie*), if we appreciate the influence on his thinking both of Fichte's approach to subjectivity, and of eighteenth century scientific developments such as galvanism in chemistry and vitalism in medicine. Reid urges us to acknowledge that Romantic psychology "opened the door" to modern psychoanalysis. He concludes his essay with the proposal that post-Kantian philosophy should be thought of as introducing or preparing the way for the further development of psychology in the nineteen and twentieth centuries.

I. Beiträge/Essays

Dieter Sturma
Philosophy of Psychology in German Idealism

Abstract. *The relationship of German Idealism to psychology is complicated. At the end of the eighteenth century there is not yet any scientific discipline capable of filling the conceptual space opened up by Kant's criticism of traditional psychology. The main current of German Idealism is characterized by a systematic approach that concedes to sub-disciplines at most provisory significance. Accordingly, it answers questions about consciousness and self-consciousness of persons only on the basis of the overarching concepts of nature, spirit, or society.*

Das Verhältnis des deutschen Idealismus zur Psychologie ist kompliziert. Im Ausgang des 18. Jahrhunderts gibt es noch keine psychologische Disziplin, die den konzeptionellen Raum hätte besetzen können, der durch Kants grundsätzliche Kritik an der traditionellen Psychologie entstanden ist. Die Hauptströmung des deutschen Idealismus kennzeichnet ein systematischer Ansatz, der disziplinären Aufteilungen allenfalls provisorische Bedeutung einräumt. Fragen nach Bewusstsein und Selbstbewusstsein von Personen werden entsprechend auf der Grundlage umfassender Bestimmungen wie Geist, Natur oder Gesellschaft beantwortet.

1 Introduction: Philosophy of Psychology and German Idealism

Since its earliest beginnings, philosophy has been occupied with the internal landscape of the human life-form, albeit without explicitly using the title "psychology." Yet, historically speaking, the philosophy of mind—including the modern philosophy of psychology—is and has always been a system of ruptures. There are almost no coherent semantic or methodological transitions between the identifiable epochs. Traditional philosophy of mind has become particularly obscured in the main currents of modern philosophy of psychology, which draws primarily on the philosophy of language and science. This is perhaps not least a consequence of the fact that in methodological terms the twentieth century is the age of eliminative reductionism whose impact can be seen within the philosophy of psychology as elsewhere.

The shift away from traditional philosophy of mind toward a scientifically oriented philosophy of psychology brought about extensive changes in the meth-

https://doi.org/10.1515/9783110673692-005

odological and thematic spectrum. While up until the age of classical German philosophy analyses of consciousness are always conducted from the perspective of a broad understanding of the world, the nineteenth century, under the influence of the emerging positivism, saw the narrowing and disciplinary fragmentation of those problems originally examined by the traditional philosophy of mind. By the end of the twentieth century, the theoretical landscape had come to be dominated by a range of eliminativist approaches, with the main focus no longer on elucidating the phenomenon of human consciousness as such, but instead on deriving it from processes investigated by the natural sciences and, especially, the neurosciences.

Classical German philosophy encountered a form of psychology assembled from the rational and empirical psychology of German school philosophy in combination with anthropological speculation. Kant brought this phase to an end with his systematic disclosure of the *Paralogisms*[1] of speculative psychology. He himself is hesitant to develop any constructive suggestions in relation to the philosophy of psychology.[2] This is largely due to the fact that he used psychological vocabulary in his systematic revision of traditional metaphysics and had to make sure that in his epistemology expressions like "transcendental apperception," "transcendental imagination," "schema" or "synthesis" are not confused with concepts for mental states.

The age of Kant and German Idealism directly preceded the disciplinary divergence of philosophy and psychology within the history of science. The attempt made in the nineteenth century to emancipate psychology scientifically under the programmatic title of a "psychology without soul" at the same time signaled the beginning of a strange relationship between philosophy and psychology characterized by mutual misunderstandings and misinterpretations.

Modern philosophy of psychology refers only very rarely to German Idealism. At most, German Idealism receives occasional mention in psychological and psychiatric works addressing the history of their disciplines, in particular

---

[1] Kant 1998b, A 341–405/B 399–428.

[2] According to Kant, his transcendental philosophy has to be kept apart from anthropology as well as from empirical and rational psychology, and he constantly emphasizes that this differences should not be blurred. Nevertheless, it is possible to treat Kant's critical philosophy of mind in a meta-theoretical move as an investigation into the necessary conditions of psychology; cf. K. Kraus 2019. But this cannot be a pretext for a relaunch of concepts of a pre-critical psychology—this applies particularly to the concept of the soul. Kant's critical philosophy has no place for a soul in a non-metaphorical sense. Kant has other means to his disposal when it comes to the rejection of eliminativist approaches, above all a critical and practical concept of self-consciousness; cf. Sturma 2018.

with regard to the groundwork it laid in the development of the theory of the unconscious. Only more recently have efforts been made within the philosophy of psychology to dissolve the artificial rivalry between these disciplines. The fact that the roots of psychology as an independent, non-philosophical discipline lie in the age of classical German philosophy is noteworthy in this context and provides grounds for re-evaluation.[3] Among other reasons, the works of Schelling and Hegel contain reflections on the natural and cultural history of consciousness and the unconscious. A path can be traced from Schelling and his followers all the way to Freud and to the psychological theory of the unconscious.

There are essentially two reasons for the complicated relationship of German Idealism to twentieth century positivistic psychology. For one thing, at the end of the eighteenth century there is not yet any scientific discipline available of filling the conceptual space opened up by Kant's criticism of traditional psychology. At this time, empirical psychology and anthropology still belonged to the metaphysical realm marked out by German school philosophy. For another thing, the main current of German Idealism is characterized by a systematic outlook that afforded sub-disciplines at most provisory significance and according to which questions about the consciousness of persons could only be answered against the background of the overarching concepts of nature, spirit, or society. The innovative moves made within philosophy in Kant's wake do not occur in the area of psychology, simply because it is not central to this systematic interest. The significance of Kant's *I think* for German Idealism is too immense to confine it to the philosophy of psychology. The great project is the monistic system—*hen kai pan* —in the face of which the subjective attitudes and circumstances of the individual person pale.

2 Kant's Critique of Psychology

As is well known, Descartes introduced a systematic distinction between the mental and the physical into modern science with far-reaching consequences. His dualism presupposes a dimension of introspection and self-referential thought that is fundamentally different to the realm of spatiotemporal events and processes. At the center of this space is according to the doctrine of rational psychology that followed on from Descartes the soul, which must in theory be kept free of any determinations that are potential predicates of physical objects. The qualities of the soul identified by rational psychology are ones apparently

---

3 Cf. Leary 1980.

shared with supernatural beings—such as substantiality, immateriality, simplicity, personhood, and immortality. Rational psychology is aware of the fact that any investigation or distinction relating to psychology, no matter how discerning or subtle, is ultimately dependent on the possibility of proving the reality of the soul. Evidence for this requirement thus features prominently in its theoretical endeavors.

In the *Critique of Pure Reason*, Kant strips these endeavors of their philosophical foundation. With critical intention he takes up the idea, which goes back to Descartes, that the *I think* is the only text of rational psychology.[4] He goes on to show that the significance of the *I think* does not lie in identifying an ego or soul as an object; it functions rather—and herein lies the key argument against rational psychology *and* Hume's egological skepticism—as the highest logical principle of propositional attitudes. For Kant, the *I think* constitutes and structures human consciousness in its entirety.

In the course of his epistemological critique, Kant explicitly refutes the rational psychology—psychology from the concept (*Psychologie aus dem Begriff*) —that is prevalent in his time. He first demonstrates that assumptions about the existence of a soul as substance result from the unjustified reification of epistemological distinctions. An unwarranted transition is made from the predicatively empty sentence *I think* to descriptive statements about a soul. Additionally, Kant is able to draw on the logical sense of the *I think* to show that, due to its constitutive function in experiential situations, an instance of thought cannot itself be an object of experience. If we wish to make it an object of thought, we always have to presuppose it. The attempt to reify it causes the subject of thought to turn around itself in a continuous circle.[5] As the principle of the constitution of human consciousness, the *I think* is the key to an epistemological understanding of all propositional attitudes, but it does not clear the way for the self-knowledge of an I or a soul. In Kant's view, psychological statements can only be employed as empirical descriptions. This judgement results largely from his

---

4 See Kant 1998b, A 343/B 401: "*I think* is thus the sole text of rational psychology, from which it is to develop its entire wisdom." Cf. Kitcher 2011, pp. 180–200.

5 See Kant 1998b, B 404: "Through this I, or He, or It (the thing), which thinks, nothing further is represented than a transcendental subject of thoughts = x, which is recognized only through the thoughts that are its predicates, and about which, in abstraction, we can never have even the least concept; because of which we therefore turn in a constant circle, since we must always already avail ourselves of the representation of it at all times in order to judge anything about it; we cannot separate ourselves from this inconvenience, because the consciousness in itself is not even a representation distinguishing a particular object, but rather a form of representation in general, insofar as it is to be called a cognition; for of it alone can I say that through it I think anything."

doctrine of inner sense, according to which experiences are necessarily subject to the condition of time. From this perspective, temporal succession is the essential structural element of mental phenomena.

Kant's epistemological project overlaps thematically and conceptually with the psychology of German school philosophy, especially in its systematic examination of the phenomenon of self-consciousness, where the methodological priority of epistemology is put to the test. This becomes obvious in the *Paralogisms* chapter of the second edition of the *Critique of Pure Reason*. Kant's position on the doctrine of the soul in German school philosophy, which encompasses both rational and empirical psychology, is not one of straightforward rejection but is characterized by terminological borrowing and strict repudiation alike. The distinction between empirical and rational psychology finds expression in the fact that in the *Transcendental Deduction* Kant's epistemology unfolds with the help of the vocabulary of empirical psychology, while the *Paralogisms* chapter undermines the foundations of rational psychology.

In order to clarify his critical idea that a concept of a substance cannot justifiably be concluded from the logical unity of self-consciousness, Kant turns to the evidence for the persistence of the soul provided in Moses Mendelssohn's *Phaedon*.[6] He considers Mendelssohn the most advanced representative of speculative metaphysics. Mendelssohn does not lay out his evidence in a manner typical of rational psychology, he instead develops the argument that the soul as an intensive magnitude cannot cease to exist as a consequence of division.[7] In his critique of Mendelssohn, Kant differentiates between extensive and intensive magnitudes and outlines a descriptive concept for incorporating the fundamental concepts of his epistemology into the philosophy of mind. He emphasizes that the soul as an intensive magnitude can certainly "be transformed into nothing [...] but by a gradual remission (*remissio*) of all its powers" (Kant 1998b, B 414). This corresponds with the descriptive finding that mental states exhibit numerous gradations, extending as far as the complete disappearance of consciousness. From this perspective, simplicity cannot be equated with timeless persistence.

Kant assesses rational psychology to be a "putative science" (Kant 1998b, A 342/B 400) built on the single sentence *I think*. Its dilemma is that it must avoid systematic recourse to empirical determinations if it is to retain its claim to the title "rational." The empirical predicates without which the self-attribution of mental states cannot take place must inevitably taint the "rational purity" of

---

6 See Mendelssohn 1979.

7 Mendelssohn 1979, pp. 89–101 [202–236].

the psychology from the concept (Kant 1998b, A 343/B 401). If, however, empirical content is renounced, self-knowledge collapses into an empty relationship with itself. The weight of the brief assertion "*I think* is thus the sole text of rational psychology" (Kant 1998b, A 343/B 401) therefore clearly rests on the expression "sole."

It is nevertheless possible to understand rational psychology as resting on the assumption that the existence and post-mortal persistence of the soul can be derived from the fact of self-consciousness. This assumption is addressed by Kant in the *Paralogisms* chapter. His epistemology would have to be considered unsuccessful from the outset if it were possible to justify passing over the objects of possible experience within philosophical psychology. His epistemological conception of the *I think* is his response to this challenge. But Kant by no means stops at rejecting the way in which the sentence *I think* is used. Instead, he goes on to demonstrate that it is not possible under *any* circumstances to extract elements of the content of self-knowledge from the *I think*.[8]

Kant's refutation of the speculative rational psychology and his contextualization of the *I think* in the *Paralogisms* chapter already makes possible the step from "I*" (*Ich*) to "I" (*ich*) called for by the analytic philosophy of language.[9] In this sense he develops a *philosophy without a soul* without committing himself to eliminativism. Kant's approach includes insights that can be used to correct aberrations of contemporary philosophy of mind. From the Kantian perspective, one has to ask whether the contemporary eliminativist approaches to self-consciousness[10] follow inevitably from the descent from "I*" to "I."

Underlying Kant's epistemology is the conviction that the theoretical perspective of the natural sciences as a whole is incapable of capturing the essential structures and phenomenal contents of experiential consciousness and self-consciousness. Non-eliminativist positions within philosophical psychology have sought to develop similarly designed approaches right up to the present day. The legacy of Kant's epistemological philosophy of mind lies in his having held fast to the special status of human consciousness and self-consciousness amid the enduring methodological critique of the psychology of his time and the successful methods of modern natural sciences. German Idealism follows Kant in his rejection both of the unjustified reification of egocentric concepts and of the poor methodological standards of the psychology of his time.

---

8 Cf. Sturma 2018, pp. 143–146.
9 Cf. Tugendhat 1979, pp. 68–90.
10 Cf. Churchland 2013, pp. 11–32.

3 Fichte: Transforming the Egological Vocabulary

Fichte, Schelling, and Hegel accepted Kant's thesis that psychology is not a scientific discipline in the strict sense and has only limited systematic potential. The German Idealists do not diverge from Kant's critical stance in relation to the traditional doctrine of the soul. They criticize Kant, however, for failing to elucidate the nature of self-consciousness as such, which he had after all elevated to the highest principle of knowledge in the form of the logical function of the *I think*. If Kant is right in stating that our epistemic claims can only ever be justified from within the structure of self-consciousness as the internal logic of human consciousness, it appears to be incomprehensible, and this is the starting point for Fichte's critique in particular, that he should leave self-consciousness unexplained in its internal nature and principal requirements.

According to Fichte, it is Kant's practical philosophy that showed him the way to "true" idealism; he identifies in it the concept of "absolute freedom" which becomes the driving force of the philosophical examination of self-consciousness. Analysis of the phenomenon of self-consciousness convinced Fichte that the concept of unconditional freedom can be interpreted as having much further-reaching implications than Kant is prepared to entertain in his practical philosophy. Building on the Kantian idea of the logic of subjectivity, of the cooperation of spontaneity and synthesis on the part of the subject of consciousness in its experiential processes, Fichte defines the fact of consciousness as being grounded in a deed-act (*Tathandlung*). In this view, consciousness is not a given state but an unconditional activity. This is particularly evident in self-consciousness, which for Fichte signifies nothing more than "I am simply active" (Fichte 1982, p. 41). In self-consciousness, intelligence contemplates itself, thereby discovering its pure act of self-realization.

This marks a radical turn in the philosophical interpretation of Descartes' philosophical discovery of the phenomenon of self-consciousness. From Descartes to Kant, the undeniable self-certainty and synthetic activity of the subject of consciousness had always been in the foreground. Fichte now states that it is insufficient to affirm the basic infallibility of self-consciousness or to bring to light functional structures of subjectivity. The statement that the I of self-consciousness determines rather than is determined from without already contains the basic figure of *true* idealism. All that is needed, therefore, is to develop this notion systematically. The point of departure must be the unconditionality of the I that becomes explicit in self-consciousness.

The self-certainty of self-consciousness is interpreted by Fichte, exemplarily for German Idealism as a whole, as an indication of the unconditionality of thought or reason. If self-consciousness is accepted as the basic epistemic structure, the unconditional self-referential activity of the I takes on almost fundamental proportions, for the opposition of that which is given and that which is thought is then dependent on the activity of the unconditioned I. Accordingly, Fichte defines the opposition of that which is given and that which is thought in consciousness as an opposition *in* and *of* consciousness. With the help of the systematic potential of formal self-reference, Fichte considers himself justified in reinterpreting ontological problems within the framework of a constellation of idealist concepts. His aim is not to provide evidence for the claim that the I literally brings the world into being. Instead, he intends to show that what is believed to be real arises not from external effects, but out of the activity of the unconditioned I and its potentially infinite determinations. It is on this activity of the I that, according to Fichte, "the possibility of our consciousness, our life, our existence for ourselves, that is, our existence as selves" (Fichte 1982, p. 202) is founded. Only on this abstract level is it possible to speak of an opposition of thought and given, subject and object, and only in this sense is the formula "the self opposes to itself a not-self" (Fichte 1982, p. 225) to be understood.

It should also be pointed out that Fichte's reflections on the I are in no way directed toward the egological vocabulary that we use to refer to ourselves in a philosophically naïve sense. Fichte's concept of the self-activity of the I does not correspond to any concrete phenomenon of self-awareness and remains inaccessible to everyday consciousness. According to Fichte, the absolute I is a speculative necessity in philosophical reflection that does not compete with the life-world over its reality; it manifests itself in a philosophical system in which the fact of intelligent and self-conscious existence is constructively explained. Taking Kant's philosophy as his point of departure, Fichte performs a conceptual ascent from the "I" (*ich*) to the "I*" (*Ich*). This approach is paradigmatic within German Idealism. It draws on an egological vocabulary to dissolve psychological self-reference in formal abstraction. In contrast to its significance in the work of Kant, the "empirical I" is no longer an important element in philosophical reflection in German Idealism. The development of speculative Idealism causes the theoretical profile of empirical consciousness to vanish, leaving psychology, from a systematic perspective, without an object of interest.

4 Schelling: History of Self-Consciousness and Beyond

It is Schelling who introduces the concept of the unconscious into German Idealism as the prehistory of the human mind. Still under the influence of Fichte's *Science of Knowledge*, he presents a theory of the soul as emerging self-consciousness:

> Thus, through its own products—imperceptible to the common eye, [yet] clear and distinct to that of the philosopher—the soul marks the path on which it gradually reaches self-consciousness. The external world lies unfolded [*aufgeschlagen*] for us, so that we may rediscover within it the history of our spirit. (Schelling 1994a, p. 90)

Schelling reinterprets the idealist model of self-reference in the terms of philosophy of nature. He points out that self-consciousness is only possible through the at least implicit relation to something other than itself and treats what is addressed in external experience as a manifestation of the "*history of self-consciousness*" (Schelling 1994a, p. 90). Initially, Schelling follows Fichte's project of a "pragmatic history of the human mind" (Fichte 1982, pp. 198–199). However, his naturalist approach soon leads to positions far beyond the idealist forms of reflection outlined by Fichte. Eventually, he becomes convinced that the philosophical concept of nature must amount to more than just a constructive instrument of the self-reference of the mind.

According to Schelling, a history of self-consciousness must necessarily encounter the "transcendental past" of the mind, for the existentially aware consciousness does not merely posit its external nature ideally, but in fact encounters it physically. Looking back on the transformations in his philosophy, Schelling describes the insight that ultimately led him away from Fichte's Idealism:

> [...] as the I becomes an *individual* I—which announces itself precisely via the "I am"—having arrived, then, at the "*I am*," with which its individual life begins, it does not remember the path anymore which it has covered so far, for as it is only the end of this path which is consciousness, it (the now individual I) has covered the path unconsciously and without knowing it. By this the blindness and necessity of its ideas of the external world is explained, as by the previous point the sameness and universality of those ideas for all individuals is explained. The individual I finds in its consciousness only, as it were, the monuments, the memorials of that path, not the path itself. (Schelling, 1994b p. 110; cf. Sturma 2000, pp. 223–228)

Nature is the unconscious mind, which is the principle that shapes nature and consciousness alike. This makes the emergence of consciousness from nature possible and ultimately explains the fact that there is a structural similarity between the numerous forms of consciousness—regardless of the manifold of their contentual differences. Schelling coins for this similarity the formula that nature must be understood as visible mind and mind as invisible nature (Schelling 1988, p. 42).[11] In his view, nature is not the other of consciousness and reason, but their temporal and logical condition. Even pure physical nature is rationally determined within; if it were not, the development from non-conscious nature to knowing and self-conscious intelligence could not have taken place. If we are to speak of the nature of reason, according to Schelling's reflections, then we also have to speak about the reason in nature. In his assessment, the constitutive conditions of consciousness and self-consciousness are to be found in their natural conditions and not in the perspective of isolated self-reference.[12]

Schelling rules out the possibility of the unconscious being delivered to interpretation via an analytic process of self-enlightenment. Philosophy, he argues, is at best in a position to reconstruct the history of self-consciousness in epochs (cf. Schelling 2000, p. 399) and speculatively to identify abstract positions that shape the relationship of nature, mind, and self-consciousness. Here Schelling turns his gaze not to formative social processes but to temporally expansive determinations of the natural history of the human life-form.

The concept of a natural history of self-consciousness relativizes the notion of a comprehensive self-interpretation on the part of subjectivity without a commitment to irrationalism. In this regard, Schelling's philosophy is more nuanced than most contemporary critiques of the idealist philosophy of subjectivity. The unveiling of the natural contexts of the human mind, as outlined by Schelling in his history of self-consciousness, occurs with the intention of exposing the false abstraction of egocentricity, which appears inevitably to accompany the subjective perspective of persons, yet without subscribing to a "back to nature" sce-

---

11 Schelling's natural history of self-consciousness has found continuation and adaption in the period of the disciplinary emergence of psychology. Worth mentioning are Carl Gustav Carus and Gustav Theodor Fechner. While Carus still operates in the field of idealism (Carus 1846 and 1866), Fechner already develops a kind of empirical approach (Fechner 1860).

12 Cf. Carus's paraphrase of the opening passage of the *System of Transcendental Idealism:* "Schelling put it quite beautifully: All motion and activity, all vital impulse, even that of nature, is only an unconscious process of thought, or happens in the form of the latter; the more in nature what is normal or conformable to law becomes apparent, by so much the more spiritual do her workings appear; optical phenomena are but a system of geometry, the lines of which are traced by the light, and the perfected theory of nature would be that by virtue of which the whole of nature should resolve itself into an intelligence." (Carus 1970, p. 72)

nario. This distinguishes the contextualization provided by Schelling's natural philosophy from the many contemporary approaches that seek to eliminate self-consciousness or have excessive expectations regarding subjectivity.

In his later philosophy Schelling drastically modifies his history of self-consciousness. The conception of human consciousness comes to be dominated not only by externalizations and egological criticism, but above all by a notion of pre-reflexivity (Sturma 1995). Schelling criticizes all the important attempts at drafting a philosophy of mind from Descartes to Fichte for being unable to break free of the limiting and limited phenomenon of self-consciousness. This applies even to his own early philosophy. From the perspective of the reflecting person, self-consciousness is inescapable. This point of view organizes the theoretical framework of the modern philosophy which finally leads to the position that "self-consciousness might merely be the modification of a higher being" (Schelling 1978, pp. 16 – 17) or can only be explained with recourse to something "of which we *can* know nothing, because the whole synthesis of our knowledge is first made precisely through self-consciousness" (Schelling 1978, p. 17).

In engaging with the foundations of self-consciousness, Schelling makes a number of revisions. In a continuation of Fichte's early *Science of Knowledge*, he initially argues that self-consciousness sets its own limits. It is not limited from without, but rather draws its limits from within. In his later philosophy, Schelling adopts a more radical position. He is no longer concerned with the internal differentiation of self-consciousness. Due to the contingent nature of finite existence, he takes self-consciousness—like reason—to be groundless. In the end, self-consciousness makes the disturbing experience that its essential determination occurs beyond itself. For this reason, Schelling regards neither self-consciousness nor the egological vocabulary as the key to human self-understanding (cf. Sturma 2004).

According to Schelling, self-consciousness can no longer locate its ground within itself and has to step outside itself if it wishes to come closer to an understanding of its place in nature. Self-consciousness is the principle of finiteness but not its ground. Ultimately, Schelling's aim is to leave behind the limitations of a finite world. Self-consciousness must therefore be understood as a principle that, due to the limited nature of its reflective perspective, points to something in which it only has a partial share.

According to Schelling's conception of pre-reflexivity, freedom and self-determination do not occur in isolated self-reference, but in personal attitudes and relationships with other people and nature in its entirety. If, within the philosophy of mind, freedom, consciousness, and action cannot be confined to the realm of explicit awareness, it is likewise necessary to go beyond the sphere of explicit deliberation and decision-making in evaluating matters of accountability and responsibility. Self-determination, then, no longer takes the form of an act of will transparent to itself and revealed through action, but that of pre-reflexive dispositions. This approach turns conventional approaches to the attribution of accountability into the opposite: persons are not held responsible for what they intend and do in a given moment; they are held responsible for what they are, for their moral and behavioral dispositions—understood in an existential or moral rather than a legal sense (Sturma 1995, pp. 165–172).

Schelling's conception of pre-reflexivity certainly allows for connections to be drawn with everyday phenomena. After all, persons experience their behavioral dispositions and habits as substantially more profound than their arbitrary reflections and acts. The inertia of dispositions points "to a life before this life" (Schelling 1936, p. 65). The dispositions and habits rely on periods of life in which persons may not yet have been in a position to exercise control over their actions. The adversity of a person's situation has for Schelling, as for Kant, no influence on her responsibility; if it did, it would not be possible to accord any metaphysical dignity to a person. There is no question that persons are influenced by their social conditions—a fact which classical German philosophy, with the exception of Hegel, pays too little attention—but morally speaking this does not mean that the behavior of persons can be reduced to the conditions under which they have to lead their lives. On this point and with recourse to Kant, Schelling adopts a decidedly different position than Hegel.

The challenge of Schelling's doctrine of freedom lies in his theory that consciousness of not having been able to act otherwise does not affect responsibility. Even this daring assertion has a phenomenal basis: a person understands herself responsible for *herself*, regardless of the conditions and contingencies in which her actions are carried out. She feels this way even if she often does not acknowledge it to herself or even when she is required to justify herself in public. The excuse "That's just the way I am," with which many criticisms or regrets are met, does nothing to soothe the conscience, for it is capable of feeling guilt even when acting otherwise is impossible. The strange state of mind in which a person feels guilty in spite of exoneration—such as in cases where other persons have unintentionally been harmed—provides empirical confirmation of Schelling's theory of pre-reflexive freedom.

5 Hegel: Nature, Soul, and the Unconscious

Hegel expands the analysis of subjective consciousness to incorporate self-criticism and the self-limitation of finite reflection. With regard to his view, that the human mind cannot be understood in itself due to its limited character, his program shares similarities with Schelling's rejection of narrow idealism. As distinguished from Schelling, Hegel's critical philosophy of mind has its orientation in society and history, not in nature. He sees psychological points of view as particularly vulnerable to the overestimation of the epistemic transparency of subjective consciousness.

In reaction to the empirical naïvety in psychological reflections, Hegel seeks to grasp mental phenomena in their contingency and mediation, and to cease treating them as if they were objects. We can already find in Hegel a version of the critique of the "myth of the given".[13] He demonstrates that the naïve dealing with phenomena as given is merely the fallacy of a dogmatist who fails to recognize the formal and contentual dependencies of the phenomenal manifestations of consciousness.

In Hegel's psychological analysis, the concept of the soul takes on a highly significant role of the theoretical turning point at which the mind emerges out of nature. In this context, he explicitly refers to the books of Aristotle on the soul (E § 378). While Cartesianism works with the dualist conception of mind and body, Aristotle addresses the soul in the wider scope of a philosophy of nature—an approach Hegel considers decidedly more appropriate. Aristotle's interpretation of the soul as entelechy, as the functional subject of the body, has a considerable impact on Hegel. Because entelechy, as an activity of the body directed toward ends, cannot transcend physical determinations and must always be immanent to them, it opens up a line of argumentation allowing for the dissolution of the strict dualism of mind and nature taught by Platonism and Cartesianism.

Hegel's psychology, the philosophy of the subjective mind, marks the transition from philosophy of nature to the philosophy of mind, which in turn—proceeding from the forms of human subjectivity explicated one after another in the *Anthropology*, the *Phenomenology of Mind*, and the *Psychology*, and via the deduction of manifestations of the objective mind such as law, morality, and social institutions—represents the speculative culmination of his philosophy, the theory of the absolute mind.

The concept of the human soul is treated explicitly in the *Anthropology*, where the investigation of the human life-form is reduced to an analysis of the soul. In the philosophy of the subjective mind, the theory of the soul serves to illustrate the transition from nature to mind, i.e. it is supposed to describe how consciousness and reason come about or have been able to come about in nature. This shows just how radical the claims of Hegelian philosophy are.

---

13 See Sellars 1997, pp. 85–88 [§ X].

Where Cartesianism and even Kant's critical philosophy posit subjectivity as an irreducible phenomenon, Hegel attempts—in this regard comparable only to Schelling—to demonstrate how subjectivity comes into existence. To this effect, the theory of the soul is assigned the demanding task of describing the emergence of consciousness and reason from nature.

The fact that consciousness and reason arise out of nature as emergent processes is a clear indication that natural processes have rational structures of their own, or at least structures compatible with reason. Hegel therefore draws no strict opposition between nature and mind; his analyses of natural processes always pertain to the significance of reason *in* nature. The semantics of Hegel's concept of the soul are accordingly located on the threshold of the forms of life and consciousness. This allows Hegel to return once again to the classical determinations of the "*anima vegetativa*" and the "*anima sensitiva*," i.e. determinations that conceive of the soul as a principle of nature that cannot be confined to the sphere of the human life-form.

According to Hegel, what distinguishes the human soul from the substance of animal life is its capacity to develop in such a way as to be explicitly determined by reason. As he says, "*Consciousness awakens* in the *soul*. It posits itself as reason*" (E § 387). And this determination by reason is realized in a trans-individual reflexivity that emerges as the general structural characteristic of subjectivity. Correspondingly, in the architectonics of philosophy as a whole, Hegel's theory of the soul, which is located in an area between philosophy of nature and the philosophy of mind, comes down on the side of mind. Although the human soul is a naturally determined phenomenon, it does not arise naturally out of nature.

It is precisely the positioning of the soul on the threshold between the realms of nature and mind that lends Hegel's arguments particular theoretical weight in light of contemporary philosophical psychology that puts a focus on the development of an integrative approach incorporating both naturalist and non-eliminative theories of mind. Moreover, Hegel is credited with having analyzed the inevitably ambivalent concept of the soul in a way that eludes overly hasty conclusions in favor of one side or the other. Hegel at least hopes to avoid a one-sided dissolution of the relationship between nature and mind in favor of demonstrating "that and how nature and mind relate to one another of their own accord" (Hegel 1971, p. 525). His account of the concept of the soul opens up the dimension of a consciousness with access to itself and to determinations of reason. The soul has the formal structure of an individuality without consciousness or understanding. The emergence of consciousness from nature is realized in the awakening of the soul, which is, however, not an awakening to self-transparent consciousness but initially only the manifestation of the unconscious.

According to Hegel, the awakening of the soul is initially still the "sleep of spirit" (E § 389), i.e. the mind awakes to unconsciousness in the soul. Hegel points out again and again that the states of the soul cannot at this point be interpreted as cases of explicit consciousness; in elucidating the states of the "feeling soul" (E § 404), he concludes: "this stage is that of the darkness of spirit, for its determinations develop into no conscious and understandable content" (E § 404).

Hegel's theory of the soul as a theory of the unconscious is more psychologically oriented than Schelling's natural theory of the unconscious. For Hegel, the unconscious is not merely the absence of states of awareness, but a psychophysical reality in itself. He explains the soul in the form of the unconscious as a real unity in which situations and events of individual life are regarded as moments within a developmental process of unity and change. In this sense, the unconscious soul is the common background that gives continuity to individual life-forms over time; it is the real unity of the biographical development and change of the rational individual. The soul is in fact potentially rational, but in its unconscious mode it has a pre-logical structure that forms the natural foundation for rational behavior.

While Schelling extends the concept of the unconscious in the context of the philosophy of nature, Hegel's theory of the unconscious amounts to an expansion of originally anthropological determinations from the perspective of social philosophy. Of key significance here is the reconstruction of the emotive constitution of the human life-form. For Hegel, this is not simply a passive and separated element of an otherwise rationally determined consciousness; it facilitates in its own right the formation of complexes of meaning and behavioral dispositions in rational individuals. For this reason, any attempt at psychological self-discovery or self-enlightenment that sharply distinguishes between a rational and an emotive realm is inadequate. Psychological analyses can only provide a restricted understanding of the natural determination of personal existence, for the mental dimension of the person is considerably more extensive than the phenomenal realm of explicit states of consciousness. The unconscious formation of personality is, according to Hegel, no way station in the history of a life, but an ever-present backdrop to personal attitudes and dispositions.

Even though, Hegel asserts in his theory of the unconscious the irreducibility of the natural history of rational individuals, he by no means conceives of the unconscious as the voice of a repressed and potentially superior nature. For all its contingency, there can be no return to nature for the individual person. Transition from nature to mind does not represent a natural transition. Once emerged, the human unconscious always comes down on the side of mind or culture.

Hegel's critique of subjectivity has far-reaching consequences for the methodical status of psychological analyses. In the end, observational or empirical psychology is nothing more than a trivial recounting of diverse aspects of the social existence of rational individuals. It ultimately only leads to a collection of trivia that is even less interesting "than enumerating the species of insects, mosses, and so on, for these latter give observation the right to take them singularly and as devoid of concepts because they essentially belong to that element of contingent separation" (Hegel 1977, p. 169). His critique of one-sidedly empirical psychology focuses above all on its status as a scientific discipline. Unreflected recourse to apparently unmediated phenomena is in Hegel's view not a scientifically justifiable method given that the very approach obscures the constitutional processes of these phenomena. In contrast with the incoherent particularization of the mind carried out by empirical psychology, Hegel wants to reintroduce "the Notion into the cognition of spirit" (E § 378).

Drawing a contrast to the coincidences of natural life, Hegel's philosophy of mind elaborates the non-natural beginnings of a rational history of humanity. For Hegel, only *Geist*, the subject of rational universality, can have a coherent development. In this regard, the gap between philosophy of nature and philosophy of mind is the point of no return for the history of humanity—a "return to nature" would be nothing other than a regression into indeterminacy. The objective of this approach is to illustrate the internal connection between nature and mind. Accordingly, he sees the beginning of the history of self-consciousness in an already rationally formed unconscious. Hegel expects a theoretical perspective of this kind to be capable of avoiding the one-sided aspects of the Cartesian theory of mind on the one hand and empirically oriented psychology on the other.

The natural and emotive constitution of humankind is not the passive foundation of an otherwise socially and rationally determined consciousness, but already affects linguistic and normative behavior. For this reason, psychological analyses can provide only a restricted understanding of the life of persons, for, according to Hegel, their mental dimension is considerably more extensive than the phenomenal realm that comes to light in states of explicit awareness.

> [A] person who has once forgotten the things he has learnt can never know the true extent of the knowledge he possesses;—these things are simply implicit in what he is, and do not pertain to his actuality, his subjectivity as such. This simple inwardness constitutes individuality, and it persists throughout all the determinateness and mediation of consciousness subsequently posited within it. (E § 403)

The realm of the unconscious formation of personality is not a transitional phase in the life of persons, but the persistent background of their attitudes and dispositions. In Hegel's account, there is no path to an analytical uncovering of unconscious formations. In this regard, he differs fundamentally from Freud and his followers. Admittedly, Hegel's philosophy can generally be described as a speculative elaboration of formations and processes that occur "behind the back" of our consciousness. However, it is not possible to conclude from this that Hegel believes self-discovery in the *subjective* sense to be possible.

A further obstacle to subjective self-discovery lies in the fact that transitions between the realms of the rational and the emotive cannot be concretely identified in human behavior. One might almost speak of conditions of indeterminacy regarding these transitions. Hegel considers this indeterminacy as characteristic of human existence. His critique of subjectivity repeatedly demonstrates that the reason for behavior attributed to a person by herself or by someone else need by no means necessarily be effective in her behavior.

6 Past and Present

Looking back on the various theoretical efforts of German Idealists to grasp the human mind conceptually, it is difficult to see the "psychology without a soul" that followed Idealism as an appropriate reaction to their speculative projects. Classical German philosophy does not derive from its critique any positivistic program for the theoretical dissolution of subjectivity; the fact that the concept of the soul is an example of psychological reification does not mean that the problems lying behind its conceptual history have been dispelled. From Kant to Hegel, attempts have been made to redefine self-reference. These reconstructions contain a potential whose critical consequences have not yet been adequately addressed, above all with regard to the numerous eliminativist approaches of contemporary philosophy of psychology.

The fact that German Idealism is systematically hardly taken into account neither in contemporary psychology nor in recent philosophy of psychology is most likely due to the initial lack of understanding for the abstract methods characteristic of idealistic systems. From a contemporary perspective, idealist systems are literally questionable because of their speculative methods and semantics. However, in this context it has to be considered that the scientific status of psychology is highly debated to this day, especially concerning its unclear disciplinary status between humanities and natural sciences as well as its methodological self-conception. In contrast, German Idealism adopts an uncompromising point of view. From the idealist perspective, the human life-form, both in its general and individual manifestations, can only be explained by means of coherentist reconstructions of abstract forms of self-reference manifested in reason, nature, history or *Geist*. Talking about humans always implies talking about the big picture or the great unsaid, thus refusing mechanistic explanations as equally short-sighted as the positivist reifications of mental qualities and objects which are still popular in psychology. Due to its semantic and epistemological naïveté, the major part of psychological research exposes itself to the critique of operating with the myth of the given or even seeking shelter in mechanist models of human consciousness. Consequently, the methodological situation of psychology actually invites considerations for fundamental revision of its self-image or self-conception—at least from an idealist perspective. Reconsidering idealism in the field of psychological research would also depend on the space conceded to mechanistic explanations, especially with regard to the neuroscientific challenges.[14]

Whereas the conceptional approach of psychology is mainly concerned with individual consciousness, or rather concrete states of consciousness, idealist systems are anti-individualistic and anti-psychological. They are interested in the human life-form and its place in the world in general, individual actors merely playing a subordinate role. Accordingly, instead of individual self-discovery or introspection, reflexivity in the form of self-reference of the space of reasons and the movement of concepts are of systematic importance.

In the course of systematic re-evaluation of self-reference, the egological and psychological vocabularies are transformed. Initially psychological concepts, i.e. concepts describing human attitudes, abilities and conditions, are elevated on an abstract level and provided with their own conceptual dynamics, especially in the case of concepts such as "I", "self", "productive imagination", "self-consciousness", or "spirit". These transformations go along with a further development of the philosophical concept of the unconscious. The unconscious in idealist systems is not an opaque remnant of the consciousness of persons—especially not with Schelling and Hegel as well as with their followers Carus and Fechner—but the historically and anthropologically decisive element in the constitution of personal life which exceeds individual manifestation by far. The unconscious in German Idealism encompasses past and present of the human life-form as a whole and relates it to the world in its entirety.

---

14 See Sturma 2016.

References

Carus, Carl Gustav (1846): *Psyche. Zur Entwicklungsgeschichte der Seele.* Pforzheim: Flammer und Hoffmann.

Carus, Carl Gustav (1866): *Vergleichende Psychologie oder Geschichte der Seele in der Reihenfolge der Thierwelt.* Wien: Braumüller.

Carus, Carl Gustav (1970): *Psyche. On the Development of the Soul.* Thompson: Spring Publications.

Churchland, Patricia S. (2013): *Touching a Nerve. The Self as Brain.* New York: Norton.

Fechner, Gustav Theodor (1860): *Elemente der Psychophysik.* Leipzig: Breitkopf und Härtel.

Fichte, Johann Gottlieb (1982): *The Science of Knowledge.* Cambridge: Cambridge University Press.

Fichte, Johann Gottlieb (1971): *Werke.* Nachdruck der von I. H. Fichte herausgegebenen Sämtlichen und Nachgelassenen Werke. Berlin: De Gruyter.

Hegel, Georg Wilhelm Friedrich (1971): "Fragment zur Philosophie des Geistes." In: *Werke* (Theorie-Werkausgabe). Vol. XI. Frankfurt am Main: Suhrkamp.

Hegel, Georg Wilhelm Friedrich (1975): *Enzyklopädie der philosophischen Wissenschaften im Grundrisse.* [E] Edited by F. Nicolin und O. Pöggeler. Hamburg: Meiner.

Hegel, Georg Wilhelm Friedrich (1977): *Phenomenology of Spirit.* Oxford: Oxford University Press.

Hegel, Georg Wilhelm Friedrich (1978): "Encyclopedia of the Philosophy of Spirit." In: M. J. Petry (ed.): *Hegel's Philosophy of Subjective Spirit.* Vol. I. Dordrecht: Reidel.

Kant, Immanuel (1998a): *Kritik der reinen Vernunft.* Hamburg: Meiner.

Kant, Immanuel (1998b): *Critique of Pure Reason.* Cambridge: Cambridge University Press.

Kitcher, Patricia (2011): *Kant's Thinker.* Oxford: Oxford University Press.

Kraus, Katharina (2019): "Rethinking the Relationship between Empirical Psychology and Transcendental Philosophy in Kant." In: Jahrbuch des Deutschen Idealismus DeGruyter: Berlin, pp. [In this volume.]

Leary, David E. (1980): "German Idealism and the Development of Psychology in the Nineteenth Century." In: *Journal of the History of Philosophy* 18, pp. 299–317.

Mendelssohn, Moses (1979): *Phädon oder über die Unsterblichkeit der Seele.* Hamburg: Meiner.

Schelling, Friedrich Wilhelm Joseph (1856–1861): *Sämtliche Werke* (Stuttgarter Gesamtausgabe). Stuttgart: Cotta.

Schelling, Friedrich Wilhelm Joseph (1936): *Philosophical Inquiries into the Nature of Human Freedom.* La Salle: Open Court.

Schelling, Friedrich Wilhelm Joseph (1967): *The Ages of the World.* New York: Columbia University Press.

Schelling, Friedrich Wilhelm Joseph (1978): *System of Transcendental Idealism.* Charlottesville: University Press of Virginia.

Schelling, Friedrich Wilhelm Joseph (1988): *Ideas for a Philosophy of Nature.* Cambridge: Cambridge University Press.

Schelling, Friedrich Wilhelm Joseph (1994a): "Treatise Explicatory of the Idealism in the Science of Knowledge." In: *Idealism and the Endgame of Theory.* Albany: State University of New York Press, pp. 61–139.

Schelling, Friedrich Wilhelm Joseph (1994b): *On the History of Modern Philosophy.* Cambridge: Cambridge University Press.

Sellars, Wilfrid (1997): *Empiricism and the Philosophy of Mind.* Cambridge, Mass.: Harvard University Press.

Sturma, Dieter (1995): "Präreflexive Freiheit und menschliche Selbstbestimmung." In: O. Höffe/A. Pieper (eds.): *F. W. J. Schelling: Über das Wesen der menschlichen Freiheit.* Berlin: Akademie Verlag, pp. 149–172.

Sturma, Dieter (2000): "The Nature of Subjectivity. Schelling's Philosophy of Nature and the Mystery of Its Origins." In: S. Sedgwick (ed.): *The Idea of a System of Transcendental Idealism in Kant, Fichte, Schelling and Hegel.* Cambridge: Cambridge University Press, pp. 216–231.

Sturma, Dieter (2004): "Person sucht Person. Schellings personalitätstheoretischer Sonderweg." In: T. Buchheim/F. Hermanni (eds.): *"Alle Persönlichkeit ruht auf einem dunkeln Grunde." Schellings Philosophie der Personalität.* Berlin: Akademie Verlag, pp. 55–70.

Sturma, Dieter (2016): "Self-Consciousness, Personal Identity, and the Challenge of Neuroscience." In: M. García-Valdecasas/J. I. Murillo/F. Nathaniel/N. F. Barrett (eds.): *Biology and Subjectivity: Philosophical Contributions to Non-reductive Neuroscience.* Basel: Springer, pp. 13–24.

Sturma, Dieter (2018): "The Practice of Self-Consciousness: Kant on Nature, Freedom, and Morality." In: E. Watkins (ed.): *Kant on Persons and Agency.* Cambridge: Cambridge University Press.

Tugendhat, Ernst (1979): *Selbstbewußtsein und Selbstbestimmung. Sprachanalytische Interpretationen.* Frankfurt am Main: Suhrkamp.

Patricia Kitcher
Kant's Moral Psychology in the Fact of Reason

Abstract. *Kant's central question in morality parallels his central question in epistemology: 'How is cognition possible?' In ethical writings he asks: 'How is morality possible?' For both cases his answers are cast in terms of the faculties necessary for the possibility of the task. I present the basics of Kant's moral psychology of reason, will and desire and then draw on that account to provide a more adequate understanding of his demonstration that morality is not chimerical, but real in the 'fact of reason' texts.*

Kants zentrale Frage in der Moralphilosophie ist parallel zu seiner zentralen Frage in der Erkenntnistheorie: ‚Wie ist Erkenntnis möglich?'. In seinen ethischen Schriften fragt er: ‚Wie ist Moralität möglich?' In beiden Fällen ist es für die Möglichkeit der Aufgabe notwendig, etwas in Form von Vermögen anzunehmen. Ich stelle die Grundlagen von Kants Moralpsychologie der Vernunft, des Willens und der Bedürfnisse dar. Anschließend gebe ich im Ausgang davon ein adäquateres Verständnis des Beweises im Text zum ‚Faktum der Vernunft', dass die Moral keine Chimäre ist, sondern real ist.

1 Kant's Three Moral Psychologies

The title of the first section of the Introduction to the *Metaphysics of Morals,* "Of the Relation of the Faculties of the Human Mind to Moral Laws," provides clear evidence that Kant assigned faculty psychology a central role in his account of morality.[1] That obvious fact has been obscured by three Kantian *dicta* that have had great currency. One is that human freedom is inexplicable. In *Groundwork 3,* Kant says that

> We can explain nothing but what we can trace back to laws whose object can be given in some possible experience [...]. Where determination by laws of nature ceases, there all **explanation** ceases as well [...]. (Ak. 4, p. 459)[2]

---

1 Engstrom (2010, pp. 33–34) drew my attention to this title.
2 References to Kant's works other than the *Critique of Pure Reason* will be given in the text by the volume and page of Kant (1900 ff.). Citations from the *Critique of Pure Reason* are in the text with the usual A/B pagination. The translations are from Pluhar 1996; translations from the *Cri-*

https://doi.org/10.1515/9783110673692-006

Since deterministic natural laws are incompatible with freedom, freedom is inexplicable, and since morally correct or incorrect action requires freedom, it too must be inexplicable (see also Ak. 5, p. 72), despite Kant's express project of explaining how the Categorical Imperative is possible (Ak. 4, pp. 419, 453). If moral action is inexplicable, then a faculty psychology of morality must fail to explain it and so is pointless. This *dictum* is also expressed in the language of Transcendental Idealism. Only phenomena are susceptible of explanation and free moral actions cannot be ranked among phenomena. Although physical actions are phenomenal, the determination of those actions through practical reasoning is noumenal and so beyond human cognition. That is, Transcendental Idealism itself implies that a faculty psychology of morality is impossible.

A second, related *dictum* is that since no theoretical knowledge of free moral action is possible, the only way that humans can know themselves to be free is practically. Although the first way of obscuring the centrality of faculty psychology to Kant's account of morality is largely his own doing, the second arises from what I take to be a misreading of what he means by a "practical" cognition of freedom (Ak. 5, p. 48; Ak. 4, pp. 455–456; cf. A 803/B 831). As we see below, the "practical proof" of freedom comes directly out of his faculty psychology, but it has not usually been read in that way. Instead, Kant's appeal to a practical proof has been understood through the lens of a contrast between the first person or agential point of view and the third person or scientific point of view, a contrast that he is alleged to have discovered. On Strawson's widely influential reading of the Paralogisms chapter, Kant's central insight was that humans self-ascribe psychological predicates on the basis of no criteria of identity whereas they ascribe them to others on the basis of bodily movements (Strawson 1966, p. 165). A serious objection to this reading is that in a passage at the beginning of the Paralogisms that is common to both editions Kant draws attention to an almost diametrically opposed claim about how humans cognize their own minds and about how they understand other minds:

> It must, however, seem strange at the very outset that the condition under which I think at all, and which is therefore merely a characteristic of myself as subject, is to be valid also for everything that thinks; and that upon a proposition that *seems empirical* we can presume to base an apodeictic and universal judgment, *viz:* that everything that thinks is of such a character *as the pronouncement of self-consciousness asserts of me.* The cause of this, however, lies in the fact that we must necessarily ascribe to things a priori all of the properties

---

tique of Practical Reason are from Pluhar (2002); in both cases, I indicate Kant's emphases through bold not italics. Translations from the *Groundwork* are from Gregor/Timmermann (2011) and translations from the *Metaphysics of Morals* are from Gregor (1996). Translations from the lectures on Metaphysics are from Ameriks/Naragon (1997).

that make up the conditions under which alone we think them. Now through no outer experience, but *solely through self-consciousness*, can I have the least representation of a thinking being. Hence objects of that sort are nothing more than the transfer of this consciousness of mine to other things, which thereby alone are represented as thinking beings. (A 346/B 404–405, my italics)

The focus of the passage is self-consciousness. That is what enables humans to cognize their own mental characteristics. To understand Kant's views of those characteristics (and how humans cognize them), we must try to figure out what, exactly, he thinks is revealed in self-consciousness.

Self-consciousness also plays an essential role in understanding other minds. Since thinking is accessible neither through outer nor through inner sense (B 153, Ak. 7, p. 134n), the only way that cognizers have of understanding others as thinkers is by using themselves as a model for them. They attribute what they cognize about their own mental activities through self-consciousness to others. In making this move, Kant is not committing the infamous single-case induction to solve the problem of other minds. His claim is not that since I know that I have a certain kind of mind, I can infer that, e.g., all humans have the same kind. He is explicit that the self-as-model for others is not an empirical generalization, but merely *seems* to be one. His concern is not with how humans know of something that it has a mind, but with how they represent something that they take to be minded—how they understand what having a mind involves.

Given that Kant thought that humans understood other minds through their understanding of their own minds, the asymmetry between the third person and first person point of view vanishes, as I argue in detail in another place (Kitcher 2013). A third person is just another first person. Still, it might seem as though Kant's emphasis on self-consciousness vindicates rather than refutes reading his invocation of a practical proof as introducing an agential point of view. Although that is true in a sense, the usual way of treating the agential perspective is simply to contrast it with the 'third person' point of view and leave it at that. As we have seen, that contrast is not true to Kant's views. More importantly, in merely gesturing at an agential perspective, scholars leave out what he takes to be revealed in self-consciousness.[3] Alternatively, interpreting Kant's emphasis on self-consciousness as highlighting an agential perspective is fine as long as there is no implied contrast with a 'third person' point of view—we are all first persons

---

[3] Even such scholarly and sensitive readers as Pauline Kleingeld (2010, pp. 69–72) and Owen Ware (2014, pp. 12–17) note Kant's appeal to agential thinking without trying to investigate what self-consciousness divulges to agents about their thinking.

—and as long as it leads to a serious exploration of what he thinks that self-consciousness divulges.

Beyond its potential for cutting off the Kantian account of moral psychology just when it should be getting underway, the appeal to the agential point of view suggests that it is just a point of view and therefore not fully correct. Sometimes this line of thinking goes so far as to claim that Kant maintained only that it seems or must seem to agents that they are capable of free moral action.[4] That reading is flatly inconsistent with what he says in the Preface to the *Critique of Practical Reason*.

> For if as pure reason it is actually practical, then it proves its reality and that of its concepts through the deed, and all subtle reasoning against the possibility of its being practical is futile. (Ak. 5, p. 3)[5]

Since pure reason is practical it can prove its reality through what it does—the practical proof—and in such a way as to eliminate all room for debate.[6] Despite talk of two worlds and two standpoints, the aim of the *Second Critique* is not to argue that, from a certain perspective, humans can be understood as capable of free moral action, but to offer irrefragable proof of the reality of pure practical reason and so of the possibility of morality.

A third *dictum* also blocks scholars from fully appreciating the importance of Kant's faculty moral psychology. Kant insists in the *Groundwork* and in the *Metaphysics of Morals* that the study of morality is utterly independent from the study of human nature. The *Groundwork* offers several versions of this point:

> [T]he metaphysics of morals is to examine the idea and the principles of a possible **pure** will, and not the actions and conditions of human willing in general, which are largely drawn from psychology. (Ak. 4, p. 391)

---

4 As Allison notes, his dual aspect reading of transcendental idealism implies that some actions merely seem to be free (Allison 1990, p. 79); Lewis White Beck tried to save Kant from transcendental idealism by suggesting that it is only necessary to take the agent (as opposed to spectator) point of view and act *as if* the maxim of the will were a sufficient determining ground of the action to be executed or omitted (Beck 1960, p. 193). In both cases, humans would not really be free or really capable of morality. Although I think this is a misreading, Kant encourages it by referring to "standpoints," e.g., Ak. 4, p. 458.

5 In the *Groundwork*, Kant notes that the use of reason in acting and abstaining presupposes freedom and so makes it impossible for the "subtlest philosophy as for the commonest human reason to rationalize freedom away." (Ak. 4, p. 456)

6 When discussing how morality is really possible or actual, Kant is not using "real" or "possible" in the sense of the categories of "reality" and "possibility" in the *Critique of Pure Reason* (A 218/B 265 ff.).

> [I]t is of the utmost importance to let this serve as a warning, that one must put the thought right out of one's mind that the reality of this principle [the Categorical Imperative] can be derived from the **particular property of human nature** [...]. [W]hatever [...] is derived from certain feelings and propensities, and indeed even, possibly, from a special tendency peculiar to human reason [...] would not have to hold necessarily for the will of every rational being [...]. (Ak. 4, p. 425)

The problem with appealing to a specific human nature is that any 'law' derived in that way would apply only to humans and further that, as dependent on nature, such 'laws' would be heteronomous rather than autonomous (Ak. 4, pp. 441–442). In the *Metaphysics of Morals*, Kant explains the proper relationship between morality and a theory of human psychology:

> With the teachings of morality [...] [the theorist] does not derive instruction in its laws from observing himself and his animal nature [...]. [Still] a metaphysics of morals cannot dispense with principles of application, and we shall often have to take as our object the particular **nature** of human beings, which is cognized only by experience, in order to **show** in it what can be inferred from universal moral principles [...] a metaphysics of morals cannot be based upon anthropology but can still be applied to it. (Ak. 6, p. 217)

Again, human psychology can play no role in laying out fundamental moral principles, but can and should enter discussions of morality when the questions are applied: How can morality be taught? How can virtue be enhanced and vice avoided?

Yet, despite the dire warnings about mixing metaphysical and psychological matters, Kant uses the language of psychology to state what is arguably his most distinctive moral doctrine: A morally good action must be done from the motive of duty (Ak. 4, pp. 397 ff.). Or in Kant's explicitly psychological terminology:

> Nothing other than the **representation of the moral law** in itself—**which of course can take place only in a rational being**—in so far as it, not the hoped for effect, is the determining ground of the will, can therefore constitute the pre-eminent good that we call moral [...]. (Ak. 4, p. 401)

This claim about morality is replete with psychological notions that are essential to its import: "representation," "determining ground," and "will." On the other hand, the claim does not depend on empirical psychology, on observations of particular human behaviors. The provenance of the claim is, instead, Kant's distinctive way of addressing philosophical questions. In the *Critique of Pure Reason*, he asks, "how is experience possible?" "how are synthetic *a priori* judgments possible?" In addressing ethics, his questions are "how is morality possible?" "how is the Categorical Imperative possible?"

It is important to distinguish these questions about the possibility of morality from the goal of the *Critique of Pure Reason* to establish that the freedom required for morality, and so morality, are possible. Kant's aim in the *First Critique* is merely "defensive," as he puts it in *Groundwork 3*; it is merely that of showing that determinism does not rule out the possibility of freedom and so of morality (Ak. 4, p. 459). As we saw in the Preface to the *Second Critique*, his goal in his ethical writings is far more ambitious. He seeks indubitable proof that pure reason is practical and thus that morality is really possible.[7] This goal and the doctrine of duty cited above are cast in the language of faculty psychology. How and why does faculty psychology enter a discussion of the real possibility of morality?

It may be useful to contrast the transcendental psychology of the *Critique of Pure Reason* with the faculty psychology of Kant's ethical writings. One central project of the *First Critique* is to explain how experience or empirical cognition is possible. Kant's focus is not on knowledge *qua* justified true belief, but on something more basic that is presupposed by knowledge—cognizing—representing an object as having some property (Watkins/Willaschek 2017). His explanation proceeds by functional analysis, by decomposing the task of cognizing into its essential sub-tasks (Kitcher 1990), which include receiving representations through the senses, forming general representations of marks or characteristics that are common to many objects and applying those general representations to received sensory representations. The analyses provide "transcendental cognition" because they reveal that empirical cognition is impossible without *a priori* representations of space and time and *a priori* principles and concepts (A 11/B 25, A 56/B 80–81, A 65–66/B 89–91, A 94/B 126). Given the tight connection between 'transcendental' psychology and the necessity of *a priori* representations in empirical cognition, the faculty psychology of Kant's ethical writings cannot be characterized as 'transcendental.'

Still, the projects are similar, because both involve functional decomposition into essential sub-tasks. In the *Groundwork*, Kant is explicit that he begins with ordinary moral consciousness (Ak. 4, pp. 392, 403, 406). He is less explicit that his starting place is not just the ordinary moral agent's judgments of right and wrong, but also her understanding of the necessary psychological conditions for moral action in the exemplary cases he considers. Through carefully chosen examples, ordinary moral consciousness is plumbed for its understanding of the ways in which psychological faculties must be aligned in morally correct action (Ak. 4, pp. 397–401).

---

7 See note 6.

Kant characterizes the first two sections of the *Groundwork* as "analytic," which are to be followed by a "synthetic" third section (Ak. 4, p. 392). These sections are "analytic," because they regress from ordinary moral cognition to the necessary conditions for morality, as ordinarily understood. The *First Critique* clarifies what such an "analytic" consists in, by contrasting the work of its Analytic of Concepts with the practice of conceptual analysis:

> By 'analytic of concepts' I do not understand their analysis, or the procedure usual in philosophical investigations, that of dissecting the content of such concepts as may present themselves, and so of rendering them more distinct; but the hitherto rarely attempted **dissection of the faculty of the understanding** itself, in order to investigate the possibility of looking for them in the understanding alone, as their birthplace, and by *analyzing the pure use of this faculty.* This is the proper task of transcendental philosophy [...]. (A 64–66/ B 89–91, my italics)

By analogy, the "analytic" sections of the *Groundwork* do not analyze the concepts of 'good' and 'evil,' but explore the possibility of morality by dissecting the faculties involved in human action into their pure and empirical uses. The general form of Kant's explanation is: Morality is possible only because faculty A functions in way 1, faculty B functions in way 2 and so forth. Such functional analyses are consistent with his dismissal of the results of empirical psychology, because they do not appeal to features that humans happen to have, but to the sub-capacities that an agent must have to have a real moral capacity.

Kant is often criticized for claiming that it is part of ordinary moral consciousness that

> I ought never to proceed except in such a way that I could also will that my maxim should become a universal law. (Ak. 4, p. 402)

A parallel criticism could be made about the faculty psychology that he attributes to the ordinary moral agent. Do ordinary moral agents think that the moral worth of an action lies in a representation of the moral law that is the determining ground of the will? Presumably ordinary agents do not think in terms of "representations" or "determining grounds" at all, even if they occasionally think about a free "will." As Kant introduces the formula of universal law in the *Groundwork*, he explains that when he claims that common human reason always has this principle "before its eyes," he does not mean that the ordinary person thinks of her moral principle at this level of abstraction, as a universal principle governing all actions (Ak. 4, pp. 402, 404). Rather, ordinary agents think of the particular action that they are contemplating as a universal law, and then philosophers characterize this practice abstractly, as testing a maxim against the possibility of its being a universal law. In a similar way, Kant's claim about ordinary agents' understanding of how the faculties must align in morally correct action would not be that they employ the language of faculty psychology, but that a philosopher can use that language to characterize their judgments about individual cases in an abstract and illuminating way. Faculty psychology enters Kant's account of the possibility of morality because he takes ordinary moral consciousness to hold that the morality or immorality of an action depends on its motive; how it enters is that he proposes to explain the possibility of morality by expressing the moral consciousness of ordinary agents about what is required for moral action in the standard vocabulary of psychological faculties (but see below, p. 9), but with his signature emphasis on the pure (non-empirical) and empirical uses of those faculties.

Although Kant's faculty moral psychology is very evident in the text, its centrality has been diminished by the presence of two competing psychological doctrines: Since moral motivation cannot be phenomenal, the only possible moral psychology would be noumenal, i. e., impossible; Kant's 'practical' proof of morality and freedom invokes the agential perspective, i. e. a perspective that cannot be studied by a third person or scientific psychology. If these alternative 'psychologies' divert attention from Kant's faculty moral psychology, his commitment to banishing observations of human psychology from discussions of foundational moral principles seems to mark the project itself as illegitimate. What I have argued in this first section is that neither the two alternative psychologies nor the rejection of observational psychology should diminish scholarly interest in pursuing Kant's faculty moral psychology and, further, that it is essential to do so, because he uses that psychology to carry out his central project of explaining how morality is possible. In section two, I will present the basics of his moral psychology and then draw on that account in section three to provide a more adequate understanding of his perennially unpopular practical demonstration of the real possibility of morality in the fact of reason texts, i. e. the Comments to § 6, § 7 and its Corollary of the *Second Critique*.

2 Faculties Required for a Moral Capacity

Kant begins to lay out the faculties required for morality and freedom in the *First Critique* as he turns from cognitive to moral matters. Without first specifying either what an ability to choose is or what a faculty of desire is, he contrasts the ability to choose of animals with a capacity for free, rational choice.

> [A]n ability to choose [*Willkür*] is merely **animal** (*arbitrium brutum*), if it cannot be determined otherwise than through sensible impulses [...]. But an ability to choose that can be determined independently of sensible impulses and hence through motivating causes that are independent of sensory impulses that are represented only by reason is called a **free ability to choose** (*arbitrium liberum*) [...]. Practical freedom can be proved through experience. For the human ability to choose is determined not merely by what stimulates, i. e. by what directly affects the senses. Rather we have an ability to overcome, through representations of what is beneficial or harmful even in a more remote way, the impressions made upon our sensible faculty of desire. (A 802/B 830, amended translation[8])

This discussion seems inconsistent. It opens with a contrast between creatures whose choices can be determined only through impulses and (presumably) those who can also be determined by something else. Then it claims that experience can show that humans have a free ability to choose. As Kant well appreciates, however, even though experience reveals that human choices are not stimulus bound, it cannot show that they do not require any sensory impulse at all.

Without explaining what a will (*Wille*) is, the *Groundwork* opens with the pronouncement that a good will is the only unconditionally good thing. Many pages later, it offers Kant's famous and problematic identification of the will with practical reason:

> Everything in nature works according to laws. Only a rational being has the capacity to act **according to the representation** of laws, i. e. according to principles, or a **will.** Since **reason** is required for deriving actions from laws, the will is nothing other than practical reason. If reason determines the will without fail ... i. e. the will is a capacity for choosing **only that** which reason independently of all inclination recognizes as practically necessary, that is, as good. (Ak. 4, p. 412)

As innumerable readers have noted, something must be wrong in this account. If the will is identical with practical reason, then how could it *not* choose what reason recognizes as good?

By contrast, the *Critique of Practical Reason* is more systematic in introducing the faculties that are critical to morality. In a note to the *Preface* Kant admits that he was not careful enough in the *Groundwork* in presenting the fundamental faculty required for action, *viz.*, that of desire. Properly understood

---

8 "*Willkür*" is usually translated as the 'power of choice,' e. g., by Pluhar (1996), but that is not an especially felicitous translation since Kant uses "*Willkür*," and not '*Willkürskraft*.' Further when he addresses the possibility of a power or faculty of choice in criticizing Carl Leonhard Reinhold (Ak. 6, p. 226), he does not use "*Willkür*," but the expression "*Vermögen der Wahl*."

[t]he **power of desire** [Begehrungsvermögen] is the [living] being's **power to be, through its representations, the cause of the actuality of the objects of these representations.** (Ak. 5, p. 9a)

The correction is needed, because on the standard psychological account, the faculty of pleasure is assumed always to be the determining basis of the faculty of desire. In that case, morality would be impossible, so Kant offers a broader and more neutral characterization. Some creatures have a capacity to be through their representations the cause of the objects of those representations. This capacity or faculty can be labeled "desire" and the question of whether desire is always determined by pleasure can be left open.

Kant's discussion of the faculties involved in morality (and in cognition and judgments of art) is even more systematic in the First Introduction to the *Critique of the Power of Judgment*. He addresses the then current controversy about how many basic faculties there are. Christian Wolff had argued from the simplicity of the soul to the conclusion that its various operations must all be expressions of a single basic power, that of representation (Meta. § 747, pp. 465–466, § 784, p. 488).[9] J. N. Tetens's *Philosophische Versuche* originally pressed for the view that there had to be more than one basic faculty, but then somewhat reversed course and conceded that possibly all could be explained by a single basic faculty of "active feeling" (PV, vol. 1, pp. 607, 609; Kitcher 2014, pp. 124–126). By contrast, Kant maintains that Wolff cannot be right:

For there is always a great difference between representations belonging to cognition, insofar as they are related merely to the object and the unity of the consciousness of it, and their objective relation, where considered as at the same time the cause of the reality of the object, they are assigned to the faculty of desire [...]. (Ak. 20, p. 206)

It is impossible to reduce all the faculties to one, because of the different ways in which the representations of different faculties figure in relations between subjects and objects. The key feature of the faculty of cognition is that its representations are means by which subjects can know objects. By contrast, the representations of the faculty of desire enable subjects to produce objects. On the other hand, although Kant argues that there must be three basic faculties (cognition, desire, and a faculty of pleasure and pain or feeling), he explains that the

exercise [*Ausübung*] of all of them [...] is always grounded in the faculty of cognition. (Ak. 20, p. 245)

---

9 I use Wolff's (1751/1983) system of giving references with the abbreviated book title, e.g., *Meta[physik]* and the paragraph, as well as by the pagination in this edition.

More precisely, the exercise of such faculties by rational beings, paradigmatically human beings, is grounded in the faculty of cognition.

Kant elaborates that although the use of, e.g., the faculty of desire is grounded in the faculty of cognition, it is not grounded in intuitions, but in principles (and so in concepts). The faculty that grounds the rational use of all faculties is

the faculty of cognition in accordance with principles. (Ak. 20, p. 245)

With the mediation through the faculty of cognition, he observes that theorists must add three "higher powers" to go along with the three basic faculties:

Faculty of cognition	Understanding
Faculty of pleasure and displeasure	Power of Judgment
Faculty of desire	Reason (Ak. 20, p. 245)

The higher powers provide the principles governing the mediating faculty of cognition. Thus, although there is mediation through the faculty of cognition, the mediation is not primarily through principles required for cognition.

Student lecture notes from Kant's metaphysics course, now dated to be around 1777–1780 (Carl 1989, p. 119), present him as arguing that 'higher' faculties require self-consciousness. Although the notes do not use the term 'higher,' the contrast is between animals who have representations only of outer sense and humans who also have an inner sense (which Kant once thought was crucial for the kind of rational cognition that was distinctive of humans [see Ak. 2, pp. 59–60]). Because animals have only outer senses

they will go without those representations that rest on inner sense, on the consciousness of the self, in short on the concept of the 'I.' They will accordingly have no understanding and no reason; for all acts of the understanding and of reason are possible only insofar as one is conscious of oneself. (Ak. 28, p. 276)

By the time of the *First Critique* Kant is clearer that the self-consciousness that is crucial to the use of concepts is not the passive consciousness that might arise from an inner sense. Rather, in judging, using a concept, the subject must be conscious of what she is doing. In his exemplary case of counting, the subject must not forget that she has been adding units together one after another or she will not be able to apply a number concept (A 103–104). It is only by consciously combining representations that a subject can apply a concept, e.g., 'four.'

> Often this consciousness may be only faint, so that we do not [notice it] in the act itself, i.e. do not connect it directly with the representation's production, but [notice it] only in the act's effect. Without this consciousness, concepts, and along with them cognition of objects, are quite impossible. (A 103–104, amended translation)

Kant's point is not that unless the subject keeps track of her counting, she might attribute the wrong number—she counted to four, but judges the number of items to be three. It is that if she were not conscious in adding the units one after another in the manner prescribed by the counting rule, then she would not be using any number concept at all, even the wrong one. The counting example is particularly clear, but all concept application has the same requirement. A subject who uses a concept must be conscious of doing so on some appropriate ground.

Having established that discursive judgment requires self-consciousness, the *First Critique* need not separately establish that inference requires self-consciousness, since inference involves judgments. In the *Logic*, Kant explains the basis that inference provides for judgments:

> By **inferring** is understood that function of thought whereby one judgment is derived from another. (Ak. 9, p. 114; see also A 303/B 359)

In inferring, a subject is conscious of making one judgment on the basis of another. As with judging, subjects do not always attend to their activity in inferring:

> Because we constantly have to make use of inference and so end by being completely accustomed to it, we no longer take note of this distinction [between immediate and mediate cognition], and frequently, as in the so-called deceptions of the senses, treat as being immediately perceived what has really only been inferred. (A 303/B 359)

Even though subjects do not always mark habitual inferences as inferences, they still distinguish perceptual judgments from mediate ones—judgments where one cognition is grounded on others. If the subject were not conscious in deriving some judgment from others, then she would be incapable of reasoning. She might, in the manner of animals, associate the sounds 'Socrates is mortal' with the sounds 'All men are mortal' and 'Socrates is a man,' but she could not infer that Socrates is mortal.

Although Kant does not offer a systematic account of the "higher power" of desire and its dependence on the faculty of cognition and on principles until the *Third Critique*, there does not appear to be any change in view. He refers to "higher powers" in the *First Critique* (A 130–131/B 169), in the *Second Critique* (Ak. 5, p. 24) and in the *Anthropology from a Pragmatic Point of View* (Ak. 7, pp. 140–

141); the *Groundwork*'s introduction of the crucial idea of acting on principle clearly draws on this conception. Rational beings have a higher power of desire that is mediated by concepts and principles in that they are able to derive their actions from principles.

Even if no new doctrine is introduced in presenting his faculty psychology explicitly in terms of "higher powers" that employ concepts and principles and so require self-consciousness, it is illuminating briefly to consider what this implies. In making judgments and in deriving action-guiding judgments from principles, a moral agent must be conscious of the grounds of those judgments and conscious of them not through inner sense, but through the conscious activity of thinking. This self-conscious mental activity supplies a very different basis for the claim that rational beings can act on principle. Here we are not dealing with an inference to the best explanation of observable behavior, as in, e. g., 'My dog must represent his water bowl and its location because he goes to it when he has not had a drink in a while.' Theorists do not maintain that humans act on principle by, e. g., watching baseball players exit the batter's box after the third strike. Theorists know that the players are following the rules —acting on principle—because the players know that, and the players know that, because they know the basis of their returning to the dugout after the third strike, because they returned on that basis. This is one of the myriad of mental activities revealed in self-consciousness.

We now have a fairly full account of the faculty psychology that Kant invokes in explaining the possibility of morality.[10] Rational beings, paradigmatically human beings, have a faculty of desire that is not bound to react to immediate stimuli and that can be mediated by concepts and principles, so they can be conscious of the grounds of their judgments, in particular, of the principles from which they derive actions. These capacities are essential to establishing the possibility of morality, because the exploration of ordinary moral consciousness in the *Groundwork* has shown that morality, as ordinarily understood, will be possible only if subjects have a higher faculty of desire or a will—a will that can be determined by principles and so by the representation of the moral law.

---

10 I have not discussed Kant's introduction of a "*Gesinnung*" in *Religion within the Bounds of Mere Reason*, or his effort firmly to separate an ability to choose (*Willkür*) from the rational will (*Wille*) in the *Metaphysics of Morals* here. In another paper, I argue these further considerations refine, but do not fundamentally alter Kant's faculty psychology of morality (Kitcher 2018).

3. The Practical Proof of the Fact of Reason

Kant is clear about what the *Critique of Practical Reason* needs to prove to establish the possibility of morality. In the Preface he explains that

[t]his *Critique* is to establish merely **that there is pure practical reason** [...]. (Ak. 5, p. 3)

The Introduction explains exactly what this means in its formulation of the question at issue:

[T]he first question is whether pure reason is sufficient by itself alone to determine the will, or whether reason can be a determining basis of the will only as empirically conditioned. (Ak. 5, p. 15)

Pure reason can be shown to be practical—there is a pure practical reason—just in case pure reason alone can determine the will or rational faculty of desire. What does 'determining the will' mean? As Kant notes, in the world of sense

causality with regard to actions of the will [...] must be cognized by reason in a determinate way, for otherwise practical reason could not actually give rise to any deed. (Ak. 5, p. 49)

To determine her will, a subject's reason must specify the action she is to take. As we have seen, there is no need for philosophy to establish that a subject's reason can determine her will. Human beings have the capacity to act from principles and anyone who can act from principles must know that she can, even if most people would not express their self-knowledge so formally. But that self-consciousness does not settle the issue of whether a subject's pure reason can determine her will; that is, it does not settle whether her reason can determine her will through principles that reason supplies from itself, or only through principles of action that are conditional on expected pleasures or pains.

Kant places an important restriction on establishing the possibility of morality. Although ordinary moral consciousness understands that the moral worth of an action depends on its motive, it is not possible even for the agent to be certain in any actual case that her motive was the moral law (Ak. 4, p. 407). He notes that people often take themselves to be doing the right thing for the right reasons, but he thinks that is because humans have a strong tendency to flatter themselves and so discount the possibility that their interest in, e.g., preserving their reputations might be providing the motivation for actions that are merely in accord with morality (Ak. 4, p. 407). He is also aware that whatever good deed might be presented to a moral skeptic or cynic, that person can always find some self-interested motive behind it (Ak. 4, p. 407).

Given this limitation, Kant does not try to show that pure reason determines action, but only that it determines the will (or willing). He signals in the Introduction that the *Second Critique* will not originally be concerned with the production of actions, but only with determinations of the will, practical judgments about what to do:

> In this [practical] use, reason deals with determining bases of the will, which is a power either to produce objects corresponding to one's representations, or, at any rate, to determine itself to bring about these objects [...], i.e., to determine its causality. For there [in the latter case] reason can at least succeed in determining the will and, insofar as the willing [*das Wollen*] alone is at issue, always has objective reality. (Ak. 5, p. 15, amended translation)

Kant appears to beg the question in the last sentence, since he claims that reason can determine the will to intend to produce a particular action, but he goes on to explain that this is the first question (and so not assumed), the question of whether pure reason can so determine the will.

The *Critique of Pure Reason* presents another limitation on any proof of morality. As noted, it maintains that humans have no access to their thinking through outer or even inner sense. What humans know about their mental characters comes from the self-consciousness that must be present in higher or rational cognition. It follows that Kant has only one avenue for demonstrating the possibility that pure reason can determine the will—that a principle of pure reason can be the basis of a practical judgment to act in a particular way. He must engage his reader in higher practical cognition, i.e., in moral deliberation.

The paragraphs of the *Second Critique* leading up to the fact of reason texts begin with an analysis of the concept of "practical law": A "practical law" must hold for the will of every rational being (Ak. 5, p. 19) and so be objectively necessary; it must be independent of any differences of inclinations across rational beings (Ak. 5, p. 20). Kant then turns to the task of dissecting principles into their pure and empirical elements. Insofar as they have an object whose reality is desired for the pleasure it would produce, principles are empirical. Kant insists that all practical principles that have an object or matter are species of the principle of self-love. He claims further that unless there were formal (i.e. non-material) principles of the will, it would be pointless to distinguish between lower and higher faculties of desire. He concludes that if a rational being is to think of her maxims as practical laws, then she must think of them as determining the will through their form (not matter) (Ak. 5, p. 27). (Again, this is the way a philosopher, not the ordinary moral agent, would describe the situation.) This conclusion is buttressed by two further claims: It is an identical proposition that

> [a] practical law that I cognize as such must qualify for the giving of universal law. (Ak. 5, p. 28)

Further, the most common understanding is able to discern whether a maxim has that form, i.e., is fit for the giving of universal law (Ak. 5, p. 27). From the conclusion about form, it follows that there will be practical laws if and only if reason has a pure part, a part that can determine the will through the mere form of a maxim, and so independently of any object connected by experience to the faculty of pleasure.

As with the first two sections of the *Groundwork*, the elucidation of what it would be for pure reason to determine the will establishes only a conditional claim: If morality is possible—if there are practical laws—then pure reason must determine the will to a specific course of action through the mere form of the maxim. In § 6, Kant raises the crucial question of human cognition of freedom and morality, and claims that human cognition of freedom and the moral law must begin with the latter.

> [I]t is the **moral law** of which we become conscious directly (as soon as we frame or draft or pose [*entwerfen*] maxims of the will for ourselves) which **first** offers itself to us, and which inasmuch as reason displays [*darstellt*] it as a determining basis not to be outweighed by any sensible conditions and indeed entirely independently of them—leads straight to the idea of freedom. (Ak. 5, pp. 29–30, amended translation)

How is this claim, which presents exactly the conclusion that Kant needs to establish, supported in the text? Here I follow Marcus Willaschek (1992, p. 186) in regarding the cases of lust and false testimony that Kant introduces in § 6 as *Gedanken* experiments designed to focus readers' attentions on the fact that when trying to figure out what to do in a morally parlous situation, *they* are conscious of the moral law as determining their wills.

As Willaschek notes, Kant concludes the *Second Critique* by reflecting on the methodological situation of the philosopher. The moral philosopher must follow the practice of chemistry and dissect examples of morally judging reason

> in repeated experiments on common human understanding [...] a procedure of **separation** of the empirical from the rational that may be found in them, this can allow us to be acquainted [*kennbar machen*] with both of them **pure** and, with certainty, what each can accomplish by itself. (Ak. 5, p. 163, amended translation; see also Ak. 5, p. 92)

The false testimony case provides a helpful thought experiment, because, as Willaschek notes, all imaginable motives of self-interest are on the other side (1992, pp. 186–187). Kant invites his readers to consider a case where a prince demanded of someone:

> on the threat of the [...] penalty of death [by immediate hanging], that he give false testimony against an honest man whom the prince would like to ruin under specious pretenses, he might consider it possible to overcome his love of life, however great it may be. He will perhaps not venture to assure us whether or not he would overcome that love, but he must concede without hesitation that doing so would be possible for him. He judges, therefore, that he can do something *because he is conscious that he ought to do it*, and he cognizes [*erkennt*] freedom within himself—the freedom with which otherwise, without the moral law, he would have remained unacquainted. (Ak. 5, p. 30, my italics)

Although I agree with Willaschek's basic approach, I think the *Gedankenexperiment* needs to be spelled out in more detail.

Kant wants to show that pure reason can determine the will independently of sensory impulses, i.e., without any considerations of present or future pleasure or pain. If the thought experiment resulted only in readers judging that they ought to not give false testimony while being conscious that no considerations of self-interest lead to that judgment, then it would not establish the efficacy of pure reason. Perhaps nothing led them to judge that they ought to not testify falsely or perhaps they were moved by sympathy for the man. Kant would dismiss the former possibility because, as rational beings, they must have some ground for their judgment; he would dismiss the latter possibility because he takes sympathy to be ultimately based in self-love and/or because it is too subjective a basis for the necessary universality of a practical law. These objections to the second possibility are, however, philosophical and do not show that someone considering the case could not think 'I ought to not bear false witness' on the ground of sympathy for other humans.[11] Kant cannot assume that there is only one basis on which someone could judge that she ought not testify falsely (even if other ways at arriving at an 'ought' can be criticized). What his faculty psychology of reasoning implies is that, *if* the subject judges that she ought to

---

11 When I read an earlier version of the paper to the FAGI group in Leipzig, Sebastian Rödl noted that Kant has ways of dismissing sympathy as the basis of an 'ought' claim. Although Rödl is correct that Kant tries to eliminate sympathy as a basis for moral judgment through considerations offered in the sections that precede the fact of reason texts, I am not persuaded by Kant that sympathy must be a form of self-love. As the text above makes clear, however, this philosophical debate is irrelevant to the psychological point that, when performing the experiment, subjects could come to believe they ought to not bear false witness on various grounds.

not bear false witness on the ground that she cannot will a world of false testimony, then she must be self-conscious in judging on that ground.

Kant presents the fact of reason doctrine as agents' consciousness of the moral law. He echoes the assertion made earlier in § 6 that practical deliberators are directly conscious of the moral law:

> The consciousness of this basic law may be called a fact [*Faktum*] of reason, because one cannot reason it out from antecedent data of reason [...] rather, it thrusts itself upon us on its own as a synthetic a priori proposition not based on any intuition, whether pure or empirical [...]. [Through this consciousness] [...] pure reason [...] announces itself as originally lawgiving (Ak. 5, p. 31, amended translation)

I take the practical proof to be constituted by the claim about the epistemic priority of the moral law, the thought experiment and the conclusion announcing a fact of reason:

To be shown: When humans, or those possessed of a rational will more generally, form an intention about what to do, they are conscious of the moral law as determining their judgment.

Thought experiment: Suppose a prince demands that you bear false witness. In deliberating about what to do in the face of this demand, you become conscious that you ought to not bear false witness, [because you cannot will a world of false witnessing.]

Conclusion: [When deliberating about what to do,] humans are conscious of pure reason as giving the moral law, as originally lawgiving, through their non-empirical consciousness of the moral law [as e. g., the basis of their practical judgment that they ought not bear false witness.]

Except for the phrases in square brackets, this account of the practical proof merely paraphrases Kant's text. Since the bracketed additions have clear warrants in the text and in his theory of judging and inferring, I take the account to be an explication rather than a reconstruction of Kant's reasoning.

An essential feature of the account is that subjects who participate in the experiment are conscious of the moral law in two different ways. First, they are conscious of its content in the concrete case: Unless I can will a world of false witnessing, I ought to not bear false witness. They become so conscious, because when they formulate their maxim—and pause to consider whether what they are doing is right, as also happens in the Groundwork's famous four examples (Ak. 4, pp. 421–423)—they ask whether their maxim conforms to practical law. Since it is analytic that if something is cognized as a practical law, then it must qualify as a universal law, they ask whether the universal law to which their maxim conforms (from which it can be derived, i. e., the universal form of their maxim) is possible as a universal law. Since they also understand that, unlike natural laws, practical laws are possible only if they can be willed,[12] the subjects are conscious that they ought to not bear false witness, unless they can will a world of false witnessing. But they are also conscious of the moral law in a second way: They are self-conscious in inferring from this instance of the moral law to the judgment that they ought to not bear false witness. This is how they have a practical cognition that their consciousness of the principle is not inert, but determines their will to a particular act, that of not bearing false witness. Although ordinary people would not use this terminology, philosophers may characterize the situation abstractly, and usefully, as a practical proof that 'act only on that maxim that your will could always hold at the same time as a principle in giving universal law' is an efficacious principle in practical deliberation. As Kant puts it in the title of §7, the moral law is a "basic law [*Grundgesetz*] of pure practical reason" (Ak. 5, p. 30), i.e., a basic principle through which pure practical reason (actually) operates.[13] It determines the will to an action that will ensue unless opposed by self-love.

Besides clarifying how the practical proof is supposed to work, Kant's faculty psychology also enables us to understand his Preface boast that he will prove the possibility of freedom and morality through a deed and in such a way that no amount of counter-argument can cast doubt on their possibility. Since practical deliberating is a species of reasoning, when subjects infer a course of action from a principle, they enjoy Cartesian certainty about the existence of the judgment and its ground. As noted, Kant has a different view about ultimate decisions to act. Even in theoretical cases where there is evidence for and against holding something to be true, the evidence must be weighed and further investigated, or not, and inclinations can lead one to put one's finger on the scale or to not continue looking for evidence that one would rather not find.[14] The situation is worse in the practical case, where the secret influence of inclinations can both lead to action and to misrepresenting one's motive as the moral one (Ak. 4, p. 407). Although the complex processes of holding a judgment to be true and reaching a final decision about how to act can be opaque and error-filled, Kant would agree with Descartes that in carrying out a single transition to a judg-

---

12 I argue for this way of understanding "conforming" to law and explain how willing enters the formula of universal law in my 2004.

13 It is a *basic* principle (*Grundsatz*) of pure practical reason, because it contains a general determination that has more particular rules under it (Ak. 5, p. 19).

14 Alix Cohen (2013) argues that Kant made an important distinction between the more or less automatic acts of judging and reasoning and the complex process of holding-to-be-true. She also drew my attention to some key passages where Kant discusses these matters in the Bloomberg logic, Ak. 24, pp. 158, 736. See also Ak. 9, pp. 73–74.

ment, such as judging '4' on the basis of counting, or in inferring that 'Socrates is mortal' on the basis of, e. g., the usual premises, subjects are self-conscious and so indubitably certain of their judgment and of the ground on which they make it.[15]

I have explicated the *Gedankenexperiment* and the special status of the fact of reason claim by appealing to Kant's theory of reasoning, but the theory is hardly unique to him. Tetens argues that self-consciousness (apperception) is essential to thinking, giving inference as an example. Inference is a matter of

> deriving one [proposition] from another, and apperceiving the dependency of the last upon the first. (PV, vol. 1, p. 371)

More recently, Paul Boghossian offers the following characterization of inference:

> reasoning [is] a mental action that a person *performs*, in which he is either *aware*, or can become aware, of why he is moving from some beliefs to others. (Boghossian 2014, p. 16)[16]

What is original with Kant is the realization that, given a familiar theory of the necessary conditions for inferring, it is possible to construct a practical proof of the efficacy of the moral law to determine the will by inviting readers to engage in practical deliberation. He constructs the experiment for maximum effect by beginning with a contrasting case of lust, where the threat of the same penalty utterly extinguishes a man's allegedly irresistible lust for his mistress. The false testimony case then demonstrates not just that the moral law can determine the will on its own, without any aid from self-love, but that it can do so even when all the interests of self-love are arrayed against it. Again, how the demonstration works is that *if* an agent infers that she ought to not give false testimony, because she cannot will a world of false testimony, then she is self-conscious in judging on that ground and so cannot not be brought to doubt that she is so judging.

Kant acknowledges that most agents would be hesitant to claim that they could resist the pull of self-love and so do what they ought; but that does not alter the fact that if they make a practical judgment about what they ought to

---

15 In a discussion of a related paper, Andrew Chignell helpfully pressed me to be clearer about how Cartesian certainty about thinking applies to the case of practical deliberation.

16 Contemporary scholars sometimes argue that there are other sorts of mental transitions that can be understood as rational, but that do not involve this sort of awareness (e. g., Susanna Siegel forthcoming). Even if these somewhat controversial proposals are established, however, they would not affect Kant's use of (conscious) inferring to demonstrate that pure reason can move the will.

do on the basis of the principle, then they cannot be brought to doubt that they have. And that is all that Kant thinks that he needs to defend the real possibility of morality—a single case where the agent derives her practical judgment about what she ought to do from the moral principle. The analysis of ordinary moral consciousness in the *Groundwork* and in the earlier parts of the *Second Critique* have already shown that the moral law is the standard by which ordinary agents measure the morality of actions and so is the highest principle of morality. All that remains to show is that it is efficacious. The practical proof suffices to defeat the skeptical objection that Kantian morality is not really possible, because only pleasure can determine the faculty of action. It also reveals the objection to be skeptical, since agents' rational faculties make them conscious not only of which actions are right and wrong, but also of the grounds of some of those judgments. The point of the thought-experiments is thus to remind readers of what they already know through their practical deliberating, *viz.*, that they can make a practical judgment that they ought to not perform an action on the grounds that they cannot will it to be a universal practice.

I have not tried to answer all the questions that have been raised about the practical proof in the fact of reason. In particular, I have not addressed the essential question of whether this pattern of practical reasoning is inculcated by education or is, as the title to § 7 claims, simply a basic law of pure reason, a law that pure reason supplies from itself. All I have tried to argue is that unless we pay attention to Kant's faculty psychology, including his views about what is revealed by self-consciousness in reasoning, we will neither understand nor appreciate his defense of the innocence of ordinary moral agents against philosophical skeptics. He does not retreat to defending freedom and morality as merely one point of view that competes with others; he taps into the self-consciousness that is required for rationality and morality to remind agents that they are as certain about deriving a judgment about what they ought to do from the moral law as they are in making any simple inference from one judgment to another.[17]

---

17 I am grateful to members of the FAGI group in Leipzig, for many helpful comments on an earlier version of this paper and to the members of Tobias Rosefeldt's group at the Humboldt University for a very lively and enlightening discussion of a related paper. I am also happy to acknowledge support from the Max Planck Institute for the History of Science while I was writing the paper.

References

Ak. | Kant, Immanuel (1900 ff.): *Kant's gesammelte Schriften*. Königlich Preußische Akademie der Wissenschaften. 29 vols. Berlin/New York: Walter de Gruyter and predecessors.

Meta. | Wolff, Christian (1751/1983): *Vernünfftige Gedancken von Gott, der Welt und der Seele des Menschen, auch allen Dingen überhaupt*. Reprint. Hildesheim et al.: Georg Olms Verlag.

PV | Tetens, Johann Nicolas (1777): *Philosophische Versuche über die menschliche Natur und ihre Entwickelung*. 2 vols. Leipzig: Weidmann.

Allison, Henry (1990): *Kant's Theory of Freedom*. Cambridge.

Ameriks, Karl/Naragon, Steve (trans. and eds.) (1997): *Immanuel Kant. Lectures on Metaphysics. The Cambridge Edition of the Works of Immanuel Kant*. P. Guyer and A. W. Wood (gen. eds.). Cambridge: Cambridge University Press.

Beck, Lewis White (1960): *A Commentary on Kant's Critique of Practical Reason*. Chicago: University of Chicago Press.

Boghossian, Paul (2014): "What is Inference?" In: *Philosophical Studies* 169. No. 1, pp. 1–18.

Carl, Wolfgang (1989): *Der schweigende Kant: Die Enwürfe zu einer Deduktion der Kategorien*. Göttingen: Vandenhoeck & Ruprecht.

Cohen, Alix (2013): "Kant on Doxastic Voluntarism and its Implications for Epistemic Responsibility." In: *Kant Yearbook* 5. No. 1, pp. 33–50.

Engstrom, Stephen (2010): "Reason, desire, and the will." In: Lara Denis (ed.): *Kant's Metaphysics of Morals: A Critical Guide*. Cambridge: Cambridge University Press, pp. 28–50.

Gregor, Mary (trans. and ed.) (1996): *Immanuel Kant. Practical Philosophy. The Cambridge Edition of the Works of Immanuel Kant*. P. Guyer and A. W. Wood (gen. eds.). Cambridge: Cambridge University Press.

Gregor, Mary/Timmermann, Jens (trans. and eds.) (2011): *Immanuel Kant. Groundwork of the Metaphysics of Morals*. Cambridge: Cambridge University Press.

Kitcher, Patricia (1990): *Kant's Transcendental Psychology*. Oxford: Oxford University Press.

Kitcher, Patricia (2004): "Kant's Argument for the Categorical Imperative." In: *Noûs* XXXVIII, pp. 555–584.

Kitcher, Patricia (2013): "Kant versus the Asymmetry Dogma." In: *Kant Yearbook* 5. No. 1, pp. 51–78.

Kitcher, Patricia (2014): "Analyzing Apperception." In: Gideon Stiening/Udo Thiel (eds.): *Johann Nikolaus Tetens (1736–1807)*. Berlin/Boston: De Gruyter, pp. 103–132.

Kitcher, Patricia (2018): "Explaining Freedom in Thought and Action." In: Violetta L. Waibel/Margit Ruffing/David Wagner (eds.): *Natur und Freiheit. Akten des XII. Internationalen Kant-Kongresses*. Berlin/Boston: De Gruyter, pp. 185–207.

Kleingeld, Pauline (2010): "Moral consciousness and the 'fact of reason'". In: Andrews Reath/Jens Timmermann (eds.): *Kant's Critique of Practical Reason: A Critical Guide*. Cambridge: Cambridge University Press, pp. 55–72.

Pluhar, Werner (trans.) (1996): *Immanuel Kant. Critique of Pure Reason: Unified Edition*. Indianapolis: Hackett.

Pluhar, Werner (trans.) (2002): *Immanuel Kant. Critique of Practical Reason*. Indianapolis: Hackett.

Siegal, Susanna (forthcoming): "Inference without Reckoning." In: Magdalena Balcerak
    Jackson/Brendan Balcerak Jackson (eds.): *Reasoning: Essays in Theoretical and Practical
    Thinking*. Oxford: Oxford University Press.
Strawson, Peter F. (1966): *The Bounds of Sense*. London: Methuen.
Ware, Owen (2014): "Rethinking Kant's Fact of Reason." In: *Philosophers' Imprint* 14. No. 32,
    pp. 1–21.
Watkins, Eric/Willaschek, Marcus (2017): "Kant's Account of Cognition." In: *The Journal for
    the History of Philosophy* 55, pp. 83–112.
Willaschek, Marcus (1992): *Praktische Vernunft: Handlungstheorie und Moralbegründung bei
    Kant*. Stuttgart: J. B. Metzler.

Katharina T. Kraus

Rethinking the Relationship between Empirical Psychology and Transcendental Philosophy in Kant

Abstract. *This paper explores the transcendental sources that Kant's philosophy is able to offer to empirical psychology as the study of the empirical aspects of the human mind. I argue that Kant's transcendental philosophy defines a set of distinctive conditions in terms of an idea of reason – the idea of the soul – which gives systematic unity to psychological knowledge. The idea of the soul primarily serves as the most general genus-concept of the domain of inner nature, i. e., the idea defines what counts as a psychological phenomenon to be investigated in empirical psychology. In addition, the idea of the soul serves as a placeholder for the complete species-concept of an individual person.*

Dieser Artikel untersucht die transzendentalen Grundlagen der empirischen Psychologie als der empirischen Lehre vom menschlichen Gemüt nach Kant. Darin wird gezeigt, dass nach Kants Transzendentalphilosophie von der Vernunftidee der Seele spezifische Bedingungen abgeleitet werden können, die allem psychologischen Wissen eine systematische Einheit verleihen. Die Idee der Seele dient dabei hauptsächlich als allgemeinster Gattungsbegriff der inneren Natur, d. h. die Idee bestimmt, was überhaupt als ein in der empirischen Psychologie zu untersuchendes Phänomen gilt. Zudem dient die Idee der Seele als Platzhalter für den vollständigen Artbegriff einer individuellen Person.

Introduction

The relationship between transcendental philosophy and empirical psychology is a notoriously difficult and controversial issue in Kant. There seems to be some consensus with regard to their distinct subject matters. Transcendental philosophy aims to uncover the necessary conditions of human cognition and morality that apply universally for every human thinker and agent. By contrast, empirical psychology – broadly speaking – seeks to explain the empirical-psychological features of human individuals, such as the actual operations of mental faculties, the temporal occurrence and causal relations of mental states, as

https://doi.org/10.1515/9783110673692-007

well as the development and display of character traits.[1] Yet commentators differ greatly over the question of how exactly the two disciplines are related.

Kant himself is at pains to keep the two disciplines apart and occasionally warns us not to confuse his transcendental philosophy with matters of psychology and not to fall back on psychological accounts, if concerned with transcendental matters.[2] In other places, Kant points out how transcendental philosophy may illuminate or resolve certain puzzles and misconceptions held by empirical psychologists.[3] In yet other places, Kant seems to suggest that empirical psychology may even promote the aims of transcendental philosophy in that it provides empirical examples and hence some corroboration for his transcendental claims about the human mind.[4]

Kant's diverse comments on matters of psychology have led commentators to propose a variety of accounts of the relationship between transcendental philosophy and empirical psychology. Some argue that they are largely distinct enterprises, even to the extent that empirical psychology may not fall under the transcendental conditions of cognition, as explicated in Kant's *Critique of Pure Reason* [henceforth *Critique*].[5] Some conclude that empirical psychology does not contain full-fledged objective knowledge (i. e., empirical cognition of objects) since it cannot be subject to the transcendental conditions of experience examined in transcendental philosophy.[6] Others see close interrelations between the two disciplines.[7] Some even concede that transcendental philosophy depends to some extent on some sort of empirical-psychological knowledge.[8] What has been

---

1 Interpreters who subscribe to this or a similar characterization include Hatfield (2006), Schmidt (2008), Sturm (2009), Kitcher (2011), and Frierson (2014).

2 E. g., A 53–55/B 77–79; A 152; A 801/B 829; Anth, Ak. 7, pp. 135n, 141.

3 E. g., A 120n; B 153; A 380; A 848/B876; Anth, Ak. 7, p. 142.

4 E. g., in the Transcendental Deduction of the Categories, Kant uses examples from perception to illustrate his arguments, e. g., the example of drawing a line, s. A 102; B 154–155.

5 Mischel (1967), Nayak/Sotnak (1995).

6 Washburn (1975), Schoenrich (1991), Westphal (2004).

7 E. g., O'Neill (1984) and Schmidt (2008) propose a clear division of labour between transcendental philosophy and empirical psychology, recognizing the autonomy of each as well as their necessary interrelation. Schmidt (2008) interprets transcendental philosophy as "the study of universal and necessary principles of empirical cognition" and, correspondingly, "empirical cognitive psychology" as "the study of the success of any given human subject in any particular activity of judgment" (Schmidt 2008, p. 463). In a similar vein, s. Hatfield (2006). Emundts (2007, p. 205) construes empirical psychology as an "art of description" regarding the relations of mental states.

8 For Frierson, the material of empirical psychology "like all experience, is governed by the general transcendental categories", while "empirical psychology also serves transcendental philosophy by laying out the empirical influences on the development and exercise of proper reason-

largely ignored in the debate is whether transcendental philosophy is able to discern a more specific set of conditions for empirical psychology in addition to (or perhaps partly in replacement of) the necessary conditions of empirical cognition. Are there distinctive conditions that follow from a transcendental investigation of empirical psychology, such as conditions on what it means to be a psychological person, to have mental states in time, and to develop an empirical character?

In what follows, I shall take seriously the view that transcendental philosophy is an investigation of the necessary conditions of *all* human knowledge, including psychological knowledge, and argue that transcendental philosophy specifies some distinctive conditions for empirical psychology. More specifically, I shall explore the transcendental sources that Kant's philosophy is able to offer for the conceptualization and cognition of psychological phenomena. For current purposes, I do not enter into a detailed discussion of the different conceptions of empirical psychology in the eighteenth century, nor do I assess the extent to which, for Kant, empirical psychology as an academic discipline could ever rise to the rank of a science.[9] Rather, I confine myself to an analysis of the type of knowledge that is produced by studying the empirical aspects of the human mind, namely *psychological knowledge*, and examine the conditions of this type of knowledge, according to Kant's Critical philosophy.

To this effect, I first introduce Kant's distinction between transcendental and empirical faculties in Section 1. In Section 2, I examine the way in which psychological knowledge is related to, but also distinct from, a specific type of experience, namely inner experience, i.e., the experience of one's own mental states. In Section 3, I argue that empirical psychology is conditioned, not only by the transcendental conditions of experience defined by the understanding, but in addition relies on more specific transcendental sources provided by reason. In

---

ing, moral virtue, and the pursuit of happiness" (Frierson 2014, pp. 49 – 59). In a similar vein, Kitcher suggests that psychological knowledge is governed by the transcendental conditions of experience, but at the same time she demands that Kant should have acknowledged that transcendental philosophy is crucially informed by empirical psychology (Kitcher 2011, p. 159). In her earlier account, Kitcher (1990) still proposes a transcendental psychology to bridge the gap between transcendental philosophy and empirical psychology.

9 It is notoriously difficult to discern the exact notion of empirical psychology that Kant in fact had in mind or would have endorsed on the basis of his transcendental philosophy. It is not always clear in his Critical writings whether he uses the term to present his own views regarding matters of empirical psychology or to criticize the views of his contemporaries, such as Wolff and Baumgarten. For a survey of the different uses, s. Kraus/Sturm (2018, pp. 212 – 215), also Hatfield (2006). For a discussion of the scientific status of empirical psychology, s. Sturm (2009), Kraus (2018), and McNulty (2018).

particular, I show that the rational idea of the soul gives an indispensable guidance for the formation of psychological predicates and hence for the acquisition of psychological knowledge. This argument finally allows me, in Section 4, to identify the specific set of conditions that Kant's transcendental philosophy offers to make empirical psychology possible.

1 Transcendental Faculties and Empirical Faculties

A centrepiece of Kant's Critical philosophy is the division of mental faculties. While Kant's view is broadly in line with the prevailing faculty psychology that was held by many of his rationalist and empiricist predecessors, Kant crucially departs from their views in developing a *hylomorphic* account of experience.[10] This account distinguishes between transcendental (or formal) and empirical (or in a broad sense "material") aspects of mental faculties contributing to experience. So Kant frequently introduces both a transcendental and an empirical variant of the major faculties, e. g., "*a priori* sensibility" (A 21/ B 35) and the "empirical sense(s)" (A 29/B 35, see Anth, Ak. 7, pp. 153ff.), the "transcendental faculty of imagination" (A102) (or "productive imagination", B 152) and the "reproductive imagination" (which "belongs to psychology", B 152), "transcendental apperception" and "empirical apperception" (A 107). According to this hylomorphic account, a faculty is still seen as carrying out a mental operation and thereby generating representations. Yet these mental operations work not only upon *given* representational content, but importantly each faculty additionally contributes a characteristic *form* through which such representational content first becomes available to the mind. The faculty of sensibility, for instance, contributes the forms of space and time; the understanding contributes the categories (e. g., substance and causality), which are derived from the pure forms of judgment (e. g., categorical and hypothetical judgment).

Kant identifies three basic mental faculties and several derivative ones. The basic faculties are the faculty of *cognition*, *desire*, and *feeling*. The derivative faculties include: the senses, memory, understanding, reason, all of which belong to the power of cognition; the higher desires (e. g., rational motives) and lower

---

10 Many eighteenth-century philosophers endorsed some version of faculty psychology, both the empiricist-minded, such as Tetens (1777), and the rationalist-minded, such as Wolff (1732) and Baumgarten (1739). For the historical context, s. Heßbrüggen-Walter (2004) and Falduto (2014).

desires (e. g., instincts, basic inclinations); the feeling of respect and the feelings of pleasure and pain, and so on. This tripartite division features prominently in Kant's lectures on rational and empirical psychology, which were closely modeled on the textbook written by Alexander Baumgarten, a resolute proponent of rational psychology.[11] In his Critical philosophy, Kant offers a transcendental justification for this tripartite structure in terms of three basic dependence relations that a faculty can have to its objects. Firstly, the faculty of cognition is directed at given, existentially independent objects in the world. Secondly, the faculty of desire aims for the realization of an object or state of affairs in the world that is represented by a desire. Thirdly, feelings of pleasure and displeasure are not directed at objects: they are subjective states in that they do not represent an object, though they may themselves be the effect of a subject's having a cognitive or conative relation to an object.[12]

According to Kant's Critical hylomorphic account of our possible experience of nature, a mental faculty can be described either transcendentally qua its *form* or empirically qua the *representation* (or *representational content*) that it produces at a certain time. The former gives us "transcendental definitions" (CJ, Ak. 5, pp. 177–178n; cf. CpracR, Ak. 5, p. 9n; CJ First Intro, Ak. 20, pp. 205–206, 230n).[13] Such transcendental definitions primarily give functional accounts: each mental faculty is defined by the characteristic mental activity by which it produces a characteristic type of representation in accordance with its form. For instance, sensibility's function is to receive sensory content in the form of space and time, the understanding's function is to generate (pure or empirical) judgments in accordance with the logical forms of judgment, and so on.

The transcendental definition of a faculty applies universally to all human beings, i.e., all beings that are assumed to have the same mental faculties.[14] In this sense, a transcendental faculty can be understood as a *type* of faculty that, characteristically, gives rise to a particular *type* of representation (i.e. a rep-

---

11 Baumgarten (1739). I will not discuss Kant's pre-critical account of rational psychology, nor his later critique and rejection thereof. For discussion, s. Hatfield (2006), Kitcher (2011), and Dyck (2014).
12 S. CJ, Ak. 5, p. 189 and CpracR, Ak. 5, p. 9n.
13 In the CpracR (Ak. 5, p. 9n), Kant argues that in ethical disputes one should presuppose definitions of the basic faculties of desire and feeling that are neutral with regard to the ethical theory that one defends. This is precisely what his "transcendental definitions" of desire and feeling are supposed to be. Although these definitions originally borrowed the very concepts of desire and feeling from psychology, psychology cannot provide such transcendental definitions. For an opposite view, s. Frierson (2014, p. 2); for further discussion, s. Kraus/Sturm (2018).
14 I leave aside any speculations about the existence of non-human beings with the same or similar mental faculties, such as angels, God, or non-rational animals.

resentation in the faculty's characteristic form) and that is can be realized by all human minds. Such transcendental definitions, though not derived from experience, can be corroborated through empirical observation of individuals.[15]

Transcendental philosophy enquires into the necessary conditions that must be in place in order for a faculty to fulfil its characteristic function. It examines each faculty and its interrelation with other faculties with respect to form. In the *Critique*, which focuses on the faculties of cognition, Kant argues that the characteristic forms of each cognitive faculty, viz. space, time, and the categories, determine the transcendental conditions of experience: these conditions *must* be fulfilled in order for the resulting cognition to be *able* to truthfully represent an object of experience.

In turn, an empirical faculty can now be understood as the concrete realization or implementation of the corresponding transcendental faculty, or function, in a human individual. The empirical faculty is the particular *token* of a transcendental faculty that operates within an individual mind and that produces the representations occurring in the individual's empirical consciousness.[16] Its representations "as modifications of the mind [...] belong to inner sense" (A 99) and hence give rise to so-called inner appearances (*innere Erscheinungen*), or what in contemporary philosophy is commonly called *mental states*. This means that the operations of empirical faculties can be observed primarily in terms of the states in empirical consciousness they produce. By actively attending to these states we can then become conscious of them in inner perception (*innere Wahrnehmung*).

Empirical psychology inquires into the nature of these empirical faculties and aims to describe how such faculties actually operate. In the *Anthropology from a Pragmatic Point of View* [henceforth, *Anthropology*], Kant states that the goal of psychological investigations is to examine the level of "appropriateness" of our empirical faculties, that is the extent to which we appropriately exercise "*[c]orrect* understanding, *practiced* judgment and *thorough* reason" (Anth,

---

15 Note that, while the transcendental definitions of the three basic faculties are presupposed *a priori* in Kant's system, their real existence in each individual case is not secured *a priori*, but has to be confirmed *a posteriori*. The resulting mental states can be described by psychological predicates (e.g., "cognitive", "conative", and "emotional").

16 Schmidt (2008) cashes out the relationship between transcendental and empirical faculties in terms of "configuration" or "structure": a transcendental faculty provides the configuration or structure of an empirical faculty, whereas the empirical faculty carries out mental operations defined by this configuration. I take her account to be broadly in line with mine.

Ak. 7, p. 198).[17] Empirical psychology derives such descriptions primarily from the self-observation of individuals and thereby pays particular attention to the *specific variations* that mental operations show both across different individuals and across different times within one and the same individual.[18] At the same time, empirical psychology pursues public knowledge and aims at generating sufficiently *general* descriptions of the workings of empirical faculties in general. In the best case, it discovers *psychological laws of experience* that capture lawful, efficient-causal relations between inner appearances, which apply to everyone or at least in all sufficiently similar cases.[19]

This first gloss of empirical psychology already reveals an intrinsic tension. On the one hand, the acquisition of psychological knowledge relies on the self-observation of individual minds with regard to their subjective states of consciousness. On the other hand, for such self-observations to give rise to objectively valid psychological knowledge, they must already rely on the availability of general psychological concepts that apply objectively across different individuals. Yet such general psychological concepts are first acquired through general psychological studies comparing different individuals. *Prima facie*, there is thus a tension between the subjective validity and specificity of self-observation, on the one hand, and the objective validity and generality of psychological concepts and descriptions, on the other hand. I explore this tension further in a closer analysis of psychological knowledge in the next section, before I then show, in Section 3, how this tension can be resolved by means of a transcendental investigation. I shall argue that this tension can be overcome if one acknowledges that both specific self-observations and general psychological descriptions presuppose a common guiding principle, namely the idea of the soul.

2 Psychological Knowledge and Inner Experience

What for Kant counts as psychological knowledge? In order to answer this question it is necessary to understand the relation of psychological knowledge to a particular type of experience, namely *inner experience*. In his Critical writings, Kant offers only scattered remarks on inner experience, covering a variety of phenomena, ranging from consciousness of one's passing perceptions, thoughts, de-

---

17 On psychology as a study of mental disorders, s. Schmidt (2008, p. 470); Frierson (2014, pp. 189–258).

18 S. "In anthropology, experiences are appearances united according to laws of understanding, and in taking into consideration our way of representing things" (Anth, Ak. 7, p. 142).

19 S. "psychology (a sum of all inner perceptions under laws of nature)" (Anth, Ak. 7, p. 141).

sires, and feelings, to the temporal determination of one's own mental states, as well as the empirical cognition of oneself qua more general psychological properties, including one's character traits.[20]

What makes all these phenomena distinctively psychological is the fact that they all involve mental states, i. e., inner appearances, though they may not be fully reducible to such mental states and may in addition have accompanying behavioural components and actions. All psychological phenomena, therefore, rely on *inner sense*, i. e., the part of sensibility "by means of which the mind intuits itself, or its inner state" (A 22/B 37). On Kant's view, mental activities produce mental states, which then occur as inner appearances under the form of inner sense, i. e., time, in empirical consciousness. These mental states are the primary objects of our *inner perception* (*innere Wahrnehmung*) or *self-observation* (*Selbstbeobachtung*).[21] Through inner perception we thus become aware of our own mental activities only in terms of their inner appearances, such as a particular perception, thought, desire, or feeling. Based on inner perception, inner experience then is experience of such inner appearances.[22] Yet inner experience requires something more if it is to be empirical cognition of oneself, that is – according to Kant's general theory of experience – if it is to yield objectively valid empirical judgments about one's psychological features.[23]

---

20 In the *Critique*, Kant also uses locutions such as "determining my own existence in time" (B xl; B 157n; B 430 – 431), "cognizing myself as I appear to myself" (B 68; B 158), and "self-cognition". Kant uses the term "*self*-cognition" (*Selbsterkenntnis*) rarely in the sense of empirical cognition of oneself (e. g., *Religion*, Ak. 6, p. 75; B 421), but more often in the sense of transcendental (or philosophical) cognition of the nature and limits of human reason (e. g., B 509; B 763; B 877; Prol, Ak. 4, p. 328; CpracR, Ak. 5, p. 86). As to more general psychological properties, s. for instance "his *inner experiences* (of grace, of temptations)" (Anth, Ak. 7, p. 134).

21 I take "inner perception" and "self-observation" to be by and large co-extensive. E. g. Anth, Ak. 7, pp. 134, 141 ff.; A 342/B 401. Kant mainly conceives of inner experience in the *narrow sense* as experience of oneself "from within" without drawing on self-directed external sources of information, such as behavioural observation or testimony of others. It should be distinguished from experience about oneself *in the broad sense*, which may additionally draw on external sources, such as the observation of one's bodily state or of one's behaviour, and the testimony of one's character traits by others. Sturm (2017) sees this broader notion mainly at play in the *Anthropology*.

22 S. "inner sense, which contains a manifold of determination that make an inner *experience* possible" (Anth, Ak. 7, p. 134n).

23 I here use the notion of *psychological features* to refer both to relatively short-lived, frequently fluctuating *mental states*, such as passing representations in empirical consciousness, and relatively stable, long-term *psychological properties* that characterize the whole person, such as character traits.

In the *Anthropology* and related notes, which contain the most detailed account of inner experience, Kant suggests that inner experience is made possible as empirical cognition by some kind of "reflection" on inner appearances. He is ambiguous as to what exactly this "reflection" consists in, as some passages suggest that it requires (a) reflection according to the concepts of the understanding or (b) reflection under general (psychological) laws of nature; other passages suggest that it requires (c) reflection yielding a concept of oneself. Each of these options is supported by one of the following passages:

(a) "an empirical intuition [becomes], through reflection and the concept of understanding arising from it, [...] inner experience" (Anth, Ak. 7, p. 142),
(b) "[inner sense] belongs to psychology (a sum of all inner perceptions under laws of nature) and establishes inner experience" (Anth, Ak. 7, p. 141),
(c) "The inner sense is not yet cognition of myself, but we must first have appearances through it, then we first make a concept of ourselves through reflection on [these appearances], which eventually results in empirical cognition, i.e., inner experience" (Refl, Ak. 18, p. 680, translation amended).[24]

This ambiguity in Kant's account of inner experience, I submit, is due to the same tension that I have diagnosed above with respect to empirical psychology. On the one hand, inner experience is had by an individual person and based on the person's subjective consciousness of her own mental states. On the other hand, inner experience, if it is to be empirical cognition of an object, makes a claim to an objectively valid judgment, i.e., a judgment that is valid for everyone and that is about some empirical reality.

In reply to this tension, Kant suggests that inner experience can be empirical cognition of an object, i.e., "knowledge of the human being through inner experience" in the passage below, only if it involves "the assertion of certain propositions that concern human nature" in general:

> [K]nowledge of the human being through inner experience, because to a large extent one also judges others according to it, is more important than correct judgment of others, but nevertheless at the same time perhaps more difficult [...]. So it is advisable and even necessary to begin with observed *appearances* in oneself, and then to progress above all to the assertion of certain propositions that concern human nature; that is, to *inner experience*. (Anth, Ak. 7, p. 143)

---

24 S. also "All my inner experience is a judgment in which the predicate is empirical and the subject is *I*" (Refl 5453, Ak. 18, p. 186, my translation).

In this passage, Kant acknowledges that observing one's own inner appearances is the indispensable starting point of any acquisition of *inner experience as empirical cognition*, but it remains insufficient if it is not at the same time assisted by general propositions concerning human nature. In self-observation, it is difficult to clearly separate one's different states and to observe them "by will" (MFNS, Ak. 4, p. 471). Moreover, self-observation easily distorts and "displaces the state of the observed object" (MFNS, Ak. 4, p. 471), is prone to error, illusions, "enthusiasm and madness" (Anth, Ak. 7, p. 132) and may involve "the tendency to accept the play of ideas of inner sense as experiential cognition, although it is only a fiction" (Anth, Ak. 7, p. 161). Due to the danger of distortions and self-manipulation, Kant advises us in the passage above to interpret our own inner appearances only within a more comprehensive theory of human nature in general. Only if we assert "certain propositions concerning human nature" in general, can we finally accomplish adequate empirical cognition of oneself. Yet having such general propositions regarding human nature already presupposes a general classification of mental states and psychological properties. That is, it presupposes general psychological knowledge.[25]

The tension can now be understood as follows: while psychological knowledge concerning human nature in general relies on inner experience of individuals as its "material" source, inner experience can be understood as objectively valid cognition of one's psychological features only if some general psychological propositions are already accepted as a background theory within which one can reliably assess the truth of one's specific inner experiences. Note, furthermore, that psychological propositions cannot be gained by simply comparing the self-observations of different individuals because for one thing self-observation concerns the private items of an individual's consciousness, which need to be communicated in order to be accessible for others. Yet such communication and subsequent comparison already presuppose a generally accepted conceptual framework by means of which mental states can be expressed.[26] Hence, accomplishing inner experience as empirical cognition already presupposes generally applicable psychological concepts, which in turn, however, can be acquired

---

25 There is some controversy as to the primacy of inner experience over general psychological knowledge in this passage. While Frierson (2014, p. 37n43) endorses that "observation of inner appearances is still the ultimate and primary basis" and is optimistic that undistorted inner experience is possible, Sturm (2009) doubts whether inner experience can ever be a reliable source of knowledge and, therefore, argues that knowledge can be produced only on the basis of a general, anthropological theory of human nature (s. Kraus/Sturm 2017, pp. 219–220).

26 Here I assume that while behavioral states may express mental states to some extent, for Kant mental states are not fully reducible to externally observable states (see Kraus 2018).

only on the basis of general psychological descriptions. Does this mutual dependence of general psychological knowledge and specific inner experience pose a vicious circle, or can we resolve this tension? I suggest that a transcendental investigation of the way in which we acquire psychological concepts, which are needed both for psychological knowledge and for inner experience, will help to disperse worries regarding any vicious circularity in Kant's account.

3 The Conceptualisation of Psychological Phenomena

The mutual dependence between general psychological knowledge and inner experience resembles the problem of empirical concept formation in general. In order to first acquire an empirical concept, we need to rely on some prior experience of particular objects that instantiate the concept. In turn, in order to take one's experience to be a true representation of an object (regarding outer or inner matters), we need to have available empirical concepts that serve as the constituents of empirical judgments.[27] Kant tackles the problem of concept formation within his theory of reason, and in particular with respect to reason's regulative principles of systematicity, as introduced in the Appendix to the Dialectic (*Critique*). In what follows, I sketch Kant's approach to empirical concept formation in general, then apply it to the case of the acquisition of psychological predicates, and finally show that this approach is capable of resolving the apparent circularity between general psychological knowledge and inner experience.

---

27 Recall that for Kant experience is empirical cognition, i. e., a judgment about a sensible object. Note that it may be possible to have experience on the basis of the categories alone, e. g., experience of spatial or temporal quantities. Yet, as soon as experience is about, or distinguishes between, specific kinds of realities (or qualities), it requires empirical concepts. In order for empirical cognition to give rise to knowledge, i. e., to taking a judgment to be true on objectively sufficient grounds, it requires conditions of adequacy (or truth conditions) of these empirical concepts (s. A 821/B 849). On the distinction between empirical cognition and knowledge in Kant, s. Watkins/Willaschek 2017.

3.1 Three General Principles of Concept-Formation

Kant famously argues that the content of our empirical concepts can never be rich enough to ensure the full determination of individual objects.[28] Rather, concepts always remain to some extent *general* representations, which relate to objects only by means of intuitions that contain common marks. In conceptualising our intuitions, we attempt to track these common marks by forming adequate empirical concepts.[29] On the one hand, we aim for concepts with increasingly broad empirical content so as to grasp more and more similarities between objects. On the other hand, we look for concepts with increasingly rich empirical content so as to grasp more and more details of a particular object.

The theory of concept formation that Kant depicts in his *Lectures on Logic* and in the Appendix to the Transcendental Dialectic (*Critique*) suggests that such specification of conceptual content can be meaningful only within a *system of concepts:* the empirical content of a concept should be understood in relation to "higher", more general concepts, to "lower", more specific concepts, and to "neighbouring" concepts that denote similar kinds.[30] The acquisition of concepts is thus more properly understood as an ongoing complex activity that is implemented in light of ongoing experience by three complementary activities: taken together the activities of generalisation, specification, and interconnection lead to an increasingly comprehensive, increasingly specific, and increasingly dense *system* of empirical concepts.[31]

To further fill in the details of his account, Kant argues, in the Appendix, that one aim of reason – the highest faculty of cognition – is to seek "a certain systematic unity of all possible empirical concepts" (A 654/B 680). Kant introduces three principles of reason that enable us to seek such a systematic unity of concepts. These are the principles of *homogeneity* (or "of the *sameness of kind* in the manifold under higher genera"), *specification* (or "of the *variety* of what is same in kind under lower species"), and *continuity* (or "of the *affinity* of all con-

---

28 A 655/B 683; L-Log/Vienna, Ak. 24, p. 911; L-Log/Jäsche, Ak. 9, p. 97. For an excellent discussion of Kant's argument for this claim, s. Watkins 2013. Kant rejects Leibniz's thesis of complete conceptual determination, according to which a complete concept fully determines individuals, but is only fully knowable by an infinite mind, viz. God.

29 I remain neutral as to whether the relevant marks are *given* in intuition or whether the marks are first *found* through synthetic activity of the mind. For insightful discussions, see Longuenesse (1998), Ginsborg (2006) and Anderson (2014).

30 Kant's idea of a systematic unity of concepts follows the "scholastic" tradition that assumes a hierarchical order in terms of higher genus and lower species concepts (s. A 652/B 680).

31 For excellent discussions of empirical concept-formation in Kant, s. Ginsborg (2006, 2017) and Anderson (2014).

cepts") (A 657/B 685).[32] The principle of homogeneity guides us in seeking, for every pair of concepts, a genus-concept defining a higher kind under which both these concepts can be subsumed. This principle serves "the interest in [enlarging] the *domain* (the universality)" of genus concepts (A 654/B 682). The principle of specification guides us in finding for every given concept further sub-concepts (or species concepts). This principle serves "an interest in *content* (the determinacy [of concepts])" by finding ever-richer species-concepts that contain ever-more fine-grained determinations of an individual object (A 654/B 682).[33] By assuming continuity between different concepts, we finally arrive at an interconnected hierarchical system that proceeds, not only vertically from elementary genus concepts to fine-grained species concepts, but also horizontally between "neighbouring" concepts.[34]

Consider, for instance, the concept 'tree'. If taken together with the concept 'shrub', we may subsume the two concepts under the common genus-concept 'plant'; if taken together with 'animal', we may subsume the two concepts under the common genus-concept 'living being'. Looking for further varieties of 'tree', we may consider lower, more specific concepts that can be subsumed under 'tree', such as 'oak', 'birch', and 'linden'. Finally, searching for continuity among concepts, we may consider further more general concepts such as 'trunk', 'root', 'branches', and 'leaves'. These concepts are, as it were, horizontally, rather than vertically, connected, and each of them is contained *in* both 'tree' and 'shrub' (which is just to say that both 'tree' and 'shrub' can be subsumed *under* them).

Primarily, these principles of homogeneity, specification, and continuity are introduced as *logical* principles of systematicity that concern only the logical relations among concepts and that abstract from the concepts' relation to objects. By means of them, reason pursues its subjective interest of acquiring a system of concepts.[35] In addition, reason – as one of the cognitive faculties – aims at a truthful description of nature, which seemingly can be accomplished by seeking a systematic unity of empirical cognitions. So Kant argues that each of the logical principles is applicable to nature only if "a transcendental principle is presupposed, through which such a systematic unity, as pertaining to the object itself, is assumed *a priori* as necessary" (A 650 – 651/B 679 – 680). Accordingly,

---

32 S. A 652–668/ B680–696; CJ, Ak. 5, pp. 185–186.

33 L-Log/Jäsche, Ak. 9, pp. 96–97; also L-Log/Blomberg, Ak. 24, pp. 240–260; L-Log/Vienna, Ak. 24, pp. 905–913; L-Log/Dohna-Wundlacken, Ak. 24, p. 755.

34 For a detailed discussion in connection to Kant's Logic lectures, s. Watkins (2013).

35 They are also called "principle[s] of parsimony" or "principle[s] of economy for reason" (A 650/B 678).

Kant defines three corresponding transcendental principles of homogeneity, specification, and continuity, which do *not* abstract from the concepts' relations to empirical objects. Hence, reason demands not only the systematic unity of concepts, but also the systematic unity of all cognition concerning nature itself.

Kant justifies the assumption of transcendental principles by arguing that reason's principles of systematicity are "objective but in an indeterminate way" (A 680/B 708). He explains this indeterminate objective validity in the following way:

> [such a principle functions] not as a constitutive principle for determining something in regard to its direct object, but rather as a merely regulative principle and maxim for furthering and strengthening the empirical use of reason by opening up new paths into the infinite (the undetermined) with which the understanding is not acquainted, yet without ever being the least bit contrary to the laws of its empirical use. (A 680/B 708)

According to this passage, reason's principles of systematicity are only regulative, rather than constitutive insofar as they complement the constitutive principles of the understanding by providing guidelines for the discovery of new pieces of cognition, without determining objects of experience as such. Regulative principles, unlike constitutive principles of the understanding, do not define conditions of the very possibility of experience and hence do not determine generic features of objects of experience. Nonetheless, they define necessary conditions of experience, namely in terms of guiding rules for the understanding, if experience is to amount to empirical knowledge.[36]

So Kant continues his line of argument by making the stronger claim that reason's principles of systematicity play an epistemic role for the justification of empirical knowledge claims. They lead reason to serve as an arbiter of empirical truth. More precisely, Kant argues that "we simply have to presuppose the systematic unity of nature as objectively valid and necessary", since otherwise we would have "no coherent use of the understanding" with regard to empirical cognition and hence "no sufficient mark of empirical truth" (A 651/B 679).[37] This

---

36 There is an ongoing debate regarding the regulative status of these principles. Some commentators take them to be merely optional guides for experience, e.g., Guyer (1990), Grier (2001); others take them to be necessary for the very possibility of experience, e. g., Buchdahl (1967), Abela (2006). Based on the textual evidence I provide above, it seems safe to assume that they are at least necessary conditions for those experiences that are supposed to give rise to empirical knowledge, i.e., empirical cognition that is taken to be true on subjectively and objectively sufficient grounds (s. fn. 38 below; also, e.g., Zuckert 2017).

37 Elsewhere, Kant explicates the coherent use of the understanding in terms of goals set by reason: reason has an "indispensably necessary regulative use, namely that of directing the un-

suggests that reason's epistemic role lies in providing principles of systematicity according to which we can test the coherence of our empirical judgments and then develop coherence criteria of empirical truth.[38]

While a further discussion and evaluation of Kant's line of argument regarding the assumption of these transcendental principles goes beyond the scope of this paper, the upshot for current purposes is as follows: For Kant, empirical concept formation and the acquisition of systematic empirical cognition can be understood as ongoing complex activities, one complementing the other. The formation of empirical concepts is viewed as an ongoing activity of systematization according to the principles of generalisation, specification, and continuity. The formation of concepts is informed by the ongoing activity of acquiring a system of empirical cognition. In light of ongoing experience, our system of empirical concepts is continuously assessed and refined as to its adequacy by adding (or revising) increasingly comprehensive genus-concepts, increasingly determinate species-concepts, and further intermediary concepts. In turn, newly acquired empirical cognition can be assessed as to its truth in light of a system of already accepted empirical cognitions, which builds on the system of empirical concepts. Based on the outcome of this assessment, the new cognition can then be asserted and added to the system, or rejected as untrue; in rare cases it may lead to the revision of already accepted cognitions.[39]

Despite making the greatest effort of completing our system of concepts, our conceptual abilities are severely limited insofar as we can never fully conceptually grasp a unique individual. Although Kant denies that we can ever be in the possession of a lowest species-concept, he affirms the existence of a highest genus-concept, the *conceptus summus* (V-Lo/Jäsche, Ak. 9, p. 97), which forms

---

derstanding to a certain goal" – a goal, which, "although it is only an idea", is needed to find the greatest unity among cognitions (A 644/B 672).

38 S. Kant's definition of knowledge in the Canon: "when taking something to be true is both subjectively and objectively sufficient it is called knowing" (A 822/B 850), whereby a reason is objectively sufficient if it is "valid for the reason of every human being to take it to be true", because it "rests on the common ground, namely the object" (A 821/B 849). On the distinction between knowledge and cognition, s. Watkins/Willaschek (2017).

39 The fact that these two activities complement one another does not necessarily imply that the resulting systems – the system of concepts and the system of cognitions (within a particular domain) – fully correspond to one another. Rather, the discussion of the conceptualization of psychological phenomena below will show that there can be concepts that do not have a correspondent in the system of cognitions, e.g., the idea of the soul (s. section 3.3).

the highest point of the system.[40] The highest genus-concept of a system of *empirical* concepts is the most general concept of a thing that falls in the domain of nature described by that system. For nature in general, this highest genus-concept is the concept 'object of experience in general'.[41] The predicates contained in this highest genus-concept can be derived from the *a priori* forms of the mind, which determine the transcendental conditions of experience, viz. the forms of space and time and the categories of the understanding (e. g., 'quantity', 'quality', 'substantiality' and '(seat of) causal powers'). What counts as an object of experience is precisely that which instantiates the highest genus-concept.

3.2 The Idea of the Soul as Concept of Reflection

Returning to psychological knowledge and inner experience, conceptualization concerns only a particular domain of nature, namely the domain of psychological phenomena, i.e., humans qua their psychological features. This domain includes all inner appearances that can occur in human empirical consciousness and be constituents of human mental life. Let us call this domain *inner nature*, or as Kant sometimes puts it, "thinking nature" (A 682/B 710; MFNS, Ak. 4, p. 467). The corresponding system of concepts is a system of psychological predicates – those predicates that describe (aspects of) inner appearances. Here it is important to note the distinction between inner nature and an individual's mental life. Inner nature comprises all possible inner appearances that can appear in any human's mental life, that is, the *sum total of all possible inner appearances*. It is the subject matter of general psychological knowledge.[42] By contrast, an individual's mental life concerns only those inner appearances that in fact belong to a particular individual and of which only that individual can have *inner* experience. It is the *sum total of someone's actual inner appearances*, i.e., those ap-

---

40 In his *Lectures*, he identifies this highest concept as the concept of "something" (L-Log/Vienna, Ak. 24, p. 911), as that of "a thing" (L-Log/Dohna, Ak. 24, p. 755), or as that of "a possible thing" (L-Log/Blomberg, Ak. 24, p. 259).

41 S. Anderson (2014, p. 368) on the concept of 'object in general' (or what he calls "Ur-concept").

42 Here I draw on Kant's definition of "nature as the sum total of all appearances (*natura materialiter spectata*)" (B 163); i.e., "by 'nature' taken substantively (*materialiter*) is understood the sum total of appearances insofar as these are in thoroughgoing connection through an inner principle of causality" (A 419/B 446). S. also Kant's definition of the "world of sense" as "the sum total of appearances, so far as it is intuited" (A 257/B 312; also A 419/B 447).

pearances that belong to one and the same person and which make her the psychological person she is.

In what follows, I argue that both the conceptualization of inner nature and the acquisition of inner experience rely on a system of psychological predicates and that such a system requires a unifying idea of reason, namely the *idea of the soul*. While this idea is crucial for both activities, it serves a different purpose in each case. In the case of inner nature, the idea of the soul serves – according to the principle of homogeneity – as the highest genus-concept that first defines the domain of inner nature, or what counts as a psychological phenomenon. In the case of an individual's mental life, the idea of the soul serves – according to the principle of specification – as a placeholder for the lowest species-concept, that is, for the empirical concept that, if it were available, would completely describe the individual person.

In the Appendix, Kant introduces the *idea of the soul* as a transcendental idea of reason that gives us a "guiding thread" for pursuing the systematic unity of inner experience and hence the "systematic unity of all the appearances of inner sense" (A 682/B 710). More precisely, the idea of the soul is needed to

> connect all appearances, actions, and receptivity of our mind [*Gemüth*] to the guiding thread of inner experience *as if* the mind [*Gemüth*] were a simple substance that (at least in life) persists in existence with personal identity, while its states [...] are continuously changing. (A 672/B 700)[43]

This and related passages in the Appendix are central to understanding how we can make sense of our inner experiences as cognitions of our mental states or of our more general psychological properties, without asserting the existence of a permanent mental substance.[44] Here it is important to note that inner experience is a special case of experience: strictly speaking, it is not experience of a substance since nothing permanent, "no standing and abiding self", is given to

---

43 S. also A 682–684/B 710–712.

44 The idea of the soul is often ignored in interpretations of Kant's psychology. Its role remains unnoted by Frierson (2014) and is marginalized by Sturm (2009, pp. 254–255, n87). There are exceptions, such as Klemme (1996), who however claims that the "as-if" model of the soul has been replaced in the B-Edition (Klemme 1996, pp. 229–234). Serck-Hanssen (2011) makes the suggestions that the idea should serve to define a "mark of the mental", but thinks that this is not the interpretation that Kant in fact develops in this passage (Serck-Hanssen 2011, p. 69). Dyck (2014) reads Kant's account of the idea as the vindication of an "impure rational psychology" in the spirit of his rationalist predecessors (Dyck 2014, pp. 199–225). None of them takes the idea of the soul to be foundational for the acquisition of either inner experience or general psychological knowledge.

inner sense that could instantiate the category of substance (A 107).[45] So *not* all categories are straightforwardly applicable to that which is given in inner sense. Therefore, inner appearances – strictly speaking – do not fall under the genus-concept 'object of experience in general', but instead require a regulative idea that substitutes for those categories that are not applicable.[46]

Recall that Kant has difficulties in the *Anthropology* in discerning which kind of "reflection" on inner appearances gives rise to inner experience: (a) reflection under a concept of the understanding, or (b) reflection under general (psychological) laws of nature, or (b) reflection yielding a concept of oneself. The passages in the Appendix now suggest that all these reflective activities can be traced back to the *reflection under the idea of the soul*. But what would this mean?

Firstly, for Kant, an idea of reason gives completeness to an empirical synthesis that cannot be completed in intuition "through its progress towards the unconditioned" (A 409/B 436). With respect to inner experience, the synthesis in accordance with the category of substance cannot be completed. Therefore, Kant introduces the idea of the soul as the concept of the "*unconditioned* of the *categorical* synthesis in one subject" (A 323/B 379).[47] The idea represents the unconditioned unity that is taken to be the ultimate condition *with respect to* all one's conditioned representations, viz. inner appearances. Since the categorical syllogism corresponds to the conditioning relation of subsistence, Kant explicates this idea as the concept of a "simple [thinking] substance" (A 672/B 700; also A 682/B 710). The idea of the soul thus primarily denotes that which is assumed as the subsistent ground in which all one's representations inhere. Moreover, the idea contains predicates such as 'personal identity' and '(seat of a) fundamental mental power' (see A 672/B 700; also A 682/B 710). These predicates of the soul are broadly in line with what has traditionally been associated with the soul.[48]

---

45 S. A 22–23/B 37; A 350; B 412–413.

46 In Kraus (2016), I argue that the categories of quantity and quality, which concerns single intuitions, can be constitutively applied to distinctively inner intuitions. By contrast, the categories of relation, which concern the relation between intuitions, including the category of substantiality, cannot be used constitutively, but must be substituted by regulative principles based on the idea of the soul (s. Kraus 2019).

47 The idea of the soul is also identified as "the concept of the absolute (unconditioned) unity of the thinking subject" (A 334/B 391; also B 348; A 353; A 406/B 432).

48 Concerning the predicates, s. in particular A 682/B 710. Yet Kant does not endorse all traditional predicates of the soul: he explicitly rejects predicates that define features beyond this life, as those of "generation, destruction or palingenesis" (A 683/B 684). Further phrases Kant uses to characterize the idea of the soul include the concepts of an "absolute subject" (A 348), the "absolute unity of a thinking being" (A 353), and the "unconditioned unity of the subjective condi-

Yet Kant departs from the rationalist tradition in arguing, secondly, that this use of the idea is only *regulative*, not constitutive. In general, transcendental ideas serve as *"regulative* principle[s] of the systematic unity of the manifold of empirical cognition" (A 671/B 699). So for Kant the predicates contained in the idea are not asserted as properties that are instantiated by a real soul-substance. Such an assertion would presuppose a constitutive use of them. Rather, they are only problematically assumed in order to guide the derivation of systematic connections between inner experiences and hence guide the determination of inner appearances:[49]

> It is not from a simple thinking substance that we derive the inner appearances of our soul, but from one another [i.e., inner appearances] in accordance with the idea of a simple being. (A 673/B 701)

In sum, this suggests that for Kant we acquire inner experience by reflecting on inner appearances under the idea of the soul in the following way: by considering inner appearances *as if* those appearances inhered in a mental substance, we can gain cognition of them and of their relations, even though such a substance can *never* be cognized on the basis of sensation, but is only problematically assumed on the basis of a transcendental idea.[50] In the following section, I explain how such a reflection under the idea of the soul plays out for the conceptualization of inner nature in general and for the acquisition of inner experience by individuals. I then explain, in Section 4, the observed tension between general knowledge of inner nature and individual inner experience.

---

tions of all representation in general (of the subject or soul)" (A 406/B 432). Further predicates contained in the idea can be discerned in accordance with the categories, as is discussed in the Paralogisms, s. A 404/B 419.

49 S.: "With [the concept of a simple self-sufficient intelligence] reason has nothing before its eyes except principles of the systematic unity <u>in explaining the appearances of the soul</u>, namely by considering all determinations as in one subject, <u>all powers</u>, as far as possible, as derived from one unique fundamental power, <u>all change as belonging to the states of one and the same persisting being</u>, and by representing all *appearances* in space as entirely distinct from the actions of *thinking*" (A 682/B 710, <u>emphasis added</u>).

50 My use of "reflection" is broadly in line with the notion of reflective judgment, that is judgment that does not determine a sensibly given object, but relates given contents in accordance with a regulative principle or idea, e. g., the idea of purposiveness for judgments about living beings (s. CJ First Intro, Ak. 20, pp. 213, 236; CJ, Ak. 5, pp. 185, 375, 385, 389, 397–401, 405). For further discussion with regard to the experience of living beings, see Nassar 2016.

3.3 The Idea of the Soul as Genus and as Species Concept

Reflection under the idea of the soul can take different forms: (1) regarding the conceptualization of inner nature in general, the idea of the soul serves as the highest genus-concept of inner nature; (2) regarding the acquisition of inner experience, the idea of the soul serves as a placeholder for the lowest species-concept of an individual person. I discuss each case in turn.

(1) The idea of the soul functions as the highest genus-concept of inner nature. Despite its regulative character, I argue, the idea of the soul serves as the highest genus-concept of inner nature in that it defines what counts as a psychological person in general. The idea defines the domain of inner nature as that which can be reflected upon under the regulative concept 'soul', that is, it defines the class of beings to whom psychological features can be ascribed. Due to the regulative character of the idea, the predicates it contains, such as '(mental) substance', 'personal identity' and '(seat of a) fundamental power', are not straightforwardly instantiated by inner appearances. But inner appearances can be reflected on under them. That is, even though there is no sensibly given substance that instantiates the idea, we can cognize *given* inner appearances and their relations in accordance with these predicates.

Each predicate thereby explicates a particular kind of unity that is approximated in inner experience. For instance, in accordance with the predicate '(mental) substance', inner appearances are trans-temporally unified *as if* they were the states of one and the same persistent mental substance, even though such a substance can never be cognized. In accordance with the predicate '(seat of a) fundamental power', all inner appearances are causally unified *as if* they were mental states originating from one and the same mental power and thus subject to a general kind of mental causation. In this way, causal relations between mental states within one and the same mind can be derived, even though such a fundamental power can never be cognized. These states may in fact even be produced by entirely distinct faculties, such as the faculties of cognition, desire, and feeling, according to the tripartite division of the mind, as discussed in Section 1.

Hence, without the regulative idea of the soul, we would not be able to recognize inner appearances as instances of mental states that can be ascribed to a psychological person (as opposed to other *kinds* of natural states, e.g., physical-material, physiological, or behavioural states). The idea of the soul serves as the highest genus-concept under which each more specific psychological predicate must be subsumed. The idea defines a whole from which a systematic unity of psychological predicates can be derived. The resulting system is applicable to all human individuals in general and reflects the interrelations between different kinds of mental states (or more general psychological properties). These interrelations correspond to the *conceptual containment relations* between psychological predicates.

In accordance with the tripartite division of transcendental faculties, as outlined in Section 1, Figure 1 schematically illustrates the function of the idea of the soul as highest genus concept, from which the system of psychological predicates originates.[51]

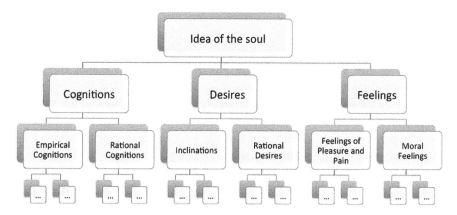

Figure 1: The idea of the soul as the highest genus concept of the system of psychological predicates in accordance with the tripartite structure of basic mental faculties.

(2) The idea of the soul serves as the placeholder for the lowest species-concept of an individual person. The idea of the soul also plays a crucial role in the acquisition of inner experience. As demanded by the principle of specification, the idea helps one to acquire a more and more determinate concept of oneself as an individual person. According to Kant's denial of the availability of lowest species-concepts, one can never obtain the complete psychological concept of oneself as a unique individual, nor of any other individual. Nonetheless, the general principle of specification guides one in searching for a more determinate empirical concept. By determining further psychological predicates that are applicable to a particular individual and adding those predicates to the existing psycholog-

---

51 My reading of the idea as a necessary condition for defining the domain of inner nature is stronger than a merely heuristic reading, such as Dyck's, according to which the idea of the soul is a useful, but to some degree contingent, device for "organizing our knowledge and directing the understanding to the discovery of new cognition" (Dyck 2014, p. 210). Similar to my reading, Serck-Hanssen (2011, p. 69) argues that the soul should be understood as defining the "mark of the mental", but she eventually denies that this is what Kant has in mind in the Appendix.

ical concept one has of oneself (or of another individual), one approximates a complete self-concept.

The idea of the soul serves as a "template" of the lowest species-concept of a psychological being. As such a template, the idea of the soul offers a sketch of the psychological species-concept of a unique individual, which is then to be progressively "filled in" with applicable psychological predicates such that the sketch approximates the complete concept of this individual. The most general predicates contained in the idea, such as '(mental/thinking) substantiality', 'simplicity', 'personal identity', and '(seat of a) fundamental mental power', define the most general outline of this sketch. Since they are assumed only problematically, they do not strictly speaking determine generic properties of psychological beings, but give guidance for finding further applicable psychological predicates. In this sense, they serve the idea's purpose of advancing one's empirical cognition of oneself. These psychological predicates range from rather specific descriptions of individual mental states, e. g., emotions, thoughts, and desires, to more general notions identifying character traits or other more global psychological properties, e. g., gratitude, honesty, and wit.

Corresponding to the conceptual containment relations within the general system of psychological predicates, the specific predicates applicable to a particular individual can be arranged within a system, as well. Taken together, these predicates give rise to a unified system, ascending from more determinate concepts specifying mental states occurring in particular moments, e. g., particular feelings, thoughts, and desires, to more general concepts defining long-term psychological properties, such as character traits, e. g., shyness, kindness, and confidence. Here the idea of the soul is the placeholder of a complete species-concept, the most determinate concept of the individual, "at the bottom" of the hierarchy. From there, potentially infinitely many, less determinate psychological predicates (of different levels of determinacy and generality) branch out.

Although a complete concept of an individual can never be fully grasped (and arguably cannot even exist) from an empirical perspective according to Kant, our conceptualizing capacities are such that we seek to approximate this concept. In light of ongoing inner experience, we approximate such a concept by determining more and more applicable psychological predicates within a systematic unity, which becomes increasingly fine-grained, dense, and general at the same time. The empirical concept towards which we thereby converge would potentially contain infinitely many psychological predicates *in it*, but only one individual falls *under it*: the unique individual person.

In sum, with respect to inner experience, the idea of the soul serves as the placeholder for the unavailable complete psychological concept of a person. It serves as a template for "filling in" this species-concept with applicable psychological predicates and hence for approximating the unity of, as well as the systematic relations among, all inner appearances that belong to one and the same person. Figure 2 schematically illustrates the function of the idea of the soul as the placeholder for the lowest species-concept of an individual person in which *all* psychological predicates ever applicable to this person are contained.

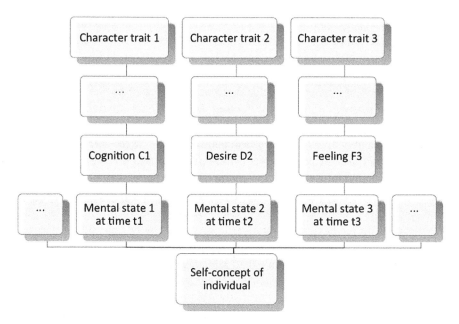

Figure 2: The idea of the soul as the placeholder for the lowest species concept, i. e., the unavailable complete concept of the individual person in which all psychological predicates applicable to this person are contained.

4 The Transcendental Sources of Psychological Knowledge

Let us now return to the mutual dependence we observed earlier between general psychological knowledge and an individual's inner experience. Given the above considerations regarding the relation between concept-formation and the acquisition of systematic cognition, I suggest that the acquisition of general psychological knowledge and the acquisition of inner experience should be understood as two ongoing complex activities, one complementing the other. In line with my considerations regarding the conceptualization of psychological phenomena, we can now see that psychological knowledge and inner experience can be understood as complementary constituents of one and the same system of empirical cognitions regarding matters of psychology, i.e. regarding humans qua their psychological features.

The worry about an apparent vicious circularity or of a possible primacy of one of these two types of cognition can be resolved if one recognizes that the two corresponding activities through which they are acquired are mutually necessary complements of another. Both activities – the acquisition of general psychological knowledge and the acquisition of inner experience as empirical cognition of myself – can operate alongside one another and complement one another, as long as both are guided by reason's overarching demand for systematic unity. For the domain of inner nature, this demand is explicated by the most general predicates contained in the idea of the soul. Both activities are thus conditioned by the same transcendental idea of reason. The complementary nature of the two activities does not explain the historical genealogy of how we – as a community of human cognizers – come to adopt certain psychological predicates or how we – as human individuals – come to acquire certain inner experiences in the first place. Rather, it addresses the issue of justification. We can start out with psychological predicates and inner experiences that we assume only hypothetically, for instance, on the basis of tradition or upbringing. The two complementary activities determine a procedure of justification by which we acquire new concepts or cognitions and revise (or even reject) already adopted concepts or cognitions. As a consequence, my inner experience of my own mental states can be empirical cognition of myself and hence can give rise to knowledge – self-knowledge as well as general psychological knowledge – only if I subject my inner experience to a general system of psychological predicates. In turn, this system reflects insights from empirical psychology and is increasingly refined through the acquisition of further psychological knowledge.

With this proposal, we can finally return to my initial question regarding the specific set of necessary conditions that Kant's transcendental philosophy offers for empirical psychology, which I have identified for the current purpose as the study of the empirical aspects of the human mind: psychological knowledge is not only made possible by the transcendental conditions defined by the categories of the understanding, but in addition it is necessarily conditioned by a transcendental idea that gives systematic unity to psychological knowledge and to the corresponding system of psychological predicates. The predicates of the idea of the soul, such as '(mental/thinking) substantiality', 'simplicity', 'personal identity', and '(seat of a) fundamental mental power', can be understood as assumptions of the most general propositions regarding human nature. Yet, these propositions should not be understood as truths that are assertable on the basis of experience; and the predicates above do not literally describe features of psychological beings. Rather, they give an outline of the inner structure of the domain of inner nature. They first span the domain of inner nature into which given empirical cognition can be integrated and classified. It is in this sense, I suggest, that the idea of the soul defines the specific transcendental sources of empirical psychology.

Kant himself explicitly draws on these transcendental sources in his *Anthropology*, which includes a study of human psychological features. There Kant presupposes a fine-grained taxonomy of mental faculties and mental capacities more generally. A taxonomy, for Kant, while showing signs of the possibility of constructing a system, is nonetheless not yet fully systematic. In general, it still lacks an *a priori* schema (or outline) of the system by means of which the position of each part within the whole can be derived *a priori* in accordance with a guiding idea.[52] Nonetheless, Kant himself emphasizes the need for systematicity with respect to matters of psychology in his *Anthropology*. There, he explicitly acknowledges that the observation of particular human beings "can yield nothing more than fragmentary groping" without a general classificatory scheme in the background (Anth, Ak. 7, p. 120). Particular observations must "be ordered and directed through philosophy" (Anth, Ak. 7, p. 120). The aim of anthropology, then, is to "gradually unite [this taxonomy] into a whole through the unity of the plan" (Anth, Ak. 7, p. 122). What this plan of anthropology exactly consists in is not entirely clear from Kant's account.[53] Nonetheless, anthropology requires "appropriate categories" and "the completeness of headings under which this or that observed human quality [...] can be" (Anth, Ak. 7, pp. 121–122).[54]

---

52 S.: "For its execution the idea needs a *schema*, i.e., an essential manifoldness and order of the parts determined *a priori* from the principle of the end." (A 832–833/B 861–862) The schema of an idea "contains the outline (*monogramma*) and the division of the whole into members in conformity with the idea, i.e., *a priori*" (A 834/B 862).

53 For a discussion of Anthropology as a science and its guiding idea, s. Brandt (1999, 2003). On the relationship between empirical psychology and anthropology, s. Kraus (2018).

54 .While Kant would certainly reject the claim that empirical psychology (as well as pragmatic anthropology) can be a proper natural science (s. MFNS, Ak. 4, p. 471), there is a controversy as to whether (or the extent to which) empirical psychology can fulfill the requirement of systematicity according to Kant's demanding concept of science (s. MFNS, Ak. 4, p. 469 and A 832–833/B 861–862). For discussion, s. Pollok (2001), Sturm (2009), and Kraus/Sturm (2017). Note that the requirement of systematicity may be – at least approximately – implemented by empirical sciences that do not have an *a priori* part and that therefore do not count as "proper" natural sciences, though perhaps as "improper" sciences, e.g., chemistry (McNulty 2015) or even empirical psychology (Kraus 2018).

From our earlier considerations, we can conclude that at least the part of anthropology that is concerned with psychological matters is guided by the idea of the soul as a highest genus-concept. Thus, Kant's *Anthropology* itself is structured in accordance with the tripartite structure of the mind and taxonomically investigates empirical psychological observations. The first part is divided into three books, each investigating one of the three basic faculties. Book I, which is concerned with the cognitive faculty, investigates the senses (and their physiological modalities) and the power of imagination (and its modalities). In it, Kant eventually offers a taxonomy of mental disorders and illnesses in accordance with the internal structure of the cognitive faculty (Anth, Ak. 7, p. 214; Ak. 2, pp. 256–260).[55] In a similar manner, Book II, concerned with the feeling of pleasure and displeasure, presents a detailed study of lower pleasures, such as the feeling of agreeableness, and higher pleasures, such as the feeling of aesthetic beauty and taste. Book III, concerned with the faculty of desire, lays out accounts of lower desires, viz. affects, and higher desires, viz. passions, and finally offers a division of the passions.

The empirical study of anthropology thus enriches the basic system of psychological predicates that is based on the transcendental definitions of the mental faculties, as sketched in Figure 1. It adds a variety of psychological capacities, which in the broader anthropological context are then viewed as aspects of behavioral and social dispositions. The transcendental definition of each basic mental faculty, as well as the empirical account of each more specific psychological capacity, can be understood only through relating them to one another within a system of faculties and capacities. This system corresponds to the taxonomy of psychological predicates that captures these interrelations in terms of conceptual containment relations. While the transcendentally defined predicates corresponding to indispensable mental faculties, such as cognition, desire (or will), and feeling, must be realized by *all* human minds, the more specific predicates describing particular psychological capacities may be realized only by *some* persons. Both kinds of predicates should be able to be corroborated by empirical observations in a science of empirical psychology, as well as in everyday life.

---

55 For a detailed reconstruction and discussion of Kant's taxonomy of mental deficiencies and illnesses, s. Frierson (2009a and 2009b).

Conclusion

In this paper, I have explored the transcendental sources that Kant's philosophy is able to offer to empirical psychology as the study of the empirical aspects of the human mind. I have argued that Kant's transcendental philosophy defines a set of distinctive conditions in terms of an idea of reason – the idea of the soul – which makes psychological knowledge possible.

With respect to empirical psychology, the idea of the soul primarily defines what counts as a psychological being whose psychological features are to be investigated in empirical psychology. The idea thus defines as the highest genus-concept the domain of inner nature. The predicates that are contained in the idea, such as '(mental/thinking) substantiality', 'simplicity', 'personal identity', and '(seat of a) fundamental mental power', can then be understood as the most general, though only problematically assumed propositions regarding human nature. As regulative principles, they give guidance for establishing a system of psychological predicates and, correspondingly, a system of psychological knowledge.

With respect to inner experience, the idea of the soul additionally serves as a placeholder for the lowest species-concept of an individual person, that is, for the empirical concept that, if it were available, would completely describe a particular individual. The mutual dependence between general psychological knowledge and particular inner experiences can then be understood as resulting from two mutually complementary complex activities that are both guided by the same regulative idea. Both the activity of acquiring psychological knowledge, and the activity of acquiring inner experience giving rise to empirical self-knowledge, rely on a system of psychological predicates and, therefore, both necessarily depend on the idea of the soul as the unifying idea of such a system.[56]

References

In citing Kant's text the following abbreviations are used:
Ak. | *Kant's gesammelte Schriften*. Königlich Preußische Akademie der Wissenschaften (ed.). Berlin: Reimer/De Gruyter 1900 ff.
Anth | *Anthropology from a Pragmatic Point of View* (1798) (Ak., vol. 7)
A/B | *Critique of Pure Reason* (1781/1787) (Ak., vol. 3 – 4)

---

56 I am grateful to all those who have given me valuable feedback on earlier versions of this paper. I thank in particular Aaron Wells, Clinton Tolley, and Eric Watkins, as well as the editors, Dina Emundts and Sally Sedgwick.

CJ | *Critique of Judgment* (1790) (Ak., vol. 5)

CpracR | *Critique of Practical Reason* (1788) (Ak., vol. 5)

MFNS | *Metaphysical Foundations of Natural Science* (1786) (Ak., vol. 4)

L-Log/Blomberg | *Logic Blomberg* (early 1770s) (Ak., vol. 24)

L-Log/Dohna-Wundlacken | *Logic Dohna-Wundlacken* (1792) (Ak., vol. 24)

L-Log/Jäsche | *Jäsche Logic* (1800) (Ak., vol. 9)

L-Log/Vienna | *Logic Vienna* (1780s) (Ak., vol. 24)

Prol | *Prolegomena to any future metaphysics that will be able to come forward as a science* (1783) (Ak., vol. 4)

Refl | *Reflections* (Ak., vols. 14–19)

Religion | *Religion within the Boundaries of Mere Reason* (1793) (Ak., vol. 6)

All translations are taken from:

Kant, Immanuel (1992 ff.): *The Cambridge Edition of the Works of Immanuel Kant.* Paul Guyer and Allen Wood (eds.). Cambridge: Cambridge University Press.

Abela, Paul (2006): "The Demands of Systematicity: Rational Judgment and the Structure of Nature". In: Graham Bird (ed.): *A Companion to Kant.* Oxford: Blackwell, pp. 408–422.

Anderson, R. Lanier (2014): *The Poverty of Conceptual Truth.* Oxford: Oxford University Press.

Baumgarten, Alexander G. (1739/1982): *Metaphysica.* 7th edition. Halle/Magdeburg: Hildesheim: Olms.

Brandt, Reinhardt (1999): *Kritischer Kommentar zu Kants ,Anthropologie in pragmatischer Hinsicht'.* Hamburg: Meiner.

Brandt, Reinhardt (2003): "The Guiding Idea of Kant's Anthropology and the Vocation of the Human Being". In: Brian Jacobs/Patrick Kain (eds.): *Essays on Kant's Anthropology.* Cambridge: Cambridge University Press, pp. 85–104.

Buchdahl, Gerd (1967): "The Relation between 'Understanding' and 'Reason'". In: *Proceedings of the Aristotelian Society* 67, pp. 209–226.

Dyck, Corey (2014): *Kant and Rational Psychology.* Oxford: Oxford University Press.

Emundts, Dina (2007): "Kant über innere Erfahrung". In: U. Kern (ed.): *Was ist und was sein soll. Natur und Freiheit bei Immanuel Kant.* Berlin: De Gruyter, pp. 191–205.

Falduto, Antonino (2014): *The Faculties of the Human Mind and the Case of Moral Feeling in Kant's Philosophy.* Berlin: De Gruyter.

Frierson, Patrick (2014): *Kant's Empirical Psychology.* Cambridge: Cambridge University Press.

Frierson, Patrick (2009a): "Kant on Mental Disorder 1: An Overview". In: *History of Psychiatry* 20, pp. 267–289.

Frierson, Patrick (2009b): "Kant on Mental Disorder 2: Philosophical Implications". In: *History of Psychiatry* 20, pp. 290–310.

Ginsborg, Hannah (2006): "Empirical concepts and the content of experience". In: *European Journal of Philosophy* 14, pp. 349–372.

Ginsborg, Hannah (2017): "Why Must We Presuppose the Systematicity of Nature?". In: Michela Massimi/Angela Breitenbach (eds.): *Kant and the Laws of Nature.* Cambridge: Cambridge University Press, pp. 71–88.

Grier, Michelle (2001): *Kant's Doctrine of Transcendental Illusion.* Cambridge: Cambridge University Press.

Guyer, Paul (1990): "Reason and Reflective Judgment: Kant on the Significance of Systematicity". In: *Noûs* 24, pp. 17–43.

Hatfield, Gar (2006): "Empirical, Rational, and Transcendental Psychology: Psychology as Science and as Philosophy". In: Paul Guyer (ed.): *The Cambridge Companion to Kant*. Cambridge: Cambridge University Press, pp. 200–227.

Heßbrüggen-Walter, Stefan (2004): *Die Seele und ihre Vermögen. Kants Metaphysik des Mentalen in der ‚Kritik der reinen Vernunft'*. Paderborn: Mentis.

Kitcher, Patricia (1990): *Kant's Transcendental Psychology*. Oxford: Oxford University Press.

Kitcher, Patricia (2011): *Kant's Thinker*. Oxford: Oxford University Press.

Klemme, Heiner (1996): *Kants Philosophie des Subjekts*. Hamburg: Meiner.

Kraus, Katharina/Sturm, Thomas (2017): "'An Attractive Alternative to Empirical Psychologies Both in His Day and Our Own'? A Critique of Frierson's *Kant's Empirical Psychology*". In: *Studi Kantiani* 30, pp. 203–223.

Kraus, Katharina (2018): "The soul as the 'guiding idea' of psychology: Kant on scientific psychology, systematicity, and the idea of the soul". In: *Studies of History and Philosophy of Science* 71, pp. 77–88.

Kraus, Katharina (2019): "The Parity and Disparity between Inner and Outer Experience". In: *Kantian Review* 24 (2), pp. 171–195.

Longuenesse, Béatrice (1998): *Kant and the Capacity to Judge*. Princeton: Princeton University Press.

McNulty, Bennett (2018): "Kant on Empirical Psychology and Experimentation". In: Violetta Waibel/Margit Ruffing (eds.): *Natur und Freiheit: Akten des XII. Internationalen Kant-Kongresses*. Berlin/Boston: De Gruyter. Vol. 4, pp. 2707–2714.

McNulty, Bennett (2015): "Rehabilitating the Regulative Use of Reason: Kant on Empirical and Chemical Laws". In: *Studies in History and Philosophy of Science* 54, pp. 1–10.

Mischel, Theodore (1967): "Kant and the Possibility of a Science of Psychology". In: *Monist* 51, pp. 599–622.

Nassar, Dalia (2016): "Analogical reflection as a source for the science of life: Kant and the possibility of the biological sciences". In: *Studies in History and Philosophy of Science* 58, pp. 57–66.

Nayak, Abhaya/Sotnak, Eric (1995): "Kant on the Impossibility of the 'Soft Sciences'". In: *Philosophy and Phenomenological Research* 55, pp. 133–151.

O'Neill, Onora (1984): "Transcendental Synthesis and Developmental Psychology". In: *Kant-Studien* 75. No. 2, pp. 149–167.

Schmidt, Claudia (2008): "Kant's transcendental and empirical psychology of cognition". In: *Studies in History and Philosophy of Science* 39. No. 4, pp. 462–472.

Schönrich, Gerhard (1991): "Kant und die vermeintliche Unmöglichkeit einer wissenschaftlichen Psychologie". In: *Psychologie und Geschichte* 2, pp. 130–137.

Serck-Hanssen, Camilla (2011): "Der Nutzen von Illusionen. Ist die Idee der Seele unentbehrlich?". In: B. Dörflinger (ed.): *Über den Nutzen von Illusionen. Die regulativen Ideen in Kants theoretischer Philosophie*. Hildesheim: Olms, pp. 59–71.

Sturm, Thomas (2009): *Kant und die Wissenschaften vom Menschen*. Paderborn: Mentis.

Tetens, Johann Nicolaus (1777). *Philosophische Versuche über die menschliche Natur und ihre Entwickelung*. Leipzig: Weidmann.

Washburn, Michael C. (1976): "Did Kant have a theory of Self-Knowledge?". In: *Archiv für Geschichte der Philosophie* 58, pp. 40–56.

Watkins, Eric (2013): "Kant on *Infima Species*". In: Alfredo Ferrarin/Claudio La Rocca/Margit Ruffing (eds.): *Kant und die Philosophie in weltbürgerlicher Absicht. Akten des XI. Internationalen Kant-Kongresses*. Berlin: De Gruyter, pp. 283–296.

Watkins, Eric/Willaschek, Marcus (2017): "Kant's Account of Cognition". In: *Journal of the History of Philosophy* 55. No. 1, pp. 83–112.

Westphal, Kenneth R. (2004): *Kant's Transcendental Proof of Realism*. Cambridge: Cambridge University Press.

Wolff, Christian (1732/1968): *Psychologia empirica*. In: *Gesammelte Werke*. Vol. II/5. Hildesheim: Olms.

Zuckert, Rachel (2017): "Empirical Scientific Investigation and the Ideas of Reason". In: Michela Massimi/Angela Breitenbach (eds.): *Kant and the Laws of Nature*. Cambridge: Cambridge University Press, pp. 89–107.

Gary Hatfield

Modern Meanings of Subjectivity: Philosophical, Psychological, Physiological

Abstract. *A recent account (by Daston and Galison) defines the modern meaning of "objectivity" in relation to "subjectivity": objectivity means, among other things, avoiding personal bias. Subjectivity denotes mental characteristics idiosyncratically peculiar to individuals. Without denying that these meanings are found in the modern period (albeit earlier than Daston and Galison suggest), this article maintains that a more profound modern meaning of "the subjective" concerns subjective conditions of perception and thought that need not or indeed cannot vary among individuals. Kant brought this more profound meaning into prominence, and it entered into scientific theories of perception of the nineteenth century. This meaning can describe an early modern "subjective turn" in philosophy and the theory of perception.*

Jüngst ist (von Daston und Galison) folgender Vorschlag zur modernen Bedeutung von „Objektivität" mit Bezug auf „Subjektivität" gemacht worden: Objektivität bedeutet, unter anderem, dass persönliche Einflussnahme vermieden wird. Subjektivität bezeichnet mentale Eigenschaften, die bei Individuen idiosynkratisch verschieden sind. Ohne dass bezweifelt werden soll, dass sich diese Bedeutungen vom achtzehnten Jahrhundert an finden lassen, wird in diesem Aufsatz die These entwickelt, dass es eine grundlegendere moderne Bedeutung die subjektiven Bedingungen von Wahrnehmung betreffend gibt, bei der die Bedingungen zwischen Individuen nicht variieren müssen. Kant hat diese Bedeutung etabliert und sie ist in die wissenschaftlichen Theorien des neunzehnten Jahrhunderts eingegangen. Diese Bedeutung markiert eine „subjektive Wende" in der Philosophie der Frühen Neuzeit in der Theorie der Wahrnehmung.

Objectivity and subjectivity, as concepts, find application in describing core features of modern science and philosophy. Epistemological, methodological, and metaphysical writings from the time of Bacon and Descartes are concerned to avoid bias in observation and description (Bacon's idols, Descartes' warning about "childhood prejudices"). There is also a trend, shot through the early modern period, of distinguishing subjective aspects of sense perception and thought from objective aspects that directly describe external objects; the distinction between ideas of secondary qualities and of primary qualities is a prime example. The relation between what the subject brings to perception and cognition (a sub-

https://doi.org/10.1515/9783110673692-008

jective component) and what exhibits objects as they are in themselves (an objective component) became a guiding theme for early modern philosophy, from Descartes to Kant. Indeed, Kant altered the question by distinguishing physical objects and their objectivity from things in themselves, placed beyond the pale, unleashing a long dialogue on subjectivity and objectivity in German philosophy and science of the nineteenth century.

This standard story rests easily on an application of the *concepts* of objectivity and subjectivity. It has been challenged by recent work that focuses on the *terms* "objectivity" and "subjectivity." In *Objectivity*, Lorraine Daston and Peter Galison (hereafter, "D&G") examine the origin of "objectivity" and its counterpart "subjectivity" in what they consider to be a "modern" (present-day) sense.[1] They find that the notion of scientific objectivity first arose in the nineteenth century (about 1860), in response to a fear among scientific practitioners that their measurements and representations were biased by individual preferences or idiosyncratically subjective attitudes and interests. Scientific objectivity arose to counter the practice of creating ideal images or exemplars of natural objects. It was a form of "mechanical objectivity" (D&G, pp. 13–19, 120), emblematically found in photography but also present in mechanized recording techniques, which avoided the idiosyncrasies of the recording scientist or scientist's assistant. On this conception, subjectivity was inherently a matter of observer variability and the attendant possibility that individual attitudes and beliefs distort observations and representations (D&G, pp. 34–35, 44).

There is much to value in D&G's elegant book, including the narrative that surrounds the invention of mechanical objectivity. Nonetheless, I believe that D&G miss the core feature of the complementary concept of *subjectivity*, as a descriptive category for modern thought (post 1600). They fail to take note of the modern idea, found in Descartes and revised in Kant, that the subject may contribute a constant element to sense perception or thought that is related to an external world but that does not picture that world as it is in itself. This is the notion of a general and pervasive subjective element, which *might* vary among individuals, but whose credentials as a subjective element *do not* depend on or require such variability. Being innocent of this notion, D&G overlook the entire "subjective turn" in modern conceptions of sense perception (and thought more generally), according to which something can be "subjective" if it pertains to the observing or cognizing subject, even if this subjective element is the same in all subjects.

---

1 As D&G put it, "The evidence for the nineteenth-century novelty of scientific objectivity starts with the word itself" (D&G, p. 29).

After summarizing more closely D&G's characterization, I explicate some main notions of subjectivity and objectivity from the eighteenth and nineteenth centuries. In accordance with D&G's own method, I track especially the terms "subjective" and "objective" and their kin. Documented historical usage requires introducing a notion of subjectivity as *pertaining to the subject* but without the implication of individual (idiosyncratic) variation. I then summarize some uses of the terms in Kant, including this notion of pertaining to the subject (without implying variation). Subsequently, I trace notions of subjectivity and objectivity into the nineteenth century, focusing on German sensory physiology and psychology in the century's first half. In this scientific literature, the Kantian notion of pertaining to the subject was deeply influential, even if the various authors disagreed with Kant and were trying to refute or correct his views on subjectivity and objectivity in perception.

1 D&G

Daston and Galison's book charts the origin of a specific form of scientific objectivity in the nineteenth century. It follows a thread of scientific practice, centered on the use of images in scientific atlases (mainly anatomical and botanical) and as illustrations or data records in physics. As such, it makes a good case for a particular historical transition from a practice of idealized depiction ("truth to nature"), to a demand that images and observations be "mechanically objective" (photographs are emblematic), to a hybrid practice of advisedly adjusting images, data records, and their interpretation in accordance with "trained judgment" (D&G, pp. 17–19). The turn to mechanical objectivity responds to the worry, already mentioned, that the biases and preferences of the observer or image-maker may distort the portrayal of nature. Although historians of anatomy, botany, and physics may question the generality of the story or some of its particular claims, the authors do make the case that their thread describes the development of one notion of objectivity, paired with a notion of subjectivity.

At the same time, in its very title, and in replies to imagined skeptics of the book's message, the authors present their topic in another light: as a history of "objectivity" *tout court*,[2] along with the contrasting notion of "subjectivity." They

---

2 D&G seek to learn "what objectivity *is*" (D&G, p. 51) prior to endorsing its pursuit. Although accepting a multi-faceted conception of objectivity – their answer to what objectivity is involves these factors: emotional detachment, automatic data recording, quantification, and an observer-independent reality (D&G, p. 29) – their focus is on objectivity as a methodological aim of sci-

support their claim that "objectivity is new" (D&G, p. 27) with a quick excursus into the history of philosophy, at first focused simply on the terms themselves. In medieval and early modern usage, they maintain, the term "'[o]bjective' referred to things as they are presented to consciousness, whereas 'subjective' referred to things in themselves" (D&G, p. 29). This is contrasted with the "modern" usage that the authors have arising in the nineteenth century, in which "subjectivity" has to do with individual minds and "objectivity" with representations or measurements of objects as they are. These terminological claims are addressed below (sec. 2). But, as the authors affirm, one need not always stay within the language of the past in describing its products (D&G, p. 421, n. 5). Accordingly, after noting that "historians of philosophy have routinely used the vocabulary of objectivity and subjectivity [in a modern sense] to analyze the works of Bacon and Descartes" (D&G, p. 423, n. 14), especially in relation to the distinction between primary and secondary qualities, D&G imply that these historians have been *conceptually* mistaken in doing so. The mistake, as they diagnose it, lies in an erroneous retrospective application of the modern terms to describe secondary qualities as "subjective" and primary qualities as "objective." But, as they would have it, the distinction between primary and secondary qualities, as understood by Descartes, was really "a distinction among purely mental entities, one kind of idea versus another – what nineteenth century authors would (and did) label 'subjective'" (D&G, p. 32). As they see it, in modern terms the distinction is wholly on the subjective side and so does not express the modern concepts of subjective as contrasted with objective. (Evaluation of their diagnosis comes below.)

Among the more telling of our authors' statements, for revealing the particularity of their own notions of objectivity and subjectivity, is their objection to applying the modern terms "objective" and "subjective" to Bacon's four idols, which, as a historian of philosophy might put it, pertain to various subjectively based limitations on or potential distortions of knowledge; the idols describe threats to objectivity.[3] Not so, according to D&G. As they see it, "only one of the four categories (the idols of the cave) applied to the individual psyche and could therefore be a candidate for subjectivity in the modern sense (the others refer to errors inherent in the human species, language, and theories, respectively)" (D&G, p. 32). Subjectivity, according to our authors, is a matter of individual

ence. As we shall see, other framing conceptions of objectivity and subjectivity were at work in at least some of the sciences.

3 Zagorin 2001, p. 390, analyzes Bacon's idols as threats to objectivity considered as "enquiry that leads to true knowledge and understanding of the world," finding it reasonable to attribute this (modern) notion of objectivity to Bacon.

variability – which is certainly one meaning that "subjectivity" can have, but not the only meaning, and not the primary meaning that historians of philosophy have intended in describing secondary qualities as "subjective," or in seeing Bacon's idols as threats to objectivity. And it is not the sense invoked in discussions of the "subjective" conditioning of perception and thought in the first half of the nineteenth century.

D&G see the nineteenth-century concepts of objectivity and subjectivity as "post-Kantian" but deny their identity with Kantian notions. For, they argue, when Kant distinguished "objective validity" from "the subjective," he used the latter "as a rough synonym for 'merely empirical sensations'," a word usage that "shares with later usage only the sneer with which intoned." Further, "for Kant, the line between the objective and the subjective generally runs between the universal and particular, not between world and mind" (D&G, p. 30). Kant can be the "grandfather" of modern usage because he (allegedly) uses the term "subjective" to mean individual or particular, and "objective" to mean universal. Again, our authors maintain that, in modern usage, "subjective" applies exclusively to individual variations, which their nineteenth-century scientists attempted to avoid by taking the subject out of the observing process in accordance with the goal of achieving "mechanical objectivity."

The next two sections examine the historical appearance of the most relevant meanings of "objectivity" and "subjectivity" in the seventeenth and eighteenth centuries, ending with Kant.

2 "Objectivity" and "Subjectivity" in Use

D&G (p. 421, n. 6) appeal to the *Oxford English Dictionary* (among other sources) to support their claim that these two terms saw something like a reversal of their philosophical meanings between the seventeenth and late eighteenth centuries, at the very least rendering questionable any extension of the modern meanings back to the earlier period. They correctly note that, in seventeenth-century usage, to speak of something "objectively" or as having "objective reality" was (often) to speak of it as an object of thought (or perhaps as an object or goal of action). The *OED* sums up this meaning of "objective" as: "Existing as an object of consciousness as distinct from having any real existence; considered only as presented to the mind" (*OED*, vol. 1, p. 1963, citing initial usages from the fourteenth and seventeenth centuries). D&G also correctly note that, in the same period, the terms "subject" or "subjective" could have the sense of a substance or independently existing thing: "Pertaining to the subject as to that in which attributes inhere; inherent; hence, pertaining to the essence or reality of a thing; real, essential"

(*OED*, vol. 2, p. 3121). D&G's "modern meaning" of "objective" generally accords with this *OED* entry: "the object of perception or thought, as distinct from the perceiving subject; hence, that is, or has the character of being, a 'thing' external to the mind; real" (*OED*, vol. 1, p. 1963) – although the OED traces this meaning back to the seventeenth century (well before D&G find it in common use). This modern meaning contrasts with "subjective" as "Relating to the thinking subject; proceeding from or taking place in the subject" (*OED*, vol. 2, p. 3121), which is found from the early eighteenth century.

The oft-invoked "reversal" of the terms would, given these meanings, be from the seventeenth-century notions of the "subject" as the thing existing independent of thought and "object" as the content of thought, to the later notion of "subject" as a thinking subject or locus of (idiosyncratically varying?) thoughts and "object" as an independently existing external object.[4] Tracking the *OED* entries, there was no simple reversal. First, seventeenth-century "objective reality" concerns the content of a thought. Hence, Descartes said that ideas present things to the intellect "objectively" or "by representation" (AT 7, p. 42; 9 A, p. 33);[5] the sun is in the intellect objectively, or as represented (AT 7, pp. 102–103). But the "thinking subject" in the later, modern sense is a locus of all thoughts and experiences (including feelings, attitudes, and volitions) and so does not have the same meaning as seventeenth-century "objective reality" understood as the object (or content) of thought. Second, the connotation of the "object" in the later, modern sense is a material object. But the seventeenth-century contrast to "objective reality" is "formal reality" (AT 7, pp. 40–41, 102). Such reality can be attributed to a subject as substance, but in seventeenth-century usage the "subject" is by no means restricted to material objects; it can include the mind or God, as immaterial beings. Hence, the modern term "object" (meaning "material object") is not a mere reversal of the earlier "subject," since the modern term "object" as invoked here does not extend to immaterial substances.

Beyond the lack of a simple reversal, there is another, more fundamental problem with the definition of the "modern subject" offered by D&G. Recall that they understand the "subjective" as something varying idiosyncratically among individuals and needing to be avoided in seeking unbiased, "objective" knowledge. In fact, this notion of the "subjective" is not contained in the first

---

4 Mention of a reversal of meanings is common: Beck 1969, p. 284; D&G, p. 31; Dewey 1902, p. 608. The *OED*, vol. 1, p. 1963, shows some caution, citing William Hamilton as describing what is "almost an exchange of sense" between the older and newer meanings.

5 Descartes' works are cited by volume and page numbers in the Adam and Tannery (AT) edition. Translations are taken, where possible, from Descartes 1984–1985. His *Principles of Philosophy* is cited as *Principles* plus Part and article number.

relevant new meaning offered in the *OED*, partially quoted above: "Relating to the thinking subject; proceeding from or taking place in the subject [...]"; the entry continues: "having its source in the mind; (in the widest sense) belonging to the conscious life" (*OED*, vol. 2, p. 3121). This meaning of "subjective" as "relating to the thinking subject" is first attested in the *OED* in 1707. It was established during the eighteenth century and is prominent in Kant's German. There is no connotation of individual variability here. In the *OED*, the notion of idiosyncratic variability that is at the center of D&G's analysis is only found in a subsequent entry (first attested from 1767): "Pertaining or peculiar to an individual subject or his mental operations; depending on one's individuality or idiosyncrasy; personal, individual" (*OED*, vol. 2, p. 3121). D&G's notions of subjectivity and objectivity are not the first (new) modern meanings either chronologically or in order of significance, but instead came second.

The genuinely first modern meaning of "subjectivity" (without idiosyncrasy) is the more profound as a descriptive category applied to the history of philosophy. With that meaning, we can speak of a "subjective turn" in the history of philosophy, first as regards the sensory qualities (in the distinction between primary and secondary qualities) and then as regards space, time, and the Kantian categories.[6] Concerning the subjectivity of the sensory qualities in the seventeenth century, the distinction between primary and secondary qualities, as found in Descartes, Boyle, Locke, and others, is not a distinction wholly on the side of the mind (as D&G suggest). Rather, the point made by these authors is that sensory ideas of secondary qualities stand in a different relation to their external causes than do sensory ideas of primary qualities. Phenomenal colors, sounds, odors, and the like do not accurately portray their causes, because there is nothing in the objects that "resembles" the experienced qualities (Descartes, *Principles*, I.66 – 70; Locke 1690, Bk. II, ch. 8, art. 15). By contrast, phenomenal shapes and sizes can, under good conditions, reveal the actual shapes and sizes of ob-

---

6 Erdmann 1890, pp. 455, 459, 620, describes Schopenhauer and Fries as admiring the "subjective turn" (*subjective Wendung*) (first modern meaning) given to philosophy by (respectively) Descartes and Kant. Falckenberg 1893, pp. 57, 347, 608, 617, notes the "subjectivity of sense qualities" as found in Kepler, Galileo, Descartes, Gassendi, and Hobbes, describes Kant as distinguishing the individual subjectivity of sense qualities from the generally subjective forms of intuition and categories, and finds Lotze and Lange promoting the doctrine that sense qualities along with forms of intuition and categories are subjective (first modern meaning). Ogilvy 1992, p. xiii, writes of the "subjective turn" promulgated in philosophy by especially Descartes and Kant: "What, in the structure of rational consciousness, is necessarily the case in order that knowledge and experience should be possible? This is the question posed by the transcendental-subjective turn that dominated philosophy from Descartes to Kant." German philosophy of the nineteenth century incorporates and responds to this subjective turn.

jects, because objects actually do have, formally and in fact, shapes and sizes. Further, secondary qualities as properties of objects are to be understood as dispositions to cause ideas (sensory experiences) of secondary qualities (color, etc.). Those dispositions involve affecting the mind, but they are not themselves mental.[7]

A further lacuna occurs in the treatment of Kant and subjectivity. D&G attribute only the second modern meaning, of idiosyncratic variability, to Kant. Further, they give him only partial credit for the modern notion of objectivity, contending that, for him, objective and subjective both lie in the mind. But, in fact, Kant was an influential purveyor of the first modern meaning, of the subjective as what depends on the subject. And not only is this notion of "subjective" not intended by Kant to be inherently bad (although it does express a limit to knowledge), it provides, in his eyes, the basis for objective knowledge (modern sense) of external things, as objects existing in space and time.

3 Kant and the Subjective

When Descartes and Locke distinguished between primary and secondary qualities, they invoked a twofold distinction between mind and world. External objects have properties that cause sensory ideas in minds, and we can know what type of properties these are with *a priori* certainty (Descartes) or through empirical arguments (Locke): they are the spatialized properties of matter (including size, shape, position, and motion). Kant offered a more intricate picture of the relation between phenomenal experience and its objects in the world: experience arises when sensations (such as color, sound, and the like) are synthesized according to the forms of intuition (space and time) and the categories of the understanding (such as substance and cause). He set up a threefold framework anent the relation between experience and external objects: experiences are had by a *subject* (a mind); they have contents that present *physical objects* existing externally; these objects as known do not reveal the properties of *things as they are in themselves*.[8]

---

7 For an overview of the distinction, s. Nolan 2011, Introduction and chs. 4–12. Also, in the cited passage from Descartes (*Principles* I.70), he distinguishes "sensations" of color from their causes in the "object" (Latin, *objectum*), revealing that the term "object" was not, in seventeenth-century philosophy, limited to its use in the scholastic technical compounds "objective reality" or "objective being," but could mean "external object."

8 Of course, Kant also allows inner experience of the self as an appearance, but our focus is on outer objects.

Kant's *Critique of Pure Reason* and *Prolegomena to Any Future Metaphysics* examine the relation between the knowing subject and the objects of knowledge. As mentioned, he concludes that we do not know things as they are in themselves but only as they appear to us. At the same time, he held that aspects of those appearances which apply to all physical objects are rooted in universal characteristics of the human subject. This is his doctrine that space and time are forms of sensibility. As D&G would have it, this means that Kant's notion of "objective validity" does not refer to external objects (that is, to the world). But in fact Kant claims, and intends to establish, exactly the opposite. We know external objects, the objects both of Newtonian physics and of everyday life, under the aspect of space and time. This way of knowing them is a condition that pertains to all human subjects. As such, the inter-subjectively shared forms of sensibility could provide, in Kant's expression from the *Prolegomena* (an "abstract" of the *Critique*),[9] the "subjective foundation of all outer appearances," that is, the foundation of all experience of external objects (Ak. 4, p. 288).[10] In the *Critique*, he notes that "Except for space, there is no other subjective representation related to something external that could be called *a priori* objective" (A 28/B 44), adding in the second edition that "from no other subjective representation can one derive synthetic *a priori* principles, as one can from intuition in space" (B 44). A similar usage occurs with the respect to his table of categories as "subjective conditions of thought" that nonetheless yield "objective validity" (A 89/B 122). In explaining how it is possible to know that the causal law applies to all possible experience, Kant averred: "the subjective laws under which alone a cognition of things through experience is possible also hold good for those things as objects of a possible experience (but obviously, not for them as things in themselves, which, however, are not at all being considered here)" (Ak. 4, p. 296).

Kant proposes that the forms of sensibility and the categories, as brought to experience by the subject, nonetheless are able to ground objective knowledge of

---

9 The first *Critique* is cited as usual with "A" and "B" for the pagination of the first (1781) and second (1787) German editions (translations are mine). The *Prolegomena* is cited as translated in Kant 2004; the pagination is to the fourth volume of the Academy edition of Kant's works (Ak.). **10** D&G, p. 30, may be reading Kant's transcendental idealism as bringing external objects into the mind. Kant has been read that way. Still, his intention was to avoid making things into mere representations and to sustain the validity of physical space and an external world (Ak. 4, pp. 288–289), in accordance with his "empirical realism" (A 29–30/B 44–45). One cannot simply assume without comment a reading that places outer objects in the mind. But, even accepting such a reading, Kant's "subjective" is no "synonym for 'merely empirical sensations'," nor does his distinction between objective and subjective generally run "between the universal and particular" (D&G, p. 30).

external objects. Here, "subjective" clearly means pertaining to the subject in general; this notion excludes idiosyncratic variation. "Objective" and "object" have two relevant meanings. Application of the forms of intuition and the categories serves as the basis for objectively valid knowledge; this is *objectivity* in the sense of universal validity, and it does not apply only to knowledge of external objects but to any judgments that appropriately apply the categories. Second, cognition may be directed toward and provide knowledge of external *objects*, as things existing in space and time.

All the same, Kant does indeed use the term "subjective" in ways that do not require universal validity. One such example arises in connection with the subjectivity of the habit-based belief that every event has a cause (e. g., Ak. 4, p. 277). Here, "subjective" mental states include those joined by mere associative processes, which operate according to associative rules in subjects, but which do not sustain the conceptual demand for universality and necessity that goes with the concept of cause and is met by the category of cause (Ak. 4, pp. 257–259, 312). Here, "subjective" means "merely subjective," that is, formed by or depending on the mental activity of the subject. It does not require idiosyncrasy. Thus, the laws of association, even if they operated with the same results in all human cognizers, would still yield merely subjective results (as at Ak. 4, p. 258; A 91–92/B 123–124; A 121; A 766–767/B794–795). A second example does invoke idiosyncrasy. Kant distinguishes merely subjective sensations, which are related to a single individual's perception and can vary among individuals, from perceptions that have been rendered objectively valid by proper application of the categories, where such perceptions constitute experience and include a demand for universal agreement among perceivers.[11] The sensations that do vary from individual to individual are "subjective" in the sense of D&G: they are subjective because they vary in an idiosyncratic way.[12]

---

11 In A, Kant maintains that "colors are not objective qualities of the bodies to the intuition of which they are attached, but are also only modifications of the sense of sight, which is affected by light in a certain way" (A 28). In the *Prolegomena* (Ak. 4, p. 299), discussing examples such as judging that the room is warm or that sugar is sweet, he labels these "merely subjectively valid judgments," which can never be made objective, in the way that judgments concerning spatial structures and causation can be rendered objective. Such judgments can vary among individuals: "I do not at all require that I should find it so at every time, or that everyone else should find it just as I do" (Ak. 4, p. 299). But the forms of intuition and the application of the categories, although "subjective" conditions of experience, do entail a demand for universal agreement (Ak. 4, pp. 298–300).

12 D&G, p. 210, note another of Kant's uses of "subjective" as varying individually, in his discussion of "subjective" inclinations in ethics.

In these cases, Kant distinguishes between mere subjectivity and universally shared subjective conditions of thought. And within the merely subjective he distinguishes dependent on the subject from dependent on the subject and varying idiosyncratically. The universal subjective conditions yield objective validity, the other two instances do not. All three cases employ the concept of a human subject. The "merely subjective" is dependent on the subject and either simply fails to yield objective validity, as in the laws of association (idiosyncrasy allowed but not required), or varies idiosyncratically as in the case of color sensations (subjectivity as individual variation). The claim that subjective conditions of thought can yield objectivity is characteristic of Kant. By his own lights, his primary critical insight was to characterize and justify this sort of subjectively based cognitive apparatus as sustaining knowledge applicable to external things.

These various Kantian notions of subjectivity were recognized in hindsight a century later. Standard reference works mark the distinction between universal subjectivity and individual variation. John Dewey, in his 1902 entry "Subject (-ive)" in Baldwin's *Dictionary*, commenting on a series of passages in Kant invoking the subject or the subjective conditions of experience, finds that Kant repeatedly describes as "subjective" "all the part played by mental activity in constituting empirical objects" (Dewey 1902, p. 608). Dewey then sorts out two aspects of this notion of the "subjective":

> A double sense is clearly contained here: on one side, this subjective is set over against the objective, when thing-in-themselves – reality in its intrinsic nature – are in mind; it is the source of the phenomenal, of that which has not unconditioned validity – tending towards the skeptical and illusory sense of the term. But, on the other hand, it is constitutive of objects as experienced, and therefore has complete (empirical) objectivity; indeed, because of its universal and necessary character, it is more "objective" than any law or object found in experience. (Dewey 1902, p. 608)

Dewey puts at least three Kantian points together: the general subjectivity of experience in relation to things in themselves; the particular or individual subjectivity of some appearances (the sensations, described here as "the phenomenal"); and the role of universal subjective aspects of cognition, the forms of intuition and the categories, in constituting the objective experience of physical objects. Other commentators emphasize a further distinction, found in Kant, between what belongs to subjects in general (e. g., associative processes), which might be deemed the *psychologically subjective* (reflecting the common psychological properties of all humans), and what belongs to the subject as knower, that is, as possessor of objective knowledge based in the forms and categories, which might be termed, with Kant, the *transcendentally subjective*.[13] That which is psychologically subjective can vary idiosyncratically, but such variability is not required for application of "subjective" to psychological states and processes. As previously mentioned, the laws of association, even if they yielded the same results in all human cognizers, would still be merely subjective. But, as in the case of color sensations, that which is psychologically subjective can be so in the sense of individual variations (yielding two forms of psychological subjectivity). Finally, objective (universally valid) experience results only when experience is subject to the categories (such as the category of cause), yielding a transcendentally subjective basis for knowledge. We find here a recognition of the three relevant Kantian instances of "the subjective" mentioned above: that which varies idiosyncratically among subjects (such as color sensations); that which pertains to all psychological subjects and perhaps can vary, but need not vary in order to be "subjective" (as with associative processes); and that which is fixed among all human subjects, in Kant's sense of transcendental subjectivity.

The next two sections look at usages of "subjective" and "objective" in the first half of the nineteenth century. One could here consider how the German Idealists and other philosophical authors (such as Fries or Schopenhauer) variously developed the Kantian universal subject. But in line with D&G's emphasis on scientific writings, I focus on uses of the terms "subjective" and "objective" in sensory physiology and psychology in the decades after 1800. I start with Goethe, who is not Kantian but whose work illustrates one way of developing the "modern" (Kantian) senses of the term "subjective." I then turn to the rich body of work in sensory physiology and psychology that adapted Kantian notions.

---

13 Eisler 1921, pp. 638–639, distinguished (1) "subjektiv" describing variation from person to person (or from one time to another in one person); from (2) "subjektiv" as the "(nicht das Individuell-, sondern) das Allgemein-Subjektive ('Intersubjektive'), d. h. das von der gleichartigen Beschaffenheit aller erlebenden Wesen (Menschen) Abhängige"; while noting (3) that this second sense has as a variant or subspecies "das Transzendental-Subjektive (S. im rein logisch-erkenntnistheoretischen Sinne) als Inbegriff von Funktionen, Gesetzlichkeiten, Geltungen, welche eine Bedingung objektiv-einheitlichen Erfahrungszusammenhangs, also Grundlagen, Voraussetzungen des Objektiven (s. d.) selbst sind." Such references to the Kantian heritage of subjectivity easily could be multiplied. For a conceptual-historical overview of the various uses of the notion of a subject in general and its relation to objectivity (including logical usage, which has not been addressed here), with considerable attention to Kant and his influence, s. Ritter and Gründer 1998, pp. 373–433. See also Karskens 1992.

4 Goethe and the Subjective

Another recent interpreter claims to find the origin of subjectivity, or of "subjective vision," in the nineteenth century. Jonathan Crary (1990) sees in Goethe and subsequent authors an invention of the subjectivity of vision. In his narrative, the seventeenth and eighteenth centuries were dominated by a model of vision based on the camera obscura, entrenched as an abstract, geometrical, one-eyed perspectival relation to the world. By contrast, Goethe, in his theory of color, emphasized the contribution of the subject to vision via physiology, a contribution that Crary marks as an historicized and embodied subject (Crary 1990, p. 14), a conception that (allegedly) undermines the objective vision of the camera obscura. This trend continued in the new physiology of two-eyed vision (as with the stereoscope). Crary's birth of subjectivity occurs with Goethe's *Farbenlehre* in 1810, fifty years before what D&G identify as the birth of "scientific objectivity" to counter subjectivity as individual bias.

Crary's story may be challenged on several fronts. Thus, the camera obscura was no model of vision for major theorists such as Descartes; rather, it was a model of the eye. But, as Descartes observed, "it is the soul which sees, and not the eye; and it does not see directly, but only by means of the brain" (*Dioptrics*, AT 6, p. 141). In Descartes' theory, the brain receives binocular input, and it responds physiologically to this input in various ways that affect the mind, according to instituted rules of nature.[14] More importantly, like D&G, Crary misses the "subjective turn" in the theory of sense perception that became prominent in the seventeenth century, a failing that undermines his easy comparison between hyper-geometrical objectivity in Descartes and lived bodily experience in Goethe. As has been discussed, this "subjective turn" was carried through to Kant, who transformed it (while rendering its terminology modern).

Having missed this generic form of subjectivity, Crary also missed the singularity of Goethe's position in the nineteenth century, including his response to Newton's conception of the relation between physical color and color experience.

Two aspects of the relation between Goethe's and Newton's color theories are especially problematic for Crary's thesis (Crary 1990, pp. 68 – 72) that the subjectivity of color is a nineteenth-century phenomenon facilitated by Goethe in opposition to Newton. First, Newton himself held that colors as experienced

---

14 Crary 1990 has no diagrams of the eye and visual physiology from Descartes' works, in which the relevant images, from the *Dioptrics* and *Treatise on Man*, typically show a binocular system and its neural physiology (s. Hatfield 2015).

are subjective, that is, are sensations whose character depends on the experiencing subject. Second, Goethe held something akin to an Aristotelian theory of colors. In more recent terminology, he was a sort of naïve realist. He held that color experience directly reveals a color reality in the surfaces of bodies or even within the eye itself. His account of the "subjectivity" of color in the case of afterimages takes on a special meaning: it means pertaining to the subject, but not because the color quality is contributed by the subject but because the really existing color property is found in the eye (in the retinal processes) of the human subject. This color is not different from external color, except in its location inside the skin.

Accordingly, in relation to Goethe, Newton had the more "subjective" view of color. Famously, Newton discovered through his prism experiments that white light contains rays of differing refrangibility or refractive index. When separated from one another, these rays appear with the colors of the spectrum. However, Newton did not ascribe to the rays themselves the very color that the subject experiences. He understood the experienced color to be an effect of the rays on the perceiver (whom we may call "the subject"),[15] induced by some property that varies with the refractive index of the rays.

> The homogeneal Light and Rays which appear red, or rather make Objects appear so, I call Rubrifick or Red-making; those which make Objects appear yellow, green, blue, and violet, I call Yellow-making, Green-making, Blue-making, Violet-making, and so of the rest. And if at any time I speak of Light and Rays as coloured or endued with Colours, I would be understood to speak not philosophically and properly, but grossly, and accordingly to such Conceptions as vulgar People in seeing all these Experiments would be apt to frame. For the Rays to speak properly are not coloured. In them there is nothing else than a certain Power and Disposition to stir up a Sensation of this or that Colour. (Newton 1718, Bk. I, Pt. II, Prop. 2, Definition, p. 108)

According to Newton, the rays are not colored if that means that they possess the very quality of red – the redness of the red, that phenomenal character that we find present to us when we see a color. As Newton goes on to explain, "Colours in the Object are nothing but a Disposition to reflect this or that sort of Rays more copiously than the rest; in the Rays they are nothing but their Dispositions to propagate this or that Motion into the Sensorium, and in the Sensorium they are Sensations of those Motions under the Forms of Colours" (Newton 1718, p. 109).

---

15 In discussing Crary as opposed to D&G, I allow latitude in retrospective applications of the terms "subject" and "subjective," as conceptually warranted in discussing Newton's theory.

Goethe understood this to be Newton's position: "Newton held that in white, colorless light in general, especially however in sun light, there are several colors (producing sensations of color) that various lights really contain, the compounding of which brings forth white light (the sensation of white light)."[16] He objected to this view because it assigns standing color values to a series of individual physical lights (of various refractive indices). As we shall see, Goethe thought of color as always arising from a particular interaction of light and dark; accordingly, colors cannot be lined up and statically assigned to individual types of light.[17]

In the modern language of subject and object colors are, according to Newton, subjective effects. They cause in us a sensation that does not reveal the underlying property of the rays that produced it; rather, it is a fact of nature that differently refracting rays cause different sensory experiences of color, in a regular way. Even though Newton did not use the term "subjective," he possessed the concept. He held, with Descartes and Locke, that colors are produced in the mind by an as yet unknown dispositional property of the rays that causes a "motion in the sensorium" that, in turn, yields a sensation of a certain character. The concept of subjectivity in play is not individual variability but generically pertaining to the subject. Color belongs to the subject in a way that could, in principle, be the same for all subjects (though it needn't be). The subject contributes the qualitative character of the color as found in the sensation.

This concept of subjectivity contrasts with Goethe's from his *Farbenlehre* (1810).[18] In the first, systematic portion of the book, Goethe distinguishes three kinds of colors: physiological, physical, and chemical. Physiological colors are produced in the observer due to effects on the retina that do not depend on a present colored object, with afterimages being the emblematic instance; the colors found in afterimages have a physiological basis in the subject's retina. Physical colors are those created in transparent and colorless media, as by looking through a prism or letting light be transmitted through a prism onto a surface.

---

16 Goethe 1810, vol. 1, p. 365, Pt. II, § 17: "Newton behauptet, in dem weißen farblosen Lichte überall, besonders aber in dem Sonnenlicht, seyen mehrere farbige, (die Empfindung der Farbe erregende,) verschiedene Lichter wirklich enthalten, deren Zusammensetzung das weiße Licht (die Empfindung des weißen Lichts) hervorbringe."

17 Sepper 1988 offers a sympathetic comparison of Goethe and Newton, focusing on the experiments with prisms and delving deeply into Goethe's methodological criticisms while noting places in which they fell short.

18 Only the first, "didactic" (or systematic) part of Goethe's book has been translated (1840/ 1970); the second, polemical part completes the first volume of the original (1810); the third, historical part, forms the second volume.

Chemical colors are such as those found in paint or dye; they produce colors of some permanency in a surface.

Goethe invoked a concept of subjectivity with respect to both physiological and physical colors. Regarding physiological colors, he says: "We naturally place these colours first, because they belong altogether, or in a great degree, to the subject* – to the eye itself" (Goethe 1840/1970, § 1, p. 1). The translator added a note containing the following gloss on the term "subject": "The German distinction between *subject* and *object* is so generally understood and adopted, that it is hardly necessary to explain that the subject is the *individual*, in this case the *beholder*; the object, *all that is without him*" (Goethe 1840/1970, § 1, p. 1, note). Here, the adjective "subjective" would mean, in Goethean terms, belonging to the subject. This, the translator tells us, would be understood to mean belonging to the individual. But in what sense of "belong," and how specific to the particular "individual"? Let us pursue these questions.

Goethe assigns these physiological colors, such as afterimages, to "the eye in a healthy state" (Goethe 1840/1970, § 3) and hence to the retina of any healthy observer. I read him as considering these colors to be of a kind with the colors in the world. They are not subjective effects in Newton's sense. Rather, they simply are colors produced in the retina as a result of some previous operation, such as staring at a bright light. Goethe's notion of subjectivity in such cases permits, but does not require, individual variation.

I read Goethe this way because of hints from the Introduction to his *Farbenlehre*. He insists that he – by contrast with Priestley's *History* (German translation, 1776), which dates progress in color theory from Newton's prism experiment – does not disparage the "ancient and less modern inquirers, who, after all, had proceeded quietly on the right road, and who have transmitted to us observations and thoughts in detail which we can neither arrange better nor conceive more justly" (Goethe 1840/1970, p. xlv). The central ancient theory for Goethe is that of Theophrastus and Aristotle. He echoes the general theoretical framework for Aristotle's theory of the perception of sensory qualities, including color, by endorsing the principle that "Like is only known by Like," which he attributes to the Ionian school of (pre-Aristotelian) natural philosophers, but which Aristotle himself affirmed. Goethe says that we should believe "that a dormant light resides in the eye, and that it may be excited by the slightest cause from within or without" (Goethe 1840/1970, p. liii). His bottom line, beyond which "no further explanation" is possible (Goethe 1840/1970, p. lviii), is that "colour is a law of nature with respect to the sense of sight," which, in his restatement, says that "colour is an elementary phenomenon in nature adapted to the sense of vision" (Goethe 1840/1970, p. liv). Color arises, as for Aristotle, through the interaction of black and white or light and dark, in a manner that receives no further explanation. All colors arise out of such interactions.[19]

These physiological colors are, according to Goethe, subject to "constant law" (Goethe 1840/1970, § 4). His text offers a set of generalizations about the response of the eye to various instances of colorless (white) light and to various colors. Within the range of these laws, individual responses vary. This fact is introduced secondarily, as a further specification of the laws described (Goethe 1840/1970, §§ 10, 23). The variations come in relation to differences among subjects: those with stronger or weaker eyes take less or more time to adjust to darkness after having been in daylight. These are not described as "deviations" from laws, but would seem to be applications of laws to particular circumstances (stronger or weaker eyes). Pathological cases do deviate from the constant laws (Goethe 1840/1970, § 4), as with color blindness (Goethe 1840/1970, §§ 103–108). But even such deviations are taken by Goethe as further evidence of "general" and "constant" laws (Goethe 1840/1970, § 102).[20] Individual variation clearly is permitted within Goethe's notion of subjectivity but is not required.

I conclude that color, for Goethe, is a basic property, elementary, admitting no deeper explanation. I also take the hint that color is the same in the eye and in the world. We can experience the colors of the world because they excite colors in the eye. They do not do this by setting up a subjective mental response, as with Newton, but by inducing the quality of color in the eye, which is of the same quality as color external to the eye. The genesis of colors and other phenomena is lawful, but there are individual variations (subject to law) as well as violations of law in pathological cases, which nonetheless confirm the lawfulness of color responses in subjects.

In Goethe's usage, then, "subjective" means pertaining to the subject but not necessarily peculiar to the subject or dependent on the subject's mind. This reading is confirmed in the physical part of the work, in Goethe's explicit contrast between subjective and objective:

---

19 In the polemical part of *Farbenlehre*, in rejecting Newton's assignment of colors to refractive values, he writes: "We have namely sufficiently shown that all colors owe their existence to light and not-light, that colors thoroughly gravitate toward darkness, that they are *skieron*" (Goethe 1810, vol. 1, Pt. II, § 25, pp. 370–371); see also Goethe 1840/1970, p. lvi. I note that some efforts have been made to articulate Aristotle's own mixture account (Sorabji 1972).

20 Goethe 1840/1970, § 101: "We know what appearances belong to the eye in a healthy state[...]"; § 102: "Morbid phenomena indicate in like manner the existence of organic and physical laws [...]."

> Throughout nature, as presented to the senses, everything depends on the relations which things bear to each other, but especially on the relation which man, the most important of these, bears to the rest. Hence the world divides itself into two parts, the human being as *subject* [*Subject*], stands opposed to the *object* [*Object*]. (Goethe 1840/1970, § 181, p. 75)

We have here Goethe's own statement of the distinction introduced earlier by the translator, between "the human being" as subject and the rest of the world as object. Goethe uses these terms to distinguish between subjective and objective experiments (Goethe 1840/1970, §§ 186 – 188, 194, 303). The first arise when the observer focuses light into his or her own eyes, for instance, by looking through a prism. Here, color may or may not arise (Goethe 1840/1970, §§ 195 – 202). It arises in cases in which what is seen through the prism includes a boundary between light and dark. Various colors appear at this boundary, through the interaction of light and dark as a result of overlapping caused by the prism. These experiments are "subjective" just because the light through the prism enters the eye directly, as opposed to falling on a screen where it might be seen by any number of observers. The color is produced "in the human being" because the light proceeds directly into the eye. But, in accordance with Goethe's Aristotelianism, the qualitative character thus produced is not contributed by a subject's mind. It is the same color property as might occur in the world on a screen that receives light; it is subjective because the light is sent into the human being (into the eye). External light awakens the color intrinsic to the eye; recall that "a dormant light resides in the eye" (Goethe 1840/1970, p. liii; see also p. lv).

Objective experiments are those in which a strong source of light, such as sunlight, is directed through a prism and falls on a surface (Goethe 1840/1970, §§ 187, 303). Goethe describes various circumstances, involving focused light and light coming through apertures of various sizes, in which a colored border appears on the surface (Goethe 1840/1970, §§ 306 – 316). These colors are "objective" because they fall outside the boundary of the skin and can be observed by all. They are no more "true" or "real" than the subjective colors.

Here, "subjective" and "objective" distinguish cases in which the light enters the eye directly or is cast on a surface for all to see. Qualitative color is something found in dyes, in light transmitted through a prism, or in the retina under specific physiological conditions. "Subjectivity" is not the specifically modern subjectivity of Descartes, Newton, or Kant, in which "pertaining to the subject" means being contributed by, or arising from, the subject's mind. It is a more general notion, of "occurring in the subject," that is, within the boundary of the skin. This gives us a fourth sense of "subjectivity," to add to the three we identified in Kant.

5 Subject and Object in German Sensory Physiology and Psychology

Goethe was on the margins of a community of researchers in sensory physiology and psychology in the first half of the nineteenth century. He received some favorable notice.[21] More generally, a community of specialists arose, trackable through mutual references and a pattern of citations of earlier works by later. This community of researchers positioned itself in relation to a Kantian framework, by asking questions about the status of spatial perceptions in representing objects and/or things in themselves. Kantian terminology, beyond "subject" and "object," included "forms of intuition."

To give a sense of these discussions, I sample two parts of this literature.[22] First, theoretical treatments of spatial perception and perception more generally that thematize subject and object, often in relation to Kant, offered as either refutation or helpful correction. The theorists included are Steinbuch, Müller, and Bartels. Second, some authors offered histories of sensory physiology, thematizing subject and object, and others offered taxonomies of theoretical positions organized around the subject–object distinction. I consider a history from Tourtual and a theoretical taxonomy from Volkmann. Taken together, these five authors demonstrate scientific engagement with notions of objectivity and subjectivity, in a modern sense, twenty-five to fifty years before the birth of scientific objectivity in D&G's historical narrative. Typically, the notion of "subject" is what we have identified as Kant's psychological subject, and "object" is an external material object.

In 1811, Johann Georg Steinbuch, a practicing physician in Heidenheim, published his *Beytrag zur Physiologie der Sinne*, focusing on spatial perception. His theory emphasized how motor activity (voluntary muscle movements, starting *in utero*) leads to the construction of a "subjective space," and it sought to explain how this subjective space would be taken to be equivalent to objective space and how this process shows, contrary to Kant, that we can know the spatial properties of things in themselves.

Steinbuch used the distinction between subject and object, or subjective and objective, in a post-Kantian sense, where "subjective" means dependent on the

---

21 Tourtual 1827, p. xviii, describes Goethe as a continuer of Aristotle's color theory. Müller 1826, pp. 28, 30, 249, 281, 289, mentioned Goethe's color theory as well as his work on comparative anatomy of vertebrates.
22 My discussion builds on Hatfield 2017, sec. 4. Hatfield 1990 situates many of these authors relative to more properly philosophical writings of the time.

perceiving subject. A subjective space arises from "the simple ideas of our simple spontaneity in the movement of our sense organs" (Steinbuch 1811, pp. ix – x). Indeed: "The simple fact that, parallel to the outer movements of the sense organs there run inner ideas of will, is the principle upon which our sensory intuition is based, and out of which our *subjective space* (the space in our intuition) arises through successive development" (Steinbuch 1811, p. x). Interaction between ideas of will and sensations from the sense organs produce ideas of lines, surfaces, and bodies (spatial ideas). Steinbuch sought to show "why the senses, all in the same manner, give their inner products to intuition in such a way that the objects of sensation *necessarily must* appear as existing outside us, and why we feel compelled to take our ideas of objects in the outer world for the object itself" (Steinbuch 1811, p. xi). He here offers to explain the relation between subjective space, or space that is found in the mental states or ideas of the subject, and the space of objects, which ultimately is the world of things in themselves (mind-independent objects). On his theory, we do not directly perceive the things in themselves, but we can trust the spatiality of our subjectively constructed representations to represent the real spatial properties of those things (Steinbuch 1811, pp. 264 – 269). Steinbuch offers an account of "subjective space" in the general psychological sense of subjectivity, as belonging to all subjects. The space is "subjective" in that it is constructed through psychological processes and belongs to the mind. But, in his view, the subjectively constructed space accurately portrays external objects as they are in themselves. Variability doesn't enter into this general account. And, despite his challenge to Kant on things in themselves, Steinbuch does not engage the notion of transcendental subjectivity.

Johannes Müller was the foremost physiologist in Germany before mid century. He worked in several areas, including on the senses. Two relevant works are his *Handbuch der Physiologie des Menschen für Vorlesungen* (1833 – 1840) and his earlier *Zur vergleichenden Physiologie des Gesichtssinnes des Menschen und der Thiere* (1826). The second chapter of Müller's comparative physiology, entitled "On the Mediation of Subject and Object through the Sense of Sight," examines how individual animals come "to intuit their sense-energies as a sensory world apart from themselves" (Müller 1826, p. 39). Initially, individual self-consciousness (the subject) knows only its own sensations and their spatial arrangement, which, in vision, is originally two dimensional and consists in an intuitive awareness of the retina itself. The positing of an external world (of objects) as a cause of these sensations requires judgment; hence, animals can't experience a world as external through sense perception alone but must rely on their intellectual faculties.

In the *Handbuch*, Müller explained the process of coming to experience an external world in connection with his ninth law of the senses, which says: "That sensations are referred from their proper seat towards the exterior, is owing, not to anything in the nature of the nerves themselves, but to the accompanying idea derived from experience" (Müller 1843, p. 716).[23] Unable to remember the initial acquisition of these ideas, we infer them by considering our current sensations and ideas:

> Through the analysis of the act of the mind that accompanies sensory activity there arise, opposed to each other, the *sentient, self-conscious subject* [*Subject*] of the modifiable body – the states of which body, whether inner or induced from without, presently become objects [*Object*] for the self-conscious subject – and the *external world*, with which the modifiable body comes into conflict. [...] The "I" sets itself as a free subject against the most intense sensations, the most tormenting pains. The limb that gives us pain can be removed and the "I" is not diminished [...]. (Müller 1833–1840, vol. 2, pp. 268–269; adapted from Müller 1843, pp. 716–717)

As a child touches its own body and other things, it finds that its own limbs are subject to its will and that they meet with resistances. The child finds a difference in touching parts of its body as opposed to other things, which leads to the awareness of some objects as fully external to it, opposed not only to the self but also separate from its sentient body (Müller 1833–1840, vol. 2, p. 536). "Subject" here is the experiencing subject, and "object" may either be the object of conscious thought (whether inner or outer) or external objects (as in the "external world").

The problem of distinguishing self from world, subjective sensation from external cause, was pervasive in the literature of sensory physiology. Carl M. N. Bartels, a practicing physician in St. Petersburg, offered *Beiträge zur Physiologie des Gesichtssinnes* (1834). He was familiar with the recent literature, including Steinbuch, Müller, and Tourtual, among others (Bartels 1834, p. v). A section entitled "On the Externalization or Objectification [*Objectiviren*] of Sensory Objects" characterized the problem of accounting for the distinction between subject and object, which are reciprocal notions. Without objectivity, no being can become aware of itself: "Only through awareness of external things and its own embodiment is a being given its feeling of existence, for the sensitive being cognizes itself and the thing sensed only in the sensation, and, conversely, in each sensation it cognizes itself and a thing sensed" (Bartels 1834, p. 10). On the origin of spatial perception, Bartels favors Steinbuch's learning account (Bartels 1834,

---

23 Where I cite Müller 1833–1840, the translation is mine. Otherwise, I follow Müller 1843. It is abridged, leaving out much of the philosophical discussion in Bk. 6 (Bk. 7 in the translation).

p. 14). But spatial perception is not needed to recognize objects as distinct from the subject; this distinction is given primitively in sensation. In this initial discussion, "subject" and "object" are used in the general sense of perceiving subject and external object; the distinction between these is the first result of "objectification."

Caspar Theobald Tourtual, a surgeon and anatomy teacher in Münster, published *Die Sinne des Menschen in den wechselseitigen Beziehungen ihres psychischen und organischen Lebens; ein Beitrag zur physiologischen Aesthetik* in 1827. He praised Steinbuch's discussion of the relation between touch and vision as especially insightful and helpful, even if he didn't agree with it (Tourtual 1827, pp. xix, 223 – 228). Most tellingly for our purposes, Tourtual organized the history of previous work on perception (philosophical, psychological, and natural scientific) into "objective," "subjective," and "intermediate" phases (Tourtual 1827, pp. xxxiv – lx). The objective phase has external objects acting on the sense organs to produce sensory ideas, with little regard for the contribution of the subject. In the subjective phase, including Descartes, Malebranche, Kant, and Müller, the activity of the subject in projecting a world comes to the fore. The intermediate phase, which Tourtual prefers, recognizes the contributions of both subject and object. When an object affects the senses, the sense organ provides subjective forms of experience (space and time) and subjective matter (colors, tastes, and the like). We live in a subjective world of intuition but refer our sensory ideas to the external world (Tourtual 1827, pp. 6 – 9). Human beings have an "inborn drive, or rather a necessity of our mental nature," to synthesize the sensations from disparate sense organs (e. g., those of touch and sight) into the sensory representation of a single external object with various (especially spatial) properties (Tourtual 1827, p. 14). Tourtual is a realist and thinks that the senses give us a good representation of the world (Tourtual 1827, pp. lx, 20). Here, the subject is a generic perceiver, "subjective" means pertaining to the subject's perception (the psychological subject, not requiring variability for its "subjectivity"), and our perceptions correspond to external objects. Presumably, Steinbuch's constructive account of the perceived spatial world would also fit in Tourtual's intermediate phase.

Alfred Wilhelm Volkmann (1836), professor of physiology in Leipzig, Dorpat, and Halle, reviewed recent work on the theory of vision. He examined Müller's theory that the distinction between subject and object is learned and depends on the mind rather than the faculty of sense (citing Müller 1826, pp. 39 – 43). He agreed with Tourtual's counterclaim that externalization is a sensory, not an intellectual or judgmental accomplishment, and that the tendency to externalize is innate. Indeed, in most matters concerning the theory of vision, he aligned himself with Tourtual.

Volkmann crystallized Tourtual's history into a taxonomy of possible positions with respect to subject and object. He felt a need to address the relation between subject and object prior to offering his own theory of vision. He found only three conceptions of this relation to be possible. First, that the outer world simply determines the sense impression, as the seal impresses the wax. Here, the object has all the activity, the senses are purely passive. Second, active sense organs render things as appearances. We perceive only the states of our sense organs and transfer these onto outer objects, a kind of projection theory. Third, sensory intuition results from the unified activity of subject and object. The third position grants activity to the senses as opposed to the intellect. This third position is exemplified in Volkmann's account of space as a universal form of intuition. In his view, this form of intuition does not arise from subjective conditions alone. Rather, "the necessity of this form of intuition allows itself to be explained through a triumph of the objective over the subjective, or, if I may be allowed, through a pre-established harmony between the two" (Volkmann 1836, p. 16). The properties of sense impressions cannot be explained simply through subjective activity, their relation to objects must be taken into account (presumably, under the view that the senses are to bring us into contact with objects). The immanent activity of the senses is responsible for the externalization of sensory objects. Again, the subject here is the general psychological subject, and objects are external objects. And again, the sense of pertaining to the subject connotes psychological equipment but does not imply that our subjective sense perceptions keep us from perceiving the world as it is.

The contrasts in these authors between "subjective" and "objective" aspects of sense perception draw on Kant's distinction but typically do not introduce the apparatus of the Kantian transcendental subject. The Kantian question of how sensory representations relate to things in themselves is rendered as a scientific question about the genesis of spatial perception and its correlation with external objects. This question continued to be discussed later in the century, by the likes of Wilhelm Wundt, Hermann von Helmholtz, and Ewald Hering (s. Turner 1994). These usages by the community of German sensory physiologists and psychologists count as a scientific invocation of notions of the perceiving subject and external objects. They are certainly "modern" senses of subject and object. "Subjectivity" becomes the activities, processes, and modes of experience found in the perceiving subject. "Objectivity" *per se* is not a focus of discussion, but "objective," "objectification," and "object" are used in the modern sense of pertaining to external objects.

6 Varieties of Subjectivity and Objectivity

In sections 1 and 2, I distinguished two modern notions of subjectivity, starting with that of D&G and contrasting it with an earlier and more profound sense:

(i) Subjectivity as resulting from individual variability among human subjects; and
(ii) Subjectivity as pertaining to the human subject in general and conditioning human perception and thought.

D&G restrict their notion of subjectivity to (i), which they date from the mid nineteenth century. We have in fact found this notion of individual variation attested in the mid eighteenth century and present in Kant.[24] Still, I do not deny that new attention was given to describing the range of individual variation in the nineteenth century (as in the work of Purkyně), or that some scientists in the nineteenth century reacted against the perceived threat that individual variation might contaminate scientific images.

My aim has been to reveal the presence of the second sort of subjectivity as a major thread in the history of modern philosophy and science extending from the seventeenth to the nineteenth centuries. Descartes, Newton, and Kant all invoke this notion with respect to aspects of sensory experience. For Descartes and Newton, it pertains to the status of color sensations. They attributed the quality of color sensations to the general features of the subject. In relation to Kant, we came to call this "psychological subjectivity," and we identified it with (ii) above. This sort of subjectivity, not requiring individual variation, remains under discussion in relation to sensory qualities (Hatfield 2003) and the subjectivity of consciousness more generally (Zahavi 2005), among other topics.

Kant developed the notion of what belongs to the subject to include a "transcendental subject" whose structure conditions and explains the possibility of human knowledge. Such conditions include space and time as forms of sensibility and the categories as sustaining cognition and knowledge. Kant advanced a philosophical thesis that there can be a subjective basis for objectively valid knowledge. He held that the domain of geometry as applied to physical objects, the very domain that served as the chief instance of non-subjectively conditioned knowledge for Descartes and Newton, was in fact subjectively based, but in a way that allowed for inter-subjective and hence objective validity. We thus have:

---

24 More generally, the idea that the senses or reason might be defective because of observer relativity or idiosyncrasies is very old; it is found in ancient skeptical tropes and is a theme in Montaigne.

(iii) Transcendentally subjective conditions that condition and explain the possibility of objectively valid knowledge.

We also found that Kant made use of subjectivity in sense (i). Further, (ii) and (iii) are paired with notions of "objectivity" as cognitive validity (which is also part of D&G's (i)). Senses (ii) and (iii) are also paired with a notion of "the object" as an external object.

In our investigation, we distinguished a fourth sense of subjectivity, as pertaining to the subject in general in a bodily as opposed to mental manner. Goethe asserted that "the world divides itself into two parts, the human being as *subject*, stands opposed to the *object*" (Goethe 1840/1970, § 181). If it is right to read Goethe's color theory as aligned with an Aristotelian theory, then although color can inhere in the subject as a physiological state of the retina, the character of that color does not arise from the subject's mind but from an interaction between light and dark, as all color arises. We need then to distinguish (ii) subjectivity as pertaining to the human subject and conditioning human perception and thought, from:

(iv) Subjectivity as pertaining to the human subject, without conditioning sensory qualities or thought or depending on the mind.

This form occurs with sensory qualities that inhere in the subject as instances of the same quality in external objects.[25] This fourth sense technically is non-Kantian, although it adapts the notion of "pertaining to the subject" in a way that could be seen as building on Kantian usage.

Finally, we examined a community of German sensory physiologists and psychologists who adopted the distinction between subjective conditions of perception and their relation to the actual properties of external objects. Here we found instances of the use of modern notions of objectivity and subjectivity in a flourishing scientific practice. These modern notions are not so much concerned with methodological issues as with the content and representational accuracy of various types of sensory ideas. An advocate for D&G might argue that perception and its relation to objects is inherently a philosophical topic and so doesn't count as a properly scientific invocation of subjectivity. To which I respond: what is a scientific topic has a history. In German physiology and psychology

---

[25] Goethe's color qualifies the human body as an instance of color quality; Steinbuch's and others' spatial perceptions include both a mental (phenomenally present) space and an external space, which do not have the same unity as do Goethe's color instances.

of the nineteenth century, scientific topics included the notion of the perceiving subject and the relation between subjective sensory perceptions and external objects.[26]

References

AT | Descartes, René (1969–1975): *Oeuvres de Descartes*. Charles Adam/Paul Tannery (eds.). 11 vols. Revised. Paris: Vrin.

D&G | Daston, Lorraine/Galison, Peter (2007): *Objectivity*. New York: Zone Books.

OED | *Oxford English Dictionary* (1971): Compact Edition, 2 vols. Oxford: Oxford University Press.

Bartels, Carl Moritz Nicolaus (1834): *Beiträge zur Physiologie des Gesichtssinnes*. Berlin: Reimer.

Beck, Lewis White (1969): *Early German Philosophy: Kant and His Predecessors*. Cambridge: Harvard University Press.

Crary, Jonathan (1990): *Techniques of the Observer: On Vision and Modernity in the Nineteenth Century*. Cambridge: MIT Press.

Descartes, René (1984–1985): *The Philosophical Writings of Descartes*, John Cottingham/Robert Stoothoff/Dugald Murdoch (eds.), 2 vols. Cambridge: Cambridge University Press.

Dewey, John (1902): "Subject (-ive)." In: James Mark Baldwin (ed.): *Dictionary of Philosophy and Psychology*. Vol. 2. New York: Macmillan, pp. 607–608.

Eisler, Rudolf (1922): *Eisler's Handwörterbuch der Philosophie*. 2nd edn. Richard Müller-Freienfels (ed.). Berlin: Mittler.

Erdmann, Johann Eduard (1890): *A History of Philosophy. Vol. II: Modern Philosophy*, Hough, Williston S. (ed.). London: Sonnenschein.

Falckenberg, Richard (1893): *History of Modern Philosophy: From Nicolas of Cusa to the Present Time*. A. C. Armstrong, Jr. (ed.). New York: Holt.

Goethe, Johann Wolfgang von (1810): *Zur Farbenlehre*. 2 vols. Tübingen: Cotta.

Goethe, Johann Wolfgang von (1840): *Theory of Colours*. Charles Lock Eastlake (trans.). London: Murray. Cited as reprinted, Cambridge: MIT Press, 1970.

Hatfield, Gary (1990): *The Natural and the Normative: Theories of Spatial Perception from Kant to Helmholtz*. Cambridge: MIT Press.

Hatfield, Gary (2003): "Objectivity and Subjectivity Revisited: Color as a Psychobiological Property." In: Rainer Mausfeld/Dieter Heyer (eds.): *Colour Perception: Mind and the Physical World*. Oxford: Oxford University Press, pp. 187–202.

Hatfield, Gary (2015): "On Natural Geometry and Seeing Distance Directly in Descartes." In: Vincenzo De Risi (ed.): *Mathematizing Space: The Objects of Geometry from Antiquity to the Early Modern Age*. Berlin: Birkhaeuser, pp. 157–192.

---

26 I thank Sally Sedgwick, Rolf Horstmann, Nabeel Hamid, and Dina Emundts for helpful comments on previous drafts.

Hatfield, Gary (2018): "Helmholtz and Philosophy: Science, Perception, and Metaphysics, with Variations on Some Fichtean Themes." In: *Journal for the History of Analytical Philosophy* 6, pp. 11–41.

Kant, Immanuel (2004): *Prolegomena to Any Future Metaphysics.* Gary Hatfield (ed.). Second edition. Cambridge: Cambridge University Press.

Karskens, Machiel (1992): "The Development of the Opposition Subjective versus Objective in the 18th Century." In: *Archiv für Begriffsgeschichte* 35, pp. 214–256.

Locke, John (1690): *An Essay Concerning Human Understanding.* London: Thomas Bassett.

Müller, Johannes (1826): *Zur vergleichenden Physiologie des Gesichtssinnes des Menschen und der Thiere.* Leipzig: Cnobloch.

Müller, Johannes (1833–1840): *Handbuch der Physiologie des Menschen für Vorlesungen.* 2 vols. Coblenz: Hölscher.

Müller, Johannes (1843): *Elements of Physiology.* William Baly (trans.). 2 vols. Philadelphia: Lea and Blanchard.

Newton, Isaac (1718): *Opticks: Or, A Treatise of the Reflections, Refractions, Inflections and Colours of Light,* London: Innys.

Nolan, Lawrence (2011): *Primary and Secondary Qualities: The Historical and Ongoing Debate.* Oxford: Oxford University Press.

Ogilvy, James (1992): "Introduction." In: James Olgivy (ed.): *Revisioning Philosophy.* Albany: SUNY Press, pp. xi–xxiii.

Priestley, Joseph (1776): *Geschichte und gegenwärtiger Zustand der Optik, vorzüglich in Absicht auf den physikalischen Theil dieser Wissenschaft.* Simon Klügel Georg (ed.). Leipzig: Junius.

Ritter, Joachim/Gründer, Karlfried (eds.) (1998): *Historisches Wörterbuch der Philosophie.* Vol. 10. Basel: Schwabe.

Sepper, Dennis L. (1988): *Goethe contra Newton: Polemics and the Project for a New Science of Color.* Cambridge: Cambridge University Press.

Sorabji, Richard (1972): "Aristotle, Mathematics, and Colour." In: *The Classical Quarterly* 22, pp. 293–308.

Steinbuch, Johann Georg (1811): *Beytrag zur Physiologie der Sinne.* Nürnberg: Schrag.

Tourtual, Caspar Theobald (1827): *Die Sinne des Menschen.* Münster: Regensberg.

Turner, R. Steven (1994): *In the Eye's Mind: Vision and the Helmholtz-Hering Controversy.* Princeton: Princeton University Press.

Volkmann, Alfred W. (1836): *Neue Beiträge zur Physiologie des Gesichtssinnes.* Leipzig: Breitkopf und Härtel.

Zagorin, Perez (2001): "Francis Bacon's Concept of Objectivity and the Idols of the Mind." In: *The British Journal for the History of Science* 34, pp. 379–393.

Zahavi, Dan (2005): *Subjectivity and Selfhood: Investigating the First-Person Perspective.* Cambridge: MIT Press.

Manja Kisner
Fichte's Moral Psychology of Drives and Feelings and its Influence on Schopenhauer's Metaphysics of the Will

Abstract. *In this article, I discuss what role the concept of feeling has in Fichte's and Schopenhauer's philosophy and how it reveals a newly arising interest in psychological topics within the period of Classical German Philosophy. I expand on this concept first by analysing Fichte's system of drives and feelings as a part of his moral psychology developed in* The System of Ethics *(1798). In the next step, I compare Fichte's view of the concept of feeling with that of Schopenhauer and argue that Fichte's conception had a strong impact on Schopenhauer's first volume of* The World as Will and Representation *(1818/19).*

In diesem Aufsatz gehe ich dem neu erwachten Interesse für psychologische Themen in der Klassischen Deutschen Philosophie nach und beschäftige mich mit dem Begriff des Gefühls in der Philosophie von Fichte und Schopenhauer. Zuerst analysiere ich Fichtes System der Triebe und Gefühle als einen Teil seiner Moralpsychologie, die er in dem System der Sittenlehre *(1798) entwickelt hat. Im Weiteren stelle ich dann den Vergleich zwischen Fichtes und Schopenhauers Begriff des Gefühls dar und zeige, dass Fichtes Philosophie einen wichtigen Einfluss auf Schopenhauers ersten Band der* Welt als Wille und Vorstellung *(1818/19) hatte.*

1 Introduction

Schopenhauer's philosophy is typically understood as a philosophy of the blindly striving, pre-reflective universal will and in this sense it seems to be clearly opposed to the philosophies of the German idealists, especially Fichte's alleged subjectivism and strong idealism. Whereas Schopenhauer recognized the influence of Plato and Kant on the development of his own thought, he repeatedly criticized German idealists and tried to distance himself from their influence. However, as I contend in this article, these explicit criticisms do not reflect an actual lack of influence on Schopenhauer's thought. Schopenhauer intensively studied Fichte's works and attended Fichte's lectures as a student at the

https://doi.org/10.1515/9783110673692-009

newly founded University of Berlin in 1811 and 1812.[1] Therefore, Fichte's relevance to Schopenhauer's development cannot be dismissed even though Schopenhauer tried to conceal it.[2]

The aim of my article is to discuss this influence and to demonstrate why Fichte's idealism and Schopenhauer's philosophy of the will have far more in common than first appearances suggest. I will focus on Fichte's 'moral psychology'[3] developed in his *System of Ethics* and on Schopenhauer's metaphysics of the will in first volume of *The World as Will and Representation* (1818/19). In particular, I will compare Fichte's and Schopenhauer's understanding of the concept of feeling. As we will see, in these works a close interconnection between psychological and philosophical use of the terms becomes particularly obvious and important.

In *The System of Ethics* Fichte develops his own "original, determinate system of drives and feelings" (GA I/5, p. 108).[4] This work, as I intend to demonstrate, greatly influenced Schopenhauer's second book of his main work and his conception of the world as will. Schopenhauer was well acquainted with Fichte's book. He had already read it during his student years and a copy was found in his library together with side notes and further commentaries.[5] However, in spite of Schopenhauer's intensive study of Fichte, very little research to date discusses this relationship in depth or emphasizes the role of the psychological concept of feeling within their respective philosophical systems. There are just two monographs in German that study Fichte's influence on Schopenhauer in detail.[6] Moreover, there are only a few articles, predominantly in German, that examine Fichte's influence on Schopenhauer, but most are general comparisons and none analyse exclusively Fichte's *System of Ethics* and Scho-

---

1 Schopenhauer's *Handschriftlicher Nachlaß* (abbreviated as HN) contains the list of Fichte's books Schopenhauer owned and commented on. Moreover, his handwritten notes on Fichte's works are also preserved and accessible. S. HN II, HN V.

2 As a student, Schopenhauer read Schelling's works as well as Fichte's. Hegel's influence on Schopenhauer, however, is less evident and in his *Handschriftlicher Nachlaß* we can find no signs of in-depth study of Hegel's work.

3 The term 'moral psychology' is of course not an expression that Fichte himself uses, but his theory of drives and feelings is in Fichte scholarship nevertheless often interpreted as a moral psychology. See for instance Kosch 2018, p. 24; Wood 2016, p. 106.

4 References to Fichte's texts are made by citing the volume and page number of Fichte's *Gesamtausgabe*. Translations are taken from Fichte 2005.

5 Schopenhauer's side notes to *The System of Ethics* are published in HN V, pp. 53–58. Moreover, in Schopenhauer's student manuscripts we can find further comments on *The System of Ethics*. S. HN II, pp. 347–352.

6 See Schöndorf 1982 and Kisner 2016.

penhauer's main work, let alone the importance of the concept of feeling in these two works.[7]

Fichte's *System of Ethics* is not the first book in which he introduces the concepts of feelings and drives.[8] For a complete assessment of the influence of Fichte's *oeuvre* on Schopenhauer's main work, we should certainly look not only at *The System of Ethics*, but also at other works that Schopenhauer knew and studied. These works range from the *Foundations of the Entire Science of Knowledge* and *Foundations of Natural Right* to Fichte's most popular work *The Vocation of Man* (1800) and to his lectures on the late *Wissenschaftslehre*, which Schopenhauer attended in Berlin in 1811 and 1812. However, to maintain the focus and because I think that Fichte's *System of Ethics* offers the most systematic presentation of his system of drives and feelings, I will concentrate only on a comparison between this book and Schopenhauer's first volume of *The World as Will and Representation*.

I present my comparison in two steps. First, I present Fichte's conception of immediate knowledge, which he introduces in the first part of his *System of Ethics*, and compare it with Schopenhauer's notion of immediate knowledge in the second book of his main work. However, even though both philosophers refer to "immediate knowledge", they use the term in different ways and for different purposes. We may be tempted to think that their philosophies point in two entirely different directions. However, when we compare Schopenhauer's understanding of immediate knowledge with Fichte's system of drives and feelings as he develops it in the second part of his *System of Ethics*, an astonishing resemblance

---

7 S. Decher 1990, pp. 45–67; Philonenko 1997, pp. 437–451; D'Alfonso 2006, pp. 201–211; Zöller 2000, pp. 200–218; Zöller 2006, pp. 365–386; De Pascale 2012, pp. 45–59; Novembre 2016, pp. 315–335; Knappik 2018, pp. 200–220. Moreover, there is one collected volume in German that discusses the influence of German idealism on Schopenhauer; four essays discuss Fichte's influence on Schopenhauer in particular. S. Hühn 2006.

8 Already in his earlier work, Fichte discusses these concepts, especially in the practical part of the *Foundations of the Entire Science of Knowledge* (1794/95), later in his second Jena presentation of the science of knowledge, known also as *Wissenschaftslehre nova methodo* (1796–1799) and in his book on the philosophy of right, *Foundations of Natural Right* (1796/1797). Schopenhauer was well acquainted with Fichte's *Foundations of the Entire Science of Knowledge* and with the *Foundations of Natural Right*; he owned both and his commentaries and side notes were preserved. Fichte's *Wissenschaftslehre nova methodo*, however, was never published during his lifetime. Therefore, all that is preserved are the student transcripts of the lectures he held at the University of Jena from 1796 to 1799. Although in these transcripts the concept of feeling and the concept of drive already play an important role, it is quite improbable that Schopenhauer could have known of Fichte's *Wissenschaftslehre nova methodo*. Therefore, the only published book from this period, which presents the main topics of the *Wissenschaftslehre nova methodo* in most detail, is his *System of Ethics*.

between the two philosophers' works becomes apparent. Therefore, in the second part of my article I present Fichte's system of drives and feelings and compare it with Schopenhauer's notion of affection, which he understands as a feeling. The similarities between their uses outweigh the differences and speak to the important influence of Fichte's philosophy on Schopenhauer's system.

2 Fichte on immediate knowledge

Fichte begins his *System of Ethics* by explaining the difference between theoretical and practical philosophy.[9] This distinction pertains to the difference between knowledge of objects and our immediate knowledge of ourselves: theoretical philosophy examines how I engage in cognition (*ich erkenne*), whereas the focus of practical philosophy is on how I act efficaciously (*ich wirke*) (Cf. GA I/ 5, p. 21). In the first case, what is subjective follows from what is objective. This means that theoretical philosophy focuses on the subject's cognition of objects and therefore "the former is supposed to agree with the latter" ("das erstere sich nach dem letztern richten soll", GA I/5, p. 21). In the second case, what is objective follows from what is subjective. Here an object (or a being) results from the subject's concept of this object and hence practical philosophy deals with how I am able to act in the world (Cf. GA I/5, p. 21). I am directly aware of myself as efficacious but only indirectly aware of other objects. Yet, Fichte also insists that these two perspectives are actually identical even though we normally conceive of them as distinct.

However, for the purpose of my analysis, I do not discuss in detail Fichte's theoretical philosophy; instead, I intend to focus only on Fichte's conception of immediate knowledge developed in his *System of Ethics*. The aim of his ethical theory is to show how we can analyse and explain the thesis "I find myself to be acting efficaciously in the world of sense" (GA I/5, p. 22).[10] In the work's first part, the "Deduction of the principle of morality", Fichte abstracts from anything sensible and focuses only on the experience of our own efficacy. In the second part, the "Deduction of the reality and applicability of the principle of morality", he then reintroduces sensible reality in his analysis and examines how we can indeed act efficaciously in the world.

---

9 For a detailed analysis of Fichte's *System of Ethics* s. Wood 2016 and Merle/Schmidt 2015.
10 Accordingly, Fichte's work is not limited only to a moral theory but tries to develop a theory of action in general.

Fichte's first part is based on the fact that something exists, which he calls "an immediate fact of consciousness" (GA I/5, p. 22) that precedes all other knowledge of objects. It is through this immediate fact of consciousness that we are directly aware of our efficacy. This means that the claim that I find myself to be acting efficaciously is more basic than any other form of knowledge. This claim is based on a pre-reflective fact of consciousness. The starting point of Fichte's deduction of the principle of morality is thus grounded in a special kind of immediate knowledge. As Fichte writes, there

> remains something within the representation of my efficacy which simply cannot come to me from outside but must lie within myself, something that I cannot experience and cannot learn but must know immediately: namely, that I myself am supposed to be the ultimate ground of the change that has occurred. (GA I/5, pp. 22–23)

Therefore, Fichte first relates my efficacy to an immediate knowledge I have about myself as the ultimate ground of the changes I experience. In further steps, he then recognizes this activity of the I as my willing: "I find myself as myself only as willing" (GA I/5, p. 37). What we as efficacious beings are immediately conscious of is our own willing. However, Fichte's claim that we find ourselves as willing subjects cannot mean that we are passive in this act. On the contrary, he understands the act of finding oneself as an act of positing. For that reason, he also equates my immediate knowledge of myself with the act of positing (Cf. GA I/5, p. 23). When I posit myself, I am immediately conscious of myself. Therefore, Fichte's I has two sides: on the one hand, I am a knowing I, which cognizes objects; on the other hand, I am a real force (*reelle Kraft*). It is in my capacity as the latter that I conceive of myself as being in the world with the ability to act efficaciously. This inner agility of the I "is something that cannot be demonstrated to anyone who does not discover it in the intuition of himself" (GA I/5, p. 26).

Hence, Fichte's method depends on the immediate knowledge we have of ourselves. However, he can never prove that others also "possess some image of activity in general, of some agility, mobility or however one may want to express it in words" (GA I/5, p. 26). This is something we can only presuppose about others on the basis of our own personal experience. The first part of Fichte's *System of Ethics* is thus built upon the method of introspection that allows him to inquire into the essence of the I.[11] When we abstract from sensible

---

11 "The path of the deduction will be as follows: we will assign ourselves the task of thinking of ourselves under a certain specified condition and observing how we are required to think of ourselves under this condition. From those properties of ourselves that we find in this way, we will then derive, as something necessary, the moral compulsion noted earlier" (GA I/5, p. 35).

reality and focus solely on our inner, immediate experience, we recognize that it is pure activity and agility that represents the true essence of the I (Cf. GA I/5, p. 42).

Fichte defines this pure activity of the I as a tendency or more precisely as "the absolute tendency toward the absolute [*absolute Tendenz zum Absoluten*]" (GA I/5, p. 45). Consequently, this activity is not a blind, purposeless tendency. Instead, the I tends to determine itself independently of any external impetus; or, if we use Kant's term, it determines itself 'autonomously'. Fichte's I is thus a striving I with a "tendency to self-activity for self-activity's sake" (GA I/5, p. 45). However, because the I strives for self-activity and self-sufficiency, this I cannot be absolutely self-determined and free from the beginning.

To sum up, the result of Fichte's investigation is that "nothing is absolute but pure activity, and all consciousness and all being is grounded upon this pure activity" (GA I/5, p. 29). As we noted, he arrives at this conclusion through his introspective method that leads us to the essence of the I as it appears when we abstract from sensible conditions. The focus of Fichte's deduction of the principle of morality hence lies on the self-positing I in its pure activity. In this way, Fichte's conception of immediate knowledge points towards a special kind of pre-reflective self-consciousness that precedes all other reflection.

3 Schopenhauer on immediate knowledge

Schopenhauer never had much appreciation for Fichte's method, which focuses on the essence of the I as a pure activity. In a side note to a passage in which Fichte points out that the essential character of the I consists in a tendency to self-activity for self-activity's sake (Cf. GA I/5, p. 45), Schopenhauer objects to Fichte's claim, writing that every I has a tendency to rest for rest's sake (Cf. HN V, p. 54).[12] But also more generally, Schopenhauer is critical of Fichte's approach, calling Fichte's philosophy an "illusory philosophy", which has "little genuine worth and inner substance" (WWR I, § 7, p. 54):[13]

> [T]he only thing that interested him [Fichte] in the whole matter was the idea of starting out from the subject, which Kant had chosen in order to show that starting out from the object, as had been done previously, was the wrong approach and made the object into a thing in itself. Fichte took this approach of starting out from the subject as the crucial thing and

---

12 "[J]edes Ich hat eine Tendenz zur Ruhe um der Ruhe willen [...]" (HN V, p. 54).
13 References to Schopenhauer's first volume of *The World as Will and Representation* (abbreviated as WWR I) are made by citing the English translation. See Schopenhauer 2010.

thought, like all imitators, that in going further than Kant here he was also doing better than him; but by going in this direction he was repeating the mistake made by the dogmatism of the past (the very thing that had occasioned Kant's critique), only in reverse. (WWR I, § 7, p. 55)

Accordingly, it is Fichte's focus on the subject that Schopenhauer criticizes most. Unsurprisingly, Schopenhauer does not follow the approach Fichte developed in the first part of *The System of Ethics*. But immediate knowledge is nevertheless crucial for Schopenhauer's second book in *The World as Will and Representation*. Like Fichte, Schopenhauer distinguishes between two kinds of knowledge: knowledge of objects and immediate knowledge. However, Schopenhauer's understanding of immediate knowledge differs considerably from Fichte's. In this section, I focus specifically on the differences in their understanding of immediacy. However, and as will become clear in the following sections, these differences are not as substantial as Schopenhauer wanted to convince us and they do not diminish Fichte's actual impact on the development of Schopenhauer's philosophy.

Schopenhauer's work *The World as Will and Representation* has a twofold structure: the world as representation and the world as will. The world as representation, which Schopenhauer presents in the first and third books of his main work, deals with knowledge of objects as representations. This knowledge cognizes objects as they appear to the knowing subject. The world as will, which he discusses in the second and fourth books, is, on the contrary, based on a special kind of immediate knowledge. This knowledge is related to a domain beyond the world of representations, which Schopenhauer calls the world as will.

Thus, the main place in which Schopenhauer introduces immediate knowledge is in the second book of his main work.[14] But already in the first book we can find a few passages that point to his later conception of immediate knowledge as well. In the first book, Schopenhauer is aware of the fact that we would not have the knowledge of representations "if we were not immediately acquainted with some effect that could serve as a starting point" (WWR I, § 4, p. 32). These effects are hence a necessary presupposition for all other knowledge of objects. However, we experience this immediate effect because we are not only knowing subjects, but also have a special acquaintance with our

---

14 In the second volume of *The World as Will and Representation* (1844), Schopenhauer relates the notion of immediate knowledge to his concept of self-consciousness. Cf. Kisner 2016, p. 83.

body. Therefore, in the first book Schopenhauer calls our body an immediate object:[15]

> So at this stage we will be treating the body as immediate object, which is to say as the representation that serves as starting-point for the subject's cognition. The body is the starting-point because we are directly acquainted with the alterations it undergoes, and these alterations precede any application of the law of causality, and thus supply it with its initial data. (WWR I, § 6, p. 41)

Schopenhauer refers here to the concept of an immediate object in order to point out that we are more than just knowing subjects, namely embodied individuals. At the same time, however, he is aware that the term 'immediate object' is actually problematic and ambiguous since the concept of an object already designates something that is not immediate, but mediated (Cf. WWR I, § 6, p. 41). With the concept of an immediate object, Schopenhauer in his first book points to a sphere of immediate knowledge, which in the second book becomes an important subject of further discussion.

Schopenhauer starts his second book with an inquiry into the essence or the content of representations and asks whether the world is more than just a bundle of representations. He thereby affirmatively maintains that representations must have a ground. We come to this conclusion not as knowing subjects, but as embodied individuals. The concept of the body, which in the first book he defined as an immediate object, hence plays a crucial role also for the establishment of the second book:

> The body is given in two entirely different ways to the subject of cognition, who emerges as an individual only through his identity with it: in the first place it is given as a representation in intuition by the understanding, as an object among objects and liable to the same laws; but at the same time the body is also given in an entirely different way, namely as something immediately familiar to everyone, something designated by the word will. (WWR I, § 18, p. 124)

Thus, 'body' is a concept with a twofold meaning. Schopenhauer's distinction between two different kinds of knowledge is a result of this twofold character of the body. The first way to look at our body is bound to our faculty of understanding; in this case, the body is an object of thought for the subject. The second way is immediate and non-conceptual; Schopenhauer calls this immediate

---

15 Schopenhauer had already introduced the concept of an immediate object in his dissertation *On the Fourfold Root of the Principle of Sufficient Reason* (1813), especially in § 21. But Fichte and Schelling also occasionally use this term although without a unified meaning. Cf. Schöndorf 1982, p. 102.

knowledge, knowledge *in concreto* (cf. WWR I, § 18, p. 127). In this case, we have a special, pre-reflective acquaintance with our body, and the body functions here as a so-called immediate object. Of course, it is only to our own body that we have access, both directly and indirectly. All other things in nature can only be cognized as representations, but not immediately.

Consequently, the concept of the body has a special status in Schopenhauer's philosophy since it opens up a domain of immediate knowledge, which is crucial for establishing the world as will. But how does Schopenhauer's conception of immediate knowledge compare with Fichte's? First, my analysis has so far shown that they both distinguish between two different kinds of knowledge – knowledge of objects and immediate knowledge.[16] They both also establish immediate knowledge on the basis of the special immediate experience we have of ourselves. To this extent, they agree and take immediate knowledge as a starting point for their philosophies. However, the ways in which they describe and define immediate knowledge are nonetheless distinct.

In Fichte's view, we are immediately conscious of ourselves as efficacious and as willing subjects, and this immediate fact of consciousness precedes all other knowledge. The focus of Fichte's introspective method is hence on the essence of the I. Schopenhauer's method, based on immediate knowledge, takes another direction. His way inward does not bring us to the essence of the I; on the contrary, it brings us to the immediate consciousness we have of our bodies. Schopenhauer hence relates his conception of immediate knowledge to a totally different inner experience, which we have as sensible beings and not when we abstract from sensible conditions, as was the case in Fichte's first book. Whereas Fichte's conception of immediacy is connected with the tendency of the I toward self-sufficiency and self-determination, Schopenhauer's focus is not on the I, but on the body. In contrast to Fichte, Schopenhauer's conception of the immediacy does not bring to expression the self-sufficiency and freedom of the I. Instead, it is the ability to feel pain and pleasure that Schopenhauer points out and relates to the body.

Therefore, with regard to the concept of immediate knowledge, Fichte's and Schopenhauer's philosophies point in different directions. Even though they both distinguish two kinds of knowledge – the knowledge of objects and a special kind of immediate knowledge – the results of their procedures are not the same, at least not at this stage of comparison.

---

16 In one of his comments on Fichte's *System of Ethics,* Schopenhauer points to Fichte's distinction between the knowing and the willing I. Thus, this difference, which is of relevance for the distinction between knowledge of objects and immediate knowledge, is something that Schopenhauer found already in Fichte's *System of Ethics.* Cf. HN II, p. 348.

4 Fichte's system of drives and feelings

On the basis of Fichte's first part of the *System of Ethics*, we get the impression that it is the pure I, abstracted from anything sensible, which is the focus of his philosophy. According to this comparison, Fichte's and Schopenhauer's approaches differ considerably. However, in the second part of *The System of Ethics* we see that Fichte's system is much more complex and does not stop with the analysis of the pure activity of the I. Here, the concept of feeling (*Gefühl*) plays a crucial role and Fichte emphasizes that we are first aware of ourselves through feeling.[17] This turn to the concept of feeling shows his philosophy in a different light; as I will argue below, it reveals much more in common with Schopenhauer's approach in his second book than we have stressed thus far. Fichte's concept of feeling hence links his philosophy to Schopenhauer's method of immediate knowledge. Let us now see how Fichte introduces the concept of feeling into his system.

In the first part of *The System of Ethics* Fichte claims that the essence of the I lies in its activity and in the striving of the I for independence and self-sufficiency. In the second part, the "Deduction of the reality and applicability of the principle of morality", however, he maintains that we can determine the activity of the I only through and by means of its opposite. As a result, the I Fichte speaks of here cannot be an absolute I, abstracted from all sensible conditions, but is our finite, limited I that always stands in relation to something that is opposed to the I, namely the Not-I. The activity that Fichte analyses in the second part is thus not a pure activity of the I, but a determined and hence limited activity:

> Activity cannot be determined by itself, and yet it must be determined if consciousness is to be possible at all. This means nothing else than the following: the activity is to be determined through and by means of its opposite, and hence by the manner of its limitation. Only in this way can one think of a manifold of activity, consisting of several particular actions. (GA I/5, p. 94)

---

17 Fichte introduces the concept of feeling into his Wissenschaftslehre already in the *Foundations of the Entire Science of Knowledge*. Afterwards, this concept, and especially the concept of the body, are relevant also to his *Foundations of Natural Right* and to his then unpublished *Wissenschaftslehre nova methodo*. The concept of feeling in Fichte's work until the year 1801 is examined in a study written by Petra Lohmann. In her book one chapter is devoted to the concept of feeling in *The System of Ethics*, but her main focus in this part is on Fichte's concept of conscience as a feeling. S. Lohmann 2004, pp. 109–140. For a study on this topic in the *Wissenschaftslehre nova methodo* s. Kottmann 1998.

As it follows from this quotation, we are conscious of our activity only insofar as this activity is a determined activity. But the determination we can explain only in relation to something that opposes the I, namely in relation to the Not-I. This opposing Not-I is crucial for the I because we cannot objectify and represent the activity of the I without this counterpart.[18] Pure activity can never be cognized as such, it is only determined activity that we cognize. Determination, however, means always also a limitation. Consequently, and in contrast to the first part of *The System of Ethics*, the I Fichte is dealing with here is not an absolute I, but a finite and limited I. Although it is still true that the essence of the I lies for Fichte in the pure activity, this is not how we actually find and experience ourselves. As he maintains, we experience determination and limitation through feeling.

Feeling is a crucial concept of the second part because Fichte explains our limited activity through this concept. The first, immediate acquaintance we have of ourselves is that we feel our limitation:

> I cannot, however, intellectually intuit, absolutely and by myself, the manner in which I am limited; instead, this is something I only feel in sensory experience. But if an activity is supposed to be limited, and if its limitation is supposed to be felt, then that activity itself must occur – occur for me, of course, and not, as it were, in itself. (GA I/5, p. 94)

When we feel our limitation, we at the same time conceive of our activity, but only as a determined and limited activity. Taken genealogically, this is how we are initially aware of ourselves. Our first acquaintance with the I is thus through the feeling of our activity. But since we can define the limitation only in relation to its opposite, Fichte's concept of feeling needs something that belongs to the Not-I. For Fichte, that I feel myself as limited means that I am not only an intelligible being, but also a sensible being. Therefore, we are able to feel our limitation thanks only to the fact that we as sensible beings have bodies.

With the concept of the body (or more generally the concept of nature or matter) in his system, Fichte describes the counterpart of the I, the Not-I: "As a product of nature, therefore, I am matter; more precisely and in accordance with what was said above, I am organized matter that constitutes a determinate whole: I am my body" (GA I/5, p. 123). As a product of nature, I am of course de-

---

18 This does not mean, however, that we can know anything about the Not-I as it is in itself – the Not-I is always thought of in connection with the I. This is something that Fichte had already demonstrated at length in the first Jena *Wissenschaftslehre*. Whenever Fichte speaks of the opposite, he always refers to it only in a negative way and from the subjective perspective, namely through the limitation of the activity of the I.

termined and not self-sufficient and free. But only as determined can we also act efficaciously in the sensible world and as such we appear as an "articulated body [*artikulierter Leib*]":

> Now, however, I am supposed to have an effect upon that stuff, the origin of which was described above. But it is impossible for me to think of this stuff as being affected by anything other than something that is itself stuff. Consequently, since I do – as I must – think of myself as having an effect on this stuff, I also become for myself stuff; and insofar as I view myself in this way, I call myself a material body. Viewed as a principle of an efficacy in the world of bodies, I am an articulated body; and the representation of my body is itself nothing but the representation of myself as a cause in the world of bodies and is therefore indirectly only a certain way of looking at my own absolute activity. (GA I/5, p. 28; cf. also GA I/5, p. 99)

Crucial to understanding Fichte's concept of the body is that he takes the body only as a "certain way of looking at [our] own absolute activity". This means that for Fichte, the body is a manifestation of the I only in the sensible world. From the subjective perspective the I appears as a pure activity, but from the objective perspective – that is, as part of the sensible world – this same I manifests itself as a body. Moreover, the body can then be defined as an instrument of the I, this is of our will, through which we can act efficaciously in the sensible world. Consequently, the will and the body are for Fichte one and the same, described from two different perspectives (cf. GA I/5, p. 29). As we will see in the next section, this identification is also crucial to Schopenhauer.

However, this focus on the finite I that feels and has a body does not deny what Fichte maintained about the essence of the I in the first part of *The System of Ethics*. The pure activity and tendency toward the absolute self-sufficiency are still the basic characteristics of the I. What he adds in the second part is that we first experience this activity in a determined way, through feeling. This means that we are not aware of the tendency directly, but only indirectly, namely as a striving to overcome our determination and limitation and to become self-sufficient. As a result, the concept of feeling points to two basic elements of Fichte's philosophy: we are through feeling immediately aware of the limitation, yet we are in this way also aware of our striving to overcome this limitation. The characterisation of the I as a tendency, and hence as a striving, is already important to Fichte's first part. But in the second part, this tendency is given another name – Fichte describes it as a drive.[19] The tendency of the I, described from the objective perspective, is a drive. Therefore, Fichte argues that the drive is "a real,

---

19 For the interpretation of Fichte's concept of drive s. Soller 1984 and Wood 2016, pp. 143–157.

inner explanatory ground of an actual self-activity" (GA I/5, p. 55). When we reflect on the striving of the I, this striving appears to us as a drive:

> If one originally thinks the I in an objective manner – and this is how it is found prior to all other types of consciousness –, then one can describe its determinacy only as a tendency or a drive, as has here been sufficiently demonstrated right from the start. The objective constitution of an I is by no means a being or subsistence; for that would make it the opposite of what it is; i.e., that would make it a thing. The being of the I is absolute activity and nothing but activity; but activity, taken objectively, is drive. (GA I/5, p. 105)

But again, we first experience this drive through feeling: "Thus, if the I is originally posited with a drive as its objective determination, then it is necessarily posited as well with some feeling of this drive" (GA I/5, pp. 105–106). At the first stage, I feel myself as driven; I do not grasp myself as free, but as determined (Cf. GA I/5, pp. 106–107). I feel a striving. However, I do not take myself as a free subject and as a cause of this striving. The feeling of the drive makes me a part of nature. Therefore, Fichte defines this feeling of the drive as a natural drive. However, natural drive is just the first, initial manifestation of the tendency of the I. Later Fichte comes to speak also about higher forms of drives, which we can no longer describe through feelings; but for the purpose of this analysis, my discussion is limited to the concepts of feeling and the feeling of the drive.

With regard to the second part of Fichte's *System of Ethics*, we can conclude that in his work Fichte does not focus solely on the concept of the I and on the pure activity of the I, but also tries to describe the I as a part of nature. The concept of feeling plays a crucial role in this task because initially, at the first stage, we do not conceive of ourselves as free and self-sufficient, but we feel ourselves as limited and determined. As a result, the first immediate knowledge we have of ourselves is linked to the experience we have of ourselves through feeling. The concept of feeling thus is an important addition to Fichte's first part since we see that we are at first and most indirectly aware of ourselves as finite, limited beings.

With the concept of feeling, Fichte incorporates into his *System of Ethics* an important psychological concept, but at the same time he defines this concept in a philosophical way and represents it as an upshot of his philosophical deduction. Even though Fichte does not refer in this book to psychology explicitly, his method nevertheless marks an important extension of topics that belong to philosophy and shows how moral psychology can be conceived as an integral part of his ethical theory. In this way, Fichte transforms Kant's moral philosophy developed in the *Groundwork* and in the second *Critique* into a system of ethics that contains as its constitutive part also a theory of drives and feelings.[20]

5 Feelings and affections in Schopenhauer's metaphysics of the will

Fichte's second part of *The System of Ethics* allows his philosophy to appear in new light. The first, immediate acquaintance that we have of ourselves is linked to the concept of feeling and is, as a result, closely bound to our sensibility. However, from this perspective, Fichte's view becomes quite similar to Schopenhauer's understanding of immediate knowledge, which I presented in the third section. Therefore, I will now expand on Schopenhauer's understanding of immediate knowledge developed in the second book and compare it with what we found in Fichte's approach in the second part of his *System of Ethics*. My main aim will be to demonstrate that also in Schopenhauer's philosophy the concept of feeling, for which he uses the term "affection", plays a crucial role.[21]

In the second book, Schopenhauer relates our immediate knowledge to the experience of our own body. Although we can perceive our body as a mere object and hence as a representation for us as knowing subjects, additionally, we also have a special, immediate acquaintance with our body. For Schopenhauer, the body is an organ through which we immediately experience the acts of our will. The motions and changes of the body that we see are, on this account, just the manifestations of the acts of the will:

> Every true act of his will is immediately and inevitably a movement of his body as well: he cannot truly will an act without simultaneously perceiving it as a motion of the body. An act of the will and an act of the body are not two different states cognized objectively, linked together in a causal chain, they do not stand in a relation of cause and effect; they are one and the same thing, only given in two entirely different ways: in one case immediately and in the other case to the understanding in intuition. (WWR I, § 18, p. 124)

Therefore, we must be immediately aware of the acts of the will; but as knowing subjects, we can also see and cognize these acts of the will as motions of the

---

20 For my analysis of the difference between Kant's idealism and Fichte's system of transcendental idealism s. Kisner 2018.

21 My comparison focuses on the immediate knowledge and the concept of feeling by Fichte and Schopenhauer, but I do not compare their notion of the will or their conception of freedom. For this s. Zöller 2006, pp. 381–386. Cf. also Metz 2006, pp. 387–399.

body. Motions of the body are hence only a visual, objective manifestation of the acts of the will. This twofold view of the body is exactly consistent with how Fichte describes the body, namely as a sensible manifestation of the will. Thus, on this basis we can infer that Schopenhauer took over Fichte's two-fold view on the body, in which what we subjectively experience as the will is objectively perceived as a body.

But the next crucial question that opens up here is the following: how does Schopenhauer understand and describe this immediate acquaintance with acts of the will? As I will argue, he does this via feeling and therefore his approach is again quite similar to Fichte's. Let me show why this is so by highlighting why Schopenhauer's concept of affection can be identified as feeling.

Schopenhauer claims that we experience the acts of the will as affections of the will.[22] But Schopenhauer does not understand the concept of affection in a causal sense; he does not refer to a cause that brings about an effect. Instead, he defines affection as feeling: "But it is quite wrong to call pain and pleasure representations: they are nothing of the sort, but rather immediate affections of the will in its appearance, the body" (WWR I, § 18, p. 125). Since pain and pleasure are feelings, it follows that feelings are immediate affections of the will, meaning that through affections we immediately experience the acts of the will. We feel the acts of the will immediately. Accordingly, Schopenhauer claims that everyone possesses knowledge of the will in concreto, through feeling (cf. WWR I, § 21, p. 134). This interpretation of affection as feeling is confirmed also by the fact that he understands affection in German as "Affekt", that is, as emotion:[23]

> The identity of body and will is demonstrated in many other ways as well, such as the fact that every violent and excessive movement of the will, i.e. every affect [Affekt] immediately agitates the body and its inner workings and disturbs the course of its vital functions. (WWR I, § 18, p. 126)

Affection or "*Affekt*" is again not a causal term. The acts of the will that we experience immediately as emotions are not the causes for the movements of the body; instead, the acts of the will and the movements of the body are one

---

22 In the second book, Schopenhauer mostly uses the concept of affection to describe this feeling that we experience on the basis of the acts of the will. However, in the first book he also gives his definition of the concept of feeling as he understands it in contrast to the concept of knowledge. Cf. WWR I, § 11, p. 76.

23 E. F. J. Payne translated the term "*Affekt*" as emotion in his translation of *The World as Will and Representation*. S. Schopenhauer 1958, p. 101.

and the same, described from two different perspectives. Directly, we experience these acts as affections – as feelings, but indirectly, as knowing subjects they appear to us as movements of the body. The feelings of pain and pleasure are therefore the most immediate and direct ways of how we experience the inner essence of our will:

> Every true, genuine and immediate act of will is instantly and immediately also the appearance of an act of the body: correspondingly, any effect on the body is instantly and immediately an effect on the will as well: it is called pain when it is contrary to the will; and it is called comfort or pleasure when it is in accordance with the will. (WWR I, § 18, p. 125)

However, we always experience these acts of the will through the body; we can feel them because we have a body. This means that we do not experience the will (or acts of the will) as they are in themselves, but only as we are aware of them through our body. In this sense, Schopenhauer can claim that being in accordance with the will releases pleasure, and being opposed to the will triggers pain.

We can conclude that what Schopenhauer calls an immediate knowledge of the acts of the will is actually our immediate experience of feelings of pleasure and displeasure. This means that the immediate consciousness we have of ourselves is that we feel. But this is exactly the same assumption with which Fichte starts the second part of his *System of Ethics*. Therefore, it holds for both philosophers that the first, immediate experience we have of ourselves is through feeling.

Fichte understood this feeling as a feeling of limitation and determination of our activity. Schopenhauer, of course, does not use the same terms of limitation and determination to describe the affections of the will. However, from his definition of pleasure and displeasure as being in accordance or contrary to the will, we see that for Schopenhauer, too, the feelings express a limitation of the will. This does not mean that Schopenhauer's will as an underlying principle of all representations is limited; this is not the case. What it does mean is that the acts of the will that we feel are already experienced through our body; hence, they manifest themselves as particular feelings and therefore are an expression of a limitation.

Schopenhauer thus understands feelings of pleasure and displeasure as both pointing out our limitations and bringing to expression our striving to overcome these limitations. This, again, is exactly the same as how Fichte understands the concept of feeling as expressing our limitation, yet pointing to the tendency of the I (or of the will) to overcome this limitation. Schopenhauer describes this view even more plastically: when we act in accordance with our will, we perceive the acts of the will through the feeling of pleasure. When we act contrary to the will, however, we feel the boundaries of our striving very strongly and experience them as displeasure.

6 Conclusion

As a result of my analysis, we can conclude that both Fichte and Schopenhauer have a similar conception of immediate knowledge, which is grounded upon a similar understanding of the concept of feeling. They both hold that through feeling we are in a most immediate way aware of the inner activity of the will, but as embodied individuals and not when we abstract from sensible conditions. Just as Fichte conceives of the finite, limited I as a part of nature, so does Schopenhauer start his second book with the fact that we as individuals are embodied and are a part of the world. Because of their strong agreement, I think it appropriate and necessary to acknowledge that Schopenhauer developed his approach established in the second book of *The World as Will and Representation* at least in part under the influence of Fichte's philosophy.

Both philosophers attribute special importance to the introspective method and to the psychological concepts connected with this method. In this way, they integrate psychological themes into their philosophical systems and try to explain them in a philosophical way. With this approach they push forward the subjective, individual and personal viewpoint which sets a new trend for the philosophers to come. Fichte and Schopenhauer no longer insist on a clear distinction between philosophy and psychology and in this they act as forerunners of thinkers such as Nietzsche, Freud and the existentialists.

By emphasizing the impact that Fichte had on Schopenhauer, however, I do not want to minimise the originality of Schopenhauer's system. On the contrary, even though Schopenhauer's philosophy developed – *inter alia* – under the influence of Fichte's system, this does not mean that their final outcomes are alike. When we come to the next step of Schopenhauer's metaphysics of the will, namely to his understanding of the will as the thing in itself, a step which I have put aside here, significant differences between Fichte and Schopenhauer become very obvious.[24] Yet despite these distinctions, their initial ap-

---

24 In this article I did not discuss Schopenhauer's metaphysics of the will as a whole which at the end identifies the will with the thing in itself. For this identification the reference to the immediate knowledge does not suffice – this is only the first step –, but also the reference to reflection is needed. As Schopenhauer stresses, we are immediately acquainted only with particular acts of the will, but not with the will as a whole. Hence, the identification of the will with

proaches, which are based on the immediate, introspective method, are nevertheless similar. It is with regard to this method that we can in my opinion claim that Schopenhauer's philosophy cannot be properly understood and evaluated without acknowledging its Fichtean debt.[25]

References

GA I/5 | Fichte, Johann Gottlieb (2005): *The System of Ethics According to the Principles of the Wissenschaftslehre* [1798]. Translated and edited by Daniel Breazeale and Günter Zöller. Cambridge: Cambridge University Press. [Paging follows Fichte's *Gesamtausgabe*, div. I, vol. 5.]

HN I–V | Schopenhauer, Arthur (1985): *Der handschriftliche Nachlaß*. 5 vols. Edited by Arthur Hübscher. München: DTV.

WWR I | Schopenhauer, Arthur (2010): *The World as Will and Representation. Volume 1* (1818/19). Translated and edited by Judith Norman, Alistair Welchman and Christopher Janaway. Cambridge: Cambridge University Press.

D'Alfonso, Matteo Vincenzo (2006): "Schopenhauer als Schüler Fichtes". In: *Fichte-Studien* 30, pp. 201–211.

Atwell, John E. (1995): *Schopenhauer on the Character of the World: The Metaphysics of Will*. Berkeley: University of California Press.

Decher, Friedhelm (1990): "Schopenhauer und Fichtes Schrift ‚Die Bestimmung des Menschen'". In: *Schopenhauer-Jahrbuch* 7, pp. 45–67.

Hühn, Lore (ed.) (2006): Die Ethik Arthur Schopenhauers im Ausgang vom Deutschen Idealismus. Würzburg: Ergon.

Janaway, Christopher (1989): *Self and World in Schopenhauer's Philosophy*. Oxford: Oxford University Press.

Kisner, Manja (2016): *Der Wille und das Ding an sich: Schopenhauers Willensmetaphysik in ihrem Bezug zu Kants kritischer Philosophie und dem nachkantischen Idealismus*. Würzburg: Königshausen & Neumann Verlag.

Kisner, Manja (2018): "Fichtes metaphysische Rezeption des kantischen transzendentalen Idealismus". In: Antonino Falduto/Heiner F. Klemme (eds.): *Kant und seine Kritiker – Kant and His Critics*. Hildesheim: Georg Olms Verlag, pp. 157–170.

Knappik, Franz (2018): "Kant, Schopenhauer und Fichte über unser Wissen von unseren körperlichen Handlungen". In: *Fichte-Studien* 45, pp. 200–220.

Kosch, Michelle (2018): *Fichte's Ethics*. Oxford: Oxford University Press.

Kottmann, Reinhard (1998): *Leiblichkeit und Wille in Fichtes "Wissenschaftslehre nova methodo"*. Münster: Lit.

---

the thing in itself is not a direct consequence of his notion of feeling but is postulated *in abstracto*. For the further discussion on this s. Young 1987; Janaway 1989; Atwell 1995.

25 I would like to thank Dennis Vanden Auweele and Jonathan Head for helpful comments on earlier version of the paper.

Lohmann, Petra (2004): *Der Begriff des Gefühls in der Philosophie Johann Gottlieb Fichtes.* Amsterdam/New York: Rodopi.

Merle, Jean Christophe/Schmidt, Andreas (eds.) (2015): *Fichtes System der Sittenlehre. Ein Kooperativer Kommentar.* Frankfurt a. M.: Vittorio Klostermann.

Metz, Wilhelm (2006): "Der Begriff des Willens bei Fichte und Schopenhauer". In: Lore Hühn (ed.): *Die Ethik Arthur Schopenhauers im Ausgang vom Deutschen Idealismus.* Würzburg: Ergon, pp. 387–399.

Novembre, Alessandro (2016): "Das ‚Losreißen' des Wissens: Von der Schopenhauer'schen Nachschrift der Vorlesungen Fichtes ‚Ueber die Tatsachen der Bewusstseins' und ‚Ueber die Wissenschaftslehre' (1811/12) zur Ästhetik von Die Welt als Wille und Vorstellung". In: *Fichte-Studien* 43, pp. 315–335.

De Pascale, Carla (2012): "Fichtes Einfluss auf Schopenhauer". In: *Fichte-Studien* 36, pp. 45–59.

Philonenko, Alexis (1997): "Fichte et Schopenhauer". In: Alexis Philonenko (ed.): *Métaphysique et politique: Chez Kant et Fichte.* Paris: Vrin, pp. 437–451.

Schopenhauer, Arthur (1958): *The World as Will and Representation* (1818/19). Translated and edited by E. F. J. Payne. Indian Hills: Falcon's Wing Press.

Schöndorf, Harald (1982): *Der Leib im Denken Schopenhauers und Fichtes.* München: Johannes Berchmans Verlag.

Soller, Alois K. (1984): *Trieb und Reflexion in Fichtes Jenaer Philosophie.* Würzburg: Königshausen & Neumann Verlag.

Wood, Allen (2016): *Fichte's ethical thought.* Oxford: Oxford University Press.

Young, Julian (1987): Willing and Unwilling: A Study in the Philosophy of Arthur Schopenhauer. Dordrecht: Kluwer Academic Publishers.

Zöller, Günter (2000): "German Realism: The Self-limitation of Idealist Thinking in Fichte, Schelling, and Schopenhauer". In: Karl Ameriks (ed.): *The Cambridge Companion to German Idealism.* Cambridge: Cambridge University Press, pp. 200–218.

Zöller, Günter (2006): "Kichtenhauer. Der Ursprung von Schopenhauers Welt als Wille und Vorstellung in Fichtes Wissenschaftslehre 1812 und System der Sittenlehre". In: Lore Hühn (ed.): *Die Ethik Arthur Schopenhauers im Ausgang vom Deutschen Idealismus.* Würzburg: Ergon, pp. 365–386.

Willem A. deVries
The Space of Intelligence

Abstract: *Hegel often uses spatial metaphors to characterize what he calls "mechanical memory". He describes it as an "abstract space" populated by "meaningless words" that co-exist in juxtaposition to each other therein. Space is the realm of the self-external, so it seems surprising that Hegel would employ such a notion at a relatively late stage in the dialectical investigation of intelligence, the realm of the internal. After establishing the prevalence of spatial metaphors in Hegel's texts dealing with mechanical memory, this essay puts forth an interpretation of Hegel's spatial characterization of mechanical memory that draws on the notion of a "logical space of reasons" to be found in the work of Wilfrid Sellars and the so-called "Pittsburgh Hegelians".*

Hegel verwendet häufig räumliche Metaphern, um das zu charakterisieren, was er „mechanisches Gedächtnis" nennt. Er beschreibt es als einen „abstrakten Raum", in dem „bedeutungslose Wörter" nebeneinander existieren. Der Raum ist für Hegel das Reich des Äußeren des Selbst, so dass es überraschend scheint, dass Hegel einen solchen Begriff relativ spät in die dialektische Untersuchung des Geistes, als dem Bereich des Inneren, einbringt. Nach der Herausstellung von Raummetaphern im Zusammenhang des Themas des mechanischen Gedächtnisses in Hegels Texten, wird in diesem Aufsatz eine Interpretation von Hegels räumlicher Charakterisierung des mechanischen Gedächtnisses vorgestellt, die sich auf den Begriff eines „logischen Raums der Gründe" stützt, der in der Arbeit von Wilfrid Sellars und den sogenannten „Pittsburgher Hegelianern" zu finden ist.

I Mental Space?

Spatial metaphors are often used to describe and even explain something mental. Such metaphors operate at several different levels. One familiar one is the notion that mental states 'contain' something, a *content*. This treats individual ideas as if they are (metaphorically) spatial. We also talk about one idea being close to another, a way of describing similarities or other associative relations be-

---

I owe thanks to Alex Holznienkemper, who helped groom my translations of Hegel's German. Thanks are also due to the editors and to the copy editor, Jaroslaw Bledowski, who helped me improve the paper with their suggestions and queries.

https://doi.org/10.1515/9783110673692-010

tween thought contents. But we can also find the mind itself, rather than its elements, treated as a kind of space within which mental events occur. The too-often used metaphor of the mental theater (Dennett calls it the "Cartesian theater"[1]) would be an example of this. Such metaphors, though popular and seemingly unavoidable, are well known to be dangerous. Physical space is populated by a large number of more-or-less well-delimited, independent (though causally connected) objects, all of which exist concurrently, sometimes changing location, sometimes ceasing or beginning their existence. There is some number of orthogonal dimensions to physical space, though this aspect of space now seems more complicated than it did before, say, 1905 and the introduction of space-time as a single unit. It has gotten even more complicated in light of even more modern theories in physics that postulate 10 or 11 dimensions (or even more) to space, most of which we cannot see.

Treating a mind as if it is itself some kind of space seems to ignore important differences between minds and the physical world. It is not so clear what the basic entities are when we talk about the mental. Are they *ideas*, are they mental *events*, are they *judgments* or *thoughts?* How do sensations fit in? Time seems to play a proportionately bigger role in understanding the mental than it does in understanding physical objects in space (though this may be an illusion). We can easily understand what is meant when we describe two ideas or thoughts as 'close' or 'far removed' from each other, but there does not seem to be any serious sense to the notion that ideas or thoughts can move around in mental space. Though it seems clear that whatever the items in mental space are, they do interact in some causal fashion, it has been fairly mysterious just how such mental causation works and whether there are laws governing such interactions as there are governing causal interaction among spatial entities.

That applying a spatial metaphor to the mind faces some obstacles is not surprising. It is clear that models and metaphors always contain disanalogies. When confronted by a spatialization of the mind, one has to ask whether the metaphor is productive or a tempting garden path that ends up fostering deeper confusion. Too often, confusion is the result.

Surprisingly, Hegel uses a spatial metaphor for mind in some of his discussions of psychology. It is surprising that he does so, I think, because space is, for Hegel, the epitome of externality. It is a structure in which everything is outside of and merely externally related to everything else. Physical objects may be essentially spatial, but their location in space and their spatial relations to other

---

1 Daniel C. Dennett: *Consciousness Explained.* New York: Little, Brown and Company, 1991, *passim.*

spatial entities are always contingent. Mind or Spirit, in contrast, is the realm of internality: Spirit is for itself, and subjectivity is an essential moment in Spirit. Furthermore, Hegel uses this spatial metaphor right before the section in his psychology discussing thought (*das Denken*), that is, it appears in his discussion of memory (*Gedächtnis*). If he had used a spatial metaphor for mind early in the dialectic (say, in the Anthropology) before working up to the relative sophistication of memory, on the border of true thought, it might have been less surprising.

The goal of this essay is to explore this metaphor in its context and show how to understand it in a way that makes sense of its use just before the examination of thought itself. Echoes of the work of Wilfrid Sellars and some of his followers will be exploited to help us make sense of this otherwise confusing metaphor.

II Setting the Table

Before getting into my interpretive discussion, it is important to clarify its textual basis. In the paragraphs on *Gedächtnis* in the *Encyclopedia*, there are only two clear cases of Hegel's referring to the mind as a kind of space. The first is in § 463. I give the Wallace's English translation first,[2] followed by the German original.[3]

> But intelligence is the universal,—the single plain truth of its particular self-divestments; and its consummated appropriation of them abolishes that distinction between meaning and name. This extreme inwardising of representation is the supreme self-divestment of intelligence, in which it renders itself the mere being, the universal space of names as such, i.e. of meaningless words.[4]

---

2 G. W. F. Hegel: *Hegel's Philosophy of Mind*. W. Wallace and A. V. Miller (trans.). New York: Oxford University Press, 1971.
3 G. W. F. Hegel: *Enzyklopädie der philosophischen Wissenschaften im Grundrisse (1830). Dritter Teil: Die Philosophie des Geistes*. In: G. W. F. Hegel: *Werke*. Vol. 10. Eva Moldenhauer and Karl Markus Michel (eds.). Frankfurt am Main: Suhrkamp, 1970 [henceforth cited as "Enz."]. The corresponding text in the critical *Gesammelte Werke* edition [henceforth cited as "GW"] is in volume 20.
4 Here is Petry's translation: "Intelligence is however the universal, the simple truth of its particular externalizations, and its accomplished appropriation constitutes the sublation of the difference between meaning and name. This, which is the height of presentative recollection, is the supreme externalization of intelligence, within which it posits itself as *being*, the universal space of names as such, i.e. as senseless words." (Hegel, G. W. F.: *Hegel's Philosophy of Subjective Spirit*. 3 vols. Michael John Petry [ed. and trans.]. Boston: D. Reidel, 1978 [henceforth cited as "Petry"], vol. 3, pp. 207–209)

> Aber die Intelligenz ist das Allgemeine; die einfache Wahrheit ihrer besonderen Entäu-
> ßerungen und ihr durchgeführtes Aneignen ist das Aufheben jenes Unterschiedes der Be-
> deutung und des Namens; diese höchste Erinnerung des Vorstellens ist ihre höchste Entäu-
> ßerung, in der sie sich als das *Sein*, den allgemeinen Raum der Namen als solcher, d. i.
> sinnloser Worte setzt.

At this point in the dialectic of memory, intelligence has particularized itself
into a collection of words that, as such, are meaningless, arbitrary collections
of sounds or symbols. In the internality of spirit, they simply exist alongside
each other, like separate, particular objects in space.

The second use of 'space' ('*Raum*') in this section of subjective spirit is in the
following paragraph, § 464, in the *Anmerkung*:

> It is not matter of chance that the young have a better memory than the old, nor is their
> memory solely exercised for the sake of utility. The young have a good memory because
> they have not yet reached the stage of reflection; their memory is exercised with or without
> design so as to level the ground of their inner life to pure being or to pure space in which
> the fact, the implicit content, may reign and unfold itself with no antithesis to a subjective
> inwardness.[5]
>
> Die Jugend hat nicht zufälligerweise ein besseres Gedächtnis als die Alten, und ihr Ge-
> dächtnis wird nicht nur um der Nützlichkeit willen geübt, sondern sie hat das gute Ge-
> dächtnis, weil sie sich noch nicht nachdenkend verhält, und es wird absichtlich oder un-
> absichtlich darum geübt, um den Boden ihrer Innerlichkeit zum reinen Sein, zum reinen
> Raume zu ebnen, in welchem die Sache, der an sich seiende Inhalt ohne den Gegensatz
> gegen eine subjektive Innerlichkeit, gewähren und sich explizieren könne.

Here the primary idea, for my purposes, is that he describes the memory of the
young as a "space" in so far as everything in it seems to be 'on the same level',
existing indifferently alongside other things in memory.

There is another allusion in the traditionally available texts that seems clearly rooted in a spatialization of the mind; it occurs in the *Zusatz* to § 462.

> Just as the true thought is the very thing itself, so too is the *word* when it is employed by
> genuine thinking. Intelligence, therefore, is filling itself with the word, receives into itself
> the nature of the thing. But this reception has, at the same time, the meaning that intelli-
> gence thereby takes on the nature of a *thing* and to such a degree that subjectivity, in its

---

5 Again, the Petry version: "It is not a matter of chance that the young have a better memory
than the elderly, and it is not only for its utility that they make use of it. Their memory is
good because they have not yet developed a thoughtful attitude and by design or otherwise
they exercise it in order to level the ground of their inwardness to the purity of the being or
space in which the thing or implicit content may expatiate and explicate itself without having
to oppose a subjective inwardness." (Petry, vol. 3, p. 211)

distinction from the thing, becomes quite empty, a mindless container of words, that is, a mechanical memory.[6]

Wie der wahrhafte *Gedanke* die *Sache* ist, so auch das *Wort*, wenn es vom wahrhaften Denken gebraucht wird. Indem sich daher die Intelligenz mit dem Worte erfüllt, nimmt sie die Natur der Sache in sich auf. Diese Aufnahme hat aber zugleich den Sinn, daß sich die Intelligenz dadurch zu einem *Sächlichen* macht, dergestalt daß die Subjektivität, in ihrem Unterschiede von der Sache, zu etwas ganz Leerem, zum geistlosen Behälter der Worte, also zum *mechanischen* Gedächtnis wird.

Here, please note that, while intelligence "receives into itself the nature of the thing", namely, the object of its thinking, in doing so, it itself becomes "quite empty" (like space itself), a mere container in which things exist alongside each other and apparently without further connection.

These three passages do not provide an extensive basis for understanding what Hegel means when he characterizes the mind, at the level of *Gedächtnis*, as a kind of space. The publication, relatively recently, of lecture notes from Hegel's courses on subjective spirit, however, show that the application of spatial metaphors to mind in *Gedächtnis* is not at all a throw-away. Hegel consistently and repeatedly talks about *Gedächtnis* in those terms in his lectures, so we have to take this talk seriously and try to make sense of it. Let me cite some of the passages from the lectures that I have in mind.

The earliest we have record of is in the lecture notes taken by Heinrich G. Hotho of Hegel's 1822 lecture course on the philosophy of subjective spirit. In the notes for § 382, the discussion is about the fact that in mechanical memory all there is are empty words and the I that binds them. Picking the text up about halfway through the notes for this paragraph, we find this in Hotho's text:

I, as I am in this array, am the empty space and the empty time, and make myself the abstract form of intuition; of externality. Space and time are the entirely empty forms of combination. As such an emptiness, I create myself in mechanical memory. This is its nature. (My translation)

Ich wie ich in dieser Reihe bin, bin der leere Raum und die leere Zeit, mache mich zur abstracten Form der Anschauung; der Äußerlichkeit. Raum und Zeit sind die ganz leeren Formen des Verbindens. Als solches Leeres mache ich mich in dem mechanischen Gedächtniß. Diß ist seine Natur. (GW 25/1, p. 134)

---

6 The Petry translation: "At the same time however, this taking up also has the *further* significance of intelligence making a *matter* of itself, so that subjectivity, in that it is difference from the matter, becomes something that is quite empty,—the spiritless reservoir of words that constitutes *mechanical memory*." (Petry, vol. 3, p. 207)

This is one of the most direct uses of the spatial (and in this case temporal) metaphor, and it is especially interesting to note its connection to both "the abstract form of intuition" and the "empty form of combination". As empty forms of combination, space and time are also abstract forms—it is only as *filled* forms of combination that they could be concrete. In Hegel's view, thus, space and time are themselves also "abstract forms of combination", since any and every particular thing is related somehow in space and time.

The next two passages come from the lecture notes taken by C. G. J. von Griesheim in 1825.

> What intelligence does here, or what this mechanical memory is an appearance of, is that intelligence has made itself into the abstract space of this externality. Intelligence has appropriated the image and given it determinate being as something posited by it, whereupon the last step is that it gives itself entirely sensuous being as the space of this externality. Words that associate in mechanical memory are like things in space, where they are indifferently next to each other and memory is the abstract support of these determinations. One commonly speaks ill of mechanical memory, because rote learning is without sense, but memory is the highest point of representation, where intelligence makes itself into beings; this is the infinite power of intelligence. (My translation)
>
> Was die Intelligenz hier thut oder wovon dieß mechanische Gedächtniß die Erscheinung ist, ist daß die Intelligenz sich zum abstrakten Raum dieser Äusserlichkeit gemacht hat. Die Intelligenz hat sich das Bild angeeignet und ihm Dasein gegeben als einem von ihm Gesetzten und die letzte Stufe ist alsdann daß sie sich das ganz sinnliche Sein giebt, daß sie der Raum dieser Äusserlichkeit ist. Die Worte die im mechanischen Gedächtniß zusammenhängen, sind wie Dinge im Raum, wo sie ganz gleichgültig neben einander sind und das Gedächtnis ist dieser abstrakte Halt dieser Bestimmungen. Man spricht gewöhnlich vom mechanischen Gedächtniß schlecht, daß das Auswendiglernen sinnlos sei, allein das Gedächtniß ist der höchste Punkt des Vorstellens, wo die Intelligenz sich selbst zum Sein macht, dieß ist die unendliche Kraft der Intelligenz. (GW 25/1, p. 525)[7]

Again, Hegel sounds the theme that in memory, words are like things in space, indifferently juxtaposed, and, I will argue, subject at least to the *possibility* of a deeper relationship that connects them in some more internal way.

---

7 A closely related passage, not quite as compact in its phrasing, appears in Petry's bilingual edition of the *Philosophy of Subjective Spirit* (Petry, vol. 3, pp. 214–215). Petry attributes it to the set of notes taken (also in 1825) by F. C. H. V. von Kehler. The von Kehler manuscript has not been made available separately in print in the *Gesammelte Werke* edition, though the edition of the von Griesheim notes includes in the editorial apparatus the variants in the von Kehler notes. The reason seems to be that von Griesheim's manuscript is a clean copy without many symbols and abbreviations, while the von Kehler manuscript is full of such things and thus more open to dispute.

Pedagogy gains deep significance through knowledge of intelligence and making such [empty] words the object of attention. Freezing the modifications of sounds is a thorough-going cultivation of abstract representation and thus the practice of memory is the constitution, the bringing-to-being of the wholly internal spatiality. What space otherwise does, placing objects next to each other, is done by intelligence, namely, containing the objectively unrelated, and thereby intelligence reveals itself as this power. (My translation)

Die Pädagogik gewinnt tiefe Bedeutung durch Kenntniß der Intelligenz und die Beschäftigung solche Worte zum Gegenstand der Aufmerksamkeit zu machen und diese Modifikationen der Laute zu fixiren ist eine gründliche Bildung der abstrakten Vorstellung und so ist die Uebung des Gedächtnisses das Bilden, zum Dasein bringen der ganz innerlichen Räumlichkeit, was der Raum sonst thut, daß die Gegenstände neben einander placirt sind, das thut die Intelligenz, nämlich das Halten des objektiv Beziehungslosen und da zeigt sich die Intelligenz als diese Macht. (GW 25/1, p. 526)

Next, there is a passage from the Stolzenberg lecture notes taken during the 1827–28 course.[8]

Memory is the empty space in which one can place all things next to each other, but it itself is the abstract power of holding this stuff together. Thus, in the mechanism of memory intelligence has given itself this objectivity; it is itself this externality – the abstract space. Intelligence has thus given itself in memory the determinations that belong to *thinking*. (My translation)

Der Gedächtniß ist der leere Raum, in den man Alles neben einander stellen kann, aber es selbst ist dann die abstracte Kraft des Zusammenhaltens dieses Stoffs. In dem Mechanismus des Gedächtnisses hat also die Intelligenz sich selbst diese Objectivität gegeben; sie ist selbst diese Äußerlichkeit – der abstracte Raum. So hat die Intelligenz sich im Gedächtniß die Bestimmungen gegeben, die dem D e n k e n angehören [...]. (GW 25/2, p. 866)

In these two passages, the thing to note is the characterization of intelligence as both a "space" and yet also a "power". We do not normally think of space as a *power*; the 'commonsense' view of space regards it as *inert*. So one of the tasks faced by an interpretation of Hegel's employment of the spatial metaphor is the reconciliation of these two characteristics.

And finally, there are passages from the lecture notes taken in 1827–28 by Johann Eduard Erdmann and Ferdinand Walter.[9] In the midst of the discussion of mechanical memory and the way (linguistic) signs behave in it, they recorded the following:

---

8 Nothing in particular is known about the student who took these notes. There were two different students with similar names studying theology in Berlin at the time, and it isn't know which of them (if either) took these notes. See GW 25/3, pp. 1182–1183.
9 Walter was Erdmann's uncle, but only 4 years older. While both were studying philosophy and theology in Berlin, they roomed together.

These signs are meaningless; insofar as I can learn an array of names or numbers by rote, insofar as it is merely a matter of memorization, I attach no meaning to them. Intelligence is the space in which these determinations exist; it is what connects them and knows them in this connection. (My translation)

Diese Zeichen sind ein Sinnloses; daß ich eine Reihe Namen, Zahlen auswendig lernen kann, sofern das nur Gedächtnissache ist, habe ich keinen Sinn, keine Bedeutung dabei. Die Intelligenz ist der Raum in dem diese Bestimmungen sind, sie ist das Zusammenhaltende derselben und das sie in diesem Zusammenhang wissende.[10]

These passages make it clear that the spatial metaphor is used consistently over the years by Hegel to describe mechanical memory, an important concept within Hegel's treatment of psychology that he believes his predecessors did not sufficiently appreciate. As I mentioned at the outset, this could seem to be surprising, given Hegel's overall treatment of Spirit and mind. The job now is to understand why Hegel thinks this is a fruitful metaphor to employ here and what work he wants it to do.

III Space Agency

Hegel characterizes mechanical memory, or more precisely, spirit at the stage or level of mechanical memory as a *space*. To understand what he is trying to tell us with that, we need to look more closely at Hegel's conception of space. What he tells us at the beginning of the philosophy of nature is that

The first or immediate determination of nature is the abstract *universality of its being outside of itself* – of its mediationless indifference, *space*. It [space] is the entirely ideal *next-to-each-other*, because it is being outside of itself, and simply *continuous*, because this outside-of-each-other is still entirely *abstract* and has no determinate difference within it. (My translation)

Die erste oder unmittelbare Bestimmung der Natur ist die abstrakte *Allgemeinheit ihres Außersichseins,* – dessen vermittlungslose Gleichgültigkeit, der *Raum.* Er ist das ganz ideelle *Nebeneinander,* weil er das Außersichsein ist, und schlechthin *kontinuierlich,* weil dies Außereinander noch ganz *abstrakt* ist und keinen bestimmten Unterschied in sich hat. (Enz. § 254)

Hegel goes on in this paragraph to criticize Kant's notion that space is merely subjective, but he agrees with Kant that space is a *form:* "so bleibt die richtige

---

10 G. W. F. Hegel: *Vorlesungen über die Philosophie des Geistes: Berlin 1827/1828. Nachgeschrieben von Johann Eduard Erdmann und Ferdinand Walter.* Franz Hespe und Burkhard Tuschling (eds.). Hamburg: Felix Meiner Verlag, 1994, p. 220.

Bestimmung übrig, daß der Raum eine bloße Form, d. h. eine *Abstraktion* ist, und zwar die der unmittelbaren *Äußerlichkeit*" (Enz. § 254). ["The correct determination remains, that space is a mere form, i. e., an *abstraction*, in particular that of immediate externality" (my translation).] Hegel goes on immediately after this to discuss the 3-dimensionality of space, which is not particularly relevant to his use of the metaphor in mechanical memory, so I won't pursue this text here further.

In § 260, he re-emphasizes his characterization of space:

> Space is in itself the contradiction of indifferent externality and undifferentiated continuity, the pure negativity of itself [...].[11]
> Der Raum ist in sich selbst der Widerspruch des gleichgültigen Auseinanderseins und der unterschiedslosen Kontinuität, die reine Negativität seiner selbst [...].

We can see the rough outline of what Hegel wants to highlight when he employs a spatial metaphor to characterize something that is not space itself. As a *form*, space is an array of possibilities, themselves distinguished only as each being different from every other – though not qualitatively, for in principle every point in space is the same as every other – they are merely numerically different. These possibilities can be occupied by independent actual items that (need) have no further intrinsic connection to each other, but simply co-exist.

Things, of course, do not just exist side-by-side in space: they are related in various ways via the part/whole relation, the relation of constitution, causal relations, etc. If there is some kind of connection among these individual items in space (say, a causal or a part-whole relation), it is not due to space itself, which remains indifferent to such things. Space, as it were, provides the stage or the arena for such relations. Space is an indifferent emptiness, an array of possibilities for various relations among various independent items. It is important, from Hegel's point of view, to recognize that understanding *what* is in space, *how* it behaves, and, especially, *why* it is there and behaves like that, always requires going above and beyond the concept of space to higher-level concepts like force, law, or purpose.

In describing mechanical memory as a space, the implication, then, seems pretty clear: in mechanical memory, it is words, fixed or frozen modifications of sound, instead of things, that enter into an analogue of possible side-by-

---

11 Petry's translation: "Space in itself is the contradiction of indifferent juxtaposition and of continuity devoid of difference; it is the pure negativity of itself [...]." (G. W. F. Hegel: *Hegel's Philosophy of Nature*. 3 vols. Michael John Petry [ed. and trans.]. London: George Allen & Unwin 1970, p. 236)

side relations. These words in mechanical memory are shorn of their meaning and thus are capable of arbitrary combinations: we can memorize by rote mere doggerel or strings of nonsense syllables. As far as mechanical memory is concerned, all relations among words are contingent. There will also be various associative relations that tie words together. Those associative relations, however, are not themselves the responsibility of mechanical memory itself. They depend on something above and beyond mechanical memory itself, just as significant relationships among spatial entities depend on something above and beyond space itself, such as relations of force, law or purpose.

So far, the parallel to space seems preserved. But Hegel also attributes some kind of force or power to the I in mechanical memory. Hegel tells us that "The I, which is this abstract being, is at the same time as subjectivity the power over the various names, the empty bond that holds arrays of them fixed in itself and in fixed order" (my translation). ["Ich, welches dies abstrakte Sein ist, ist als Subjektivität zugleich die Macht der verschiedenen Namen, das leere Band, welches Reihen derselben in sich befestigt und in fester Ordnung behält" (Enz. § 463).][12] He also tells us that intelligence "has made itself into the abstract space of this [mechanical] externality" in which "memory is the abstract support of these determinations [i.e., words]" (GW 25/1, p. 525). Classically, however, space has been thought of as quite inert on its own: there are no forces exerted by space on its own; space doesn't *support* anything; it contains them.[13] The idea that intelligence constitutes a force, "the abstract power of holding this stuff together" (GW 25/2, p. 866), seems to go beyond the spatial metaphor by attributing force or power to intelligence, raising it above a merely abstract form of an empty array of possibilities.

But I think this twist is entirely consistent with Hegel's treatment of space. As I pointed out above, space does not itself account for all the various kinds of relations that objects in space can exhibit, part/whole, constitution, causation. It can at most account for mere juxtaposition, but even then it does not itself explain *why* things are juxtaposed the way they are. That requires invocation of a more complex relationship such as causation. Causation is a higher-level relation, involving spatial, temporal, and modal characteristics; even mechanical causation, we can say, is at both a dialectically and spiritually more advanced

---

12 Petry's translation: "It is the ego that constitutes this abstract being, and as subjectivity it is at the same time the power over the different names, the empty bond which fixes series of them within itself and retains them in a stable order" (Petry, vol. 3, p. 209).

13 The idea that space is itself entirely inert seems to be on the way out, under the influence of quantum mechanics. In fact, relativity mechanics itself requires a fundamental re-thinking of the nature of space.

level than merely spatial (or merely temporal) relations. Mechanical causation is itself the lowest form of causal relation. Chemical and teleological relations are dialectically higher forms. Indeed, to really understand what is there in space and why it is thus-and-so requires a deeper comprehension of Spirit. One does not understand nature fully until one comes to understand nature as the essential prerequisite, the necessary staging ground, of spirit. One does not fully understand nature, in Hegel's view, until one can see Spirit moving within it.

Something similar is going on in mechanical memory. Mechanical memory itself can account only for the production, co-existence or immediate temporal succession of words in an utterance, but such a mechanized memory itself affords the subject (or an outside spectator) no understanding of the thought and reason that may (or may not) be expressed in that verbal production. That kind of rational comprehension comes only when one understands the higher relationships expressed in those words. This is to see the Spirit moving within those words, to understand their point, their purpose.

Hegel rightly insists on the importance of mechanical memory, because he recognizes that our higher rational powers are grounded on the acquisition of deeply-seated, programmed habits of response (to both words and objects) that occur without any thought, even as they constitute essential prerequisites for the development and expression of thought. These habits of response are not innate, though the ability to acquire such habits is part of our biological armory. This is now a widely recognized point, but the notion that these verbal behaviors must be automated in us and occur without consciousness and without forethought or prior intention was not, in Hegel's time, widely appreciated.

Though Hegel makes an important point here in emphasizing the necessary automation of basic verbal responses, he seems to think that such automation will always show up as accentless, mechanized speech.

> A composition is, as we know, not thoroughly conned by rote, until one attaches no meaning to the words. The recitation of what has been thus got by heart is therefore of course accentless. The correct accent, if it is introduced, suggests the meaning: but this introduction of the signification of an idea disturbs the mechanical nexus and therefore easily throws out the reciter. (Wallace translation)
>
> Man weiß bekanntlich einen Aufsatz erst dann recht auswendig, wenn man keinen Sinn bei den Worten hat; das Hersagen solches Auswendiggewußten wird darum von selbst akzentlos. Der richtige Akzent, der hineingebracht wird, geht auf den Sinn; die Bedeutung, Vorstellung, die herbeigerufen wird, stört dagegen den mechanischen Zusammenhang und verwirrt daher leicht das Hersagen. (Enz. § 463, *Anmerkung*)

Schoolboy recitations of memorization assignments may well exhibit this kind of robotic speech pattern; we all have an image of a school child frozen in place at the front of a class or audience, face scrunched, robotically reciting some memorized passage. But that is hardly the universal character of memorized recitations. Consider, for instance, a company of well-trained, accomplished actors. They will have learned their roles by heart, but are anything but flat and affectless in delivering their lines. Actors usually do have to gain a purely mechanical mastery of their parts as part of the process of learning the role, but no good actor stops there. They move beyond affectless recitation to infuse the text with feeling and contextually appropriate behavior, bringing it to life.

We can fit the phenomenon of good acting into Hegel's scheme, it seems to me, fairly easily. I think it actually supports Hegel's analysis. In the actor, the mechanized associations that have been learned are indeed brought into play, just as they are in normal, responsive speech and action. They are, in a sense, at a higher level in that the actor consciously and intentionally sets about acquiring these habits; they are not learned unconsciously by absorption from an enveloping social context. But these associations and habits of response must still embed themselves deeply in the actor, become 'natural' to her. Only then can the actor be sufficiently free to re-infuse those verbal habits with meaning—indeed, with two levels of meaning, the meaning they have for the character in situation, and the meaning they have as a portrayal of the character in context of a production. That there are two levels of meaning connected with two different patterns of association can be seen when something goes wrong in the production. A good actor will stay in character and react appropriately, for example, to a miscue or a piece of the stage set breaking. But if there is something major—fire in the theater or something else disastrous—the character is abandoned and the actor's own behavior re-asserts itself. Being able to stay in character in the face of miscues and other problems is possible only to the extent that the actor truly learned the role by heart and made the character's activity natural, even if only second (or is it now third?) nature.

In any case, our capacity to memorize mechanically, to keep together otherwise arbitrary strings of symbols and connect them in arbitrary ways to experience, regardless of their meaning, affords us a space or arena within which these otherwise merely contingently related 'things' can be organized or subjected to a higher power. As in nature, the higher power organizing things in physical space is Spirit, so in mind, the higher power organizing things in the space of mechanical memory is the I, intelligence individualized as a subjective spirit.

As I argue below, it would be a mistake to think that the space of mechanical memory is entirely subjective, each single individual subjectivity having its own particular such 'space'.

IV The Space of Reasons

So, in mechanical memory, intelligence takes the form of an abstract space in which apparently independent entities (in this case, words) exist in apparent indifference to each other, yet *can* also be subject to multiple different forms of connection to each other, and those at several different levels. At the bottom level are connections forged by the acquisition of habits; these can be entirely arational, merely causal. This is purely mechanical memory. But within the space provided by mechanical memory, the connections among the entities populating it can also be informed by or embody understanding and reason. They thereby rise above the level of mechanical memory, but they do not thereby escape it altogether: without mechanical memory, understanding and reason could not gain a foothold in an otherwise animal subjectivity.

What I now want to emphasize is a point that I think is there in Hegel's texts, but not pushed to the forefront and made prominent. This is that the space created by mechanical memory is itself something universal. This is quite evident in the first quotation I gave above from Enz. § 463, but it deserves fuller spelling out. Universals, in Hegel's view, are always ones over manys, but the scope of the many can itself vary significantly. Sometimes what's universal can be a one over a very restricted range of manys—say, just the many ideas or representations in a single subjective spirit, an individual person. But I do not believe that this is the form of universality Hegel has in mind for the universal that is intelligence.

Intelligence is possible only as a socially distributed phenomenon. Any one person's intelligence is, at least in part, a function of connections of inheritance, transmission, and communication among other intelligences more generally. There is no reason to believe that the abstract space populated by words in mechanical memory is necessarily restricted to individual subjective spirits, each entirely divorced from all the others. Words themselves are communal possessions. A sound associated habitually with some circumstance that causally evokes it (or that it evokes) does not thereby become a *word*. It becomes a word only when the connection is repeated and, indeed, becomes systematic within a linguistic community, tied to other words and circumstances in more-or-less complex patterns of association that ultimately are recognized to have normative force (namely, the right and the wrong ways to use the words).

Thus, though it may be the case that in each human being there is an abstract "space" populated by words that can, in mechanical memory, be connected in arbitrary patterns, this structural feature of human kind subserves the fact that, and makes sense only because, humans are essentially social creatures that belong to linguistic communities and come to use words in norm-governed ways.

Viewed this way, the "abstract space" that Hegel postulates in association with mechanical memory sounds a good deal like the precursor to or presupposition of what Sellars (as well as such of his followers as Brandom and McDowell) called the "logical space of reasons."[14] The logical space of reasons, of course, is not a space in which items sit independent of each other in arbitrary juxtaposition. It is a space in which there are preferred pathways connecting one thing to another and disconnecting some things from others. Relations of implication and relations of evidential relevance tie items together and permit a kind of dynamism in which one can be said to move within that space from one position to another. Relations of contrariety and contradiction keep items distant from each other, blocking movement between them, even while tying them together with the bonds of mutual relevance.

The logical space of reasons is, of course, an abstract 'space' constituted of possible positions or locations that are defined by their connections and relations to other possible positions or locations. That abstract 'space' can exist *for us*—enter our consciousness as something we are aware of—only because there is a more primitive space of complex causal connections among human utterances and responses. This more primitive space is not 'natural' in the sense of innate, though the capacity to acquire such a causally complex set of structured responsive capacities is innate. The complex, structured responsive capacities must be acquired, and their acquisition provides the basis on which other, no longer merely causal relationships between utterances and responses can be built.

What Hegel has seen better than any of his forebears (even his empiricist predecessors) is the need for a level of mechanically habitual responsive associations that provide the infrastructure within which or on top of which reason can build its own structures. Sellars describes this complex relation between automatic habit and concept fairly well:

> [...] while the process of acquiring the concept of green may—indeed does—involve a long history of acquiring *piecemeal* habits of response to various objects in various circumstances, there is an important sense in which one has no concept pertaining to the observable

---

14 See Wilfrid Sellars: "Empiricism and the Philosophy of Mind" [henceforth cited as "EPM"]. In: *Science, Perception and Reality.* London: Routledge and Kegan Paul, 1963, § 36, p. 169. See also John McDowell: *Mind and World.* Cambridge, MA: Harvard University Press, 1994, *passim*; Robert B. Brandom: *From Empiricism to Expressivism: Brandom Reads Sellars.* Cambridge, MA: Harvard University Press, 2015, *passim*.

properties of physical objects in Space and Time unless one has them all—and, indeed, as we shall see, a great deal more besides. (EPM, § 19, p. 148)

Thus, [...] Jones's ability to give inductive reasons *today* is built on a long history of acquiring and manifesting verbal habits in perceptual situations, and, in particular, the occurrence of verbal episodes, e. g. "This is green," which is superficially like those which are later properly said to express observational knowledge [...]. (EPM, § 37, p. 169)

In Hegel's portrayal, the play of automatic habits becomes visible to us through the phenomenon of rote memorization, but it is clear that it is not (and cannot be) limited only to such scenarios. Hegel sees rote memorization as, not quite a break-down in the mind, but at least a reversion to and revelation of a lower stage that is normally occluded from our sight by its typical involvement in a complex, higher-level phenomenon. That lower stage, the automatizable connections we can acquire among words, turns out to be a crucial pre-requisite for the higher-level (in this case cognitive) phenomena that it is typically lost within.

V Conclusion

Hegel's treatment of memory and the fact that merely mechanical memory plays such an important role for him can be very confusing for those who approach Hegel ready to find a deeply committed, stereotypical idealist in his texts.[15] Such a view (I'm tempted to say 'prejudice') blinds one to the deeply naturalistic threads in Hegel's philosophy. The interpretation of Hegel as a pure-bred idealist that results is far thinner than Hegel's richly textured philosophical fabric deserves.

My interpretation of mechanical memory helps us better understand Hegel's description of thought (*Das Denken*) in Enz. § 465.[16] Intelligence is re-cognitive

---

15 One book stands out for recognizing the importance of these issues in Hegel: John McCumber: *The Company of Words: Hegel, Language, and Systematic Philosophy*, Evanston, IL: Northwestern University Press, 1993.

16 γ). *Das Denken* § 465

Die Intelligenz ist *wiedererkennend*; – sie *erkennt* eine Anschauung, insofern diese schon die ihrige ist (§ 454); ferner im Namen die Sache (§ 462); nun aber ist für sie *ihr* Allgemeines in der gedoppelten Bedeutung des Allgemeinen als solchen und desselben als Unmittelbaren oder Seienden, somit als das wahrhafte Allgemeine, welches die übergreifende Einheit seiner selbst über sein Anderes, das Sein, ist. So ist die Intelligenz *für sich an ihr selbst* erkennend; – *an ihr selbst* das *Allgemeine*; ihr Produkt, der *Gedanke* ist die Sache; einfache Identität des Subjektiven und Objektiven. Sie weiß, daß, was *gedacht* ist, *ist*; und daß, was *ist*, nur *ist*, insofern es Gedanke ist (vgl. § 5, 21); – *für sich*; das *Denken* der Intelligenz ist *Gedanken haben*; sie sind als ihr Inhalt und Gegenstand.

(*wiedererkennend*) because there are already forms of cognition present in intuition and imagination.[17] The grasp of things enabled by language is unique, though: in it intelligence grasps a universal that truly belongs to it, a universal that is immediate (as embodied in words and immediate habitual responses) and yet truly and concretely universal (as governed by rules and directed towards a contextually appropriate purpose, which is to say, as an item in the logical space of reasons). Linguistic abilities, the capacity to occupy positions and maneuver in the logical space of reasons, is not yet the end of the dialectic, for there is still much to be added concerning the appropriate social structures and purposes subserved by intelligence. But how practical intelligence picks up the banner is a story for a different day.

My effort here has been to enrich our reading of Hegel by connecting him to an important thinker of our recent past whose influence is still present in current debates. Hegel's philosophy of mind is far from antiquated or irrelevant to modern concerns.

References

Enz. | Hegel, G. W. F. (1970): "Enzyklopädie der philosophischen Wissenschaften im Grundrisse (1830). Dritter Teil: Die Philosophie des Geistes". In: G. W. F. Hegel: *Werke*. Vol. 10. Eva Moldenhauer und Karl Markus Michel (eds.). Frankfurt am Main: Suhrkamp.

The Wallace translation:

Intelligence is recognitive: it cognizes an intuition, but only because that intuition is already its own (§ 454); and in the name it rediscovers the fact (§ 462): but now it finds its universal in the double signification of the universal as such, and of the universal as immediate or as being—finds that is the genuine universal which is its own unity overlapping and including its other, viz. being. Thus intelligence is explicitly, and on its own part cognitive: virtually it is the universal—its product (the thought) is the thing: it is a plain identity of subjective and objective. It knows that what is thought, is, and that what is, only is in so far as it is a thought (§§ 5, 21); the thinking of intelligence is to have thoughts: these are as its content and object.

17 I haven't said anything about – or even mentioned – these faculties elsewhere in this paper. There simply isn't space enough to do so here. I have discussed them elsewhere: "Subjective Spirit: Soul, Consciousness, Intelligence and Will". In: Allegra de Laurentis/Jeffrey Edwards (eds.): *The Bloomsbury Companion to* Hegel. London: Bloomsbury Publishing, 2013, pp. 133–156; "Sensation, Intuition, Space, and Time in Hegel's Philosophy of Subjective Spirit". In: Susanne Herrmann-Sinai/Lucia Ziglioli (eds.): *Hegel's Philosophical Psychology*. Oxford: Routledge, 2016, pp. 214–227; and, of course, *Hegel's Theory of Mental Activity*. Ithaca, NY: Cornell University Press, 1988. Full text available online at: https://mypages.unh.edu/sites/default/files/wad/files/hegels_theory_of_mental_activity_complete.pdf1

EPM | Sellars, Wilfrid S. (1956): "Empiricism and the Philosophy of Mind". [Presented at the University of London in Special Lectures in Philosophy for 1956 under the title "The Myth of the Given: Three Lectures on Empiricism and the Philosophy of Mind"]. In: Herbert Feigl/Michael Scriven (eds.): *Minnesota Studies in the Philosophy of Science*. Vol. I. Minneapolis: University of Minnesota Press, pp. 253–329.
Reprinted in: Sellars, Wilfrid S. (1963): *Science, Perception and Reality*. London: Routledge and Kegan Paul, with additional footnotes [cited edition].
Published separately as: Brandom, Robert (ed.) (1997): *Empiricism and the Philosophy of Mind: with an Introduction by Richard Rorty and a Study Guide by Robert Brandom*. Cambridge, MA: Harvard University Press.
Also reprinted in W. deVries/T. Triplett: *Knowledge, Mind, and the Given: A Reading of Sellars' "Empiricism and the Philosophy of Mind"*. Cambridge, MA: Hackett Publishing, 2000.
GW | Hegel, G. W. F. (1968 ff.): *Gesammelte Werke*. In Verbindung mit der Deutschen Forschungsgemeinschaft herausgegeben von der Nordrhein-Westfälischen Akademie der Wissenschaften und der Künste. Hamburg: Felix Meiner Verlag. Vols. 25/1–3 (2008, 2011, 2016): *Vorlesungen über die Philosophie des subjektiven Geistes*. 3 vols. Christoph Johannes Bauer (ed.). Hamburg: Felix Meiner Verlag.
Petry | Hegel, G. W. F. (1978): *Hegel's Philosophy of Subjective Spirit*. 3 vols. Michael John Petry (ed. and trans.). Boston: D. Reidel.
Brandom, Robert B. (2015): *From Empiricism to Expressivism: Brandom Reads Sellars*. Cambridge, MA: Harvard University Press.
Dennett, Daniel C. (1991): *Consciousness Explained*. New York: Little, Brown and Company.
deVries, Willem A. (1988): *Hegel's Theory of Mental Activity*. Ithaca, NY: Cornell University Press. Full text available online at: https://mypages.unh.edu/sites/default/files/wad/files/hegels_theory_of_mental_activity_complete.pdf
deVries, Willem A. (2013): "Subjective Spirit: Soul, Consciousness, Intelligence and Will". In: Allegra de Laurentis/Jeffrey Edwards (eds.): *The Bloomsbury Companion to Hegel*. London: Bloomsbury Publishing, pp. 133–156.
deVries, Willem A. (2016): "Sensation, Intuition, Space, and Time in Hegel's Philosophy of Subjective Spirit". In: Susanne Herrmann-Sinai/Lucia Ziglioli (eds.): *Hegel's Philosophical Psychology*. Oxford: Routledge, pp. 214–227.
Hegel, G. W. F. (1971): *Hegel's Philosophy of Mind*. W. Wallace and A. V. Miller (trans.). New York: Oxford University Press.
Hegel, G. W. F. (1970): *Hegel's Philosophy of Nature*. 3 vols. Michael John Petry (ed. and trans.). London: George Allen & Unwin.
Hegel, G. W. F. (1994): *Vorlesungen über die Philosophie des Geistes: Berlin 1827/1828. Nachgeschrieben von Johann Eduard Erdmann und Ferdinand Walter*. Franz Hespe und Burkhard Tuschling (eds.). Hamburg: Felix Meiner Verlag.
McCumber, John (1993): *The Company of Words: Hegel, Language, and Systematic Philosophy*. Evanston, IL: Northwestern University Press.
McDowell, John (1994): *Mind and World*. Cambridge, MA: Harvard University Press.

Andreja Novakovic

Hegel on Passion in History

Abstract. *Hegel claims that nothing truly great has ever been accomplished in history without passion. In this paper I aim to explain what he means by passion and why he holds it in such high esteem, even though he thinks that its great contribution is limited to historical contexts. I consider the role of passion in the cunning of reason, proposing that passion be understood as a concrete expression of reason. I also argue that passion illuminates the structure of motivation in general, specifically the relationship between "universality" and "particularity" embodied in what Hegel refers to as the matter-at-hand. Finally, I turn to the peculiarity of passion, showing that passion in the historically relevant sense differs from other motives because it is invested in an unrealized cause and involves the sacrifice of ordinary life.*

Hegel behauptet, dass in der Geschichte nichts Großes ohne Leidenschaft erreicht worden ist. In diesem Beitrag wird erklärt, was Hegel unter Leidenschaft versteht und warum er sie so hoch einschätzt, obwohl er ihre Bedeutung auf die Geschichte begrenzt sieht. Das Verhältnis von Leidenschaft und der List der Vernunft wird bedacht und der Vorschlag gemacht, dass man die Leidenschaft als einen konkreten Ausdruck der Vernunft betrachten soll. Weiterhin wird dafür argumentiert, dass Leidenschaft die Struktur von Motivation im Allgemeinen ausdrückt, genauer die Beziehung von ,Allgemeinheit' und ,Besonderheit', die in dem, was Hegel als die Sache bezeichnet, verkörpert ist. Zum Schluss wird die Eigentümlichkeit der Leidenschaft betrachtet und gezeigt, dass Leidenschaft im historisch relevanten Sinne sich dadurch auszeichnet, dass sie auf unverwirklichte Ziele gerichtet ist und das Opfern des Alltags erfordert.

§ 1 Introduction

"We must say that, in general, nothing great in this world has been accomplished without passion" (VPG, p. 38). This is an assertion that comes from Hegel himself and appears in the Introduction to his Philosophy of History. Although it is one that any Google search of Hegel quotes will yield, reading it is always a little jarring: could *Hegel* have written this? Isn't he a critic of all those things associated with passion, like enthusiasm, fervor, frenzy? Doesn't it contradict his basic temperament and the temperament he recommends? But he quickly adds: "Passion is seen as something that is not quite right, something that is more or less

https://doi.org/10.1515/9783110673692-011

bad: the human being should have no passions. Passion is also not quite the fitting term for what I want to express here" (VPG, p. 38). My aim in this paper is to explain what Hegel does want to express with this term and why he penned this general proposition in its favor. He identifies passion as a psychological phenomenon (E III § 473) because it belongs among the natural capacities and forms of activity of individuals (E III § 229R). But he also criticizes those who adopt a "psychological view of history" (PR 124R; NHS, p. 463) and cite the passions of historical agents as a reason to discredit their motives on moral grounds.

In the context of his philosophy of history, passion appears in connection with two of his notorious doctrines: the cunning of reason and the world-historic individuals. According to Hegel, the passions of world-historic individuals are the means through which reason realizes its goal. The picture that suggests itself is one according to which passion is best embodied in individual heroes and is best understood and *vindicated* as a vehicle of rational advancement, part of reason's "cunning" (VPG, p. 49). In § 2 I will address this conception of passion's function in history, arguing that the cunning of reason needs to be understood differently from what we might initially expect. Passion should not be seen as a mere tool, but rather as a concrete expression of reason. It has the power to contribute to the advancement of reason because it expresses, however misguidedly, a commitment to rational progress. Hegel's position turns out to be the inverse of Hume's: reason is not a slave to passion, but its master.

What makes Hegel's account of passion so compelling, however, is that it has implications beyond his philosophy of history. As I will argue, passion has the power to illuminate the structure of motivation in general. Although Hegel definitely does not think that all human beings act passionately, or that they should, he suggests that passion can expose a structure present in ordinary motives. When I act, I take an interest in something and thus regard this something as a good thing to do, as having objective, *universal* value in my estimation. But since it is also my personal, *particular* interest, I am likewise trying to satisfy myself in its accomplishment, which means that it matters to me whether it is I (or someone else) who brings it about. Passion, despite its peculiarities, accentuates the relation between these two aspects – "universality" and "particularity" in Hegel's vocabulary – which Hegel thinks can be discerned in all motives for action. In § 3 I will suggest that their relation can be captured through the term *die Sache* or "the matter-at-hand", to which Hegel alludes in the *Philosophy of Right*, but analyzes in greater depth in his *Phenomenology of Spirit*.

It is nonetheless striking that Hegel reserves the term "passion", at least in the relevant sense, for his philosophy of history.[1] Passion is, according to Hegel, an admirable and redeemable feature of *historical* actions only. So in § 4 I will address the differences between the motivations behind passionate actions and those behind actions in stable social contexts. Hegel emphasizes that passion involves sacrifice of everyday life, that pursuing it requires foregoing conventional forms of happiness, including purposes that are deemed valuable by everyone else. Hence passion tends to look especially self-absorbed when compared to mundane motives. But I will argue that the supposed selfishness of passion is an artifact of the limited perspective of both parties involved, especially that of its bystanders. In fact passionate individuals also act for the sake of the matter-at-hand. The difficulty lies in the fact that their matter-at-hand is partly a possibility that is yet to be realized, which makes it by default more abstract than those for the sake of which we usually act.

One of the advantages of the account of passion in history that I will offer is that it is sufficiently general to disentangle Hegel's philosophy of history from the "great man" view[2], to which it appears to succumb. On my interpretation, passion need not be embodied in world-historic individuals, if these are understood as lone wolves standing at the head of states, people like Napoleon. Sometimes the agents of progress are not individuals who are sacrificing everyday life, but individuals for whom conventional forms of happiness are not genuine options. These individuals might be better described as fighting for a world in which conventional forms of happiness will become possible, or at least possible for a greater number of people, which is at the same time a world in which passion will no longer be needed. This is the irony of passion in Hegel's sense: it aims at its own self-overcoming.

Another advantage of my account is that it can expose an unexpected consequence of Hegel's insistence on the need for passionate individuals in his philosophy of history. When considering past cases of progress, it is easy to conclude that progress is inevitable, due to sweeping forces that are beyond *anyone's* control, whether those working for or against them. This is the view of progress that, to name one example, current narratives of the civil rights movement

---

1 In his *Philosophy of Right,* Hegel does sometimes mention passion, but it usually appears on a list alongside other "natural" determinations of the will. For example: "But the as yet abstract and formal freedom of subjectivity has a more determinate content only in its *natural subjective existence* – its needs, inclinations, passions, opinions, fancies, etc." (PR § 123). Here passion seems to just mean a more intense interest than mere inclination.
2 This phrase is generally ascribed to Thomas Carlyle's conception of history, but Hegel's doctrine of world-historic individuals tends to be associated with it as well.

have encouraged.[3] Given Hegel's own commitment to necessity in history, it might appear as if he shares this view. But what Hegel's philosophy of history demonstrates is that progress is not inevitable, because historical processes are not fully self-sufficient. They depend on the cooperation of elements that are better ascribed to nature: just as a tree cannot grow on infertile soil, humanity cannot progress unless passionate individuals are born, people capable and willing to throw themselves fully into its advancement, and this is not to be taken for granted.[4]

§ 2 Reason in History

I begin with Hegel's doctrine of the cunning of reason, which is the context in which passion is first introduced. In his lectures on the subject, Hegel recommends viewing history as a rational process, a process in which "reason rules" (VPG, p. 20), but in a *cunning* sort of way. What makes this process rational is that reason manages to achieve its own internal goal through changes of historical scope.[5] Hegel claims that the rational goal of history is freedom, and as we move from one epoch to another, the human species can be described as becoming freer and freer. But this is not just a process of approximating a fixed goal, a goal given fully in advance. The human species becomes freer and freer because it is attaining a better and better grasp of what freedom is. Hegel defines freedom as "being by oneself in another" (E I, p. 84), as finding oneself objectively confirmed. Since this is only an abstract structure, it takes the length of history to discover what precisely it requires, specifically which social conditions must be in place to support this self-relation. This means that freedom is not a determinate criterion that is ready to hand at the outset and could have been used in

---

3 Theoharis 2018 compellingly argues that the civil rights movement has been misused in order to discourage current political movements and to promote the view that the progress the civil rights movement achieved was due to the strength of American values, and not to the fearlessness and perseverance of many individuals.

4 This brings Hegel's philosophy of history closer to Kant's, since Kant also identifies a natural element needed in order to make the idea of progress more plausible, though for Kant it is the unsociable sociability of human beings. If Hegelian progress depends on the relatively rare capacity for passion, rather than on a fixture of human nature, it would seem to be even less inevitable than Kant's.

5 Sedgwick 2018 shows why Hegel holds that a philosophy of history, if it is to provide a genuinely historical explanation, must offer a developmental narrative that appeals to internal (rather than external) purposes. She also explains why Hegel believes that it is only his Hegelian idea of freedom that can serve as an internal purpose of historical development.

evaluating given epochs, but a standard that first becomes determined through the very process of its realization.[6] Hence Hegel defines world history as "progress in the *consciousness* of freedom" (VPG, p. 32).

He is well aware that this conception of history will seem highly counter-intuitive to many. If we focus on the facts, what we discover instead is a lot of seemingly random violence. It is thus important to him that we recognize this as a philosophical reconstruction of history, not an empirical study of it. While such a reconstruction cannot proceed without any basis in fact (it is *not* an *a priori* endeavor)[7], it is nonetheless highly selective in which facts it incorporates. Although Hegel holds that history really is such a rational process, that this is not just a comforting view of it that we should adopt in order to maintain hope, he admits that this is visible only from a highly philosophical perspective, a perspective that he himself assumes and develops, and a perspective that omits much, maybe most of what actually happened.

Hegel thinks that if we take his project provisionally on board, we will see that passion is going to play a vital role in this process. At face value history looks like a "theater of passions", which serve as sources of its "violence and unreason" (VPG, p. 34). But his philosophical reconstruction invites a shift in perspective that allows us to see passion as a means for rational progress. What we discover is that reason needs passion because, without it, reason would remain inert, abstract, a mere thought, a mere "ought". Here is a passage meant to explain reason's dependence on passion:

> A principle, but also rule or law, is something inner, which as such is not – no matter how true it may be in itself – completely actual. Purposes, rules, etc. are in our thoughts, initially in our inner intentions, but not yet in reality. What is implicit in itself is a possibility, a

---

6 Pinkard 2017 rejects this characterization of Hegel's philosophy of history as a teleological process aiming at freedom, since freedom was not a value to which pre-modern epochs subscribed. Pinkard describes such a reading as "lazy" and "empirically vacuous" because it means that we are supposed to be able to explain historical change simply by pointing to an epoch's failure to achieve freedom (Pinkard 2017, pp. 2–3). But I think it is important to emphasize that Hegel describes this process as one of *determination*. So even if freedom is a goal that is directing and unifying this process, which Hegel holds, it is not one that could have been fully grasped in advance of its achievement.

7 Alznauer 2018 presents a different account of Hegel's methodology, arguing that his philosophy of history has an *a priori* component: although Hegel cannot deduce specific individuals like Napoleon, he can deduce historical epochs without appeal to experience. The problem with this reading is that it makes it difficult to explain why Hegel's philosophy of history must be retrospective, in other words, why it does not allow us to make predictions about future developments. Also, Hegel does claim that "we must take history as it is; we have to proceed historically, empirically" (VPG, p. 22).

capacity, but not yet something that has emerged out of its interiority into existence. For reality a second moment has to be added, and that is the activation, actualization, which has as its principle the will and human activity in general. (VPG, p. 36)

Passion is supposed to supply this "second moment" that is necessary in order to make a rational principle real, at least when we are dealing with a principle that calls for a radical reorganization of social life. This is, in brief, the cunning of reason – that reason proceeds indirectly, by utilizing something other than itself in order to actualize itself.

The doctrine of the cunning of reason, although widely identified as Hegel's position, has received surprisingly little scholarly attention. It seems to be generally assumed that Hegel's point is pretty obvious, namely, that historical agents contribute to progress even though they have no intention of doing so. They are acting out of self-interest, pursuing wealth or honor or glory or whatever will advance their personal standing in the world. But despite the fact that they do not have much regard for the ends of reason, their actions end up contributing to its progress nonetheless. This is supposed to show that people do not need to share the ends of reason, do not need to intend them, in order for their actions to have rational consequences and in this way aid reason's advancement. In fact, reason is so clever, so *sly*, as to turn their self-seeking desires into a motor for its own development.[8]

There are indeed clear precedents for this conception of progress, according to which progress is unconsciously and unintentionally achieved through individuals who are consciously and intentionally pursuing other ends. One precedent is Kant's philosophy of history, specifically in his essay "Idea for a Universal History with a Cosmopolitan Purpose", in which Kant claims that

individual human beings and even entire nations little suspect that, by pursuing their own intention, each according to his own sense and often in opposition to each other, they are unwittingly directed by the intention of nature, which they do not know, and which their work is advancing, and for which, even if they knew what it was, they would not care much.[9]

According to Kant, it is the unsociable sociability of human nature, the competitive drive to advance one's own standing at each other's expense, that can be

---

8 This version can be found in Tucker 1956, who calls passion the "irrational element in human nature" that is "self-regarding in nature" (Tucker 1956, p. 269). He claims that passion differs from other interests because it does not aim at happiness, but at greatness, and can thus be summed up as a passion for "self-aggrandizement" (Tucker 1956, p. 270).
9 Kant 1977, p. 33.

seen as the vehicle of progress. Although none of us intends the betterment of the world, our individual and competitive drives bring it about anyway.

Is Hegel's appeal to passion as the means of reason supposed to work in the same way? Is he saying that people do not need to deliberately share the end of reason, that they can be oblivious of or indifferent to it? In fact there seems to be a precedent in Hegel's own account of civil society. In this account, as it is usually understood, Hegel holds that participants in the economic market do not have to be concerned with the good in order to contribute to it. Each member is pursuing a "selfish [*selbstsüchtig*]" end (PR § 183), to make a living and maybe also realize his own unique tastes and talents, while nonetheless contributing to something of objective value, which Hegel calls the universal wealth.[10] In this way, particularity, which is the primary principle of civil society, is supposed to aid the principle of universality, which (although unconscious and unintended) in turn redeems this selfish activity. It looks to be Hegel's version of Adam Smith's "invisible hand", according to which "each man in earning, producing, and enjoying on his own account is *eo ipso* producing and earning for the enjoyment of everyone else" (PR § 199).[11]

Although there are parallels between economic and world-historic activities, to which I will return, I do not think that the above description captures the relation between passion and reason in the context of history. Passion is not a means of reason, if it is taken to be internally unrelated to that for which it is being used. My suggestion is that we think of passion as a concrete expression of reason, as a way of directing one's energy toward ends more specific than the actualization of reason as such. When Hegel claims that reason without passion is abstract, he means that reason must become embodied in passion, manifest in it, if it is to be real. Without passion, reason would be a mere thought, a mere "ought". But passion actualizes reason because it assumes its end. This means that passions are not mere tools to be found among our natural resources that are indifferent to the purpose to which they are put. It also means that passions do not come with purposes of their own. Without reason, passion would remain without direction, without a goal.

My evidence comes from Hegel's emphasis on "thought" and on "universality" in his characterization of psychological phenomena, of which passion is an example. As Hegel puts it, "We cannot ever refrain from thinking, in this way we differ from the animal; and there is thinking in our sensations, in our knowing

---

10 Not all selfish pursuits contribute to universal wealth, but only those that are integrated into the "system of needs" and accord with professional norms.

11 Tucker 1956 explicitly notes this apparent similarity between Hegel's philosophy of world history and Smith's economic theory (Tucker 1956, pp. 275–277).

and cognizing, and in the drives and in the will, to the extent to which these are human" (VPG, p. 20). This seems to be equally true of passion, that there is thinking in passion.[12] Another way that Hegel puts it is by saying that passions are "infused" with or "permeated" by the universal.[13] What exactly this means, specifically in the case of passion in contrast to some of the other phenomena on his list, will require unpacking. These remarks nonetheless indicate that passion cannot be fully captured by the above description. They lend support to my suggestion that passion is better described as a concrete expression of reason.

I should admit that when Hegel mentions passion, he brings it into overt connection with the aims of "particular interests" and "selfish intentions" (VPG, p. 38). I think he emphasizes this aspect of passion because he is trying to explain what makes passion potent enough to propel historical change. In other words, passions are not impartial or detached. This is supposed to clarify how those in their grip become motivated to perform actions that come at a high cost to themselves and others. But Hegel has another reason for emphasizing this particular, interested aspect of passion. What he suggests is that it tells us something about motivation more generally, a feature of action that needs to be acknowledged and given its fair due. Hence this historical role of passion leads him to draw some broad conclusions:

> The activity, which brings [principles] into work and existence, is human need, drive, inclination, and passion. Bringing something into action and being indicates that I am invested in it; I have to be involved in it, I have to be satisfied by its achievement. A purpose for which I am supposed to be active has to in some way [*auf irgend eine Weise*] be my purpose; I have to thereby satisfy my purpose at the same time, even if the purpose, for the sake of which I am active, also includes many other sides that have nothing to do with me. It is the infinite right of the subject that it find itself satisfied in its activity and work. If human beings are supposed to be interested in something, they must themselves be involved in it and find their own self-feeling satisfied in it. (VPG, pp. 36–37)

This reference to the "infinite right of the subject" suggests that Hegel is articulating a rightful demand, a demand which he thinks prior epochs have failed to

---

12 In the "Psychology" Hegel claims that inclinations and passions have "the rational nature of spirit as their basis" (E III § 474), though they remain natural determinations and their content could be either good or evil.

13 A similar passage appears in the second Preface to the *Science of Logic:* "in our day it cannot be repeated often enough that it is through thinking that the human being differs from the animal. In everything that becomes something inner, a representation in general, that he makes into his own, language has penetrated, and whatever he bring to language and expresses in language contains a category concealed, combined or developed" (WL, p. 20).

accommodate.[14] It is the demand that I be given room to pursue my individual interests and particular concerns.[15]

Particularity is nonetheless only one side of passion, and given the way Hegel characterizes passions in history, it would be one-sided to neglect the universality that infuses and permeates them as well. As I suggested, reason is manifest in the purposes that passions pursue. This means, on the one hand, that I am representing this purpose under a category, a category that is independent of the specific individual pursuing it, and hence in principle open to others to pursue. If I am fighting for the "revolution", this is a general purpose, not one that is unique to me, even if I happen to be alone in fighting for it. But it means, on the other hand, that I am representing this purpose as valuable, as worthy of pursuit, whether by me or another. It is this evaluative aspect that renders passion a concrete expression of reason as an uptake of and commitment to its end. Here is a passage that points in this direction:

> I will therefore say passion and mean the particular determinacy of character, insofar as these determinations of willing do not have only a private content, but are that which drives and motivates universal deeds. Passion is initially the subjective and to that extent the formal side of energy, of will, and of activity, whereby the content or purpose remains as yet unspecified; but the same is true of one's own conviction, insight, and conscience. Everything always depends on which content my conviction or which purpose my passion has, whether this one or that one is truly genuine. But conversely, if it is truly genuine, then it belongs to it that it enters into existence and becomes actual. (VPG, pp. 38–39)

I take Hegel to be saying that, while I am pursuing my individual interests and particular concerns, I am simultaneously pursuing those purposes that I take to be "genuine" in the sense of objectively good. By drawing a parallel between passion and conviction, he means to indicate their close connection: passion has a universal purpose because it always also expresses my conviction about what

---

14 This right becomes incorporated into a rational form of ethical life: "the individual must in fulfilling his duty in some way [auf irgend eine Weise] simultaneously find his own interest and satisfaction, or settle his own account, and a right must accrue to him out of his situation in the state whereby the universal matter-at-hand [die allgemeine Sache] becomes his own particular matter-at-hand [seine eigene besondere Sache]. Particular interest should really not be set aside or even suppressed, but should instead be made harmonious with the universal, through which it itself and the universal are preserved" (PR § 261R).

15 This lesson of passion is something that Avineri notes when he writes that "the relationship between passion/interest and reason, always implied by historical action according to Hegel, is becoming more explicit and recognized in modern times [...]. This relationship thus becomes itself a criterion for the degree of historical development of any given society" (Avineri 1973, pp. 392–393).

is truly valuable. We might even say that passions have a cause, an object held to be *so* valuable that it becomes all-consuming.

Of course, passions might be invested in a bad cause, in the wrong cause. My passions could be confused, misled, misguided. So, the fact that I take myself to be pursuing rational requirements does not mean that I am right about this. Maybe I am aiming at a universal purpose which is not one, because the state of affairs I passionately pursue is not genuinely worth achieving.[16] This is why Hegel holds that actual, real, genuine reason is more than the sum of its parts, why he thinks that it necessarily exceeds what is contained in individual intentions. Its cunning consists in guaranteeing that these bad or false conceptions of what is universal do not entrench themselves in existence, that they are not permanently enforced.[17]

In short, I reject on Hegel's behalf the picture according to which those passionate individuals that contribute to progress are preoccupied with their purely personal goals – their wealth or honor or glory – while progress happens behind their backs, so-to-speak. While there is something to this picture, since it foregrounds that passion does seek self-satisfaction, it omits the fact that passion also contains a commitment to rational progress to the extent to which it expresses a commitment to the universal, to that which is truly good, valuable, worthwhile, even when it fails to grasp it fully, or correctly. In this way passion exposes the structure of motivation in general, that motivation always includes *both* aspects, what Hegel calls "particularity" and "universality". Even if most actions would not count as passionate in the strict sense, for reasons to which

---

16 In his "Psychology" Hegel suggests that passions can be either good or evil, depending on their object, though which one they are can only be determined in the context of Objective Spirit (E III § 474). Unfortunately, when it comes to actions that take place at the cusp of historical change, the social institutions needed in order to evaluate a passion's object are not yet established. It is worth noting that there are also more mundane forms of evil, which involve taking my own self-satisfaction to be so valuable that I am right to prize it above all else. This would be to reduce universality to particularity, to deny that a goal needs to have any positive aspect beyond being satisfying to me, which would fit Hegel's characterization of wrongdoing more generally (see fn. 19). But it is difficult to imagine that this form of evil could pertain to passions, since it is not clear that it makes sense to say that someone is *passionately* devoted to the pursuit of self-satisfaction – in part because self-satisfaction is not a coherent goal in the first place (s. fn. 21).

17 I am highlighting one aspect of the cunning of reason, that whatever falls short of being how it ought to be is doomed to perish in the long run. This is an optimistic conviction that Hegel voices in various contexts (for example, in PR § 270 A). But there is also another aspect of the cunning of reason, that the productive consequences of historically significant actions exceed what was contained in the purpose according to the description under which it was initially intended.

I will later return, passion allows us to see that action has its source in interest, which cannot be cashed out in purely self-interested terms. It is always also an interest in something else, something that I take to merit interest, in addition to any personal satisfaction in its attainment. He states all of this in no uncertain terms in the following passage:

> One must avoid a misunderstanding here: when we reproach [the individual], we mean that he is looking for his private advantage, without regard for the universal goal, which he uses as an occasion for his private advantage, or which he even sacrifices for his private advantage; but when someone is active for the sake of something [*die Sache*], that person isn't just interested in general, but interested *in it*. Language expresses this difference correctly. (VPG, p. 37)

§ 3 The matter-at-hand

Next, I turn to Hegel's claim that being interested means being interested in *something*, that it is only this relation to a "something" that makes my interest into an interest in the first place, and that this tells us something about the structure of motivation in general. As the above passage already indicates, what I am interested in when I act is *die Sache* or the matter-at-hand. This concept of the matter-at-hand appears in various contexts in his social and political philosophy, usually in the lecture notes. Here is one example: "When I will what is rational, I act not as a particular individual, but in accordance with the concepts of ethical life in general: in an ethical act, I validate not myself, but the matter-at-hand [*die Sache*]" (PR § 15 A). And here another: a properly socialized individual "does not have the self-consciousness of his own particularity, but has it only in the universal. This must be done, so I want to do it – for the sake of the thing [*die Sache*], not for my own sake, must the thing be done" (VRP, p. 291).

One reason Hegel privileges the matter-at-hand is that it refers to an object. The German term "*die Sache*" can also be translated as "the thing" in the sense of something other than myself to which I am responding, which is demanding a reaction. Although I will continue to refer to it as the matter-at-hand, Terry Pinkard has also translated it as the "thing that matters".[18] This translation is helpful because it indicates that Hegel's account of motivation will require an objective dimension, that we cannot make adequate sense of motivation, if we think of it purely in terms of subjective states. Another reason Hegel privileges the matter-at-hand is that it implicates the concrete features of the relevant situation. It ex-

---

18 Pinkard 2018.

presses the thought that, when I am moved to act, I am usually not acting for the sake of an abstract conception, but am responding to what matters in a specific context. Hegel would describe this as discerning the universal *in* the particular, or as pursuing some good thing or another, rather than "the good". But an equally important reason he privileges the matter-at-hand is that it implicates me as a specific individual. The matter-at-hand is also a matter-at-hand because it matters to me, even if it is true, as the passages suggest, that I am rarely self-aware of this fact in the moment of action.

This last aspect is the topic of Hegel's discussion of the matter-at-hand in the *Phenomenology of Spirit*, which appears in his chapter on Reason. This chapter is concerned with a question similar to that of his philosophy of history, namely, what it takes to realize reason, to make it manifest in the world. Reason in this chapter is understood in individualistic terms, so it is a conception of reason of which Hegel is himself critical. What he does is to emphasize that even an individual intention must be the sort of thing that is intelligible to others and so make implicit reference to them. I want for my action to be a direct, yet recognizable expression of what I meant to be doing. This means that my purpose must be universal in the sense of falling under categories that others can grasp, and additionally grasp as valuable, as possessing some positive aspect.[19] But it turns out that my purpose cannot be merely a generally valuable end, if it is to be recognizable to others as *mine*.

The matter-at-hand enters the picture as a way of giving myself a purpose that is not so flimsy as to be easily "obliterated [*ausgelöscht*]" by others (PG § 405). The problem that the matter-at-hand is supposed to solve is that, according to a purely individualistic conception of intention, an individual agent will

---

19 Hegel offers a strikingly similar argument in the Morality chapter of his *Philosophy of Right*. He seeks to show that, once we start with the concept of a purpose, we are led to that of an intention, and eventually to conscience and the good. Wrongful actions are going to display a discrepancy between the purpose contained in the action in question and my particular purpose in doing it. In other words, people do not commit wrongful actions for the sake of the type of action that it is, but for the sake of some extraneous benefit that is supposed to accrue in their performance. "Murder and arson, for example, are as universal not yet my positive content as a subject. If someone has perpetrated crimes of this kind, one asks why he has committed it. The murder was not committed for the sake of murder, but some particular positive purpose [*ein besonderer positiver Zweck*] was also present. If we were to say, however, that the murder happened from bloodlust, then this lust would already be the positive content of the subject as such, and the deed would be the satisfactions of the subject" (PR § 121 A). Interestingly enough, Hegel claims that the why-question can only ever be answered with reference to some *positive* end and that this is equally true in cases of wrongdoing. I take this is to be Hegel's version of the Guise of the Good.

regard other people's achievements as mere occasions for the realization of her own intentions. Such a process of mutual obliteration indicates that reason is not being successfully realized in the domain of being, the domain of permanence. This means that we need to find something sufficiently independent of each individual's personal ends that can serve as a subject of shared concern. The matter-at-hand thus represents an effort to give my actions an objectively recognizable purpose. The matter-at-hand becomes my aim. When I act, I am doing it for the sake of the matter-at-hand. What matters is the matter-at-hand. So even if my individual achievements do not last, I nevertheless intended what happened to them, because my commitment was and remains to the matter-at-hand.

Since Hegel connects the matter-at-hand to work, I will illustrate it in the context of a specific professional sphere, say, the academy. Let us imagine that my work is devoted to Hegel scholarship, that it is for the sake of Hegel scholarship that I do what I do. If I were asked why I am writing the things I write, I might say, "I am doing this for Hegel's sake, or for the sake of the truth about Hegel". Or I might say something to the effect that I want to contribute to processes I believe to be valuable, processes like scholarly progress. If I am sufficiently in the grip of this frame of mind, I should not even mind being proven wrong by other scholars. Hegel compares this to the attitude of children who enjoy getting beat up because they themselves provoked it (PG § 413). Like Hegel's children, I should welcome the correction, if what matters to me is that I participate in something that will endure, even when my individual contribution to it becomes discredited or surpassed.

But why exactly does it matter to me that I participate in scholarship? In other words, why do I have to be the one to do it? If I am writing it for Hegel's sake, then it should not matter who gets him right, whether it be me or someone else. Hegel identifies this as a puzzle raised by this attitude toward the matter-at-hand: if I did not care at all about who it is who gets him right, why am I doing it? Why do I take it to be worth *my* time? He concludes that this attitude is deceptive:

> Others therefore take his activity as an interest in the matter-at-hand as such and to be an interest in the aim of bringing about the *matter-at-hand as it exists in itself*, regardless of whether this is done by himself or by the others. No matter that they accordingly point out that the matter-at-hand has already been brought about by themselves (or, if not, they offer their assistance and actually provide it), still the former consciousness is already far beyond the point where they think he is supposed to be. What interests him about the matter-at-hand is what it has to do with his *own* engagements, and when they become fully aware that was what he meant by "*the matter-at-hand*", they find that they have been deceived. However, their haste to offer their assistance in fact itself consisted in nothing but

their own desire to see and to show off not the *matter-at-hand* but merely *their own* activities, i.e., they wanted to deceive the others in exactly the same manner in which they complain about having been deceived. (PG § 416)

It could sound as if Hegel is saying that people who claim to care about the matter-at-hand are hypocrites who do not care about it. But Hegel's target is a righteous attitude that claims to care *only* about the matter-at-hand, about the matter-at-hand *itself*, "*die Sache selbst*". Hegel's point is not that no one ever cares about it, but that these righteous devotees misrepresent their own motivations in a one-sided way. What matters to *anyone* acting for the sake of the matter-at-hand is both, that the matter-at-hand get done and that I be the one to do it. I would not be doing it, if it did not matter to me that it be accomplished. But I also would not be doing it, if I were completely indifferent to who accomplishes it. The matter-at-hand is itself a coin with two sides.

It is for this reason that I believe the matter-at-hand to be integral to Hegel's account of "interest", and hence of motivation. As Hegel puts it, when I am interested in something, I am interested in *something*, in a matter distinguishable from me. This something manifests universality by reflecting which general purpose I take to be good, valuable, worth pursuing. But when I am interested in something, it is also true that I am the one who is interested in it, that I am seeking self-satisfaction in its accomplishment, and that it therefore matters to me that I be the one to do it. In short, I am moved by this something only if it is *my* interest, something that reflects my particularity, too. I am deliberately leaving this aspect of particularity open-ended, for it could be filled out in different ways. It could be that I want the matter-at-hand, that I enjoy it, that it gives me pleasure. Or it could be that I am the only one around, or that I am best positioned to do it – in short, that my circumstances single me out – so that if I really want to see it get done, I better do it myself. Hegel's view is not so narrow as to reduce particularity to inclination, as if I cannot be moved to act unless I expect that the desires I already have will be thereby satiated.

Hegel's aim in this chapter from the *Phenomenology of Spirit* is to identify the elements that need to be present in order for a deed to count as motivated, as interested. What I am suggesting is that these elements are in equal measure "universality" and "particularity". Universality alone, though essential, would not suffice, since the realm of the objectively valuable usually exceeds what I as an individual am even able to, let alone moved to accomplish. I believe many things to be good things to do, from running marathons to writing poetry, without being motivated to do most of them. So why am I writing about Hegel instead of fighting for the revolution? This decision need not reflect what I believe to be of higher value, objectively speaking. Rather, my choice of profession incorporates my particularity, perhaps my specific predispositions and predilections, in addition to my convictions about which lines of work are worthwhile.

I mentioned that there are parallels between economic and world-historic activities, which have to do with the fact that they are both forms of *work*, even if some are financially compensated and others are not. There is a similar sense of devotion involved, which is perfectly compatible with finding personal satisfaction in doing them. That said, there is something about working within a stable social context that shows the matter-at-hand in its proper place as an object that is actual. To repeat, Hegel ascribes the following attitude to socialized individuals: "this must be done, so I want to do it – for the sake of the matter-at hand, not for my own sake, must the matter-at-hand be done" (VRP, p. 291) and "I act not as a particular individual, but in accordance with the concepts of ethical life in general" (PR § 15 A). As I read such passages, Hegel is issuing a warning against treating universality and particularity as two mutually exclusive sources of motivation that play a self-conscious role in deliberation. Under ordinary circumstances, I am not doing much more than responding to the situation, which is already shaped by a whole host of role obligations specific to me. I am not engaging in reflection in order to find out what I believe to be a good thing to do, or which way I in particular incline.[20]

A waiter, for example, has a lot to do while attending to the matter-at-hand, from taking orders, to serving dishes, to delivering checks, etc. He is responding to the objective requirements of his situation. Of course, it would still be true that he is doing it because he sees it as worth his time, and so as reflective of his interest, whether or not he experiences his job as a vocation. But these rather abstract considerations play at most a role when he is applying for the job, or maybe when he is talking himself out of quitting it. While he is busy being a waiter, he is rarely thinking about them. It is now that his attention is fully absorbed by the matter-at-hand, which is already an embodiment of his particularity and universality. It is for this reason that Hegel states that individuals who inhabit social roles do not have their particularity before their eyes but are fully focused on the universal. The universal is now manifest in situational requirements that are simultaneously objective and relative to me.

In the Morality chapter of the *Philosophy of Right* Hegel thus emphasizes the extent to which particularity and universality are inextricably intertwined, inseparable in actuality, even if distinguishable in thought. Although it is the "particular aspect [that] gives the action its subjective value and interest for me" (PR § 122), it would be a mistake to think that my purpose is either one or the other,

---

20 See Novakovic 2017, pp. 29–30.

either self-satisfaction or an end which is valid in and for itself (PR § 124). Self-satisfaction, which Hegel claims is *always present* when the work is done, is not a possible end in its own right, but becomes incorporated into objective ends and is only attainable in conjunction with their accomplishment.[21] Hegel thus argues that a hunt for the *true motive* concealed by the deed and the temptation to locate it in subjective satisfaction is itself motivated by an insincere moralism (PR § 121 A; EIII § 474R). It is the same moralism he discerns in what he disparages as the "psychological view of history":

> Now this principle of particularity is admittedly a moment in an antithesis and at first at least *just as much* identical with the universal as distinct from it. But abstract reflection fixes this moment in its difference from and opposition to the universal, and so produces a view of morality as a perennial and hostile struggle against one's own satisfaction, as in the injunction: "Do with repugnance what duty commands." This same understanding produces that psychological view of history which contrives to belittle and debase all great deeds and individuals by transforming into the main intention and effective motives [*Triebfeder*] of actions those inclinations and passions, which were simultaneously satisfied by the substantial efficacy, along with fame and honor and other consequences – indeed that whole particular aspect which it has declared in advance to be inherently bad. (PR § 124R)[22]

§ 4 Peculiarity of Passion

Last, I turn to the peculiarities of passionate actions, specifically Hegel's claim that passion has a special role to play in motivating actions of historical significance. If all actions are interested in this double-sense, what sets passionate actions apart? Hegel states that passion differs from all other interests because it is

---

21 This seems to be a version of the paradox of hedonism: that happiness cannot be an end in its own right, but can only be attained as the side-effect of pursuing of other valuable ends. It also suggests that evil actions, when they involve confusing particularity for universality, are self-undermining.

22 In this remark Hegel also claims that "such reflection fixates on the subjective side of great individuals [...] and overlooks their substantial element in this edifice of vanity; – it is the view of the psychological valet, for whom there are no heroes, not because the latter are not heroes, but because the former is only a valet" (PR § 124R). See also VPG, p. 48. This is a point he already made in as early as the "*Landstände-Schrift*": "the so-called hidden motives and intentions of particular individuals, anecdotes and subjective impressions were taken to be most important in the psychological view of history, which was popular until recently. This view has, however, now become discredited, and history strives again, according to its dignity, to present the nature and path of the substantial matter-at-hand and to know the character of the agents from that which they do" (NHS, p. 463).

an interest that comes at the cost of all other interests, something which other interests usually do not. He gives the following definition:

> We call an interest a passion insofar as the entire individuality, to the neglect of all other interests and purposes one has and can have, places every last fiber and ounce of will in the service of an object [*Gegenstand*] and concentrates all of its needs and powers in this purpose [...] what I understand by this word "passion" in general is human activity from particular interests, from special purposes, or (if you like) from self-seeking intentions, and indeed such that human beings invest the entire energy of their willing and of their character at the cost of what else can be a goal, even of everything else. (VPG, p. 38)

He offers a similar definition in his "Psychology", in which he characterizes passion in purely formal terms as a subject's investment of all "living spiritual interest, talents, character, enjoyment in *one* content" (E III § 474). Both emphasize that passion involves an overwhelming and exclusive devotion to one goal (E III § 473), which suggests that passions are in principle incompatible with living integrated and varied lives. According to this definition, a passionate person would be someone who is fully devoted to a single object, whatever it may be.

This is in any case a familiar conception of passion, emphasizing that passions are overwhelming and exclusive in ways in which other motives are not. But when Hegel claims that passion is "not quite the fitting term for what [he] wants to express here" (VPG, p. 38), he has something even narrower in mind. I want to suggest that passion in his philosophy of history includes constraints on its possible object and that this changes what he means by passion in this context. Hegel wants the term to designate the placing of the individual's entire energy in the service of a goal that lies beyond those socially available. An interest would then be a passion only if it calls for sacrifice of ordinary life, not just in terms of neglect, but of outright opposition. This would make passion essentially revolutionary, which means that it would be inappropriate to describe waiters or scholars as "passionate" in the relevant sense, at least under normal circumstances.[23] I think that Hegel prefers this conception of passion in the historical context because he wants to single out that rare motive capable of performing this arduous role of uprooting an established social order and thus ushering the next step in the advancement of reason.

---

23 This is not to deny that there are people who display a formally similar devoting to conventional goals by placing their entire energy into being a waiter or a scholar. Although Hegel would not consider such devotion to be "passionate" in this narrower sense, he might find it perfectly acceptable in the context of ethical life. There could also be people who pursue conventional goals in ways that exceed available possibilities, perhaps by demanding that these goals become more widely available. I will give examples of this latter case below.

In § 2 I argued that passions, despite their peculiarities, tell us something about the structure of motivation in general. Now I want to suggest that it might be precisely in virtue of their peculiarities that they make this structure so vivid. Passion can help us see the interdependence between universality and particularity because, in passion, it looks like they have come apart. First, passionate actions are so all-enveloping, consuming one's whole sense of self, that they tend to appear especially selfish to others. As Hegel puts it, "This particular [passionate] content is so bound up with a human being's will that it comprises everything that determines him and is inseparable from him, then it is through it that the human being is who he is" (VPG, p. 38). So, it can appear as if you are sacrificing everything, all of your role obligations, for your own individual self-actualization. Hegel thinks that this is the reason that passion is usually regarded as wrong or bad, to be eradicated or subdued. From the standpoint of those who value these other goals, it may seem like a highly self-absorbed life, a life lived at the expense of other valuable pursuits.

But Hegel thinks that this would be "to overlook their substantial element in this edifice of vanity" (PR § 124R), for passions are no less expressive of one's commitment to the universal. Like other interests, they are an interest in *something* and derive their orientation from one's convictions about what is good, valuable, worthwhile. The difference is that these convictions are often opposed to the interests of those whose particular purposes are supported by the status quo, in whose survival they are thus invested. This is why passionate actions look, on the one hand, so indifferent to particularity in the sense of the needs and desires we ordinarily have – the need for intimacy, the desire for stability, etc. It is also why they look, on the other hand, so indifferent to universality in the sense of what is recognized as valuable – family, career, etc. In the *Philosophy of Right* Hegel cautions that "he who does not know to despise public opinion, as he here and there hears it, will never achieve what is great" (PR § 318 A). While passions are devoted to a cause, it is a cause whose legitimacy is not already widely acknowledged. Indeed, Hegel describes it as a cause that might not even be visible to others, that might not be cognitively available to them, if it is only now beginning to dawn.

Although Hegel voices some reservations about the term "passion", he chooses it because it connotes two relevant features of the motive in question: that passion involves suffering, since it requires risking struggle, retaliation, and alienation, and that passions have a passive dimension when they are responsive to objective requirements. This latter feature is what makes passions so ambivalent, since some passions are misguided and fail to track genuinely objective requirements. It is often difficult, though not always impossible, to tell whether or not they are indeed on the side of progress. If the passion is sufficiently innovative in its aim, this might not be something that either the agent or the bystanders can conclusively determine. But when reconsidered in retrospect, we can see that some passionate people were responsive to the matter-at-hand.

For example, Rosa Parks was responding to what the situation required when she refused to get up from a segregated seat. She was reacting to the injustice of her circumstances. But she was also acting on behalf of a vision that had and has not yet been adequately realized, challenging the established order to uphold the principle of equality to which it was ostensibly committed. In order to understand her seemingly humble act, it is important to acknowledge the vast scope of her vision. Rosa Parks was a lifelong activist who fought against oppression both in the US and abroad. The Montgomery bus boycott she helped initiate demanded not just racial integration in public spaces, but also the employment of Black bus drivers, in this way addressing the issue of job discrimination. And Parks recounted that, on that momentous day the bus driver told her to move, she was thinking about the acquittal of the men who murdered Emmett Till, so she also had criminal justice on her mind.[24]

As her example illustrates, the universal purpose of passion is in part a *vision*, not yet an actual object, even when it is developed in reaction to the matter-at-hand. It is the more abstract, the farther it is from being institutionally realized. While this does not mean that passion cannot express true convictions about what is good, it does mean that passion's purpose is still just a thought, an "ought", which makes it all too easy to dismiss or ignore. In one of Hegel's favorite formulations he describes the majority as "valets" eager to accuse historical agents of base motives, especially when it comes to those whose epoch we share.[25] But he believes that this is simply due to our own limitations, because we ourselves cannot see, or are not interested in seeing the principle that is animating their deeds.

This brings me to Hegel's doctrine of world-historic individuals as the "great men" of world history, to repeat this infamous phrase. It is important to keep in

---

24 See Theoharis 2018, pp. 123 – 141. "In diluting it to a bus seat – to something palatable, narrow, and finished – the fable conveniently makes the movement less relevant for where we are today and misses its far-reaching challenge" (Theoharis 2018, pp. 140 – 141).

25 In addition to the "*Landstände-Schrift*", the *Lectures on the Philosophy of History*, and the *Philosophy of Right*, Hegel repeats the same phrase in the *Phenomenology of Spirit*: "There are no heroes for the valet; but not because the former is not a hero, but because the latter is – a valet, who deals with him not as a hero, but as someone who is eating, drinking, dressing himself, and in general in the individuality of his needs and representations" (PG § 665). Here Hegel emphasizes that the valet is unable to see the hero as a hero because he is interacting with him as a particular individual.

mind that Hegel has an exceedingly narrow conception of world history. Only those events that propelled radical paradigm shift in the *consciousness of freedom* – so shifts from "freedom of one" to "freedom of some" to "freedom of all" – are included (VPG, p. 31). His criteria for world-historic individuals are correspondingly extremely demanding. Hegel seems to think that there were to date a total of four world-historic individuals in the strict sense: Socrates, Alexander, Cesar, and Napoleon. Since this restriction on whose deeds count as historically significant severely limits the continuing relevance of his project, I will instead consider agents who acted on a smaller scale, but also contributed to the realization of freedom. Even when they did not introduce major paradigm-shifts in the consciousness of freedom, they did shift public awareness of what it takes to institute freedom for all.

One thing to note about such individuals is that they might not be much easier to identify during their own time. We can only determine who contributed to the realization of freedom after the relevant actions and their purposes have unfolded. Sometimes (though not always) we have to wait and see whose animating principles will stand the test of time, will vindicate themselves as rational in actuality. And even when we can know that someone is indeed pursuing a purpose that is genuine in Hegel's sense, as in Rosa Park's case, there is no way to predict whose actions will leave a mark, since their historical impact is often a matter of luck.[26] Why is it that we have a statue in celebration of Rosa Parks, but not one in celebration of Mae Mallory? Mallory fought for desegregation in New York City, provoked by a visit to her son's overcrowded and rundown school and the sight of its filthy toilets that would not flush. While she was also responding to the matter-at-hand, her purpose was no less genuine, and her passion comparably strong, the boycott she helped organize did not succeed in desegregating New York's public schools.[27]

---

26 Avineri 1972 identified an "epistemological difficulty" in the way Hegel characterizes the perspective of world-historic individuals: "We thus find Hegel describing the world historical individuals as alternatively, (i) wholly conscious of the idea of history and its development, (ii) only instinctively conscious of it and (iii) totally unaware of it" (Avineri 1972, p. 233). If we follow my suggestion, these statements cease to appear in tension with each other. World-historic individuals are pursuing ends that they take to be required of them and they are aware that their actions will be met with opposition. To this extent, they can be said to be conscious that their actions have the potential to be historically significant. But they cannot be conscious of the actual historical significance of their action, since this consciousness can only ever be retrospective.

27 Cf. Theoharis 2018, pp. 40–48. It is worth mentioning that the success of passionate actions is also indebted to the movements of which they are a part. Although Hegel places great significance on individuals as the sole sources of historical change, this seems based on his political

Despite the fact that neither the intensity of a passion nor its intended aim can serve as a determinate criterion by which to identify the agents of progress during their own time, we discover something striking about their passionate actions, namely, that talk of sacrifice bespeaks a privilege that many actual historical agents did not have. If we take someone like Napoleon as the paradigm of the passionate individual, it might make sense to say that he had the option of pursuing conventional forms of happiness and chose to forgo those for the sake of an unrealized cause, in his case the mere possibility of modernizing Europe's institutions.[28] Other people are, however, pursuing unrealized causes and mere possibilities because conventional forms of happiness are not available to them.

An example might be Richard and Mildred Loving, the subject of a recent film called "Loving".[29] The Lovings were an interracial couple who got married in Washington D.C. in 1958 and were subsequently banished from their home state of Virginia, where interracial marriage was illegal. The Lovings turned out to be reluctant agents of progress, so not an ideal example of passion. What they wanted more than anything else was to lead ordinary lives, to be married, raise a family, work on a construction site, spend time with relatives. But segregation prevented them from attaining what to other people might look like utterly mundane purposes. After years of frustration Mildred Loving writes a letter to Bobby Kennedy, which gets forwarded to the ACLU and eventually initiates "Loving v. Virginia", a Supreme Court ruling against all miscegenation laws. Richard Loving is quoted as saying, "We thought about other people, but we are not doing it just because somebody had to do it and we wanted to be the ones. We are doing it for *us* – because we want to live here".[30]

Even those more passionate in their commitment to civil rights might be described as similarly provoked by the obstacles in their personal way, like Rosa Parks herself, whose daily humiliations culminated in a moment when she

---

philosophy and his argument that states require leaders, even if just a symbolic figurehead like the monarch.

28 Napoleon fits Hegel's description of world-historic individuals as primarily "practical" men whose direct concerns were strategic (VPG, p. 46). For instance, Napoleon did not immediately recognize the historical significance of the storming of the Bastille, and he initially straddled his divided loyalties to France and Corsica until it became clear which political project was the more likely to succeed. But this does not mean that he did not come to identify with the principle he helped actualized. For example, Napoleon stated, "They seek to destroy the Revolution by attacking my person. I will defend it, for I am the Revolution" (Roberts 2014, p. XXXVI).

29 I am grateful to Alex Madva for suggesting this example.

30 From an interview with Life Magazine, 1966. http://time.com/3731628/richard-and-mildred-loving-reluctant-civil-rights-heroes/

had had enough, when she had been pushed as far as she could be pushed.[31] Although those of us whose family life is not perpetually threatened by institutionally sanctioned forms of violence might see someone like Martin Luther King as a neglectful parent, he was fighting for a social order in which people would not have to compromise their other obligations in the way he did. The "valets" were quick to proclaim that King was in it for the money, for personal gain. And what he had to endure was aimed to undermine his devotion to the cause, from the numerous bombings of his house to the anonymous letter recommending that he commit suicide, mailed by the FBI shortly before his assassination.

Given that passion is doomed to involve suffering and requires the strength to weather it, it is not going to be a motive of which everyone is capable. It can only strike root in those who possess traits like fearlessness and perseverance. Most people, even when they see that the circumstances call for a reaction, and even when their own lives are severely circumscribed as a consequence, lack the courage to confront them. I opened with the acknowledgment that progress, as Hegel understands it, is indebted to the cooperation of nature, because it presupposes the existence of passionate individuals as its fertile soil. As Hegel would put it, history needs heroes, people with extraordinary qualities of character, even when those include the "capacity to make ordinary people feel that they were capable of doing extraordinary, history-making deeds" (as both Napoleon and Rosa Parks illustrate).[32] He would add that a rational social order, which is reason's cunning goal, is also one in which heroes have no place.[33]

We are now in a position to appreciate why passion in Hegel's sense is a passing phenomenon restricted to contexts of historical change, why it is not something he felt he needed to incorporate into his conception of fully rational ethical life. Although in his social and political philosophy Hegel does talk about the infinite right of subjects to pursue that which interests them, he does not think that this means that individuals should be able to sacrifice all of their role obligations for the sake of abstract principles. But ethical life is precisely that at which passionate individuals themselves aim, whether or not they fully grasp it as such. What they are in fact committed to, however implicitly, is a

---

31 From Parks' notes: "I had been pushed around all my life and felt at this moment that I couldn't take it any more" (Theoharis 2018, p. 175).

32 Roberts 2014, p. XXXV.

33 Hegel is reluctant to appropriate the term "virtue" in his account of ethical life for precisely this reason, because he thinks it suggests heroism: "if we speak less about virtue nowadays than before, the reason is that the ethical is no longer so much the form of a particular individual" (PR § 150 A).

state that will be so inclusive, just, and stable that people will be able to find a range of their interests satisfied in it and that they can go about pursuing valuable purposes without having to fear that their efforts will be routinely thwarted. So even though passion is for Hegel responsible for everything truly great in this world, passion aspires to its self-overcoming, to a world so great that passion itself will become obsolete in it.[34]

References

PR | G. W. F. Hegel: *Grundlinien der Philosophie des Rechts*. In: G. W. F. Hegel: *Werke*. Eva Moldenhauer und Karl Markus Michel (eds.). Vol. 7. Frankfurt am Main: Suhrkamp, 1970.

PG | G. W. F. Hegel: *Phänomenologie des Geistes*. In: *Werke*. Vol. 3. Frankfurt am Main: Suhrkamp, 1970.

VRP | G. W. F. Hegel: *Vorlesungen über Rechtsphilosophie: 1818 – 1831*. Vol. 1. Karl-Heinz Ilting (ed.). Stuttgart-Bad Cannstatt: Frommann-Holzboog, 1973.

VPR | G. W. F. Hegel: *Vorlesungen über die Philosophie des Rechts: Berlin 1819/1820*. Hamburg: Felix Meiner, 2000.

VPG | G. W. F. Hegel: *Vorlesungen über die Philosophie der Geschichte*. In: *Werke*. Vol. 12. Frankfurt am Main: Suhrkamp, 1970.

NHS | G. W. F. Hegel: *Nürnberger und Heidelberger Schriften 1808 – 1817*. In: *Werke*. Vol. 4. Frankfurt am Main: Suhrkamp, 1970.

WL | G. W. F. Hegel: *Wissenschaft der Logik I*. In: *Werke*. Vol. 5. Frankfurt am Main: Suhrkamp, 1969.

E I | G. W. F. Hegel: *Enzyklopädie der philosophischen Wissenschaften im Grundrisse I*. In: *Werke*. Vol. 8. Frankfurt am Main: Suhrkamp, 1970.

E III | G. W. F. Hegel: *Enzyklopädie der philosophischen Wissenschaften im Grundrisse III*. In: *Werke*. Vol. 10. Frankfurt am Main: Suhrkamp, 1970.

[All translations are mine. Some passages from the *Philosophy of Right* were translated with the help of the Cambridge Edition, edited by Allen Wood.]

Alznauer, Mark (2018): "Hegel on the Conceptual Form of Philosophical History". unpublished manuscript.

Avineri, Shlomo (1972): *Hegel's Theory of the Modest State*. Cambridge: Cambridge University Press.

Avineri, Shlomo (1973), "The Instrumentality of Passion in the World of Reason: Hegel and Marx". In: *Political Theory* 1. No. 4, pp. 388 – 398.

Kant, Immanuel (1977): "Idee zu einer allgemeinen Geschichte in weltbürgerlicher Absicht". In: *Schriften zu Anthropologie, Geschichtsphilosophie, Politik und Pädagogik*. Frankfurt am Main: Suhrkamp, pp. 33 – 61.

---

34 Many thanks to Katie Gasdaglis, Alex Madva, Oksana Maksymchuk, Karen Ng, the Philosophy Department at University of California, Berkeley, and the Post-Kantian European Philosophy Seminar at Oxford University for helpful comments and suggestions.

Novakovic, Andreja (2017): *Hegel on Second Nature in Ethical Life*. Cambridge: Cambridge University Press.

Pinkard, Terry (2017): *Does History Make Sense: Hegel on the Historical Shapes of Justice*. Cambridge, MA: Harvard University Press.

Pinkard, Terry (2018) (translator): *Georg Wilhelm Friedrich Hegel: Phenomenology of Spirit*. Cambridge: Cambridge University Press.

Roberts, Andrew (2014): *Napoleon: A Life*. New York: Penguin.

Sedgwick, Sally (2018): "Innere versus äußere Zweckmäßigkeit in Hegels Philosophie der Geschichte". In: *Hegel-Studien* 51, Hamburg: Felix Meiner, pp. 11–28.

Theoharis, Jeanne (2018): *A More Beautiful and Terrible History: The Uses and Misuses of Civil Rights History*. Boston: Beacon Press.

Tucker, Robert C. (1956): "The Cunning of Reason in Hegel and Marx". In: *The Review of Politics* 18. No. 3, pp. 269–295.

Julia Peters

Hegel and Goethe on the Symbolism of Color

Abstract. *According to a central thesis in Hegel's philosophy of psychology, all states, processes and activities that belong to the life of the human mind are expressions of self-consciousness. Against this background, I examine Hegel's claim that human external sensation affords a bodily, sensuous form of self-awareness. I argue that in order to understand this claim, we need to consider the discussion in Hegel's anthropology of how external sensation—specifically, color sensation—assumes symbolic meaning by relating to the emergence of moods in the perceiving human subject. I demonstrate that Hegel draws on Goethe's* Theory of Color *in order to argue both for the general connection between color perception and moods, and for the specific connections that occur between individual colors and particular moods.*

Eine zentrale These in Hegels Philosophie der Psychologie besagt, dass alle Zustände, Aktivitäten und Vorgänge, die zum Leben des menschlichen Geistes gehören, von Selbstbewusstsein charakterisiert sind. Vor diesem Hintergrund befasst sich der vorliegende Beitrag mit Hegels These, dass menschliche Sinneswahrnehmung eine Form von körperlich-sinnlichem Selbstbewusstsein mit sich bringt. Ich zeige, dass diese These verständlich wird im Lichte von Hegels Diskussion der menschlichen Farbwahrnehmung in seiner Anthropologie, insbesondere seiner Ansicht, dass wahrgenommene Farben durch das Hervorrufen von Stimmungen im menschlichen Subjekt symbolische Bedeutung erlangen. Ich zeige außerdem, dass Hegel sich in dieser Ansicht in mehrerlei Hinsicht auf Goethes Farbenlehre *stützt.*

In his *Philosophy of Right*, Hegel draws a distinction between two ways in which human beings relate to their body. On the one hand, insofar as we are agents, we use our body as an instrument in order to pursue all kinds of purposes. On the other hand, there is a more basic relationship we have to our body: there is a sense in which I *am* my body, and this is true independently of whether I ever come to act with or through it by using it as an instrument.[1] In the context of

---

1 This distinction between two ways of relating to the body becomes explicit in Hegel's contrasting formulations "I am *alive* in this *organic* body, which is my undivided external existence [*Dasein*]" and "I possess *my life and body* like other things [*Sachen*]" (PhR § 47).

https://doi.org/10.1515/9783110673692-012

the *Philosophy of Right*, Hegel introduces this distinction in order to point out that independently of whether a person is a bodily *agent* or not, her body is a constitutive part of what is being protected by the commandment of right to "respect others and oneself as a person" (PhR § 36). That is to say, it is not permissible to harm or instrumentalize a person's body even if the person has not (yet) acquired the ability to act with her body (for instance, if she is an infant, or severely handicapped). Hegel describes this basic sense of identity with one's body in the following words: "While I am alive, my soul (the concept and, on a higher level, the free entity) and my body are not separated; my body is the existence [*Dasein*] of freedom, and I sense [*empfinde*] in it." (PhR § 48)[2]

I believe that the point Hegel is making here is plausible and important, both as an observation about the most fundamental way in which we relate to our body, and as a claim regarding the moral and political consequences of this observation. Moreover, this is a point which one is likely to overlook if one ascribes to Hegel the Kantian view that being a person starts with being an agent who can use her body as an instrument. In the following, my focus will be on the former, that is, on Hegel's claim that there is a sense in which we *are* our body even before we start using it as an instrument of action. While this may strike us as an immediately plausible way of describing our relation to our body, the passage just quoted also indicates that in Hegel this idea is supported by a complex theoretical underpinning. In the background of this view stands a theory that conceives of the human body not just as a natural organism, but as the existence of "I" and of "freedom". The passage also gives us a hint concerning one important element of this theory: Hegel's account of "sensation".[3] One of the ways in which my experience that I *am* my body becomes manifest, Hegel seems to suggest, is in having sensations. Against this background, two questions arise: how can we understand, with Hegel, the human body as the immediate existence of I (and freedom)? And what is the role of sensation in this account of the human body?

The first of the two questions just raised seems, at first sight, especially pressing. We are used to associating Hegel's conception of the self with his theory of consciousness, according to which the I is essentially self-conscious, while self-consciousness is a form of certainty of oneself *as opposed to* all external objects (see Enz. § 413). Here, in contrast, the I is supposed to be present *in* an object, the body. Furthermore, we are used to associating Hegel's conception of

---

2 Translation altered.

3 'Soul' and 'sensation' are central concepts in Hegel's Anthropology. In PhR § 47 Hegel points out that his conception of the person or self as immediately embodied builds on his discussion of spirit as soul in his Anthropology.

freedom with his theory of agency, more specifically with his conception of free will (see PhR §§ 5–8). This conception tends to emphasize—in Kantian spirit— the importance of *negating* all of one's bodily determinations in order to act free- ly. Here, in contrast, freedom is said to have its existence *in* a body which as such does not even yet constitute the person as a bodily agent.

I would like to suggest that we will be able to make progress in answering the first question by tackling the second, more specific one first. The hypothesis underlying this suggestion is the following: sensation has for Hegel a double na- ture: it involves on the one hand a bodily state, and on the other hand a mental or *geistig* phenomenon. However, crucially, the fact that it is both bodily and *geistig* is not to be understood in a dualistic sense, as if the *geistig* and the bodily aspect of sensation were two separate elements, to be accounted for from differ- ent methodological points of view (presumably, the philosophy of nature on the one hand, the philosophy of *Geist* on the other). Rather, Hegel wants to show—or so I want to argue—that in sensation, we encounter a bodily form of *Geist:* a bod- ily state which, as such, also has an inseparably *geistig* aspect (and vice versa). Applying the terminology from the passage quoted above, this means, more spe- cifically, that in sensation, we encounter a bodily form of I or self-awareness.[4] Stretching the term a little, we may even say that in sensation, we encounter a bodily form of freedom.[5] And this is going to be important in explaining, with Hegel, why we have a relation to our body which can be captured in the state- ment 'I *am* my body': in sensation (among other phenomena), the body itself af- fords a kind of self-consciousness (and therefore freedom). It will be my task in the rest of the paper to render this suggestion more intelligible and concrete.

In order to address both of our questions, we now need to shift to a different textual basis than the *Philosophy of Right:* to Hegel's Philosophy of Subjective

---

4 One may wonder at this point whether this form of self-awareness is limited to human beings, or whether it can be found in non-human animals as well on Hegel's account. In my view, Hegel holds that self-awareness of the kind we will discuss below is limited to human beings. However, it is difficult to answer the question of what underlies this limitation in Hegel's view, and wheth- er he is justified in assuming that non-human animals are excluded from this kind of cognitive accomplishment. As we shall see below, the self-awareness we will be concerned with essential- ly involves the grasp of certain symbolic connections between colors and moods. From this point of view, in order to answer the question at hand, one would have to find a way of assessing whether or not animals possess the ability to grasp this form of symbolism.

5 In Enz. §§ 382–383, Hegel explains that while freedom is essential to *Geist* in his view, he means by freedom the property of "relating of itself to itself," as well as the activities of "man- ifestation" and "revelation." In the following, I will not explore any further the connection Hegel draws between self-consciousness and freedom, focusing instead on the connection between sensation and self-consciousness.

Spirit, and more specifically to its first part, his Anthropology, where he gives his most extensive account of sensation in particular, and of the most fundamental relations between self and body more generally (or so I would describe the general trajectory of the argument in Hegel's Anthropology).[6] At this point, I would also like to narrow down the focus of my argument. As we are going to see shortly, the category of sensation for Hegel is surprisingly broad: it comprises both input we receive through our five senses—sight, hearing, smell, taste, and touch—and affective states such as anger, shame or joy, which we express through our body. While I will say a few words about how Hegel motivates this broad definition of the category of sensation, I eventually want to focus on his account of sensation as delivered through our five senses, especially through the sense of sight. This is warranted by the fact that the sense of sight, and especially color sensation, turns out to play a crucial role in Hegel's account of how sensation affords bodily self-awareness. Furthermore, in working this out, we will venture into exciting and uncharted territory. For, as I will try to show, in order to understand how visual sensation—especially the sensation of color—affords a form of bodily self-consciousness for Hegel, we will need to look into an obscure part of Hegel's theory of sensation, which commentators have hardly taken note of: Hegel's reflections on the symbolism of color. I will argue that these considerations form an essential part of Hegel's theory of sensation. Furthermore, I will try to demonstrate that and how his conception of the symbolism of color is heavily influenced by Goethe's theory of color.

---

6 Our task here is complicated by the fact that we have several versions of Hegel's Anthropology: we have three editions of his *Encyclopedia of Philosophical Sciences* (1817, 1827, and 1830). In addition, we have a number of lecture transcripts from Hegel's lectures on the Philosophy of Subjective Spirit in Berlin in 1822–1827/28. Finally, we have the *Zusätze* to the Philosophy of Spirit compiled from different lecture transcripts and edited by Ludwig Boumann. My strategy in the following will be to rely mainly on the 1830 text of the *Encyclopedia*, but to also make free use both of various lecture transcripts and the *Zusätze*. When focusing on the lecture transcripts, this will allow me to pay attention to the development of Hegel's thoughts throughout the different years (which gets lost in the compiled version of the *Zusätze*). Since some of the *Zusätze* are fairly long, when quoting from them, I use the following citation scheme: Enz. § x, page number (German edition)/page number (English edition). All translations of passages from the lecture transcripts are my own.

1 Hegel on internal and external sensation

Central to Hegel's discussion of sensation in all its different versions is a distinction between two forms of sensation. In the 1830 *Encyclopedia* version, he introduces this distinction in the following passage:

> What the sentient soul finds within itself is, on the one hand, the natural and immediate, as within the soul ideally and made its own. On the other hand, and conversely, what originally belongs to being-for-self (i.e. to what is, when further deepened and absorbed in itself, free mind and the I of consciousness) is determined to natural *bodiliness*, and is thus sensed. In this way two distinct spheres of sensation emerge. One type of sensation is at first a determination of bodiliness (e.g. of the eye or of any physical part whatever), which becomes sensation by being driven *inward*, *recollected* in the soul's being-for-self. The other is the sphere of determinacies originating in the mind and belonging to it, which, in order to be sensed, in order to be as if found, become *embodied.* (Enz. § 401)

He later goes on to label the second kind of sensation "internal sensation" (Enz. § 401, *Zusatz*, p. 102/73); I will refer to the first kind, which is equivalent to perception through our five senses, as "external sensation" (in the *Zusatz* to § 401, Hegel explicitly uses both terms, "internal" and "external" sensation, in complementary fashion). At first sight, it may appear that Hegel's distinction between two different spheres of sensation is based on a distinction between two kinds of causal chains leading in opposite directions: on the one hand, states of the body cause determinations of the soul (external sensation); on the other hand, "determinacies originating in the mind" cause bodily states (internal sensation).[7] I believe that this interpretation of Hegel's distinction is misguided. The main problem with this reading is that it suggests a picture according to which the 'inner' (mental states, states of the soul) and the 'outer' (bodily states and processes) are constituted independently of each other, and stand in a merely external, causal relation. However, I believe that one of the most important aspects of sensation for Hegel is that in sensation, body and soul (outer and inner) are more closely related than that. As I want to show in more detail below, his view is that the body contributes a formal determination to the particular sensation, and in doing so, affects or determines its content. In sensation, a bodily process is therefore neither just the cause, nor just the effect of a mental state (a state of the soul); rather, it determines the content of the relevant mental state. In

---

7 I understand 'cause' here in the sense of 'efficient cause'. Accordingly, the notion that body and soul are related as causes in a broader sense of the term is not affected by the following argument.

other words, in sensation, a state of the soul is partly *constituted* by being embodied (in a certain way); being embodied (in a certain way) is what gives the sensation its particular content. I believe that this is what Hegel has in mind when he states: "Sensation in general is the healthy participation of the individual mind in its bodiliness." (Enz. § 401)

When it comes to internal sensation, avoiding a causal reading is particularly difficult. What Hegel refers to with this term are affective states that are *expressed* in bodily processes, such as shame (expressed in blushing), sadness (expressed in crying) and joy (expressed in laughing or smiling). Here again, however, his idea is not that shame, sadness, and joy have a certain phenomenal quality and cognitive content independently of being embodied, which then, in a second and separate step, also becomes manifest in the body. Rather, his view seems to be that their particular form of embodiment partly constitutes their definite quality and cognitive content. Feeling ashamed, for instance, does not cause blushing. Rather, my blushing contributes to the way it is like for me to be ashamed.[8]

I would suggest that it is precisely this content-determining role of the body which is shared in Hegel's view by states such as blushing from shame on the one hand, and having external sensuous experiences on the other hand. *This is what motivates Hegel to group such otherwise heterogeneous phenomena into one category, the category of sensation*. At the same time, this means that sensation for Hegel is *essentially* a state in which the 'outer' partly determines the content of the 'inner'. In the following, I am going to concentrate on external sensation and work out how the content-determining role of the body becomes manifest in this case.

---

8 Because the way in which an affective state is embodied determines its cognitive and qualitative content in his view, Hegel faces the theoretical task of showing what precisely its typical form of embodiment contributes to the qualitative and cognitive content of an affective state. For instance, Hegel raises the question of why sadness is expressed in crying, rather than, say, in coughing or goose bumps. But in contrast to the 18th and 19th century physiologists who he is studying, such as J. H. F. Autenrieth, he does not consider this as a causal question, i.e. a question about the causal chains through which inner states are connected to external bodily processes. Rather, Hegel's view seems to be that the shedding of tears adds something to the qualitative and cognitive content of being sad. Specifically, it brings with it a feeling and awareness of the dissolution of one's identity which forms part of feelings of deep sadness. In this way, it draws our attention to the fact that the self as a whole is at stake when we're sad. If this is correct, it renders support to the thesis that sensation (in this case, internal sensation) affords a bodily form of self-awareness in Hegel's view. On Hegel's non-causal account of the expression of affective states, see also Wolff 1992, p. 191.

One of Hegel's guiding ideas in his discussion of outer sensation is that our five senses form a system: "The senses form the simple system of specific corporeal functions" (Enz. § 401). What he means by this is that each sense is distinguished by a certain form which in turn determines the content of the sensuous input delivered through this particular sense. Furthermore, the different forms, when taken together, constitute a whole—a system. As we will see shortly, the formal determination contributed by the sense modalities goes beyond the simple fact that what is delivered through sight is something visible, what is delivered through hearing is audible, what is delivered through touch is touchable, etc. Throughout his different lecture courses on Subjective Spirit in 1822–1827/28,[9] Hegel is experimenting with different ways of how precisely to conceive the system of the five senses. What remains constant throughout, however, is that his systematization revolves around different ways in which the sensing subject senses *herself* in receiving input of different sensory modalities. For instance, Hegel consistently associates the sense of sight with the form of "ideality". In his 1827/28 lecture course, he describes this form in the following way:

> When we see, we see an object. But we do not sense the eye; it is not present in this process, except when it is weak or sick. In that case, our bodiliness is determined in some way; but not in the case of healthy seeing. The content is thrown out of ourselves, what we see is Being, it is in space [...].[10]

When we see something, we are fully focused on the object we see; we do not sense *ourselves* as seeing the object. "The sense of sight is purely theoretical, we do not sense ourselves in it",[11] as Hegel also puts it. Accordingly, the seeing subject has no sense of itself as standing in opposition to, or being limited by, the object. This is why Hegel is using the notion of ideality for this form of perception: it is marked by the absence of a sense of opposition between subject and object.

Hearing, too, is associated with the form of ideality: just as in the case of sight, the subject does not sense herself in hearing a sound. Accordingly, there is no sense of opposition between subject and object involved ("Seeing and

---

9 See Hotho 1822; Griesheim 1825; Stolzenberg 1827/28.

10 "Wenn wir sehn, sehn wir einen Gegenstand; aber wir empfinden das Auge nicht; es ist nicht dabei; außer wenn es matt, krank ist; unsre Leiblichkeit ist irgendwie dabei bestimmt; beim gesunden Sehn aber nicht; der Inhalt ist ein aus uns hinausgeworfner, was wir sehn ist das Sein, es ist im Raum [...]." (Stolzenberg 1827/28, pp. 656–657)

11 "Der Sinn des Gesichts ist ein ganz theoretischer, wobei wir uns selbst nicht empfinden." (Stolzenberg 1827/28, p. 657)

hearing is sensationless in this sense",[12] Hegel writes). Smell and taste, by contrast, are associated with the process of the *dissolution* of bodiliness or reality: in smelling smells and tasting tastes, Hegel argues, we experience objects as being involved in a process of dissolution. In some versions of the argument, this leads him to toy with the idea that in smelling and tasting, we sense the world as overcoming and "dissolving" its characteristic as a rigid obstacle or limit to the self (see Griesheim 1825, p. 290). Finally, touch is conceived as the sense of totality, in which the sensing subject senses both herself and an object in opposition to herself: "Only for feeling, therefore, is there strictly an Other subsisting for itself, an individual entity for itself, confronting the senser as a similarly individual entity for itself" (Enz. § 401, *Zusatz*, p. 106/75).[13]

In sum, then, each sense modality, and the sensory input delivered through it, is characterized by a certain form. This form, more specifically, is a way or mode in which the sensing subject senses herself in receiving sensuous input. The self-sensing of the sensing subject comes in degrees: while the subject—as something in distinction from the object—appears to be fully absent in the senses of ideality (sight and hearing), it is fully present in the sense of touch (or smell and taste). It is important to note, furthermore, that the form embodied by a sense modality substantially determines the content delivered through it on Hegel's account. That the sense of sight is the sense of ideality means that its primary object is light and—since Hegel holds with Goethe, as we will see in more detail below, that color emerges through the interaction of light and dark-

---

12 "Sehn und Hören ist empfindungslos in diesem Sinn." (Stolzenberg 1827/28, p. 659)

13 Here I follow largely the account of the system of the senses given in Hegel's 1827/28 lectures, in the final version of the Encyclopedia, as well as in the 1822 lecture course. In 1825, by contrast, Hegel offers a different version of the system. In this alternative version, he conceives of sight as the only sense which has the form of ideality. He understands touch as the sense of "pure reality" or "difference", on the ground that in touch, one senses only the resistance or opposition of the object of sensation (see Griesheim 1825, p. 290). Both smell and taste are here conceived as senses characterized by a form in which this strict opposition between ideality (sight) and reality (touch) is overcome: in smelling smells and tasting tastes, Hegel argues, we experience objects as being involved in a process of dissolution, and hence as overcoming the opposition between subject and object of sense (see Griesheim 1825, pp. 290 – 291). Finally, hearing is similar to sight in that we do not sense ourselves when we hear a sound; at the same time, Hegel here does not use the term "ideality" in reference to hearing, presumably because when hearing a sound, we are not directed towards an external object (which can then be said to be idealized), but towards something which is subjective in itself. The main difference between Hegel's two attempts at systematizing the five senses, then, concerns the senses of touch on the one hand, and smell and taste on the other: while in the 1825 account, the senses of smell and taste come closest to representing the totality of sensing subject and sensed object, this function is transferred to the sense of touch in the final and 1822 version.

ness—color. For due to its immateriality, light can be sensed without sensing an opposition between oneself and the object: it is an "ideal element" (Enz. § 401, *Zusatz*, p. 106/75): it "expands on all sides into the immeasurable distance, is absolutely weightless" (Enz. § 401, *Zusatz*, p. 106/75). Similarly, what we sense through our sense of touch—heaviness, as well as qualities such as "the hard, the soft, the rigid, the brittle, the rough, the smooth" (Enz. § 401, *Zusatz*, p. 106/75)—are different ways in which a subject comes to sense objects as offering *resistance* to herself. Sensing hardness, for instance, is a way of sensing an object as resisting me. From Hegel's point of view, describing the content of a particular sensation as merely a simple, atomic, sensuous quality ('redness', 'hardness', 'warmth', etc.) would thus be a misleading abstraction. In reality, on Hegel's account, the qualitative content of each sensation is 'permeated' with form, and thereby constitutes part of a system.

The fact that we have five senses, and specifically these particular five senses, depends on our physiology, the constitution of our body—the senses form the system of "specific corporeal functions" (Enz. § 401), as Hegel puts it. It is due to our bodily constitution, then, that sensation has certain formal determinations, which in turn determine its content. We can see at this point how the body assumes the role of constituting the content of sensation in the case of outer sensation: each of our five senses is associated with a form which in turn determines the content of what we sense.

2 External sensation and self-awareness

The idea that each modality of bodily sensation embodies a certain form is of great importance for Hegel, given his overall program in his philosophy of spirit. It is undeniable that in external sensation, the sensing subject is passive in receiving external sensuous input. Up to a certain degree at least, it is not for the subject to determine whether the outside world confronts her with smoothness or brittleness, with warmth or cold, with yellow or blue. At the same time, Hegel makes clear at the beginning of his introduction to the Philosophy of Spirit that on his account, it belongs to the essence of spirit to engage in the "activity" of "idealization" or "assimilation": "All activities of mind are nothing but various ways of reducing what is external to the inwardness which mind itself is, and it is only by this reduction, by this idealization or assimilation of the external that mind becomes and is mind" (Enz. § 381, *Zusatz*, p. 21/12). One way of understanding this "activity" of assimilation is in terms of a formal contribution by the sensing subject, as specified in our preceding discussion of the sense modalities. Stating the upshot of this discussion in more general terms, Hegel's idea is that the sensing subject is never simply a *tabula rasa* that passively receives sensory input impinging on it from outside. Rather, the sensing subject and her sensory modalities embody a system, and anything that is received as sensory input from outside must be in accord with this system. In this way, the sensing subject assimilates the external by making it accord with its own formal determinations.[14]

However, from Hegel's own point of view, there is an important element missing from the account we have given so far. When Hegel associates spirit with the assimilation of what is external, this in fact captures only one aspect of a more complicated picture. As he makes clear, spirit's assimilation of what is external has a higher end or *telos*: it is aimed at self-awareness. Spirit assimilates what is external only because and insofar as this assimilation amounts to, or culminates in, self-awareness:

> Earlier, we posited the distinctive determinacy of mind in *ideality*, in sublation of the otherness of the Idea. If now, in §383 above, 'manifestation' is given as the determinacy of mind, this is not a new, not a second, determination of mind, but only a development of the determination discussed earlier. For by sublation of its otherness, the logical Idea, or the mind that is in itself, becomes for itself, in other words, revealed to itself. (Enz. § 383, *Zusatz*, p. 27/17)

Now, even if the five senses form a system that determines the form and (thereby) partly the content of our sensuous input, this in itself does not seem to be sufficient to explain how such 'assimilation' of the external amounts to self-awareness. To be sure, it follows from Hegel's account that there is a sense in which the sensing subject, when sensing anything at all, senses herself. She does so in so far as she therein senses her own formal contribution to what she is sensing. However, this does not seem to be sufficient for self-awareness: it only shows that sensation is self-directed in itself, or *de facto*, but not that its self-directedness becomes apparent to the subject. One might point out, though, that at least the sense of touch involves self-sensing proper on Hegel's account. In touching things, we experience the world as offering resistance to our touch, and this involves a sense of ourselves as that which the world resists. Yet this seems to offer merely a *negative* sense of oneself: one senses limits, obstacles, resistance to oneself. Such a negative self-awareness may be necessary for self-awareness proper, but is presumably not sufficient. Accordingly, our ac-

---

14 It is important to note that "activity" here must not be taken literally, as if the soul was an agent performing certain operations on a given material. Rather, it is active merely in the sense that it contributes a formal determination to a given sensuous input.

count as developed so far is missing an important element: it does not show how the system of the five senses as such can give rise to a sensuous, bodily form of self-awareness.

However, that such self-awareness must be present in sensation in Hegel's view not only follows from his overall systematic agenda in the philosophy of spirit (as sketched above), but also becomes clear from his statements concerning sensation more specifically, such as the following:

> When the soul senses, it deals with an immediate determination that just *is*, a determination only found by the soul, not yet produced by it, internally or externally given and so not dependent on it. But *at the same time* this determination is immersed in the soul's universality and is thereby negated in its immediacy and so posited ideally. (Enz. § 399, *Zusatz*, p. 96/68)

Hegel associates the soul with "universality" in this passage, stating that any immediate determination given to the senses must be "immersed" in the soul's universality. This is consistent with many other passages in the *Encyclopedia*, where Hegel contrasts the "substantial universality" (Enz. § 413) associated with the "concrete self-feeling" characteristic of the soul with the "abstract universality" (Enz. § 413) characteristic of the self-thinking I, or self-consciousness in its fully developed form. There is a contrast, but also continuity here: what the soul senses when it senses itself is more concrete and "substantial" than what the I thinks when it thinks itself. Nevertheless, just like the I's self-thinking, the soul's self-sensing must amount to a kind of sensuous awareness of oneself *as* universal. But what precisely does such an awareness consist in, and how does it come about?

We can find an answer to this question in an extensive passage which is contained, with some variation, in all versions of the lecture transcripts, and in the *Zusätze*, and which Hegel alludes to in § 401.[15] The account of sensuous self-awareness offered in this passage may be said to come in three moves (this is more or less true for all versions of the argument, with the exception of the 1825 version, where Hegel focuses on the third move). These are not so much three steps in one continuous argument as they are two tentative steps in the direction of the account which is finally given in the third move. I will discuss the first and second move in this section, and dedicate the next section exclusively to the third and decisive move.

---

15 In the following, I am going to take the *Zusatz* as my main source, and draw on the lecture transcripts whenever it is helpful to do so. The relevant passage can be found in Hotho 1822, pp. 56–59; Griesheim 1825, p. 302; Stolzenberg 1827/28, pp. 661–665.

As a first step, Hegel notes—in Aristotelian fashion—that sensation has a measure of intensity, "beyond which the sensation becomes too strong and therefore painful, and below which it becomes imperceptible" (Enz. § 401, *Zusatz*, p. 106/76). This inherent measure of the intensity of sensation, Hegel argues, testifies to the fact that there is a "relation of the impression to the subject's determinedness-in-and-for-itself, a certain determinacy of the subject's sensitivity,—a reaction of subjectivity to externality, and so the germ or beginning of inner sensation" (Enz. § 401, *Zusatz*, pp. 106–107/76). Hegel's thought seems to be the following. The fact that sensation has an internal measure shows, again, that sensation is not merely a passive process through which something external is imprinted on the subject. Rather, sensation involves a reaction of the subject towards an external input, in the sense that the subject contains inner limits (upper as well as lower limits, one might say) beyond which it no longer engages the given sensuous input. In other words, the subject itself determines, to a certain degree, what it even 'accepts' as a given sensuous input. Furthermore, Hegel points out that the inherent measure of sensation is shared across all members of a species. Different animal species have different inherent measures of sensation, and human sensation has its own characteristic measure: "Already by this internal determinacy of the subject, man's outer sensing is distinguished more or less from that of animals. Some animals can, in certain circumstances, have sensations of something external that is not yet present for human sensation. Camels, for example, can even scent springs and streams miles away" (Enz. § 401, *Zusatz*, p. 107/76). Against this background, one might then argue that there is a sense in which the subject, whenever sensing anything, does not just sense external sensuous input, but senses this external input *as* limited by itself, or *as* subjected to its own measure. This measure, moreover, is a universal measure in the sense that it is shared by all members of its own species. However, as Hegel himself seems to recognize, this latter step is far from convincing. The measure of the subject appears to be a merely negative, limiting condition; and while it is true that anything that falls outside of the internal limit of the subject cannot be sensed, it is far from clear that everything which falls within the limit is therefore sensed *as* circumscribed by an inherent measure. Furthermore, even if the latter was the case, and even though the measure can be said to be universal in the indicated sense, it is not clear that the animal also senses it *as* universal (the animal does not sense that it shares its own measure of sensation with all members of its own species).

Accordingly, Hegel takes a second step. Sensations, he points out, are sensed *as* pleasant or unpleasant. This moves us closer toward the account we are looking for. To sense something as pleasant or unpleasant is to implicitly relate or compare it to an internal standard of what is good or bad for oneself. It involves, as Hegel puts it, a "comparison, more or less interwoven with reflection, of outer sensation with our nature determined in and for itself, whose satisfaction or non-satisfaction by an impression makes the impression in the first case a *pleasant*, in the second case an *unpleasant*, sensation" (Enz. § 401, *Zusatz*, p. 107/76). Importantly, the internal standard to which the pleasant or unpleasant sensation is implicitly compared can be said to be universal in two senses. On the one hand, the pleasantness or unpleasantness affects the organism *as a whole*, because it functions as an indicator of what is conducive to the whole organism's health and survival.[16] In the pleasant or unpleasant sensation, then, the organism as a whole comes to sense itself as a whole. Furthermore, this standard can also be said to be universal in a second sense. What for an individual is healthy or unhealthy, conducive to survival or not, is determined by its "nature", as Hegel puts it in the passage quoted above, which in turn is shared by all members of the same species. Accordingly, the standard implicitly invoked here is universal both in the sense that it pertains to the organism as a totality, and in the sense that it applies to all members of the same species.

Hegel emphasizes that the sensation of pleasantness and unpleasantness has immediate practical valence for the sensing subject. That is to say, to sense something as pleasant or unpleasant is as such to feel a drive to seek or avoid it (see Enz. § 472). Although Hegel does not say so explicitly, one may speculate at this point that this practical import of the pleasant and unpleasant constitutes precisely its deficiency from the point of view of our present argument, and makes it necessary for Hegel to move on to a third consideration. The sensation of something as pleasant or unpleasant points beyond itself, one might say, towards an activity: either the activity of seeking or of avoiding that which causes the sensation. Sensing something as pleasant or unpleasant is therefore not a state which is complete in itself. Rather, it is a means to an end: to the end of life-preserving, self-directed activity. Accordingly, the sensing subject can never stay at rest in the self-awareness afforded by her pleasant or unpleasant sensation, but has to move on to pursue an activity directed at a determinate end.

---

16 See also Enz. § 472. Hegel takes care to note that this sense of what is healthy or conducive to survival or not is unreliable: "Many things can be pleasant that are detrimental to our health; likewise, sometimes something useful is unpleasant. This is why this instinct is something inferior, it is deceptive for human beings; we are therefore not limited to it; rather, we depend on our understanding." ("Es kann uns vieles angenehm sein, was schädlich für die Gesundheit ist; es ist manchen auch etwas unangenehm, was nützlich ist. Dieser Instinkt ist darum auch etwas untergeordnetes, Menschen trügerisches; darum sind wir nicht auf ihn beschränkt sondern wir sind an unseren Verstand gewiesen." [Stolzenberg 1827/28, p. 662])

3 Hegel on moods and the symbolism of color

We are now in a position to consider Hegel's third argumentative step. Since this is the most important step in the context of our overall argument, this entire section is dedicated to spelling it out in detail. At this point, Hegel finally presents a positive argument to the effect that external sensation is intrinsically connected to a form of self-awareness. One central notion Hegel introduces at this stage of the argument is the notion of mood (*Stimmung*):[17]

> What we have to consider at this stage is simply and solely the *unconscious* relatedness of outer sensation to the mental interior. Through this relation there arises in us what we call *mood*,—an appearance of the mind of which, admittedly, we find an analogue in animals (just as we find an analogue of the sensation of the pleasant or unpleasant and of the arousal of urges by impressions), but which (like the above-named other mental appearances) at the same time has a peculiarly human character and which moreover becomes something anthropological, in the narrower sense we have indicated, by being something not yet known with full consciousness by the subject. (Enz. § 401, *Zusatz*, p. 106/76)

He then continues by introducing a second crucial notion, the notion of the symbol:[18]

> [A]t the standpoint to which we have so far brought the development of the soul, external sensation itself is what arouses the mood. But this effect is produced by outer sensation in so far as an inner meaning is immediately, i.e. without conscious intelligence needing to intervene, associated with it. By this meaning, the external sensation becomes something *symbolic*. (Enz. § 401, *Zusatz*, p. 106/77)

By evoking a mood in the sensing subject, external sensations assume a symbolic meaning. In order to see why this constitutes a key move in the context of our present argument, let us start by considering in more detail the notion of mood. What is crucial for our purposes is that Hegel is assuming—quite plausibly, I would suggest—that a mood not only affects an organism as a whole, but is also felt by the organism *as* affecting itself as a whole. When we are in a gloomy mood, we feel that each of our thoughts, plans and efforts is stifled by this feel-

---

17 The German word "Stimmung" has a connotation which is absent from the English word "mood": for something to be "gestimmt" can mean for it to be 'tuned' in such a way that it resonates with something that is tuned in the same way. As will become apparent below, I believe that this connotation is important in Hegel's account. For the sake of convenience, I will nevertheless maintain the English translation here.
18 Both notions, Stimmung and the symbol, can be found in Hegel's discussion throughout the different lecture transcripts.

ing. When we are in an exuberant mood, we feel that each of our activities and thoughts is invigorated by this feeling. It is essential to a mood that it spreads out to affect the organism as a whole.[19] In being in a mood, we become aware of ourselves as a totality. What is more, however, in contrast to the pleasant and unpleasant sensation, and in contrast to more determinate and intentionally directed feelings, a mood has no immediate practical import. Being in a certain mood does not as such imply having the drive to pursue a particular course of action, either in seeking or in avoiding something.[20] There is a sense, then, in which being in a mood, in contrast to undergoing a pleasant or unpleasant sen-

---

[19] It is illuminating to consider in this context that Hegel returns to the topic of moods in his discussion of madness in later paragraphs in the Anthropology. Put in the most general terms, madness is for Hegel the state of a subject in which her identity and self-consciousness is 'assailed' by some particular determination that illegitimately lays claim on the subject as a whole. As a result, the subject finds herself in the 'contradictory' condition of being both a proper self or I (who does not identify with any of her particular determinations, but can put them into systematic order and distance herself from them), *and* finding her selfhood captured by some particular determination: "In this way the subject finds itself in the *contradiction* between its totality systematized in its consciousness, and the particular determinacy in that consciousness, which is not pliable and integrated into an overarching order. This is *derangement*." (Enz. § 408) In order for madness to be possible, accordingly, two conditions have to be fulfilled: 1) the subject already has to be a proper self or I; 2) the particular determination that besets her cannot just be a normal feeling, affect or conviction, but it must have an inherent tendency towards totality, towards laying claim on the subject as a whole. Otherwise, it could not even present itself as a competitor to the sane, rationally integrated, proper self—hence there would be no contradiction. As Hegel points out, moods—such as melancholia—have precisely such an inherent tendency towards totality, which is why they can constitute a form of madness. See Hegel's discussion of melancholia: Enz. § 408, *Zusatz*, p. 175/124. In his discussion of Hegel's conception of mood in relation to Kierkegaard's and Heidegger's, Paul Cruysberghs criticizes Hegel's tendency to insist that all forms of selfhood that are not fully reflective and conceptual eventually need to be sublated, *aufgehoben,* in a more rational, higher mode of self-consciousness (see Cruysberghs 2015). This may be correct as a reading of the ultimate trajectory of Hegel's account of human sensuous, bodily and affective life. However, what is too often overlooked is the fact that the need to sublate human sensuous life only arises, from Hegel's point of view, precisely because the latter gives rise to its own mode of selfhood, thus emerging as a potential threat and competitor to the sane, rationally integrated self, rather than remaining at a purely sub-personal level of operation. My aim in this paper is to shed light on how this is possible in Hegel's view.
[20] One might object that if I am in a bad mood, I am driven to avoid what is responsible for it— similarly to the way I am driven to react to an unpleasant sensation. However, while some moods may be pleasant or unpleasant, most moods do not have such a determinate hedonic value; this will become more obvious when we look at some of Hegel's concrete examples of moods below.

sation, is not a means to an end, but a self-sufficient state. A mood is a state of self-awareness, and it is complete as such.[21]

Let us consider, next, the notion of the symbol.[22] The crucial idea here is that moods are sensed in the face of external sensations:

> Now the mental sympathies aroused by the symbolic nature of impressions are something entirely familiar. We get that sort of thing from colours, sounds, smells, tastes, and also from what is for the sense of touch.[23]—As regards *colours*, there are grave, gay, fiery, cold, sad, and soothing colours. (Enz. § 401, *Zusatz*, p. 108/77)

Even though Hegel suggests in this passage that each of the five sense modalities can have symbolic significance, the examples he discusses in detail are all examples of the symbolism of color: seeing a particular color is associated with a certain mood. Again, we need to appreciate that Hegel is not just making a causal claim to the effect that the perception of a color can trigger a certain mood in us. Rather, he wants to draw attention to the fact that the sensuous experience of a particular color opens up a whole field of associations, feelings and thoughts for us which we experience as being expressed in this color. When I see black (*ceteris paribus*), notions such as grief, gloom, perhaps solemnity, occur to me. I may think of the night, of fears and grievances experienced in the dark, and so forth. In this way, the experience of black 'spreads out' and brings into view a totality of meaning associated with this experience. Note that this totality also unifies the different sense-modalities which Hegel has so far considered in isolation from each other. Colors are experienced as cold or warm, as fresh or dull. In seeing a color and experiencing the mood associated with it, our sensation spreads out such as to make itself felt in our sensory system as a whole, unifying the different sense modalities in one particular sensation. The experience of a particular color, then, does not just bring about or lead to a certain mood; rather, the color is experienced *as* permeated with a mood.

---

21 John Russon notes that the notion of mood plays a crucial role in Hegel's conception of a sensuous, bodily form of self-awareness which, as Russon writes, "precedes the distinction between subject and object" (Russon 2009, p. 42). However, Russon does not offer an explanation as to why mood in particular is a mode of sensibility that gives rise to selfhood for Hegel. Similarly, Lucien Ionel refers to moods as the most basic, sensuous forms of the mind's self-reference within Hegel's account (Ionel 2017, p. 1594). I agree with this, but I believe that this claim stands in need of explanation.

22 Hegel makes clear that the symbol as understood in the present context is to be distinguished from the symbol as discussed in the *Lectures on Aesthetics*, where it consists in an external object that functions as a certain kind of sign: see Enz. § 401, *Zusatz*, p. 108/77.

23 Translation altered.

Just like the formal determinations arising from the system of the five senses, mood is a form which affects or 'tinges' the content of our sensuous experience.

I believe that Hegel here makes contact with our common sense intuitions, as expressed in our practice of describing our moods by means of terms referring to color and light: for instance, we say 'I'm in a dark mood today'; 'Everything seemed grey to her'; 'I feel blue' etc.[24] Underlying this practice must be the assumption that there is something about the mood which admits of, invites, or even requires descriptions in terms of color- and light-expressions. If one now raises the question of what grounds such descriptions, pointing to a brute causal fact about human psycho-physiology ('As a matter of fact, the perception of grey makes us gloomy') would not seem to offer a satisfactory answer. Rather, there seems to be something about the internal quality and content of a mood which warrants describing it in reference to certain color-descriptions—an affinity, or "sympathy", as Hegel puts it, between the color and the mood.

However, if nothing further can be said at this point as to why such an internal relation between the color and the mood occurs—if no reason can be given, for instance, as to why we describe a certain mood as 'black'—we would find ourselves in a situation where we must admit that there appears to be a deep, internal (rather than merely a causal, external) relation between a mood and the sensation of a color, but no explanation for this fact. I am not sure that Hegel can avoid this situation altogether: at least some of the deep relations between moods and colors remain unexplained, even in his account. I will come back to this issue below. Rather than focus on this negative case, however, I want to consider the fact that on the whole, Hegel seems to be intent on offering an explanation for the internal relations between certain color perceptions and moods. He seeks to do this, I want to show, with the help of Goethe and his theory of color. Hegel never mentions Goethe's name in his discussion of the symbolism of color in the Philosophy of Subjective Spirit, but it is clear that Goethe's theory is his main point of reference here. In fact, Goethe is a natural ally for Hegel in this context, because one of the main results of Goethe's theory is that the essence of color manifests itself equally in the subjective realm of color perception (what Goethe calls "physiological colors") and in the objective realm of the physical and chemical colors. Goethe demonstrates that with regard to the phenomenon of color, there is a correspondence between human perception and the physical world: both are determined by the essence of color and the

---

24 Furthermore, as Hegel points out, there is an established artistic practice of symbolizing certain attributes of persons through particular colors: for instance, "Painters have always painted Mary with a blue coat, and Joseph as a man with a red coat." ("Mahler haben die Maria immer mit blauem Mantel, den Joseph als Mann mit rotem Mantel gemahlt." [Hotho 1822, p. 56])

inherent regularities that follow from this essence.[25] Drawing on Goethe, I want to suggest, Hegel sets out to show that there is also an affinity between the human perception of color and human self-awareness (human inner mental life, the life of spirit), mediated through moods.[26]

Let us begin with what are perhaps the most obvious examples, white and black. Hegel writes: "[T]here are serious colors and cheerful, serene colors; also certain colors for the expression of grief: not green, red etc., but black and white, the colorless."[27] And, in more detail:

> Thus for the expression of grief, of inner gloom, of the nightfall of the mind, we take the colour of night, of the darkness not brightened by light, colourless *black*. Solemnity and dignity are also denoted by black, because in it the play of contingency, of manifoldness and mutability finds no place. Pure, luminous, serene *white*, on the other hand, corresponds to the simplicity and serenity of innocence. The proper colours have, so to speak, a more concrete meaning than black and white. (Enz. § 401, *Zusatz*, p. 108/77)

It is a central thesis of Goethe's theory that darkness and light are opposite poles the interaction of which—through the mediation of turbid (*trübe*) media—makes colors emerge (see *Zur Farbenlehre*, § 368).[28] For Hegel, this account of light and darkness helps explain why a particular mood is associated with white: precisely because white (like black) is simple, it symbolizes simplicity and innocence.[29] Hegel makes it clear that in this respect, he agrees with Goethe, against Newton: "White is the simple, and it corresponds to innocence. One can feel in a certain way that white is something simple, in spite of Newton, who takes white to be composed out of seven colors."[30]

---

25 See Förster 2012, pp. 266–272.

26 Goethe's *Zur Farbenlehre* contains a section on the "Sinnlich-Sittliche Wirkung der Farbe". Hegel draws partly on this section, and partly on the whole of the *Farbenlehre* in order to bring out the affinity between moods and colors.

27 "[E]s gibt ernste Farben und fröhliche, heitere Farben, gewisse Farben zum Ausdruck der Trauer, es ist nicht grün, roth pp sondern schwarz und weiss, das Farblose." (Griesheim 1825, p. 302)

28 Herein lies one of the major differences between Goethe's theory and Newton's *Opticks:* for Newton, light as such contains all the colors, while darkness consists simply in the absence of light. For a discussion of whether and to what extent Hegel sides with Goethe against Newton, see Michael John Petry 1987.

29 In fact, Goethe's account of white is more complicated than Hegel presents it here: white, for Goethe, is not simply pure light, but "the last opaque degree of [colorless semitransparance]." (*Farbenlehre*, §494)

30 "Das Weisse ist das Einfache, und entspricht auch der Unschuld, dass das Weisse etwas einfaches ist davon hat man ein bestimmtes Gefühl trotz Neuton, der weiss aus sieben Farben macht." (Griesheim 1825, p. 302)

Similarly, the simplicity of black can help explain why black symbolizes solemnity and dignity: solemnity and dignity imply the elimination of "the play of contingency, manifoldness and mutability". Of course, the obvious problem at this point is that since both white and black are simple, one cannot explain in light of their simplicity alone why one of the two colors is associated with sadness and depression, the other with innocence and serenity. While everyone will agree that states of depression and sadness are appropriately symbolized by the color black, it is not clear to me that Hegel (or Goethe) has an explanation to offer for this fact. To speak of sadness as the "nightfall of the mind" is a metaphorical way of speaking which already describes the state of sadness in reference to color concepts (darkness, gloom). It is not obvious that our shared perception that sadness is adequately associated with darkness can be shown to be grounded in something which sadness and the color black have in common in a more literal sense. It seems to me, then, that here we have reached something like an anthropological bedrock. We cannot justify the association between blackness and sadness any further than by just pointing it out and letting it speak for itself. Presumably, something similar is true also for the association between whiteness and gaiety and serenity.

As a further example of how Hegel draws on Goethe in order to explain the symbolism of color, consider the color pure red. "*Purpurrot*", Hegel writes, "has ranked from time immemorial as the royal colour; for this is the most powerful colour, the most striking to the eye,—the interpenetration of bright and dark in the full strength of their unity and their opposition."[31] (Enz. § 401, *Zusatz*, p. 108/ 77) Regarding *Purpurrot*, Goethe writes that "whoever is acquainted with the prismatic origin of red, will not find it paradoxical if we assert that this color partly *actu*, partly *potentia*, contains all the other colors." (*Farbenlehre*, § 793) It is precisely the prismatic origin of red, as conceived by Goethe, which Hegel draws on in order to explain why red symbolizes strength, power, royalty. Starting from the thesis that all colors materialize through the interaction of light and darkness, Goethe demonstrates that the two original colors are yellow and blue: if darkness is seen through a bright, turbid medium, blue emerges (see *Farbenlehre*, § 155); if, reversely, light is seen through a dark, turbid medium, yellow emerges (the sun seen through turbid vapors appears yellow: see *Farbenlehre*, § 154). If yellow and blue are mixed in equal proportions, the result is green.

---

31 Wallace/Inwood's translation of "Purpurrot" as "purple" is misleading. As will become apparent below, what Hegel—following Goethe—has in mind is a pure red. Goethe comments on the terminology: "We are to imagine an absolutely pure red, like fine carmine suffered to dry on white porcelain. We have called this color 'purpur' by way of distinction, although we are quite aware that the purple of the ancients inclined more to blue." (Farbenlehre, § 792)

By altering the level of density of the turbid medium, both green and blue are turned into novel hues. If the medium through which yellow is seen becomes more dense, yellow is increased to yellow-red. If, on the other hand, the density of the medium through which blue is seen is decreased, blue is turned into blue-red (*Farbenlehre*, § 150). Accordingly, both original colors, blue and yellow, approximate red via decreased or increased density of their medium. However, it is only when yellow-red and blue-red are combined or mixed that pure red, or *Purpurrot*, emerges (*Farbenlehre*, §§ 703–704). *Purpurrot* is a unique color, because in contrast to yellow and green, as well as to all the hues derived from concentration or de-concentration of the latter, it contains both of the original colors within itself. Since it comprises two opposite poles, one might say that *Purpurrot* contains the highest degree of inner differentiation of all colors. At the same time, it also embodies the complete unity of the opposite poles contained within it: in pure red, the opposite hues of yellow and blue are no longer apparent as such. Yellow and blue are, to use a familiar Hegelian term, *aufgehoben* in pure red. The color red, then, may be legitimately described as the most powerful color, as it embodies the greatest possible unity within the greatest possible diversity.[32] As Goethe puts it, summarizing what he calls the "sinnlich-sittliche Wirkung" of red:

> We have remarked a constant progress or augmentation [towards red] in yellow and blue, and seen what impressions were produced by the various states; hence it may naturally be inferred that now, in the junction of the deepest extremes, a feeling of satisfaction must succeed; and thus, in physical phenomena, this highest of all appearances of colour arises from the junction of two contrasted extremes which have gradually prepared themselves for a union. (*Farbenlehre*, § 794)[33]

Let us take stock. The central point I wish to extract from the above discussion is the following: when seeing black, white, or red—or blue, yellow, and green—we

---

32 In this instance, too, Hegel notes his agreement with Goethe and disagreement with Newton: "Newton says red is also not distinguished within itself; white, he says, is the most difficult and purest color, because all the others are mixed within it. But the true determination of red is that it is an interpenetration of both types of turbidity." ("Newton sagt roth ist auch ein Nichtunterschiednes; das weiss sagt er ist die schwierigste und reinste Farbe, weil alle darin gemischt sind, die wahre bestimmtheit des Roths ist dass es eine Durchdringung von beiden Weisen der Trübung ist." [Stolzenberg 1827/28, p. 663])

33 The theoretical synergy between Hegel and Goethe in the explanation of color symbolism is most striking with regard to the cases just discussed, black/white and red. However, in the different lecture transcripts and in the *Zusätze*, Hegel draws on Goethe in order to explain the symbolism of yellow, green and blue as well; though his discussion tends to be shorter and more elliptical with regard to these colors.

do not just receive a visual sensory input on Hegel's account. Rather, we are at the same time 'tuned' in a certain way,[34] such that we find ourselves 'in the mood' to associate a totality of meaning with this color. While some of these associations may remain inexplicable, Hegel draws, as we have seen, on Goethe's theory of color in order to offer a ground for the affinities between certain colors and moods. The fact that a color is associated with a totality, a comprehensive field of meaning, explains why Hegel is speaking of moods in this context: it is characteristic of moods, as we have seen, that they affect a subject in its totality—including the totality of its sensory modalities—and make the subject aware of itself *as* a totality. In light of this, we can now also see how Hegel's account of the symbolism of color constitutes the final and decisive step in his discussion of sensory self-awareness as reconstructed above. Colors are associated with moods. In experiencing a mood, a subject comes to sense herself as a totality —she becomes aware of herself as a universal. Accordingly, we may say that on Hegel's account, subjects do not just see colors, but sense *themselves* as seeing colors. In virtue of the inner affinity between colors and moods, when seeing a color, subjects cannot help but become aware of themselves as a sensing totality.

Summarizing the argument of the preceding three sections, we can say that Hegel's account of sensuous self-awareness contains two crucial elements. To begin with, Hegel develops his account of the system of the five senses, according to which each sense-modality determines the form and thereby (in part) the content of the sensory input we receive. What this shows is that in paradigmatic cases of external sensation, sensation is not a process in which a passive subject is affected and altered by an external impression. Rather, the subject contributes form and content to the input it receives—the subject 'assimilates' the external, as Hegel puts it. This already brings into view a form of self-directedness of the sensing subject in any sensation: in sensing anything, the sensing subject always senses its own formal contribution therein. However, this in itself does not yet give us an account of how the subject gains proper self-awareness in this process of assimilation.

Hegel offers such an account by arguing, secondly, that in addition to the form it assumes in virtue of being part of the system of the five senses, sensation (here especially: color sensation) assumes the form of moods. Just like the formal determinations accruing from the systematic ordering of the five senses, this

---

34 In German, one might say: "Schwarz stimmt mich traurig"—and this brings out a connotation of *Stimmung* which is absent from the English term 'mood'. Here the idea is that one resonates with an external input in virtue of an inherent affinity—like a tuning fork that resonates when the standard pitch sounds.

form permeates and determines the content of sensation. This explains why there is an inherent affinity between the content of the sensation of a certain color and the corresponding mood—we sense the mood *in* the color, and vice versa. However, the form of mood is also special, because it is the form of universality, and therefore of self-awareness: experiencing a color as tinged with a mood is to experience it as seen by a sensing totality. Goethe's theory of color offers support to Hegel's project of connecting color perception, moods and self-awareness in two respects. On the one hand, Goethe's theory is congenial to the very idea that to grasp the essence of color means to understand both its external, physical and chemical constitution, and the way it becomes manifest to the perceiving human subject. Hegel expands on the second aspect of Goethe's theory, seeking to explain how and why the subject of human color perception becomes aware of herself as a unified subject in the perception of color. On the other hand, Hegel believes he can explain why particular colors are associated with specific moods by drawing on Goethe's account of the essence and prismatic origin of individual colors.

4 Conclusion

We started with Hegel's claim that we relate to our body not merely as an instrument for the active pursuit of goals, but also, more fundamentally, as something we identify with primary to even becoming bodily agents. Underlying this claim, I suggested, is his view that the body affords a peculiar form of self-awareness. In the preceding discussion, I tried to make good on this suggestion by reconstructing Hegel's discussion of sensation, especially of external sensation. If my reading is on the right track, then Hegel's theory of the symbolism of color —i.e. the idea that color-sensations are inherently associated with and permeated by moods (according to principles which can be derived from Goethe's theory of colors)—turns out to be a crucial building block in this view. In the moods that permeate bodily (color)sensation, we first come to sense ourselves *as* selves (or as beings that can legitimately lay claim to being ancestors of a proper self-thinking I).[35]

35 I would like to thank the participants of a conference on 'Goethe and Philosophy', held in Tel Aviv in December 2017, for helpful feedback on this paper, especially Anastasia Berg, James Conant, Eckart Förster, Eli Friedlander, Eva Geulen, Wolfram Gobsch, Keren Gorodeisky, Johannes Haag, Andrea Kern, Thomas Khurana, Guido Kreis, Doug Lavin, and David Wellbery. I would also like to thank Dina Emundts and Sally Sedgwick for their helpful comments and suggestions.

References

Works by Hegel:

Enz. | Hegel, Georg Wilhelm Friedrich (1986): *Enzyklopädie der philosophischen Wissenschaften im Grundrisse (1830). Dritter Teil: Philosophie des Geistes. Mit den mündlichen Zusätzen.* Frankfurt a. M.: Suhrkamp.

PhR | Hegel, Georg Wilhelm Friedrich (1986): *Grundlinien der Philosophie des Rechts.* Frankfurt a. M.: Suhrkamp.

Hotho 1822/Griesheim 1825 | Hegel, Georg Wilhelm Friedrich (2008): *Gesammelte Werke. Vol. 25/1: Vorlesungen über die Philosophie des subjektiven Geistes. Nachschriften zu den Kollegien der Jahre 1822 [H. G. Hotho] und 1825 [K. G. J. Griesheim].* Edited by C. J. Bauer. Hamburg: Felix Meiner.

Stolzenberg 1827/28 | Hegel, Georg Wilhelm Friedrich (2011): *Gesammelte Werke. Vol. 25/2: Vorlesungen über die Philosophie des subjektiven Geistes. Nachschriften zu dem Kolleg des Wintersemesters 1827/28 [Stolzenberg] und sekundäre Überlieferung.* Edited by C. J. Bauer. Hamburg: Felix Meiner.

Hegel, Georg Wilhelm Friedrich (2007): *Hegel's Philosophy of Mind.* Translated by W. Wallace and A. V. Miller, with revisions and commentary by M. J. Inwood. Oxford: Oxford University Press.

Hegel, Georg Wilhelm Friedrich (1991): *Elements of the Philosophy of Right.* Edited by Allen W. Wood. Translated by H. B. Nisbet. Cambridge: Cambridge University Press.

Other sources:

Cruysberghs, Paul (2015): "Mood against Reason? From Hegel via Kierkegaard to Heidegger". In: *Hegel-Jahrbuch* 2015. No. 1, pp. 186–191.

Förster, Eckart (2012): *Die 25 Jahre der Philosophie.* Frankfurt a. M.: Klostermann.

Farbenlehre | Goethe, Johann Wolfgang (1998): *Goethes Werke. Hamburger Ausgabe in 14 Bänden.* Edited by Erich Trunz. Vol. XIII: Naturwissenschaftliche Schriften I. München: C. H. Beck.

Goethe, Johann Wolfgang (1840): *Goethe's Theory of Colours.* Translated by Ch. L. Eastlake. London: Murray.

Ionel, Lucien (2017): "Moods between Intelligibility and Articulability. Re-examining Heidegger's and Hegel's Accounts of Affective States." In: *Philosophia* 45, pp. 1587–1598.

Petry, Michael John (1987): "Hegels Verteidigung von Goethes Farbenlehre gegenüber Newton." In: Michael John Petry (ed.): *Hegel und die Naturwissenschaften.* Stuttgart/Bad Canstatt: Frommann-Holzboog, pp. 323–348.

Russon, John (2009): "Emotional Subjects: Mood and Articulation in Hegel's Philosophy of Mind." In: *International Philosophical Quarterly* 49, pp. 41–52.

Wolff, Michael (1992): *Das Körper-Seele-Problem. Kommentar zu Hegel, Enzyklopädie (1830), § 389.* Frankfurt: Klostermann.

Georg Sans SJ
Hegels Psychologie der Religion

Abstract. *Der Aufsatz untersucht die Bedeutung psychologischer Kategorien für Hegels Berliner* Vorlesungen über die Philosophie der Religion. *Entsprechend dem Verhältnis des theoretischen Geistes (Intelligenz) zum praktischen Geist (Wille) unterscheidet Hegel zwei Dimensionen des religiösen Bewusstseins: Das theoretische Moment des Glaubens bilden die zur religiösen Vorstellungswelt gehörenden propositionalen Gehalte; das praktische Moment des Glaubens ist der Kultus. Darunter versteht Hegel die auf den willentlichen Selbstverzicht des Subjekts gegründete Erfahrung der mystischen Einheit mit dem Absoluten. Gezeigt werden soll, dass sich der propositionale zum fiduziellen Glauben verhält wie der theoretische zum praktischen Geist.*

The essay investigates the significance of psychological categories for Hegel's Berlin Lectures on the Philosophy of Religion. *In accordance with the relation between theoretical spirit (intelligence) and practical spirit (will), Hegel distinguishes two dimensions of religious consciousness: The theoretical moment of faith comprises the world of religious representations and its propositional content; the practical moment of faith is the cult. By the latter, Hegel means the experience of mystical union with the absolute, based on the subject's voluntary self-renunciation. It will be shown that the relation between propositional and fiducial faith mirrors the relation between theoretical and practical spirit.*

Hegels Philosophie der Religion wurde in der Vergangenheit vor allem aus theologischer und aus metaphysischer, kaum hingegen aus psychologischer Sicht betrachtet. Aus theologischer Perspektive befasste man sich mit Hegels Rekonstruktion insbesondere des Christentums und stritt über ihre Vereinbarkeit mit der kirchlichen Dogmatik. Das metaphysische Interesse richtete sich auf die religiösen Vorstellungen vom Absoluten und deren Verhältnis zur absoluten Idee als philosophischem Begriff. Dagegen blieb die psychologische Dimension der Religion vielfach unterbelichtet. Ohne die Bedeutung des theologischen und des metaphysischen Aspekts zu schmälern, will ich im Folgenden die Rolle der Psychologie für ein angemessenes Verständnis der Hegelschen Religionsphilosophie herausstellen. Zu diesem Zweck werde ich zunächst darlegen, wie Hegel seine Berliner *Vorlesungen über die Philosophie der Religion* nach Kategorien gegliedert hat, die der Philosophie des subjektiven Geistes, genauer dem Abschnitt über die Psychologie entstammen. Anschließend will ich untersuchen, welche Gestalten des theoretischen und des praktischen Geistes Hegel zur Kennzeichnung des re-

https://doi.org/10.1515/9783110673692-013

ligiösen Bewusstseins einsetzt. Dabei wird sich ergeben, dass sich das Wesen der Religion für Hegel keineswegs auf das Hervorbringen bestimmter Arten von Vorstellungen des Absoluten beschränkt. Vielmehr besitzt die Religion neben ihrer theoretischen auch eine praktische Seite, nämlich die Vereinigung des gläubigen Subjekts mit dem Unendlichen.

Dem theoretischen und dem praktischen Moment der Religion entsprechen meines Erachtens die beiden Formen des propositionalen und des fiduziellen Glaubens. Der propositionale Glaube (*fides quae*) umfasst die zur religiösen Vorstellungswelt gehörenden Gehalte. Als fiduziellen Glauben (*fides qua*) bezeichnet man herkömmlicherweise die personale Haltung des Vertrauens gegenüber Gott.[1] Ebenso wenig wie das zwischenmenschliche Vertrauen lässt sich das gläubige Vertrauen auf Gott in bestimmte Überzeugungen und ein unmittelbares Gefühl der Gewissheit auflösen. Vielmehr schließt der fiduzielle Glaube praktische Vollzüge mit ein. An die Stelle des personalen Vertrauens tritt bei Hegel die Erfahrung der Einheit mit dem Absoluten. Er beschreibt den fiduziellen Glauben nicht nach dem Vorbild interpersonaler Beziehungen, sondern stellt ihn als mystisches Erleben dar. Zur praktischen Seite der Religion zählt Hegel deshalb diejenigen Handlungen, mittels deren der Gläubige zum Bewusstsein seiner Einheit mit Gott gelangt.

Das aus Hegels Psychologie geläufige Motiv der Absage des Einzelnen an seine partikularen Interessen und Neigungen zugunsten der Allgemeinheit des vernünftigen Wollens kehrt in der Religionsphilosophie wieder. Durch den willentlichen Selbstverzicht schafft das Subjekt die Voraussetzung für die Erfahrung der mystischen Einheit. Wie sich der theoretische und der praktische Geist nicht voneinander trennen lassen, so sind der propositionale und der fiduzielle Glaube wechselseitig aufeinander verwiesen. Hegel entwickelt die Momente des religiösen Glaubens in Anlehnung an das Verhältnis von Intelligenz und Wille. Die Religion erschöpft sich nicht in theoretischen Überzeugungen, sondern enthält als praktische Dimension den Kultus, durch den sich das endliche Subjekt seiner Einheit mit dem Absoluten bewusst wird.

---

1 Zum Begriff des fiduziellen Glaubens siehe Audi 2008.

Subjektiver Geist und Religion

Die Gliederung von Hegels Philosophie der Religion gab der Forschung von jeher Rätsel auf.[2] Zwar hat sich die Ausgangslage seit Walter Jaeschkes kritischer Edition der *Vorlesungen* merklich gebessert. Doch besteht weiterhin keine völlige Klarheit, welche Prinzipien die Anlage dieses Systemteils im Einzelnen bestimmen. Halten wir zunächst fest, worüber Einvernehmen herrschen dürfte. Die Philosophie des absoluten Geistes behandelt unterschiedliche Weisen, wie wir Menschen als endliche Subjekte des Unendlichen oder Absoluten innewerden. In Kunst, Religion und Philosophie haben wir es laut Hegel weniger mit drei Arten von Gegenständen zu tun als mit drei Formen, in denen ein und derselbe Gegenstand auftritt. Aus diesem Befund ergibt sich zwanglos die Einsicht, dass der Wandel der Erscheinungsweisen des Absoluten mit den Formen zu tun hat, in denen sich der subjektive Geist auf Objekte bezieht. Bereits in der *Phänomenologie des Geistes* kennzeichnet Hegel die Religion dadurch, dass sie es im Gegensatz zur Philosophie nicht mit Begriffen, sondern mit Vorstellungen zu tun habe.[3]

Für seine Berliner *Vorlesungen* erarbeitete Hegel eine von der Philosophie der Religionen des Altertums unabhängige Ästhetik. Dabei gewann die Unterscheidung zwischen Anschauung und Vorstellung zusehends an Bedeutung. Im Manuskript der *Vorlesung* von 1821 erklärt Hegel die Differenz von Kunst, Religion und Philosophie durch die Form ihres jeweiligen Verhältnisses zum Absoluten, nämlich die Bestimmungen „α) der unmittelbaren Anschauung, β) der Vorstellung, γ) des Denkens" (VPR 1, S. 143). Die Trichotomie von Anschauen, Vorstellen und begrifflichem Denken fällt in die Philosophie des subjektiven Geistes. In der *Enzyklopädie* von 1827 untergliedert Hegel den theoretischen Geist in α) Anschauung, β) Vorstellung und γ) Denken.[4] Die Anlage der Philosophie des absoluten Geistes im Ganzen folgt demnach der hegelschen Erkenntnistheorie.[5]

---

2 Einen Überblick über die ältere Forschung gibt Jaeschke 1983, S. 69–147. Einen neueren Stand bietet Jaeschke 2016, S. 413–437.
3 Vgl. GW 9, S. 407–408 sowie dazu Sans 2016b.
4 Ähnlich gliedern bereits die Nachschrift Hotho von 1822 (vgl. GW 25/1, S. 122–137) und die Nachschrift Griesheim von 1825 (vgl. GW 25/1, S. 490–531). In der Heidelberger Enzyklopädie von 1817 beginnt der theoretische Geist noch mit dem „Gefühl" (vgl. HEnz §§ 369–372), während Hegel die „Anschauung" als Moment zur Vorstellung schlägt (vgl. HEnz §§ 373–383). Hegel hat die Überschrift des ersten Abschnitts später in „Anschauung" geändert (vgl. Enz § 446–450), wohl um der Gefahr einer Verwechslung mit dem praktischen Gefühl vorzubeugen. Außerdem ergibt sich dadurch in der Psychologie die den Gestalten von Kunst, Religion und Philosophie entsprechende Trias von Anschauung, Vorstellung und Denken. – Zur Entwicklung siehe Stederoth 2001, S. 337–348.

Umso bemerkenswerter ist angesichts dessen der Befund, dass Hegel zur Gliederung der Religionsphilosophie nicht auf den subjektiven Geist, sondern auf die *Wissenschaft der Logik* zurückzugreifen scheint. Er rechtfertigt den Aufbau mit dem Verweis auf die Begriffs- und die Ideenlehre der subjektiven Logik. Nach der Darlegung des Begriffs der Religion im ersten Teil der *Vorlesungen* folgt im zweiten Teil die Untersuchung verschiedener endlicher Erscheinungsformen von Religion. Im dritten Teil stellt Hegel eine Religion, nämlich die christliche, als diejenige heraus, in der Begriff und Gegenstand so übereinstimmen, wie es seine Auffassung von der Idee erfordert. „Der Begriff der Religion ist noch nicht Religion, wie sie existiert; die bestimmte Religion, eben weil sie bestimmt ist, entspricht noch nicht dem Begriff. [...] Erst die unendliche Religion ist es, die dem Begriff entspricht; dies ist die vollendete, christliche Religion" (VPR 1, S. 55). Die zitierten Sätze schildern die aus der hegelschen Philosophie vielfach bekannte dreigliedrige Abfolge eines abstrakten Allgemeinen, dessen Teilung in mehrere endliche Besondere und deren Rückkehr zu der ursprünglichen Einheit.

Die Untergliederung jedes der drei Teile der *Vorlesungen* – Der Begriff der Religion, Die bestimmte Religion und Die vollendete Religion – folgt einem vergleichbaren Muster. Hinter ihm kann man die Struktur der subjektiven Logik erblicken. Der subjektive Begriff realisiert sich zur Objektivität und kehrt von dort zurück zur Einheit der Idee. Die aus der Begriffslehre der *Logik* geläufigen Momente finden sich in den einzelnen Teilen der Abhandlung wieder. Am deutlichsten gilt das für die Darstellung des Christentums als die vollendete Religion. Dort spricht Hegel beispielsweise von der Entwicklung des absoluten Geistes in den drei Formen „der Allgemeinheit", „der Partikularisation, des Seins für Anderes" und „der absoluten Einzelheit, des absoluten Beisichseins" (VPR 3, S. 120). Die Momente des Allgemeinen, des Besonderen und des Einzelnen verbindet er wiederum mit den drei göttlichen Personen. Der Allgemeinheit entspricht „Gott der Vater" (VPR 3, S. 204); das Besondere oder Andere sei „bestimmt als Sohn" (VPR 3, S. 216); das dritte Moment ist „der Heilige Geist, der Geist in seiner Gemeinde" (VPR 3, S. 199).

Die trinitarische Deutung der drei Momente des Begriffs wurde berühmt, weil Hegel in den religionsphilosophischen Vorlesungen des Jahres 1831 die drei Sphären oder Elemente als das „Reich des Vaters", das „Reich des Sohnes" und das „Reich des Geistes" kennzeichnete (VPR 3, S. 280 – 281). Die ersten Herausgeber seiner Werke übernahmen diese Bezeichnungen kurzerhand in die Über-

---

5 Walter Jaeschke hat die Vermutung geäußert, den Formen des absoluten Geistes komme „zumindest eine heuristische Funktion für die Formulierung der Philosophie des subjektiven Geistes" zu (Jaeschke 1983, S. 112).

schriften der drei Teile der Abhandlung über die absolute Religion. Dadurch entstand bei Generationen von Lesern der Eindruck, Hegels Darstellung des Christentums sei eine Art Trinitätslehre. Daran ist so viel richtig, dass Hegel als ausgebildeter Theologe in der Dreifaltigkeit den Kern der christlichen Gottesauffassung erblickte. Aber der Philosoph bediente sich keineswegs der christlichen Dogmatik, um die Religion als Gestalt des absoluten Geistes zu erweisen. Im Gegenteil verwendete Hegel die Elemente seiner eigenen Begriffs- und Ideenlehre zur Aufdeckung der Entsprechung zwischen christlicher Religion und spekulativer Philosophie.

Obwohl Hegel die Einteilung der Religionsphilosophie also hauptsächlich im Rückgriff auf die subjektive Logik zu rechtfertigen scheint, wäre es ein Irrtum zu meinen, die Kategorien des subjektiven Geistes spielten dabei gar keine Rolle. Im Gegenteil hält Hegel an der bereits in Jena vorgenommenen Zuordnung der einzelnen Elemente der Religion zu den verschiedenen Vermögen des Subjekts unverändert fest. In der *Phänomenologie des Geistes* hatte er den Abschnitt über die offenbare Religion seinerseits in die drei Elemente des Denkens, der Vorstellung und des Selbstbewusstseins gegliedert. Die Darstellung des Christentums beginnt mit dem reinen Gedanken des göttlichen Wesens. In der Vorstellung wird das Absolute sich selbst ein Anderes und tritt in das endliche Dasein. Dadurch bricht zugleich der Gegensatz des Bewusstseins zwischen dem gläubigen Subjekt und seinem religiösen Gegenstand auf. Das dritte Moment der Entwicklung ist „die Rückkehr aus der Vorstellung und dem Anderssein oder das Element des Selbstbewusstseins selbst" (GW 9, S. 409). Eine ähnliche Einteilung findet sich in den Berliner *Vorlesungen* wieder, wie ich nun zeigen möchte.

Gemäß dem Manuskript teilt Hegel die vollendete Religion in die Abschnitte „A. Abstrakter Begriff" (VPR 3, S. 5), „B. Konkrete Vorstellung" (VPR 3, S. 12) und „C. Gemeinde, Kultus" (VPR 3, S. 69) ein. Innerhalb der Vorstellung unterscheidet er wiederum drei Sphären, die er das „Element des Gedankens" (VPR 3, S. 16), das „Element des Andersseins" (VPR 3, S. 27) und das „Moment der Rückkehr" (VPR 3, S. 28) nennt. An dem Moment der Rückkehr unterscheidet Hegel noch einmal zwei Seiten, nämlich die Erscheinung der göttlichen Idee zum einen „als ein [sc. einzelner] Mensch" und zum anderen „als wirkliches allgemeines Selbstbewusstsein" (VPR 3, S. 69). Mit dem allgemeinen Selbstbewusstsein meint er die christliche Gemeinde, in der sich die Einheit des endlichen Geistes mit dem göttlichen Geist vollendet.

Die *Vorlesung* von 1824 bringt eine systematische Vereinfachung. Der dritte Abschnitt entfällt, so dass nur noch die beiden Abschnitte „A. Metaphysischer Begriff" (VPR 3, S. 108) und „B. Konkrete Vorstellung" (VPR 3, S. 119) übrigbleiben. Die Gemeinde wird innerhalb der Sphäre der Vorstellung abgehandelt, und zwar als das dritte Element. Der Ausdruck „Vorstellung" ist hier in einem weiteren Sinn zu verstehen, denn ebenso wie in dem Manuskript von 1821 erörtert Hegel unter dieser Überschrift als das erste Element den Gedanken und als das zweite Element die Vorstellung im engeren Sinn. Von allen drei Elementen des Christentums erklärt er, sie seien „bestimmt in Rücksicht auf das subjektive Bewusstsein" (VPR 3, S. 120). Mit Blick auf die Gemeinde heißt es sodann, das dritte Element sei „das der Subjektivität als solcher" (VPR 3, S. 120–121). Die Kennzeichnung ist gemäß dem bisher Gesagten so zu verstehen, dass es erst unter dem letzten Gliederungspunkt um das gläubige Subjekt geht. Nachdem im Element des Gedankens die begrifflichen Voraussetzungen für die religiöse Erkenntnis des Absoluten als Geist geschaffen wurden und im Element der Vorstellung Gott als etwas Äußerliches erschien, fällt unter das dritte Element die Gegenwart Gottes im menschlichen Gemüt, „das Geistige jetzt seiend in diesem Individuum" (VPR 3, S. 121).

Eine gewisse Verdoppelung bleibt freilich bestehen, weil unter der Überschrift „Metaphysischer Begriff" nichts anderes verhandelt zu werden scheint als unter der Überschrift „Konkrete Vorstellung" in dem Element des Gedankens, nämlich „der Begriff Gottes und die Einheit desselben mit der Realität" (VPR 3, S. 109), kurz „die absolute Idee" (VPR 3, S. 118) oder „die Idee Gottes" (VPR 3, S. 122). Diese Unstimmigkeit bringt Hegel in der *Vorlesung* von 1827 durch eine weitere Vereinfachung der Gliederung zum Verschwinden. Er verzichtet auf die Einteilung der vollendeten Religion in zwei Abschnitte und begnügt sich mit den drei Elementen. Sie handeln von Gott als der absoluten Idee, und zwar insofern er „für den Gedanken, für das Denken überhaupt" sei (Erstes Element), insofern er „für den endlichen, äußerlichen, empirischen Geist, für die sinnliche Anschauung, für die Vorstellung" sei (Zweites Element), und insofern er „für die Empfindung [...], im Innersten des subjektiven Geistes" sei (Drittes Element). Die Elemente der vollendeten Religion seien nichts anderes als „die dreierlei Verhältnisweisen des Subjekts zu Gott" (VPR 3, S. 197–198). Hegel rechtfertigt die Dreiteilung mit dem Hinweis auf die Natur des menschlichen Geistes:

> Wir wissen von unserem Geist, dass wir erstens denkend sind ohne diesen Gegensatz, die Entzweiung in uns, dass wir zweitens der endliche Geist sind, der Geist in seiner Entzweiung, Trennung, und drittens, dass wir der Geist in der Empfindung, Subjektivität sind, in der Rückkehr zu sich, die Versöhnung, das innerste Gefühl. (VPR 3, S. 198)

Die Gliederung der Berliner Religionsphilosophie ist nur vor dem Hintergrund der Formen des subjektiven Geistes zu verstehen. Dessen Einteilung führt Hegel auf die Momente des Begriffs und damit auf die subjektive Logik zurück. Von den drei Elementen sei „das erste der Boden der Allgemeinheit, das zweite der Boden der Besonderheit, das dritte der der Einzelheit" (VPR 3, S. 198). Den Elementen des Denkens und der Vorstellung entsprechen, wie schon erwähnt, die Vermögen des theoretischen Geistes oder der Intelligenz. Das dritte Element, so mein Vorschlag, lässt sich dem Bereich des praktischen Geistes zuordnen. Der Zusammenhang wird wegen des mehrdeutigen Gebrauchs, den Hegel von dem Ausdruck ‚Gefühl‘ macht, nicht sofort sichtbar.[6] Um die Bedeutung des praktischen Geistes für die Religionsphilosophie zu erkennen, soll nun ein Blick auf den ersten Teil der *Vorlesungen* geworfen werden.

In seinem Manuskript beginnt Hegel den ersten Teil mit einer empirischen Beschreibung dessen, was wir gewöhnlich unter Religion verstehen, nämlich das „Bewusstsein von Gott überhaupt" (VPR 1, S. 95). Das religiöse Bewusstsein tritt in den Formen des Gefühls, der Vorstellung und des Wissens auf. In ihnen erscheint Gott jeweils als Gegenstand und insofern als ein dem Subjekt „Fremdes, Äußeres". Obwohl es sich um Formen der Intelligenz handelt, spricht Hegel von einem „ungeistigen Verhältnis" und stellt ihm das „Verhältnis des Willens" gegenüber. Dieses zeige sich in den Empfindungen sowohl der Furcht als auch der Liebe. Durch die letztere erfahre sich der Mensch als eins mit dem Unendlichen. Die Versöhnung mit Gott ist für Hegel „ein Tun, Handeln, mehr zugleich äußerliches oder inneres, überhaupt der Kultus" (VPR 1, S. 98). Wie Hegel betont, gehören der äußere Vollzug und das innere Erleben der Religion zusammen. Weder die fromme Praxis noch der religiöse Gehalt dürfen auf ein privates Gefühl reduziert werden. Die Religion auf bloße Innerlichkeit zu stellen, habe „den Kultus vernichtet, und ebenso wie das Herausgehen aus seinem subjektiven Herzen zu Handlungen, auch das Herausgehen des Bewusstseins zu einem objektiven Wissen; eins ist aufs innigste mit dem anderen verbunden" (VPR 1, S. 101).

Der erste Teil der *Vorlesung* von 1824 endet mit einem Abschnitt über „Die Realisierung des Begriffs der Religion" (VPR 1, S. 227), der in „α) Die Vorstellung Gottes" (VPR 1, S. 230) und „β) Der Kultus" (VPR 1, S. 237) gegliedert ist. Zur Erklärung der Gliederung nennt Hegel die beiden Aspekte „die theoretische" und „die praktische Seite" der Religion. Die erste Seite bestimmt er als „die Weise der Vorstellung [...] der göttlichen Erscheinung, des göttlichen Seins". Sie setzt die Unterscheidung zwischen dem endlichen Subjekt und Gott als dem Gegenstand des subjektiven Bewusstseins voraus. Die zweite Seite dagegen ist „die Tätigkeit des Aufhebens der Entzweiung" (VPR 1, S. 230). Durch die Überwindung des Gegensatzes zwischen dem religiösen Bewusstsein und seinem Gegenstand kommt es zur Vereinigung des Menschen mit Gott. Dies geschieht im Kultus als dem „praktischen Verhältnis", in dem „der Unterschied, die Entzweiung des Subjekts mit dem Gegenstand aufgehoben werden soll" (VPR 1, S. 236).

---

6 Das Gefühl tritt als Gestalt sowohl des theoretischen Geistes (vgl. Enz §§ 446–448) als auch des praktischen Geistes auf (vgl. Enz §§ 471–472). Siehe dazu Stederoth 2006.

Hegel entnimmt der Psychologie nicht nur einzelne Schlagworte zur Kennzeichnung der verschiedenen Vermögen des Geistes, sondern erarbeitet an ihrem Leitfaden die Gliederung seiner Philosophie der Religion. Wie der subjektive Geist, so ist auch die Religion durch die Verbindung der theoretischen mit der praktischen Dimension, der Intelligenz mit dem Willen gekennzeichnet. Das wird noch deutlicher, wenn man den ersten Teil der *Vorlesung* von 1824 mit der Fassung aus dem Jahr 1827 vergleicht. Ähnlich wie die Darstellung des Christentums als vollendete Religion erfährt auch die Abhandlung über den Begriff der Religion eine Vereinfachung. Zum Begriff der Religion gehören nun die drei Abschnitte „A. Der Begriff Gottes" (VPR 1, S. 266), „B. Das Wissen von Gott" (VPR 1, S. 277) und „C. Der Kultus" (VPR 1, S. 330). Während das Wissen von Gott dem theoretischen Geist zugeordnet werden kann, entspricht der Kultus dem praktischen Geist. Das Wissen von Gott ist weiter untergliedert in die unmittelbare Gewissheit, das Gefühl, die Vorstellung und das Denken. Hegel beschreibt das theoretische Verhältnis als die Versenkung des Subjekts in seinen Gegenstand. Erst durch die Reflexion auf diese „verhältnislose Beziehung" tritt der Gegensatz zwischen dem Ich und Gott ins Bewusstsein. Mit der Reflexion „geht das praktische Verhältnis an, worin ich für mich bin, dem Gegenstand gegenüberstehe und jetzt meine Einigkeit mit ihm hervorzubringen habe" (VPR 1, S. 330).

Die Entsprechungen zwischen der Philosophie des subjektiven Geistes einerseits und den religionsphilosophischen Vorlesungen andererseits lassen kaum einen Zweifel zu, dass Hegel die Religion mittels psychologischer Kategorien darstellt. Die Religion umfasst neben dem theoretischen Bewusstsein des Absoluten auch das praktische Moment der Vereinigung mit dem Unendlichen. Der die religiösen Vorstellungen prägende Gegensatz zwischen Gott und Mensch wird im Kultus überwunden. Wie die Psychologie in die Einheit des theoretischen und des praktischen Geistes, so mündet die Religion in die Einheit der Vorstellungen mit dem Kultus. Ohne die praktische Dimension, in der Intelligenz und Wille zusammenkommen, bliebe die Versöhnung mit Gott etwas rein Passives, zu dem das endliche Subjekt keinen eigenen Beitrag zu leisten vermag. Dass zur Religion neben der Theorie auch die Praxis gehört, dass der Glaube eine Betätigung nicht nur der Intelligenz, sondern auch des Willens bedeutet, soll im Folgenden genauer ausgeführt werden. Abweichend von der Anordnung der *Vorlesungen* beginne ich mit dem Element der Vorstellung. Daran schließt sich die Behandlung des religiösen Gefühls an, insofern dieses die theoretische Gewissheit des Glaubens verbürgt. Am Ende wende ich mich dem Kultus und der durch ihn hervorgebrachten Erfahrung der mystischen Einheit mit Gott zu.

Religiöse Vorstellungen

Im Religions-Kapitel der *Phänomenologie des Geistes* bestimmt Hegel das Vorstellen als „die synthetische Verbindung der sinnlichen Unmittelbarkeit und ihrer Allgemeinheit oder des Denkens" (GW 9, S. 408). Versteht man die Definition im Sinn der kantischen Lehre von der Synthesis des Urteils, verbindet sich in dem, was Hegel ‚Vorstellung' nennt, die Anschauung eines Gegenstandes mit einem allgemeinen Begriff, unter den das Einzelne gefasst wird. Doch geht es Hegel nicht um empirische Allgemeinbegriffe oder Kategorien des Verstandes. Die Vorstellung steht nicht als abstraktes Allgemeines sozusagen stellvertretend für die konkreten Einzelnen. Es kommt Hegel im Gegenteil auf die Repräsentation komplexer Gedanken durch sinnlich Gegebenes an. Deshalb spricht er von dem Gedanken als der Bedeutung einer Vorstellung oder Anschauung. Bereits in der Einleitung zur *Enzyklopädie* heißt es plakativ:

> Vorstellungen überhaupt können als Metaphern der Gedanken und Begriffe angesehen werden. Damit aber, dass man Vorstellungen hat, kennt man noch nicht deren Bedeutung für das Denken, noch nicht deren Gedanken und Begriffe. Umgekehrt ist es auch zweierlei, Gedanken und Begriffe zu haben, und zu wissen, welches die ihnen entsprechenden Vorstellungen, Anschauungen, Gefühle sind. (Enz § 3 Anm.)

In der Vorstellung, so lässt sich die Position Hegels knapp wiedergeben, erhält etwas unmittelbar Angeschautes einen begrifflichen Gehalt. Der dritte Abschnitt der Philosophie des subjektiven Geistes schildert ausführlich, wie sich die Intelligenz vom Gefühl – sei es Empfindung, sei es Anschauung – über die verschiedenen Stufen des Vorstellens zum Gedanken erhebt. Das eigentliche Ziel, das Hegel mit seiner Psychologie verfolgt, besteht in der Entwicklung des Denkens und des selbstbestimmten Wollens aus den unmittelbaren Formen des Geistes. Die Vorstellung dient ihm dabei zum einen als Stufe des Übergangs; zum anderen stellt sie die Formen bereit, in denen sich die Tätigkeit des Denkens ihrerseits vollzieht.[7] So werden aus den Anschauungen äußerer Gegenstände in der Erinnerung zunächst innere Bilder. Die Phantasie kann solche Bilder wiederum mit neuen Anschauungen verknüpfen.

Wenn sich der Geist einer Anschauung bedient, um einen bildlich vorgestellten Gehalt unter sie zu fassen, gebraucht er die Anschauung als Zeichen. Unter einem Zeichen versteht Hegel „ein Bild, das eine selbständige Vorstellung der Intelligenz als Seele in sich empfangen hat, seine Bedeutung" (Enz § 458). Das

---

7 Zu der folgenden Darstellung vgl. Enz §§ 451–464. Siehe außerdem die Kommentare von Inwood 2007, S. 480–514 und Rometsch 2007, S. 174–217.

Zeichen ist demzufolge „irgendeine unmittelbare Anschauung, die einen ganz anderen Inhalt vorstellt, als den sie für sich hat" (Enz § 458 Anm.). Um eine besondere Art von Zeichen handelt es sich bei den Worten unserer Sprache. Sie verbinden eine Lautfolge oder ein Schriftzeichen mit einer durch sie bezeichneten Vorstellung. Sobald wir den Dingen einen Namen geben, kommt es zur „Verknüpfung der von der Intelligenz produzierten Anschauung und ihrer Bedeutung" (Enz § 460). Das Gedächtnis macht aus der einmaligen Verknüpfung etwas Bleibendes. Zeichen und Bezeichnetes bilden fernerhin eine Einheit, in welcher „der Inhalt, die Bedeutung, und das Zeichen identifiziert, eine Vorstellung sind" (Enz § 461).

Wenn Hegel die Religion dem Vorstellen zuordnet, geht es ihm nicht bloß um den Befund, dass in der Religion gewisse Bilder, Zeichen oder Worte gebraucht werden. Der spezifische Vorstellungscharakter der Religion besteht vielmehr darin, dass der durch die religiöse Sprache bezeichnete Inhalt selbst wiederum die Form des Vorstellens, das heißt der Verknüpfung einer Anschauung oder Vorstellung mit einem durch sie bezeichneten Gedanken oder Begriff besitzt. Wenn die griechische Mythologie von Zeus erzählt, gebraucht sie nicht nur das Wort ‚Zeus' oder ein Bild des Göttervaters als Zeichen für den realen Gott, sondern die wahre Bedeutung aller Vorstellungen des Gottes Zeus liegt für Hegel in dem philosophischen Gedanken des Absoluten. In der Religionsphilosophie tritt die Form des Vorstellens gewissermaßen doppelt auf, nämlich zum einen in dem gewöhnlichen Sinn als die Verknüpfung bestimmter Zeichen mit einem gedanklichen Gehalt, zum anderen in dem spezifisch religiösen Sinn als eine Weise der Darstellung des Absoluten in den Gestalten des endlichen Geistes.

Obwohl in der Religion sämtliche Formen des theoretischen Geistes – also Gefühle, Vorstellungen und Gedanken – auftreten, handelt es sich bei ihnen allen um Arten der Vorstellung des Absoluten. Am ausführlichsten erörtert Hegel die Vielzahl der Formen des religiösen Bewusstseins im ersten Teil seiner *Vorlesung* von 1827. Was die Vorstellung angeht, bestimmt er sie allgemein als „ein Bewusstsein von etwas, das man als Gegenständliches vor sich hat" (VPR 1, S. 292). Zur Tätigkeit des Vorstellens gehört wesentlich, dass ihr Gegenstand ursprünglich in der Anschauung gegeben sein muss. Wie Hegel in der Psychologie darlegt, bildet der Geist aus der Anschauung die höheren Stufen der Vorstellung, nämlich Bilder, Zeichen und Namen. In der Religionsphilosophie unterscheidet er außerdem zwischen Vorstellungen auf sinnlicher Grundlage und solchen auf gedanklicher Grundlage.[8]

---

[8] In seinem Manuskript nennt Hegel die ersten ‚Bilder' und reserviert den Ausdruck ‚Vorstellungen' für die letzteren (vgl. VPR 1, S. 147–149).

Die einfachste Art religiöser Vorstellungen sind „sinnliche Formen, Gestaltungen". Insofern ihr Inhalt „aus der unmittelbaren Anschauung genommen ist, können sie Bilder überhaupt heißen". Um Vorstellungen oder Bilder handelt es sich deshalb, weil wir uns bewusst sind, dass sie zwei Seiten haben, „einmal das Unmittelbare und dann, was damit gemeint ist, das Innere" (VPR 1, S. 293). Ohne auf Einzelheiten einzugehen, bezeichnet Hegel die religiösen Bilder als Symbole, Allegorien und Metaphern. Als Beispiele nennt er die gleichnishafte Rede vom Zorn Gottes, den Mythos von der Formung des Menschen durch Prometheus oder die Erzählung vom Baum der Erkenntnis im Paradies.[9] Sie alle besitzen eine von dem unmittelbar Angeschauten „verschiedene Bedeutung" (VPR 1, S. 293). Das gilt auch für die christliche Vorstellung von der Zeugung des Sohnes durch den Vater. Die Trinitätslehre erläutert das innere Wesen Gottes mittels einer Analogie aus der Biologie.

> ‚Sohn', ‚Erzeuger', gibt die Vorstellung von einem bekannten Verhältnis, das, wie wir wohl wissen, nicht in seiner Unmittelbarkeit gemeint sein, sondern ein anderes Verhältnis bedeuten soll, das ungefähr diesem gleicht. (VPR 1, S. 293)

In den Bereich des Sinnlichen und der Bilder fällt für Hegel ferner alles, „was als Geschichtliches zu nehmen ist" (VPR 1, S. 294). Damit meint er nicht in erster Linie die griechische Mythologie und die Götter Homers, aus denen wir doch „nicht rechten Ernst" machten, sondern vor allem die Geschichte Jesu Christi, die „eine göttliche Geschichte ist, und zwar so, dass es im eigentlichen Sinn Geschichte sein soll" (VPR 1, S. 294). Hegel deutet das Geborenwerden, Leiden und Sterben Jesu als ein äußerliches Geschehen, das ein göttliches Tun zum Inhalt habe. Wie in der Geschichte eines Staates die „wesentlichen sittlichen Mächte" zum Ausdruck kommen, die sein Schicksal bestimmen, so offenbare sich in den Begebenheiten des Lebens Jesu von Nazareth eine „absolut göttliche Handlung" (VPR 1, S. 294 – 295). Im dritten Teil der *Vorlesung* von 1824 geht Hegel näher auf die Geschichte Jesu ein. Inhalt dieser Geschichte ist „der einzelne unmittelbare Mensch, in aller Zufälligkeit und in allen zeitlichen Verhältnissen und Bedingungen". Dem gläubigen Bewusstsein erscheine darin die „Einheit des Endlichen und Unendlichen" und zugleich die „Entäußerung der Idee" (VPR 3, S. 147).

Zu den religiösen Vorstellungen zählt Hegel neben den Bildern und der Geschichte auch „nichtsinnliche Gestaltungen". Sie stellen einen komplexen geistigen Inhalt „in einfacher Form" dar. Zur Erläuterung verweist er auf die Vorstellung von der Erschaffung der Welt. In ihr verbinde sich der „unendlich mannigfache Komplex" der endlichen Dinge mit dem Gedanken von Gott als dem

---

9 Vgl. VPR 1, S. 293 – 294 sowie ausführlicher VPR 3, S. 40 – 44; 224 – 228.

Ursprung ihres Daseins (VPR 1, S. 295–296). Gleichwohl fällt die Abgrenzung zu der sinnlichen Vorstellung von der Zeugung des Sohnes Gottes durch den Vater nicht leicht. Zwar betont Hegel, mit dem Satz „Die Welt ist erschaffen" bezeichneten wir „eine ganz andere Art der Tätigkeit als sonst eine empirische" (VPR 1, S. 296). Doch geht es bei der Lehre von den göttlichen Personen so wenig um ein empirisches Verhältnis wie in der Theologie der Schöpfung. Mit dem Ausdruck „zeugen" ist nicht anders als mit dem Wort „erschaffen" eine metaphysische Beziehung gemeint. Der Unterschied zwischen den beiden Vorstellungen beruht darauf, dass die Welt nicht aus einem schon vorhandenen Stoff entsteht, der von Gott nur noch geformt oder bearbeitet würde. In dieser Hinsicht entspricht das Erschaffen der Welt weder dem Erbauen eines Hauses noch dem Gestalten einer Skulptur. Weil in der Wirklichkeit unserer Erfahrung nichts aus nichts entsteht, ist die Erschaffung der Welt durch Gott die Vorstellung von einer nichtsinnlichen Tätigkeit.[10] Insofern sich lebendige Wesen aus Zellen entwickeln, die bereits da sind, handelt es sich bei der Zeugung hingegen um die Vorstellung von einer sinnlichen Tätigkeit. Das gilt selbst dann, wenn diese Vorstellung auf etwas Geistiges bezogen wird, nämlich den Hervorgang der zweiten göttlichen Person.[11]

Das religiöse Gefühl

Geht man von dem Begriff der Vorstellung aus, wie ihn Hegel in der Philosophie des subjektiven Geistes entwickelt, könnte man erwarten, dass es sich bei den in der Religionsphilosophie erörterten Gefühlen um diejenigen Anschauungen oder Empfindungen handelt, auf deren Grundlage das religiöse Bewusstsein seine Vorstellungen ausbildet. Um bei den zuletzt genannten Beispielen zu bleiben, braucht das gläubige Subjekt die Anschauung eines Vaters oder die Empfindung elterlicher Zuwendung, damit es sich Gott unter dem Attribut der Väterlichkeit vorstellen kann; weil der Mensch die Erfahrung künstlerischer Produktivität macht, entwickelt er die Vorstellung von der Erschaffung der Welt durch Gott. Gleichwohl ist derartiges mit dem religiösen Gefühl nicht gemeint. Vielmehr verbindet Hegel in der Religionsphilosophie mit dem Begriff des Gefühls die Annahme eines unmittelbaren epistemischen Zugangs zum Absoluten. Seine Position ist nicht leicht zu fassen, da er sie in ständiger Auseinandersetzung mit der *Glaubenslehre* seines Berliner Kollegen Friedrich Schleiermacher darlegt und

---

10 In der Vorlesung von 1824 beschreibt Hegel das Erschaffen als „eine unbestimmte Vorstellung, die so den spekulativen Zusammenhang Gottes und der Welt auf allgemeine Weise ausdrückt" (VPR 1, S. 235). – Zu Hegels Begriff der Schöpfung siehe De Nys 2009, S. 87–95.

11 Diese Lesart verdanke ich Maximilian Scholz.

bei jeder sich bietenden Gelegenheit gegen die Gefühlstheologie seiner Zeitgenossen polemisiert.[12]

Obwohl sich religiöse Überzeugungen nicht durch den Verweis auf Gefühle rechtfertigen lassen, schreibt Hegel dem Gefühl eine wesentliche Funktion für das religiöse Leben zu. In den *Vorlesungen* von 1824 und 1827 unterscheidet er näher zwischen dem unmittelbaren Wissen von Gott und dem religiösen Gefühl. Die Trennung bleibt unscharf, denn der Inhalt ist in beiden Fällen der gleiche, nämlich Gott. Dazu passt, dass die Philosophie des theoretischen Geistes nur einen einzigen Modus der Unmittelbarkeit kennt. In der Anschauung, so die *Enzyklopädie*, erscheint der Geist „als fühlender" (Enz § 446). Hegel umschreibt das Fühlen als ein „unmittelbares Finden". In ihm sei das Moment der „Aufmerksamkeit" des Geistes mit dem der „Gefühlsbestimmtheit als ein Seiendes" vereinigt (Enz § 448). Der Geist schaut den Inhalt seiner Empfindung unmittelbar an. In der Religionsphilosophie erläutert Hegel den Zusammenhang zwischen der subjektiven Bestimmtheit des Gefühls und seinem Objekt am Beispiel der Härte:

> Ich fühle Hartes; wenn ich so spreche, so ist Ich das eine, das zweite ist das Etwas, es sind ihrer zwei; das ist der Ausdruck der Reflexion. Das Gemeinschaftliche ist die Härte. Es ist Härte in meinem Gefühl, und auch der Gegenstand ist hart. Diese Gemeinschaft existiert im Gefühl; der Gegenstand berührt mich, und ich bin erfüllt von dieser Bestimmtheit des Gegenstands. (VPR 1, S. 176)

Dass Hegel in der Religionsphilosophie das unmittelbare Wissen einer vom Gefühl getrennten Betrachtung unterzieht, hat hauptsächlich mit der Glaubensphilosophie Friedrich Heinrich Jacobis zu tun, von der sich abzusetzen Hegel ebenfalls bestrebt ist. Eine durch keine begrifflichen Gründe vermittelte Gewissheit heißt für Jacobi „Glauben": „Dies unmittelbare Wissen hat Jacobi Glauben genannt; [...] wir glauben, dass ein Gott ist, insofern wir unmittelbar von ihm wissen" (VPR 1, S. 168). Im unmittelbaren Wissen verschmilzt gewissermaßen das Sein des Ich mit dem seines Gegenstands. „Wir sagen, es ist so gewiss, wie ich bin; das Sein des Gegenstands ist zugleich mein Sein" (VPR 1, S. 169). Sobald jedoch das Subjekt auf seinen Gegenstand reflektiert, wird es sich des Unterschieds bewusst, der es von jenem trennt. Mit dem Aufbrechen des Unterschieds zwischen dem Ich und seinem Gegenstand wird auch die unmittelbare Gewissheit fraglich. Das Subjekt beginnt an seinem Gegenstand zu zweifeln und nach Gründen für dessen Sein zu suchen (vgl. VPR 1, S. 173 – 175).

---

[12] Dass die Auffassung Hegels nicht so weit von der Schleiermachers entfernt liegt, habe ich in Sans 2016a gezeigt.

In der *Vorlesung* von 1827 zieht Hegel die Konsequenz aus dem Gesagten und erklärt, dass es ein unmittelbares Wissen recht verstanden gar nicht gibt, sondern wir unser fehlendes Bewusstsein von der Vermittlung für unmittelbare Gewissheit halten. „Unmittelbares Wissen ist das Wissen, bei dem wir das Bewusstsein der Vermittlung nicht haben; aber vermittelt ist es" (VPR 1, S. 305). Was vom unmittelbaren Wissen übrig bleibt, ist demnach die subjektive Gewissheit eines Gefühls. Darauf richtet sich in Hegels Augen der philosophische Glaube Jacobis. Für ihn sei Glauben „die Gewissheit, sofern sie Gefühl und im Gefühl ist" (VPR 1, S. 282). Einem solchen Gefühl der Gewissheit stellt Hegel die Erkenntnis der Wahrheit gegenüber. Um etwas als wahr zu erkennen, bedarf es der Vermittlung durch Begriffe. Erst wenn ich die zureichenden Gründe einer Sache kenne, verdient mein Wissen objektiv genannt zu werden. Dagegen bildet Jacobis Glaube an Gott „eine Gewissheit, die man hat ohne unmittelbare sinnliche Anschauung, ohne diese sinnliche Unmittelbarkeit und zugleich, ohne dass man die Einsicht in die Notwendigkeit dieses Inhalts hat" (VPR 1, S. 284).[13]

Wenn Hegel gleich im Anschluss an das unmittelbare Wissen von Gott auf das religiöse Gefühl zu sprechen kommt, handelt es sich nicht um eine neue Gestalt des Geistes. Unmittelbares Wissen und Gefühl sind vielmehr zwei Weisen, wie dasjenige, was in der Psychologie ‚Anschauung' heißt und sich zunächst auf sinnlich wahrnehmbare Gegebenheiten bezieht, religiös verstanden werden kann. Die Religion hat – genauso wie Recht und Moral – ihre eigene Form der Unmittelbarkeit. Religiöse Überzeugungen können mit dem Gefühl der Gewissheit gepaart sein. Im Gegenzug zu Jacobi stellt Hegel allerdings klar, dass die unmittelbare Gewissheit als solche keine epistemische Rechtfertigung darstellt. Der Inhalt des Gefühls bedarf einer angemessenen Begründung. Hegel kritisiert sowohl Schleiermacher als auch Jacobi letztlich für ihren Verzicht auf die begriffliche Vermittlung des religiösen Glaubens.

Der Inhalt des Gefühls kann verschiedenster Art sein. Die unmittelbare Wahrnehmung von Farben oder Tönen fällt ebenso darunter wie die Empfindung von Glück oder Dankbarkeit. „Wir haben Gefühl von Recht, von Unrecht, Gott, Farbe; mein Gefühl ist Neid, Hass, mein Gefühl ist Feindschaft, Freude; es findet sich darin der widersprechendste Inhalt; das Niederträchtigste und das Vortrefflichste, Edelste, hat seinen Ort darin" (VPR 1, S. 176). Die Form des Gefühls ist keineswegs auf eine bestimmte Klasse von Gegenständen beschränkt. Insbeson-

---

13 In seiner Auseinandersetzung mit Jacobi versäumt Hegel nicht, dessen Glaubensphilosophie von der Religion abzugrenzen. Das „trockene Abstraktum des unmittelbaren Wissens" sei „nicht mit der geistigen Fülle des christlichen Glaubens, weder nach der Seite des gläubigen Herzens und des ihm einwohnenden Heiligen Geistes noch nach der Seite der inhaltsvollen Lehre, zu verwechseln noch für diese Fülle zu nehmen" (Enz § 63 Anm.).

dere ist das Gefühl nicht an die Vorstellung materieller Dinge gebunden, sondern auch „alles im Menschen, dessen Boden der Gedanke, die Vernunft ist, kann [...] in die Form des Gefühls versetzt werden" (VPR 1, S. 179). Aus der Mannigfaltigkeit des Inhalts folgt für Hegel die Gleichgültigkeit der Form. Wenn alles Mögliche gefühlt werden kann, sagt die Tatsache, im Gefühl zu sein, noch nichts über einen Gegenstand aus. Das Gefühl entscheidet weder über die Beschaffenheit des Inhalts, noch verbürgt es dessen Wahrheit.

Das Gefühl „ist also eine Form, in der der Inhalt gesetzt ist als etwas vollkommen Zufälliges". Daher wäre es ein Irrtum zu meinen, die Verwurzelung im Gefühl zeichne die Religion gegenüber anderen Vorstellungen oder Gedanken aus. Insofern Gott „in unserem Gefühl" sei, erklärt Hegel bündig, habe er „nichts vor dem Allerschlechtesten voraus", das ebenso gefühlt werden könne wie das Wahre, Schöne und Gute. Ferner bezieht sich das Gefühl nicht nur auf Wirkliches, sondern es umfasst „auch Erdichtetes, vollkommen Erlogenes, Eingebildetes". Oft genug ist das Gefühl ein Ort der Selbsttäuschung. „Ich kann mir einbilden, ein edler, vortrefflicher Mensch zu sein, fähig zu sein, alles aufzuopfern für Recht, für meine Meinung, kann mir einbilden, viel genutzt, geschafft zu haben – aber es ist die Frage, ob es wahr ist" (VPR 1, S. 177). Wer sich lediglich auf sein Gefühl verlässt, verabschiedet sich gewissermaßen aus dem Raum der Gründe. „So einen Menschen muss man stehen lassen", rät Hegel. „Er zieht sich in seine Partikularität zurück, denn mit dem Appellieren an das eigene Gefühl ist die Gemeinschaft zwischen uns abgerissen" (VPR 1, S. 178).

Da Hegel zufolge nicht die Form, sondern einzig der Inhalt ein Gefühl von anderen unterscheidbar macht, muss dieser Inhalt seinerseits in einer weiteren Form vorliegen, die nicht diejenige des Gefühls ist. Gefühle können nur dann beurteilt und miteinander verglichen werden, wenn sie in Verbindung mit Vorstellungen und Gedanken auftreten.[14] Das gilt nicht zuletzt für die Religion. „Insofern das Religiöse nur als Empfindung sein soll, so verglimmt die Religion zum Vorstellungslosen wie zum Handlungslosen und verliert allen bestimmten Inhalt" (VPR 1, S. 128). Die theoretische Dimension der Religion besteht in der Einheit

---

14 In Hegels Manuskript findet sich die treffende Beobachtung, dass Empfindungen durch die Vorstellungen lebendig erhalten werden, mit denen sie einhergehen. „Die Empfindung ernährt sich und macht sich fortdauernd durch die Vorstellung; sie erneuert und zündet sich daran wieder an; Zorn, Unwillen, Hass ist ebenso geschäftig, durch die Vorstellung der mannigfaltigen Seiten ihres Unrechts, des Feindes usf., als die Liebe, Wohlwollen, Freude, durch die ebenso vielfachen Beziehungen des Gegenstands, die sie vor sich bringt, zu unterhalten und beleben; ohne an den Gegenstand des Hasses, des Zorns zu denken, wie man sagt, oder der Liebe usf., erlischt die Empfindung und Neigung; schwindet der Gegenstand aus der Vorstellung, so verschwindet die Empfindung" (VPR 1, S. 127).

von Vorstellung und Gefühl. Die Einheit kann begrifflich gedacht werden, muss es aber nicht.[15] In der *Vorlesung* von 1827 ordnet Hegel der Form des Gefühls die „subjektive Seite, die Gewissheit von Gott", der Form der Vorstellung „die objektive Seite, den Inhalt der Gewissheit" zu (VPR 1, S. 291). Das religiöse Gefühl stellt sich nicht unwillkürlich und ohne äußeren Anlass, sondern stets im Zusammenhang mit bestimmten Vorstellungen ein. Die Aufgabe der Theologie besteht angesichts dessen in der Befragung der Religion auf ihren begrifflichen Gehalt. Erst in Gedanken, so Hegel, lassen sich wahre Vorstellungen von falschen trennen. Dass eine Vorstellung von Gott an ein bestimmtes Gefühl geknüpft ist, rechtfertigt nicht ihren Inhalt. Die einen mögen bei einem als gütig vorgestellten Gott Geborgenheit finden, während andere sich vor einem als grausam vorgestellten Gott ängstigen. Solange weder die Annahme der Güte Gottes noch die seiner Grausamkeit begründet ist, kann keines der beiden Gefühle den Vorrang beanspruchen.

In der *Enzyklopädie* fordert Hegel, die Trennung zwischen Gefühl und Denken zu überwinden zugunsten der Einsicht, dass „im Menschen nur *eine* Vernunft im Gefühl, Wollen und Denken ist". Zugleich gelte es anzuerkennen, dass „die Ideen, die allein dem denkenden Geist angehören – Gott, Recht, Sittlichkeit – auch gefühlt werden können" (Enz § 471 Anm.). In Angelegenheiten, welche die Existenz des ganzen Menschen betreffen, spielen Vernunft und Gefühl zusammen. Damit beugt Hegel einer Engführung des religiösen Glaubens auf das Fürwahrhalten bestimmter Propositionen vor. Insofern religiöse Überzeugungen mit dem Gefühl der Gewissheit gepaart sind, berühren sie den Gläubigen in seiner ganzen Person. Während die Vorstellung und das Denken eher der Seite des Objektiven und Allgemeinen zuzurechnen sind, gehört das religiöse Gefühl zur Seite der Besonderheit des einzelnen Subjekts. Ausdrücklich spricht Hegel von der „anthropologischen Seite" und der „Seite der Leiblichkeit". Beim Gefühl „kommt auch das Blut in Wallung, es wird uns warm ums Herz" (VPR 1, S. 286). Hegel betrachtet die emotionale Dimension eingebettet in psychosomatische Zusammenhänge. So wichtig die begriffliche Rechtfertigung sein mag, entscheidet in seinen Augen das Gefühl darüber, ob ein Mensch hinter seinen Überzeugungen steht. „Man sagt mit Recht, man soll Gott im Herzen haben", erklärt Hegel in der *Vorlesung* von 1824, um dann hervorzuheben, dass das Gefühl „nur momentan, flüchtig" sei, durch die Bezugnahme auf das Herz hingegen die „fortdauernde, feste Weise meiner

---

15 Gedanken und Begriffe liegen der Religion auch dann zugrunde, wenn sich der Gläubige ihrer nicht bewusst ist. Während man einem einfachen Menschen, der zu seiner Religion keine abstrakten Überlegungen anstellt, nicht den Glauben absprechen kann, wird man einen Intellektuellen, der die religiösen Vorstellungen gedanklich durchdringt, ohne etwas dabei zu empfinden, kaum für fromm halten.

Existenz" angesprochen werde. Mit dem Herzen verbinden sich die „Grundsätze oder Gewohnheiten" einer Person, die „Art meiner Handlungsweise" (VPR 1, S. 179–180).

Unter der Überschrift „Das weiter bestimmte Bewusstsein" bringt die *Vorlesung* von 1824 eine Reflexion über den Gehalt des religiösen Gefühls. Hegel beginnt mit dem Erleben der eigenen Endlichkeit, die sich in der menschlichen Bedürftigkeit zeigt. Als lebendiges Wesen erfährt sich der Mensch „äußerlich abhängig vom Anderen" – sei es die Luft, die wir atmen, sei es die Nahrung, mit der wir unseren Hunger stillen, seien es die Mitmenschen, auf deren Hilfe wir jederzeit angewiesen sind. Hegel räumt ein, dass Furcht oder Schmerz den Auslöser religiöser Vorstellungen bilden können, macht in Anspielung auf Schleiermacher aber zugleich deutlich, dass unser Gefühl der Bedürftigkeit unmöglich das Wesen der Religion ausmachen kann. „Wenn man sagt, die Religion beruhe auf diesem Gefühl der Abhängigkeit, dann müssen auch die Tiere Religion haben, denn sie fühlen diese Abhängigkeit" (VPR 1, S. 184). Der Mensch hat mit den Tieren die Fähigkeit gemeinsam, im Bewusstsein einer Schranke bereits über diese hinauszugehen. Eine Grenze gibt es nur für ein Wesen, für das es zugleich ein Jenseits der Grenze gibt. Ein lebendiges Wesen „hat Bedürfnisse, aber zugleich ist es Trieb, diese Negation des Selbst aufzuheben" (VPR 1, S. 185). Anders als die Tiere verbindet der Mensch mit dem Bewusstsein seiner Begrenztheit den Gedanken eines unendlichen Anderen. „Das Unendliche, dies mein Gegenstand, ist das Nichtendliche, Nichtbesondere, Nichtbeschränkte, das Allgemeine überhaupt" (VPR 1, S. 186). Der Mensch erfährt sich als abhängig von dem Unendlichen, das ihm nicht nur Furcht einflößt, sondern dessen Güte er auch sein Bestehen verdankt. Dennoch bleibt der Gedanke eines solchen Gottes für Hegel unterbestimmt. „Gott ist ein Jenseits, wir können ihn nicht fassen". Die Religion löst sich auf in ein „sehnsuchtsvolles Streben" nach dem unendlichen Anderen (VPR 1, S. 187–188).

Kultus und Mystik

Hegels Einteilung der Psychologie in den theoretischen und den praktischen Geist ahmt die alte Unterscheidung zwischen dem Erkenntnisvermögen einerseits und dem Begehrungsvermögen andererseits nach. Während die Erkenntnis dessen, was ist, dem Verstand obliegt, richtet sich der Wille auf das, was sein soll. Hegel überträgt das Verhältnis der Intelligenz zum Willen dergestalt auf die Religion, dass dem theoretischen Geist die religiösen Vorstellungen, dem praktischen Geist der Kultus entsprechen. Im Vorspann zur Psychologie beschreibt Hegel das Wesen des subjektiven Geistes so, dass seine Produkte „im Theoretischen das Wort und im Praktischen (noch nicht Tat und Handlung) Genuss" seien (Enz § 444). Die beiden Dimensionen lassen sich in der Religion leicht wiederfinden. Während die theoretische Seite alles umfasst, was dem sichtbaren oder hörbaren Ausdruck religiöser Vorstellungen dient, gehören zur praktischen Seite der Religion die Erfahrung des Kultus sowie der mystischen Einheit mit dem Absoluten.

Mit dem Übergang vom theoretischen zum praktischen Geist verbindet Hegel zugleich das Motiv der Rückkehr aus dem Gegensatz des Bewusstseins zur Einheit des Selbstbewusstseins. Im Kultus wird Gott nicht mehr als ein Gegenüber des Subjekts vorgestellt, sondern der Mensch erlebt sich selbst als eins mit dem Absoluten. Die Aufhebung des Gegensatzes zwischen Gott und Mensch bildet den Zweck des Kultus. Das gläubige Subjekt verfolgt die Absicht, „das positive Gefühl des Teilhabens, der Teilnahme an jenem Einssein sich zu geben aus jener Entzweiung, und seiner Positivität zu genießen". Dabei unterscheidet Hegel ein „wesentlich äußerliches, öffentliches Handeln" von einem „inneren Handeln des Gemüts" (VPR 1, S. 98). Mit dem ersten meint Hegel alle Arten ritueller Handlungen, bei dem anderen denkt er an den Weg der Bekehrung des einzelnen Menschen.[16] Bemerkenswert ist, dass Hegel den kirchlichen Gottesdienst nicht gegen die private Frömmigkeit ausgespielt wissen will.[17] Vielmehr beklagt er die unter seinen Zeitgenossen verbreitete einseitige Betonung des subjektiven Glaubens, bei der „aller Kultus in dies bloße Empfinden zusammenschrumpft" (VPR 1, S. 101).

Im ersten Teil der *Vorlesungen* gibt Hegel einen Überblick über die verschiedenen Formen des Kultus. Dabei weicht die Systematik aus dem Jahr 1824 merklich ab von der Ordnung von 1827. Während sich Hegel in dem früheren Jahrgang an der Entwicklung der nichtchristlichen Religionen des Altertums orientiert, hält er sich in der späteren Fassung an das Christentum. Der gemeinsame Nenner der beiden Fassungen ist der Gedanke des Opfers, verstanden als ein bewusster Verzicht des Menschen und damit als die Lösung von den Bindungen an das Endliche. Je nach Stufe der Religion vollzieht sich die Aufgabe mehr im materiell-konkreten oder im geistig-übertragenen Sinn. Durch seine Erhebung über das Endliche öffnet sich der gläubige Mensch für das Absolute. Die Einheit des Endlichen mit dem Unendlichen ist gemäß dem Zeugnis der religiösen Vorstellung bereits Wirklichkeit und muss von dem einzelnen Subjekt nur noch nachvollzo-

---

16 In seinem Manuskript spricht Hegel einerseits von den „Sakramenten", andererseits von der „Heilsordnung" (VPR 1, S. 99). Der letztere Ausdruck steht im Protestantismus für die verschiedenen Stufen der Rechtfertigung und Heiligung des Sünders durch die Gnade Gottes.

17 In diesem Sinn trifft zu, „dass Hegel im Unterschied zu dem gewöhnlichen Kultusbegriff, der darunter nur äußere, öffentliche Religionshandlungen versteht, einen geistigen Kultusbegriff entwickelt" (Dellbrügger 1998, S. 313).

gen werden. Der Kultus ist demzufolge „die Tätigkeit des Hervorbringens und des Bewusstseins dieser Einheit und des Genusses dieser Einheit, dass das, was im Glauben an sich ist, vollbracht werde, und dass es gefühlt und genossen werde" (VPR 1, S. 248).

Die Einheit mit dem Absoluten kann nur gefühlt und genossen werden, wenn das Subjekt seine sonstigen Interessen und Neigungen aufgibt oder zurückstellt. Daher nennt Hegel den Kultus „praktisch" in dem Sinn, „dass der Zweck in mir realisiert sei gegen mich, meine besondere Subjektivität" (VPR 1, S. 249). Der Schwerpunkt der religiösen Praxis liegt auf dem Hervorbringen der mystischen Einheit. Mit dieser Deutung stellt sich Hegel dem Modell eines moralischen Glaubens bei Kant oder Fichte entgegen. In der Religion geht es weniger um das sittlich Gute, das der Mensch bewirken soll, als um die Erfahrung der Teilhabe am Absoluten. Die Bedingungen dafür schafft das Subjekt durch Entsagung und Opfer. Je deutlicher der Gegensatz zwischen Mensch und Gott sowie seine Überwindung hervortreten, desto näher kommt der Kultus dem wahren Wesen von Religion. In den nichtchristlichen Religionen zeigt sich die Spannung im Verhältnis zwischen Natur und Geist. Hegel drückt sie so aus, dass sowohl Gott „mit einer Naturbestimmtheit gesetzt" als auch der freie Mensch „mit einer Naturbestimmtheit befangen" sei (VPR 1, S. 252). Deshalb herrscht zunächst der Eindruck vor, eine Überwindung des Gegensatzes sei gar nicht erforderlich. In Anspielung auf die Naturreligion spricht Hegel von dem „heiteren Kultus" (VPR 1, S. 253). Er ist gekennzeichnet durch ein „ursprüngliches Versöhntsein" oder, was für Hegel das gleiche bedeutet, einen „Mangel des Bedürfnisses des Versöhntseins" (VPR 1, S. 259).

In der afrikanischen „Religion der Zauberei" versuchen die Gläubigen, durch magische Praktiken den Gang der Natur zu beeinflussen. Der gemeinschaftliche Kultus bestehe in einem „Zustand des Außersichseins", der herbeigeführt wird, indem die Menschen ihre Sinne durch „Tanz, Musik, Geschrei, Fressen, selbst Mischung der Geschlechter" betäuben (VPR 2, S. 202). Der Buddhismus hingegen zielt auf das „ruhige Insichsein" des Subjekts. In Asien herrsche die „Begierde zur Begierdelosigkeit, zu opferloser Entsagung" (VPR 2, S. 212). Sie zeigt sich etwa im Rückzug der Mönche aus dem öffentlichen Leben, wenn diese „das formelle Opfer des äußerlichen Besitzes" vollziehen (VPR 1, S. 255), ohne von dem Verzicht im Inneren getroffen zu werden. Der Naturreligion stellt Hegel die Religion der Kunst gegenüber. In ihr besitze der Geist das Übergewicht, „so dass die natürliche Seite als unterworfen, als idealisiert durch die geistige Einheit vorgestellt wird" (VPR 1, S. 257). Das Opfer nimmt nun die Gestalt der „Arbeit des Menschen" an, der das Kunstwerk erschafft. Durch die „Anstrengung der Partikularität des Selbstbewusstseins" bringt er seine Vorstellung des Absoluten „äußerlich zur Anschauung" (VPR 1, S. 258). In der griechischen „Religion der Schönheit" erkennt der Mensch die Götter als geistige oder sittliche Mächte an und macht sie vorstellig „in Preisen, Festen, Triumphen, Schauspielen, Dramen, Gesängen usf." (VPR 2, S. 384). Die Verehrung der Götter bedeutet zugleich eine Selbstdarstellung des Menschen.

An dieser Stelle treten die ersten „Störungen" (VPR 1, S. 261) der Einheit von Natur und Geist auf. Der Mensch weiß zwar um die sittliche Pflicht im Allgemeinen, aber sein eigenes, zufälliges Schicksal im Besonderen bleibt ihm entzogen. Er überlässt sich der göttlichen Vorsehung oder versucht, durch Orakel sein Schicksal zu ergründen (vgl. VPR 2, S. 387–388). Hegel spricht von dem Erfordernis eines „Abbüßens"[18] und einer nicht aufgelösten „Trauer", die über allen Festen mit ihren Genüssen schwebe (VPR 1, S. 261). Der ganze Ernst des Schicksals zeige sich im Tod des Menschen. Hegel erinnert an den antiken Totendienst: „So sind die Manen das Unversöhnte, was versöhnt werden muss; sie müssen gerächt werden" (VPR 1, S. 262).[19] Die wahre Versöhnung liegt für Hegel nicht in der natürlichen und sorglosen Einheit, sondern geht durch die Erfahrung des Negativen, sei es in der Widerfahrnis von Unglück, sei es im Verüben eines Verbrechens. Erst mit der „Umkehr" (VPR 2, S. 390) trete das Geistige am Menschen hervor. In dieser Hinsicht weist der Kultus der heidnischen Religionen voraus auf das Christentum. Wenn etwa die Mysterien von Eleusis der Suche Demeters nach ihrer von Hades geraubten Tochter Persephone gedenken, so Hegel, dann hat dieser Vorgang „die höhere Bedeutung, wie in der christlichen Religion, von Auferstehung" (VPR 2, S. 393).

In der *Vorlesung* von 1827 setzt Hegel den christlichen Gottesdienst ausdrücklich in Bezug zu dem dogmatischen Lehrstück von der *unio mystica* (vgl. VPR 1, S. 333). Die theologischen Debatten über den Zusammenhang zwischen der Rechtfertigung des sündigen Menschen, der Gemeinschaft der Gläubigen mit Christus und der Einwohnung des Heiligen Geistes in der Gemeinde waren dem Berliner Philosophen seit Tübinger Studienzeiten vertraut.[20] Zur genaueren Kennzeichnung des inneren Kultus gebraucht er den Begriff der Andacht. Darunter ist nicht einfach die Überzeugung von der Existenz Gottes oder das Nachdenken über Religion zu verstehen, sondern Andacht „ist vorhanden, wenn der Glaube lebhafter wird, wenn das Subjekt betet, wenn es nicht bloß gegenständlich mit diesem Inhalt beschäftigt ist, wenn es sich hineinversenkt" (VPR 1, S. 333).

---

18 Im zweiten Teil der Vorlesung erwähnt Hegel Agamemnon, der „ein Menschenopfer veranstaltet, um günstigen Wind zu erhalten" (VPR 2, S. 394), und seine Tochter Iphigenie der Göttin Artemis zum Pfand gibt.

19 Achill zum Beispiel „schlachtet so eine Anzahl Trojaner, um die Manen des [sc. von Hektor getöteten] Patroklos zu versöhnen durch das Blut der Feinde" (VPR 2, S. 396).

20 Zur Lehre von der *unio mystica* im Altprotestantismus vgl. Nüssel 2000, S. 239–292.

Ferner beschreibt Hegel die Andacht als die „Entfernung der Vorstellungen". Die Erfahrung der mystischen Einheit mit Gott ist nicht etwas Passives, sondern das Subjekt muss aktiv die Bedingungen dafür schaffen. Zur Andacht gehört „diese Energie, Gewaltsamkeit, gegen das sonst interessierte Bewusstsein sich in der Wahrheit festzuhalten" (VPR 1, S. 334).

Was die äußerlichen Formen des christlichen Kultus anbelangt, dienen sie dem Hervorbringen des Gefühls der Versöhnung, wenn auch nicht auf geistige, sondern auf sinnliche Weise. Wer sich mit dem Unendlichen vereinigen will, muss sich über das Endliche erheben. Indem das Subjekt auf etwas von sich verzichtet, wird es frei für die Verbindung mit Gott. „So wird von dieser Negation, dem Opfer, zum Genuss, zum Bewusstsein fortgegangen, sich vermittels ihrer in Einheit mit Gott gesetzt zu haben" (VPR 1, S. 334). Ihren sinnfälligen Ausdruck findet die Einheit des gläubigen Christen mit Gott im Sakrament des Abendmahls. Durch die Feier des Opfertodes Jesu ereignet sich

> der Genuss, das Bewusstsein dieser göttlichen Gnade, das Bewusstsein, Bürger im Reich Gottes zu sein – das, was mystische Union genannt ist, das Sakrament des Abendmahls, wo auf sinnliche, anschauliche Weise dem Menschen gegeben wird das Bewusstsein seiner Versöhnung mit Gott, das Einwohnen und Einkehren des Geistes in ihm. (VPR 3, S. 166)

Als die „höchste Form im Kultus" bezeichnet Hegel indes die Opferung und Reinigung des eigenen Herzens. Damit meint er einen Prozess, der in religiöser Sprache „Reue und Buße" heißt (VPR 1, S. 334) und bei dem es nicht mehr auf die äußere Tätigkeit, sondern auf die innere Haltung des Subjekts ankommt. Der Mensch soll seine Leidenschaften aufgeben und alle partikularen Interessen hintanstellen. „Dies Moment der Entsagung kommt dann in der positiven Religion konkret in der Gestalt von Opfern vor; hier betrifft zwar diese Negation mehr das Äußere, hat aber Beziehung wesentlich auf das Innere, wie dies bei der Buße, Reinigung, Reue noch mehr hervortritt" (VPR 1, S. 250). Hinter dieser Formulierung steht der unter anderem im Christentum verbreitete Glaube, dass die geistige Einheit mit Gott nicht nur die Lösung der Bindungen an das Sinnliche, sondern auch die Anerkenntnis eigenen Versagens voraussetzt.

> Hier ist die Forderung, dass das Herz breche – d.h. der unmittelbare Wille, natürliches Selbstbewusstsein soll aufgegeben werden, und damit hängt dann zusammen mit dieser Bestimmung der Freiheit, dass hier im Subjekt erscheinen kann und muss der Geist, wie er wahrhaft an und für sich ist. (VPR 1, S. 263)

Das Verständnis der Ausführungen Hegels zum Kultus wird erschwert durch den Umstand, dass er am Ende der Philosophie der Religion zugleich den Übergang von der Religion zur Philosophie bewerkstelligen will.[21] Was die Religion im Modus der Vorstellung betrachtete, bringt die Philosophie in die Form des Begriffs. Daher, so scheint es, geschieht die wahre Erkenntnis des Absoluten nicht im religiösen Glauben, sondern durch philosophisches Denken. Folgerichtig bezeichnet Hegel die Philosophie als einen „beständigen Kultus" (VPR 1, S. 334). Doch damit nicht genug. Am Ende der *Vorlesungen* deutet Hegel außerdem einen Übergang von der Religion zur Sittlichkeit an. Der Schritt kommt überraschend, geht die Sittlichkeit doch sowohl in der *Phänomenologie des Geistes* als auch im enzyklopädischen System der Religion voraus. Berücksichtigt man freilich die Abhängigkeit der Religionsphilosophie von der Philosophie des subjektiven Geistes, wird der Zusammenhang verständlich. Denn auf die Psychologie folgt im System die Philosophie des objektiven Geistes oder Rechtsphilosophie. Der Abschnitt über den praktischen Geist gipfelt in dem Bewusstsein der Freiheit des Subjekts von seinen zufälligen Neigungen und der Selbstbestimmung des Willens. „Die wahre Freiheit ist als Sittlichkeit dies, dass der Wille nicht subjektive[n], d. i. eigensüchtige[n], sondern allgemeinen Inhalt zu seinen Zwecken hat" (Enz § 469 Anm.).

Insofern der Kultus die praktische Seite der Religion bildet und dem praktischen Geist in der Psychologie entspricht, hat der Übergang von der Religion zur Sittlichkeit seine Entsprechung in dem Abschnitt der *Enzyklopädie* von 1830 über den freien Geist.[22] Dort stellt Hegel ausdrücklich die Verbindung zur christlichen Religion her. Durch das Christentum sei die Idee der Freiheit „in die Welt gekommen". Gemäß dem christlichen Glauben habe das Individuum „einen unendlichen Wert", da jeder Einzelne „Gegenstand und Zweck der Liebe Gottes, dazu bestimmt ist, zu Gott als Geist sein absolutes Verhältnis, diesen Geist in sich wohnen zu haben, d. i. dass der Mensch an sich zur höchsten Freiheit bestimmt ist" (Enz § 482 Anm.). In der rechtlichen und sittlichen Ordnung sieht Hegel die objektive Verwirklichung der Freiheit. Durch sie erscheint der göttliche Geist in der menschlichen Gesellschaft. Deshalb nennt Hegel neben der Philosophie auch die Sittlichkeit als den „wahrhaftesten Kultus" (VPR 1, S. 334).

Das die Sittlichkeit mit der Philosophie verbindende Stichwort ist die Freiheit. Als freies kommt das Subjekt „zum Bewusstsein seiner Unendlichkeit in sich" (VPR 1, S. 262). Im protestantischen Christentum ist die Freiheit das Produkt der Versöhnung des Menschen mit Gott.[23] Der religiösen Erfahrung der Einheit mit Gott entspricht das philosophische Erkennen des Absoluten. Religion und Phi-

---

21 Zum viel diskutierten Verhältnis von Philosophie und Religion siehe zuletzt Mooren 2018.
22 Zur Entstehung des Abschnitts siehe Jaeschke 2016, S. 321.
23 Vgl. VPR 3, S. 106–107 und S. 198 sowie VWG, S. 501–502.

losophie haben zu ihrem gemeinsamen Gegenstand „das Wahre in seiner höchsten Gestalt als absoluten Geist, als Gott" (VPR 1, S. 334–335; vgl. Enz § 1). Deshalb kommt es in der Philosophie nicht weniger als in der Religion darauf an, dass sich der Mensch „seiner Subjektivität entschlage, der subjektiven Einfälle der einzelnen Eitelkeit" (VPR 1, S. 335). Was Entsagung und Opfer in der Religion bezwecken, leistet in der Philosophie die Voraussetzungslosigkeit des reinen Denkens.

Indem Hegel zugleich einen Bezug der Religion zur Sittlichkeit herstellt, macht er deutlich, dass die Erhebung zum Absoluten den Menschen nicht aus seinen weltlichen Lebenszusammenhängen herausreißt. Im Gegenteil soll das Allgemeine, mit dem sich das endliche Subjekt eins weiß, zugleich die gesellschaftliche Wirklichkeit prägen. Nach christlicher Auffassung darf der Glaube an Gott nicht von der Liebe zum Nächsten getrennt werden. Der religiöse Mensch braucht das Endliche nicht zu fürchten, sondern verhält sich „zum Weltlichen, Wirklichen als bei sich selbst seiende, in sich versöhnt seiende, schlechthin feste und unendliche Subjektivität" (VPR 3, S. 262). An die Stelle der drei mönchischen Gelübde von Ehelosigkeit, Armut und Gehorsam tritt für Hegel die aktive Gestaltung des Lebens in der Familie, des beruflichen Erwerbs und der staatlichen Ordnung.[24]

Wenn Hegel die religiöse Erfahrung mystischer Einheit mit der Sittlichkeit in Verbindung bringt, liegt darin keineswegs ein Reduktionismus. Die Religion soll ebenso wenig von der Sittlichkeit verdrängt wie durch die Philosophie ersetzt werden. Weder das philosophische Denken noch das sittliche Handeln tut der Eigenständigkeit des religiösen Bewusstseins einen Abbruch. Indem Hegel die praktische Seite der Religion als die Erhebung des Menschen zu Gott in Kultus und Mystik beschreibt, greift er vielmehr auf das theologische Motiv des fiduziellen Glaubens zurück. Als solchen bezeichnet die christliche Tradition das Vertrauen auf Gott und die Tätigkeiten, mittels deren der Mensch Anteil an der von Gott gewirkten Versöhnung zu gewinnen vermag. Dieses Geschehen, das in der Theologie ‚Rechtfertigung' heißt, ist nichts Privates, sondern setzt eine Gemeinschaft von Gläubigen voraus. „Das Letzte des Kultus ist dann eben, dass das Individuum diesen Prozess mit sich selbst durchläuft und so bleibt Mitglied der Gemeinde, in der der Geist lebendig ist" (VPR 3, S. 263). In der kirchlichen Gemeinschaft entwickeln sich die Lehren und Überzeugungen, welche die theoretische Seite der Religion oder den propositionalen Glauben ausmachen. Propositionaler Glaube und fiduzieller Glaube, theoretische Vorstellungen und religiöse

---

24 Vgl. VPR 3, S. 169–170 und S. 264–265 sowie VWG, S. 466.

Praxis gehören für Hegel ebenso eng zusammen wie theoretischer Geist und praktischer Geist, Intelligenz und Wille.

Literatur

Enz | Hegel, Georg Wilhelm Friedrich. (1992). *Enzyklopädie der philosophischen Wissenschaften im Grundrisse (1830)*. In: GW 20. [Zitiert nach Paragraphen.]

GW | Hegel, Georg Wilhelm Friedrich. (1968–). *Gesammelte Werke*. 31 Bände. In Verbindung mit der Deutschen Forschungsgemeinschaft herausgegeben von der Nordrhein-Westfälischen Akademie der Wissenschaften und der Künste. Hamburg: Meiner.

HEnz | Hegel, Georg Wilhelm Friedrich. (2001). *Enzyklopädie der philosophischen Wissenschaften im Grundrisse (1817)*. In: GW 13. [Zitiert nach Paragraphen.]

VPR | Hegel, Georg Wilhelm Friedrich. (1983–1985). *Vorlesungen über die Philosophie der Religion*. 3 Bände. Walter Jaeschke (Hrsg.). Hamburg: Meiner.

VWG | Hegel, Georg Wilhelm Friedrich. (1996). *Vorlesungen über die Philosophie der Weltgeschichte*. Karl Brehmer (Hrsg.). Hamburg: Meiner.

Audi, Robert. (2008). „Belief, Faith, and Acceptance". In: *International Journal for Philosophy of Religion* 63, S. 87–102.

Dellbrügger, Günther. (1998). *Gemeinschaft Gottes mit den Menschen. Hegels Theorie des Kultus*. Würzburg: Königshausen & Neumann.

De Nys, Martin J. (2009). *Hegel and Theology*. London: T & T Clark.

Inwood, Michael J. (2007). *A Commentary on Hegel's Philosophy of Mind*. Oxford/New York: Oxford University Press.

Jaeschke, Walter. (1983). *Die Religionsphilosophie Hegels*. Darmstadt: Wissenschaftliche Buchgesellschaft.

Jaeschke, Walter. (2003; ³2016). *Hegel-Handbuch. Leben – Werk – Wirkung*. Stuttgart: Metzler.

Mooren, Nadine. (2018). *Hegel und die Religion. Eine Untersuchung zum Verhältnis von Religion, Philosophie und Theologie in Hegels System*. Hamburg: Meiner.

Nüssel, Friederike. (2000). *Allein aus Glauben. Zur Entwicklung der Rechtfertigungslehre in der konkordistischen und frühen nachkonkordistischen Theologie*. Göttingen: Vandenhoeck & Ruprecht.

Rometsch, Jens. (2007). *Hegels Theorie des erkennenden Subjekts. Systematische Untersuchungen zur enzyklopädischen Philosophie des subjektiven Geistes*. Würzburg: Königshausen & Neumann.

Sans, Georg. (2016a). „Frömmigkeit als unmittelbares Wissen von Gott. Hegel und Schleiermacher". In: *Zeitschrift für Theologie und Kirche* 113, S. 156–170.

Sans, Georg. (2016b). „Philosophische Begriffe ohne religiöse Vorstellungen sind leer. Hegel über das Wissen vom Unbedingten und den Glauben an Gott". In: Felix Resch (Hrsg.). *Die Frage nach dem Unbedingten. Gott als genuines Thema der Philosophie*. Dresden: Text & Dialog, S. 385–400.

Stederoth, Dirk. (2001). *Hegels Philosophie des subjektiven Geistes. Ein komparatorischer Kommentar*. Berlin: Akademie Verlag.

Stederoth, Dirk. (2006). Art. „Gefühl". In: Paul Cobben/Paul Cruysberghs/Peter Jonkers/Lu de Vos (Hrsg.). *Hegel-Lexikon*. Darmstadt: Wissenschaftliche Buchgesellschaft, S. 220 – 222.

Johannes-Georg Schülein

,Der Geist ist nicht das Höchste'
Schellings Psychologie in den *Stuttgarter Privatvorlesungen* von 1810

Abstract. *Schellings* Stuttgarter Privatvorlesungen *von 1810 enthalten im Grundzug eine Theorie der menschlichen Psyche. Die zentrale These besagt, dass nicht der Geist das höchste Prinzip der menschlichen Psyche, des menschlichen Seins oder gar der Welt sei; vielmehr sei die Seele das Höchste. Der Aufsatz legt eine argumentorientierte Rekonstruktion der Schelling'schen Psychologie vor und zeigt, inwiefern seine Hauptthese im Kontext zweier Annahmen zu sehen ist: einem in der Tradition des Christentums verwurzelten Vertrauen in Erlösung durch Liebe sowie der Annahme einer in der Tradition des Platonismus verwurzelten Form von Teilhabe. Mit diesen Annahmen begibt sich Schellings Psychologie in einen aufschlussreichen Gegensatz zu Hegel und Freud.*

Schelling's 1810 Stuttgart seminars *contain in a nutshell a theory of the human psyche. His major claim is that spirit is not the highest principle, neither of the psyche nor of life or the world in general. Rather, it is the soul that is supreme for Schelling. This essay provides an argument-based reading of Schelling's psychology and shows how his major claim depends on two points: a trust in salvation through divine love rooted in Christianity, and the supposition that we have access to this love through a kind of emotional participation rooted in Platonism. Despite considerable similarities, these points demonstrate how sharply Schelling's theory of the psyche contrasts with those of Hegel and Freud.*

Als Psychologie bezeichnen wir heute vor allem eine Wissenschaft, die sich mit den vielfältigen Facetten unserer Psyche, unseres mentalen und emotionalen Lebens, seinem Funktionieren, seinen Pathologien befasst. Dem Wortsinn nach meint ,Psychologie' indessen allgemein ,Lehre von der Seele (gr. ψυχή)' und kann entsprechend sehr viel mehr sein als die wissenschaftliche Befassung mit dem Psychischen, wie wir es heute kennen. In seinen *Stuttgarter Privatvorlesungen* von 1810 hat Schelling eine bemerkenswerte Psychologie in beiden Bedeutungen vorgelegt, die in der Forschungsdiskussion bislang nur eine randständige Rolle spielt: Einerseits unterzieht er die menschliche Psyche einer differenzierten Betrachtung, andererseits und zugleich legt er eine Seelenlehre im erweiterten Sinn vor. Beides hängt eng miteinander zusammen. Im Zentrum seiner Ausführungen findet sich die These, dass nicht etwa der Geist das höchste Prinzip der

https://doi.org/10.1515/9783110673692-014

menschlichen Psyche, des menschlichen Seins oder gar der Welt insgesamt sei. Höher als der Geist stehe die Seele, in Wahrheit sei sie ‚das Höchste‘.

In der ersten Bedeutung situiert Schelling den menschlichen Geist in einem Gefüge weiterer psychischer Instanzen und weist auf eine psychopathologische Basis des Geisteslebens hin. Seine Ausführungen gipfeln in der radikalen Behauptung, dass der Wahnsinn die Basis des menschlichen Geistes sei. Auf dieser Basis kann der Geist zwar durchaus aufblühen, er droht aber stets auch zu unterliegen. Grundsätzlich gilt, dass Geist für Schelling keine stabile, sondern eine abhängige, fragile Instanz ist. Auch wenn er es nicht explizit tut, liegt auf der Hand, dass er sich mit der Depotenzierung des Geistes gegen die ungleich affirmativere Position wendet, die in der klassischen deutschen Philosophie insbesondere von Hegel vertreten wird. Insofern kann Schelling aus der Perspektive vernunftskeptischer Debatten im 20. und 21. Jahrhundert, die gerade in der Philosophie Hegels wenig mehr als einen übersteigerten Totalitarismus der Vernunft sehen, ausgesprochen modern wirken. Wie in der Forschung inzwischen mehrfach gezeigt wurde, sind in verschiedenen Schriften Schellings geist- und vernunftkritische Überlegungen zu finden, die u. a. psychoanalytische Positionen Freuds antizipieren.[1] Das gilt auch für die *Stuttgarter Privatvorlesungen*. Es ist überraschend, dass Schellings Psychologie aus diesem Text zumeist bloß beiläufig als eine Ergänzung der Konzeptionen des Unbewussten in der Freiheitsschrift (1809) und den *Weltalter*-Entwürfen (1811–1815) behandelt wird.[2] Dabei

---

1 Vgl. zu Schelling und Freud allgemein Fyttches These, dass die Geschichte der Psychoanalyse einer „radical revision" bedürfe, insofern man u. a. bereits bei Schelling „many of the characteristic idioms associated with psychoanalytic theory in the twentieth century" finden könne (Fyttche 2012, S. 1 u. 3). Etwas zurückhaltender wertet McGrath 2012 die Parallelen zwischen Schellings Freiheitsschrift und Freud aus, wobei er die Bedeutung Jakob Böhmes betont. Inwiefern die *Stuttgarter Privatvorlesungen* als Ergänzung zu der Freiheitsschrift und den *Weltaltern* einbezogen werden, zeigt sich etwa bei Žižek 1997. Bowie 2010 konzentriert sich indessen auf die psychoanalytischen Implikationen des *Systems des transzendentalen Idealismus* und der frühen Naturphilosophie. Vgl. in diesem Zusammenhang auch die debattenprägenden Studien von Marquard 1987 sowie 1975, S. 22, wo es zum frühen Schelling prägnant heißt: „Freuds Psychoanalyse – kann man sagen – ist in wichtigen Teilen die entzauberte Gestalt der Naturphilosophie Schellings."

2 Die m. W. ausführlichste Rekonstruktion der Stuttgarter Psychologie Schellings hat Müller-Lüneschloß 2012, S. 257–277, im Rahmen ihrer Studie zu den *Stuttgarter Privatvorlesungen* vorgelegt, allerdings ohne auf Freud Bezug zu nehmen. Sie stützt ihre Analysen auf dasselbe Textmaterial, das auch im Folgenden verwendet wird, bezieht darüber hinaus aber noch Schellings *Clara* ein. Des Weiteren hat McGrath eine knappe Rekonstruktion der Stuttgarter Psychologie in zwei Appendizes seiner Studie beigefügt (McGrath 2012, S. 190–195). S. auch die Rekonstruktion von Oesterreich 2002, der Schellings Psychologie, ohne auf Freud Bezug zu nehmen, als „Rationalitätskritik" interpretiert, die keiner „‚romantischen‘ Vorliebe für das sogenannte ‚Irratio-

enthalten die *Stuttgarter Privatvorlesungen* eine eigenständige, von Schelling so klar wie sonst wohl nirgends ausgeführte Theorie der menschlichen Psyche, in der er drei Instanzen unterscheidet, die mit *Es*, *Ich* und *Über-Ich* bei Freud freilich nicht deckungsgleich, aber vergleichbar sind.[3]

Die zweite Bedeutung, in der Schelling auf eine charakteristische Weise Psychologie als Seelenlehre im erweiterten Sinn betreibt, markiert indessen einen substantiellen Unterschied zu Freud. Dass Schelling gerade die Seele und nicht den Geist als ‚das Höchste' behauptet, geht damit einher, dass er die psychische Gesundheit des menschlichen Geistes von dessen Unterwerfung unter die Seele abhängig macht. Entscheidend ist, dass der menschliche Geist vermittelt über die Seele letztlich einem göttlichen Prinzip untergeordnet wird. Allein dem Wirken eines solchen Prinzips, das Schelling ‚Liebe' nennt und das in den Seelen der Menschen latent vorhanden sein soll, traut er es zu, die Gesundheit der Psyche und des Geistes sicherzustellen. Die vernunft- und geistkritischen Implikationen der Schelling'schen Psychologie sind dergestalt auf eine theosophische Harmonievorstellung hin orientiert. So geneigt man heute sein mag, den menschlichen Geist als eine fragile Instanz zu betrachten, so schwer dürfte es vielen – Freud eingeschlossen – fallen, diese Fragilität durch göttlichen Beistand für überwindbar zu halten. Dass Schelling in der Tiefenschicht der Psyche den Wahnsinn freizulegen beansprucht und zugleich eine absolute, durch eine göttliche Seele vermittelte Genesung von ihm für möglich hält, ist jedoch der systematische Grundzug seiner Psychologie, den es ernst zu nehmen gilt, auch wenn man ihm skeptisch gegenübersteht. Diesen Grundzug in einer argumentorientierten Rekonstruktion herauszuarbeiten und kritisch zu reflektieren, ist das Anliegen dieses Beitrags.

Dazu wird zuerst Schellings systematisches Argument für die Subordination des Geistes unter die Seele dargestellt, das seine Psychologie insgesamt informiert (1). Vor dem Hintergrund der Stellung, die er dem Menschen in der Welt überhaupt zuweist (2), kann sodann Schellings psychologische Sicht des gesun-

---

nale', sondern der modernen Problematik korrumpierter Rationalität" (Oesterreich 2002, S. 42) entspringe.

3 Ähnlich genau widmet sich wohl nur das sog. „Anthropologische" bzw. „Psychologische" Schema" der menschlichen Psyche, das Ehrhardt 1989, S. 16 – 22, auf der Basis einer Reinschrift herausgegeben hat und das in modifizierter Form auch in SW X, 289 – 294, erscheint. Wesentlich für die vorliegende Argumentation ist jedoch, dass die Seele dort dem Geist untergeordnet zu sein scheint, indem Schelling Geist als den „eigentliche[n] Zweck, was sein soll, worin sich der Wille durch den Verstand erheben, wozu er sich befreien und verklären soll" (Ehrhardt 1989, S. 17), beschreibt. Die Seele erscheint lediglich als eine passive, der Geist als eine aktive Vereinigung der psychischen Instanzen (Ehrhardt 1989, S. 21). Zur Rekonstruktion des Schemas vgl. Hennigfeld 2002, S. 1 – 22, insb. S. 8 u. 11, sowie Müller-Lüneschloß 2012, S. 257 – 259.

den, weil der Seele unterworfenen (3), und des kranken, weil der Seele nicht unterworfenen Geistes untersucht werden (4). Charakteristisch für den Menschen ist nach Schelling, dass er eine natürliche und eine geistige Seite in sich auf eine spannungsgeladene Weise vereint. Es ist diese Spannung, die in der menschlichen Psyche zum Austrag kommt und sich in Schellings Augen einzig dadurch bewältigen lässt, dass die göttliche Seele eine Autorität über den menschlichen Geist ausübt. Am Ende des Aufsatzes (5) steht eine kritische Würdigung, in der Schellings Auffassung von der Seele im Kontext eines von christlicher Liebe inspirierten Versöhnungsideals, das dem Menschen über eine Art platonischer Teilhabe zugänglich werden soll, interpretiert wird. Den Schlussstein bildet ein skizzenhafter Ausblick auf den von Schelling implizit kritisierten Hegel, der den Rekurs auf ein göttliches Prinzip vermeidet und stattdessen einen entschieden diesseitigen Umgang mit den Pathologien der Psyche vorschlägt.

1 Schellings These und Hauptargument

Schelling führt seine These zur Hierarchie zwischen Geist und Seele folgendermaßen ein: „Es ist zwar die gewöhnliche Meinung, daß der Geist das Höchste im Menschen sey. Allein daß er es durchaus nicht sein kann, folgt daraus [...]" (AA II/8, 158; SW VII, 467). Lässt man das Argument zunächst noch außer Acht, spricht Schelling in diesem Zitat über eine offensichtlich verbreitete Auffassung, wobei ein konkreter Bezug sich besonders aufdrängt: 1807, drei Jahre bevor er in Stuttgart seine Privatvorlesungen hält, hat Hegel bekanntlich die *Phänomenologie des Geistes* veröffentlicht und erklärt, dass Geist „der erhabenste Begriff" und „das Absolute als *Geist*" zu betrachten sei. Es gelte: „Das Geistige allein ist das *Wirkliche*" (HGW 9, 22). Obwohl er ihn nicht erwähnt, liegt es nahe, dass Schelling sich, wenn er dem Geist abspricht, ‚das Höchste' zu sein, gegen Hegels philosophische Auszeichnung des Geistes als des ‚erhabensten Begriffs' wendet. Insofern kann auch Schellings These, was anstelle des Geistes in Wahrheit ‚das Höchste' sei, als der Versuch verstanden werden, eine Alternative sowohl zur verbreiteten Meinung über die Bedeutung von Geist im Allgemeinen als auch zur Philosophie Hegels im Besonderen zu entwerfen: „Dieses Höchste", erklärt Schelling, „ist die *Seele*." (AA II/8, 160; SW VII, 468) Auf den Bezug zu Hegel ist am Ende dieses Aufsatzes noch einmal zurückzukommen.

Schellings Hauptargument für die These, dass die Seele und nicht der Geist ‚das Höchste' sei, stützt sich darauf, dass er eine Fehlbarkeit des Geistes, nicht aber der Seele annimmt. Er führt aus, dass der Geist nicht ‚das Höchste' sein könne, weil „er der Krankheit, des Irrthums, der Sünde oder des Bösen fähig ist" (AA II/8, 158; SW VII, 467). Wenn also die Fehlbarkeit des Geistes in seiner Anfälligkeit für die genannten Defekte besteht, zeichnet sich ab: Was immer ‚das Höchste' ist, es muss etwas sein, das sich solche Defekte nicht zuziehen kann. Am Beispiel der Krankheit und des Bösen erläutert Schelling, dass die Seele tatsächlich immun gegen jede Form von Negativität und Mangel sei: „Man spricht von Seelenkrankheiten. Allein dergleichen gibt es nicht. Nur das Gemüth oder der Geist kann krank seyn" (AA II/8, 160; SW VII, 468); „Man sagt wohl auch im gemeinen Leben von einem Menschen: er hat eine böse, eine schwarze, eine falsche Seele" – aber, so Schelling, „eine schwarze Seele heißt *keine* Seele" (AA II/8, 160; SW VII, 469). Positiv gewendet ist für ihn die Seele nicht einfach nur „gut, sondern ist die Güte selbst" (AA II/8, 160; SW VII, 469). Das ausschlaggebende Argument lautet somit: Da der Geist, anders als die Seele, anfällig für Defekte ist, steht die Seele über ihm.

Unschwer ist die starke Voraussetzung zu erkennen, die in dieses Argument eingeht: Schelling betrachtet die Seele als eine gänzlich positive, von Negativität völlig ungetrübte Instanz. Während eine Fehlbarkeit des Geistes aufgrund seiner Anfälligkeit für Irrtum, Krankheit, moralische Übel usw. anzunehmen kaum kontrovers sein dürfte, ist sicherlich nicht auf die gleiche Weise evident, weshalb man mit Schelling auch eine maximale Reinheit der Seele postulieren sollte. Festzuhalten ist, dass Schellings Argument für die Hierarchie zwischen Geist und Seele nicht allein von der Annahme einer Fehleranfälligkeit des Geistes, sondern genauso von der Annahme eben dieser Reinheit der Seele abhängt. Es drängt sich daher die Frage auf, wie die Annahme einer derart reinen Seele zu rechtfertigen ist. Bevor dieser Frage im fünften Abschnitt nachgegangen werden kann, ist Schellings Konzeption des Psychischen zu rekonstruieren.

2 Der Mensch zwischen Natur und Geist

Schellings Bemerkungen zu Geist und Seele sind vor dem Hintergrund seiner Positionierung des Menschen im Ganzen einer göttlichen Weltordnung zu sehen, die er in den *Stuttgarter Privatvorlesungen* darlegt. Er skizziert in diesen Vorlesungen einen Systemgrundriss, wobei er weniger ein philosophisches System im eigenen Namen *zu entwerfen* als vielmehr das „System der Welt" selbst *zu finden* und angemessen darzustellen beansprucht (AA II/8, 68; SW VII, 421). Das gesuchte System, das der Welt selbst eignen soll, gründet sich auf ein selbsttragendes Prinzip, das sich „in jedem Theil des Ganzen reproducirt" (AA II/8, 68; SW VII, 421). Dieses Prinzip soll die Welt nicht nur als Ursache begründen, sondern es soll sich darüber hinaus auch in eben der Welt manifestieren, die von ihm begründet wird. Schelling gibt diesem Prinzip die Namen ‚das Absolute', ‚Gott' oder auch ‚das Urwesen'. Sachlich kennzeichnet er es als eine Einheit, die zugleich einen Gegensatz birgt: Was ‚Gott', ‚das Urwesen' oder ‚Absolute' heißt, sei nicht etwa als eine reine Identität zu begreifen, sondern als „das lebendige (einen Gegensatz in sich enthaltende) Band des Idealen und Realen" (AA II/8, 108; SW VII, 440). In Gestalt des Idealen und Realen thematisiert Schelling grundlegende philosophische Gegensätze wie Seele und Leib, Denken und Sein sowie insbesondere Geist und Natur. Sein allgemeiner Anspruch ist zu zeigen, dass diese Gegensätze in einer Einheit zusammenhängen, die durch das göttliche Absolute gestiftet wird. Da dieses Absolute sich in der Welt manifestiert, birgt grundsätzlich alles, was in der Welt existiert, den Gegensatz des Idealen und Realen in sich.

Anders als er es ab 1801 in seinen identitätsphilosophischen Schriften mehrfach inspiriert von Spinoza getan hat, vertritt Schelling in den *Stuttgarter Privatvorlesungen* keinen reinen Substanzmonismus mehr. Er betrachtet Gott nun nicht mehr als die eine unpersönliche Substanz der gesamten Wirklichkeit. Zwar soll Gott immer noch Substanz sein, aber zugleich auch über Persönlichkeit verfügen. Diese Gottesauffassung arbeitet Schelling maßgeblich in der Freiheitsschrift von 1809 aus, auf die der Text der Stuttgarter Vorlesungen immer wieder rekurriert. Man kann die Vorlesungen als den Versuch deuten, zu zeigen, wie die in der Freiheitsschrift entworfene Auffassung eines persönlichen Gottes das Ganze der geistigen und natürlichen Wirklichkeit metaphysisch prägt.[4] Das philosophische Zentrum dieses Ansatzes liegt in der Unterscheidung zwischen Gott als *Existierendem* und Gott als *Grund* von Existenz. Mit dieser Unterscheidung behauptet Schelling, dass der Grund von Gott als einem existierenden Wesen in Gott selbst liegt, Gott in seiner Existenz also von nichts außer ihm abhängig ist. Damit orientiert er sich nach wie vor an der *Causa-sui*-Struktur, die Spinoza in der ersten Definition der *Ethica* angibt und Gott als der einen Substanz der Wirklichkeit zuspricht.[5] Allererst dadurch, dass Gott sich auf diese Weise in seinem Sein selbst zu gründen vermag, kann er im System der Welt die Rolle des von Schelling geforderten selbsttragenden Prinzips spielen. Schellings nähere Auffassung besagt, dass dieser Grund nicht im Sinne rein logischer Selbstbegründung zu deuten, sondern vielmehr „zu etwas Reellem und Wirklichem zu machen" und zwar konkret *als Natur* zu betrachten sei (AA I/17, 129; SW VII, 358). Die Natur ist in Schellings Augen mithin der Grund, auf den Gott in seinem Existieren bezogen bleibt. Es kommt nun darauf an, wie Schelling im Zusammenhang mit dieser Realauffassung des Naturgrundes die *Causa-sui*-Struktur als ein potentiell

---

4 S. zum Verhältnis der Stuttgarter Privatvorlesungen zur Freiheitsschrift Baumgartner/Korten 1996, S. 105, sowie Sommer 2012, S. 133–144.

5 Vgl. zu Schellings Ontologie in ihrem Spinoza-Bezug, dem hier nicht genauer nachgegangen werden kann, die kritischen Rekonstruktionen Sandkaulens 2004, S. 40–47, und Sommers 2012, S. 109–133.

spannungsgeladenes Gefüge deutet: Den Grund als Natur und damit als etwas Reales zu begreifen, läuft in seinen Augen auf die Annahme von etwas hinaus, „was in Gott selbst nicht *Er selbst* ist" (AA I/17, 130; SW VII, 359). In Gestalt des Naturgrundes gründet sich Gott nach Schelling auf etwas in ihm, das etwas anderes als er selbst ist. Dadurch, dass ein Grund in Gott angenommen wird, der von Gott zugleich verschieden und getrennt bleibt, wird eine Spannung in den Gottesbegriff eingetragen. Diese Spannung vermag Gott noch zu versöhnen, im Menschen entfaltet sie jedoch eine potentiell destruktive Kraft.

Die in Gott angelegte Spannung ist wesentlich für Schellings Ontologie, seine Kosmologie und in der Folge auch für die Psychologie, die er in den *Stuttgarter Privatvorlesungen* vertritt. Der Naturgrund fungiert nach Schelling – erstens – nicht nur als Grund von Gott selbst, sondern auch als Grund aller Dinge: als die „unergreifliche Basis der Realität, der nie aufgehende Rest, das, was sich mit der größten Anstrengung nicht in Verstand auflösen läßt, sondern ewig im Grunde bleibt. [...] Ohne dies vorausgehende Dunkel gibt es keine Realität der Kreatur; Finsternis ist ihr notwendiges Erbteil" (AA I/17, 131; SW VII, 360). Aus diesem dunklen Grund aller Realität stamme insbesondere der „Eigenwille der Kreatur", aufgrund dessen Lebewesen als Individuen selbstisch agieren (AA I/17, 133; SW VII, 363). Gott als dunklem Naturgrund gegenüber steht – zweitens – Gott als Existierender, der, wie Schelling sich ausdrückt, „im reinen Lichte" wohne (AA I/17, 131, SW VII, 360). Die Lichtmetapher ist mit Rationalität und Geist verbunden. Er zeichnet das Licht „als Prinzip des Verstandes" aus (AA I/17, 133; SW VII, 362), der auf das Allgemeine und Universale bezogen sei. Gott als Existierender verfügt auf vollkommene Weise über das Licht des Verstandes und teilt dieses Licht zugleich allem Seienden mit, so dass sich die folgende kosmologische Grundthese ergibt: Alles Seiende birgt in sich „ein doppeltes Prinzip, das jedoch im Grunde nur Ein und das nämliche ist", eben jenes doppelte Prinzip, das auch Gott prägt (AA I/17, 133; SW VII, 362): Eine Bindung an eine natürliche, dunkle, irrationale und selbstische Realität einerseits, eine Partizipation an geistiger, transparenter, rationaler und auf Allgemeinheit gerichteter Idealität andererseits.

Das System der Welt, das Schelling darzustellen beansprucht, untergliedert sich insgesamt in einen naturphilosophischen Teil, in dem das reale, natürliche Prinzip überwiegt, und einen geistphilosophischen Teil, in dem das ideale, geistige Prinzip überwiegt. Die Naturphilosophie beginnt mit einer Betrachtung der Schwere und des Lichts, bevor sie in einer Theorie des organischen Lebens kulminiert, das sich schließlich im Menschen vollendet. An der Spitze der Natur stehend sei der Mensch „die Krone der Schöpfung" (AA II/8, 130; SW VII, 453), er besetze innerhalb der Natur nämlich exakt die Stelle, „wo das geistige Leben eigentlich aufgehen" würde und „das Leibliche als sanfte Unterlage sich dem Geistigen fügen" müsse (AA II/8, 140; SW VII, 458). Erst durch den Menschen eröffnet sich demnach eine echte geistige Welt, in der es Staat und Religion gibt und sich auch die Frage nach der menschlichen Psyche sowie einem Leben nach dem Tod stellt. Schelling wendet sich allen diesen Fragen zu. Prägend bleibt dabei stets die eigentümliche Position des Menschen auf dem Scheitelpunkt von Natur und Geist. Im Hinblick auf Schellings Psychologie sind drei Punkte wesentlich.

Erstens nimmt Schelling keine Gleichrangigkeit von Natur und Geist, Realem und Idealem an, sondern es gilt: „Das Ideale ist der Dignität nach höher als das Reale." (AA II/8, 82; SW VII, 427) „[D]ie ganze Natur ist nur die Staffel, die Unterlage der geistigen Welt, sie ist daher [...] nicht um ihrer selbst willen" (AA II/8, 132; SW VII, 454). Für uns Menschen gehe es mithin darum, dass „wir uns in uns selbst scheiden, uns uns selbst entgegensetzen, uns mit dem besseren [geistigen; J.S.] Theil von uns selbst über den niedrigeren [natürlichen; J.S.] erheben" (AA II/8, 96; SW VII, 433). „Wer sich von seinem [natürlichen; J.S.] Seyn nicht scheidet, dem ist das [natürliche; J.S.] *Seyn* das Wesentliche, nicht sein inneres höheres, wahres [geistiges; J.S.] Wesen." (AA II/8, 100; SW VII, 436) Das Ziel ist nach Schelling somit, die geistige gegenüber der natürlichen Seite des Menschen zu stärken. Präzise besteht die Herausforderung darin, die „*Gewalt*, die das Aeußere [und Natürliche; J.S.] in diesem Leben über das Innere hat" (AA II/8, 142; SW VII, 459 – 460), geistig zu bewältigen.

Zweitens versteht Schelling das reale und natürliche als ein *unbewusstes*, das ideale und geistige als ein *bewusstes* Prinzip. Was er recht früh in seinen Vorlesungen über diesen Zusammenhang sagt, enthält einen Hinweis darauf, wie eine geistige Bewältigung unserer Naturverhaftung konkret gelingen könnte: „In uns sind zwei Principien, ein bewußtloses, dunkles, und ein bewußtes. Der Proceß unserer Selbstbildung [...] besteht [...] immer darin, das in uns bewußtlos Vorhandene zum Bewußtseyn zu erheben, das angeborene Dunkel in uns in das Licht zu erheben, mit Einem Wort zur Klarheit zu gelangen." (AA II/8, 96; SW VII, 433) Bewusstsein beginne dort, wo sich das bewusste Prinzip über das Unbewusste zu erheben vermag. Wir gewinnen demnach eine Macht über die Natur, indem wir sie intellektuell durchdringen, sie uns bewusstmachen und eben dadurch geistig bewältigen. Schelling meint: „Das ganze Leben ist eigentlich nur ein immer höheres Bewußtwerden" (AA II/8, 96; SW VII, 433), wobei die volle Klarheit im irdischen Leben wohl kaum zu erreichen sein dürfte, „immer bleibt noch ein dunkler Rest" (AA II/8, 96; SW VII, 433). Die Herausforderung besteht vor diesem Hintergrund darin, die Macht des menschlichen Geistes soweit wie möglich über die Natur auszudehnen. Wie in der Theorie der Psyche deutlich wird, ist Schelling der Überzeugung, dass der Mensch dazu grundsätzlich nicht ohne den Rekurs auf ein göttliches Prinzip in der Lage ist.

Drittens beschreibt die Stellung des Menschen zwischen Natur und Geist den Ort der menschlichen Freiheit:

> Dadurch also, daß der Mensch zwischen [...] der Natur und [...] Gott in der Mitte steht, ist er
> von beiden *frei*. Er ist frei von Gott dadurch, daß er eine unabhängige Wurzel in der Natur
> hat, frei von der Natur dadurch, daß das Göttliche in ihm geweckt ist, das mitten in der Natur
> über der Natur. Jenes kann man das eigne (natürliche) Theil des Menschen nennen, wodurch
> er Individuum, persönliches Wesen ist; dieses sein göttliches Theil. Dadurch ist er *frei* – im
> menschlichen Sinn –, daß er in den Indifferenzpunkt gestellt ist. (AA II/8, 140; SW VII, 458)

Es ist hier nicht angezeigt, Schellings komplexe Theorie der Freiheit zu rekonstruieren. Aufgrund dieses Zitats ist lediglich festzuhalten, was sich für Schellings
Psychologie als maßgeblich erweist: Die Freiheit des Menschen besteht in einer
relativen Unabhängigkeit von der Natur einerseits, von Gott andererseits. Wenn
Schelling in diesem Zusammenhang davon spricht, das Göttliche sei im Menschen erweckt worden, dann geht es im Kern um die Erweckung von Geist. Die
Formulierung zeigt an, dass der Geist im Menschen zwar erweckt, aber nicht auch
schon voll verwirklicht ist. Voll verwirklicht ist Geist nur in Gott. Der Geist Gottes kann indes kein Geist sein, der sich von der Natur völlig abgewandt hätte,
schließlich gehört sie zu seinem Sein. Deutlicher als in den Stuttgarter Vorlesungen wird in der Freiheitsschrift, worin Gott und Mensch sich für Schelling
unterscheiden: Der Unterschied besteht nicht darin, ob Geist vorliegt oder nicht,
sondern in der Form von Einheit, die der Geist mit der Natur jeweils bildet. Diese
Einheit ist, wie Schelling in der Freiheitsschrift erklärt, in Gott „unauflöslich", im
Menschen aber „zertrennlich" (AA I/17, 134; SW VII, 364). Der Geist Gottes ist nach
Schellings Auffassung in der Lage, sich so über die Natur zu erheben, dass er
diese zugleich völlig zu durchdringen und auf umfassende Weise zu bewältigen
vermag. Er geht eine unauflösliche Einheit mit der Natur ein. Eben das gelingt
dem menschlichen Geist nicht. Er hat zwar teil am göttlichen Geistprinzip, sein
Geist sieht sich aber stets in den Konflikt mit einer widerständigen Natur gezogen, der er als ein menschliches und damit leibliches Wesen verhaftet bleibt.
Insofern Schelling die relative Unabhängigkeit gegenüber Gott und Natur als
menschliche Freiheit beschreibt, zeigt diese Freiheit letztlich die Zwischenstel-
lung und damit auch die Unvollkommenheit des Menschen an. In Gott sind Natur
und Geist versöhnt, im Menschen stehen sie in einem Spannungsverhältnis – und
eben dieses Spannungsverhältnis kommt in der menschlichen Psyche zum Austrag.

3 Schellings Theorie der gesunden Psyche

Wenn Schelling allgemein von Geist spricht, bezieht er sich auf die an die Natur
anschließende und von ihr zugleich abgehobene Sphäre des Idealen. Da er dem
Geist als idealem Prinzip eine Priorität gegenüber der Natur als realem Prinzip

einräumt, kann der Eindruck entstehen, dass Geist sehr wohl eine Art ‚Höchstes‘ wäre. Dieser Eindruck wird dadurch noch verstärkt, dass Schellings psychologische Ausführungen zu Seele und Geist gleichermaßen innerhalb des idealen geistphilosophischen Systemteils stehen und insofern auch die Seele als eine Form von Geist im Allgemeinen erscheint.[6] Theorieimmanent lässt sich der These, dass die Seele ‚das Höchste‘ sei, nur dann Sinn abgewinnen, wenn wir zwischen Geist im engeren Sinn und Geist im Allgemeinen unterscheiden und im letzteren Fall einen unterminologischen Gebrauch des Geistbegriffs für die Sphäre des Idealen überhaupt unterstellen. Die Hierarchie, die Schelling behauptet, besteht in Wahrheit zwischen zwei Prinzipien, die beide als Figurationen des Idealen bzw. von Geist im Allgemeinen präsentiert werden: zwischen *Geist im engeren Sinne* und *Seele*.

Der Geist im engeren Sinne und die Seele sind für Schelling Instanzen der menschlichen Psyche, oder wie man in Anlehnung an Freud sagen kann: des ‚psychischen Apparats‘. Die Parallelen, die Schellings Konzeption zu derjenigen Freuds aufweist, sind durchaus überraschend und lassen Schelling in Ansätzen als einen Wegbereiter der Psychoanalyse erscheinen. Ähnlich wie in Freuds zweiter Topik, in der er ab 1923 zwischen *Es*, *Ich* und *Über-Ich* unterscheidet[7], zeichnet sich der psychische Apparat des Menschen nach Schelling ebenfalls durch drei Instanzen bzw. „Potenzen oder Seiten" aus (AA II/8, 154; SW VII, 465): Zu der *Seele* und dem *Geist* (im engeren Sinn) tritt das *Gemüt*. Die Hierarchie, die Schelling zwischen Seele und Geist annimmt, setzt sich über den Geist im engeren Sinn bis zum Gemüt fort: Die Seele ist die höchste, der Geist die mittlere, das Gemüt die basale psychische Instanz. Bemerkenswert ist hierbei einerseits, wie sehr Schellings Auffassung des Geistes und des Gemüts dem gleicht, was Freud als Ich und Es beschreibt. Andererseits fällt auf, wie tiefgreifend zugleich der Unterschied ist, der zwischen der Seele bei Schelling und dem Über-Ich bei Freud besteht. Da Schellings Theorie der Psyche im Verhältnis zu Freud ein deutliches Profil gewinnt, lohnt es sich, zumindest kursorisch Parallelen und Unterschiede anzuzeigen.

Grundlegend für Schellings Psychologie ist, dass sich zwischen Gemüt, Geist und Seele jenes Spannungsverhältnis zwischen Geist und Natur niederschlägt,

---

6 Zudem schließen die *Stuttgarter Privatvorlesungen* mit Ausführungen zu einem Leben nach dem Tod, in dem recht unvermittelt nicht mehr ‚Seele‘, sondern ‚Geist‘ der leitende Begriff ist. Dass es sich hierbei um eine spannungsvolle Konzeption handelt, liegt auf der Hand. Müller-Lüneschloß 2012, S. 258, erwägt, ob die Psychologie samt ihrer affirmativen Seelenlehre früher entstanden und dann in die Vorlesungen eingefügt sein könnte. Zur Unsterblichkeitslehre vgl. Oesterreich 2002, S. 45–50, sowie Müller-Lüneschloß 2012, S. 268 u. 277–294.
7 Erstmals dargelegt hat Freud die zweite Topik in „Das Ich und das Es" (FGW XIII, 235–290).

das die Stellung des Menschen in der Welt überhaupt prägt. Das Gemüt verbindet den Menschen am stärksten mit der Natur. Schelling beschreibt es als „das Bewußtlose des Menschen" (AA II/8, 158; SW VII, 467), „das dunkle Princip" (AA II/8, 154; SW VII, 465) des psychischen Apparats, durch das dieser auf eine noch gänzlich intransparente Weise mit der Welt der natürlichen Realität verbunden ist. Dergestalt sei das Gemüt „eigentlich das Reale des Menschen", ohne das der Mensch „nichts zeugen oder erschaffen" könne (AA II/8, 156; SW VII, 466). Wenn Schelling schreibt, der Mensch stehe vermittelt über sein Gemüt „von der realen Seite in Rapport mit der Natur, auf der idealen in Rapport mit der höheren Welt, aber nur in dunkelm Rapport" (AA II/8, 154; SW VII, 465), ist klar, dass er nicht etwa annimmt, der Mensch wäre im Gemüt unmittelbar eins mit der Natur. Vielmehr ist das Gemüt bereits eine elementare Form von Geist, die jedoch auf eine besonders enge Weise mit der Natur verbunden bleibt. Diese Naturbindung kommt in den drei Formen zum Ausdruck, die das Gemüt seinerseits in sich birgt. Schelling unterscheidet erstens die *Sehnsucht*, die ihre stärkste Ausprägung in der Schwermut habe und das „Dunkelste und darum Tiefste der menschlichen Natur […] in ihrer tiefsten Erscheinung" sei (AA II/8, 156; SW VII, 465); zweitens die *Begierde*, die innerhalb des Gemüts dem, was den menschlichen Geist eigentlich ausmache, am nächsten komme, sich aber noch als allgemeine Triebhaftigkeit in Form von „Sucht, Begierde, Lust" zeige (AA II/8, 156; SW VII, 466). Diese triebhafte Begierde sei „etwas Unauslöschliches", „jede Befriedigung gibt [ihr] nur neue Kraft, d. h. noch heftigeren Hunger" (AA II/8, 156; SW VII, 466); drittens das *Gefühl* als „das Höchste des Gemüths, das Herrlichste, was ein Mensch im Gemüth haben, und was er über alles schätzen soll" (AA II/8, 156; SW VII, 466). Insgesamt zeigt sich die Sphäre des Gemüts als naturgebundene, begierdegeleitete, genauso unbewusste wie unpersönliche Tiefenschicht des psychischen Apparats. Ein Bezug zu dem, was Freud als ‚Es' bezeichnet, drängt sich unweigerlich auf (FGW XIII, 247–255).

Der Geist (im engeren Sinne) macht den zweiten Aspekt des psychischen Apparats aus und steht bei Schelling für „Bewußtheit" und „das eigentlich Persönliche im Menschen" (AA II/8, 158; SW VII, 466). Insofern sie Bewusstsein ist und die Sphäre des Persönlichen abdeckt, läuft diese Sphäre weitgehend parallel zu dem, was Freud in der zweiten Topik als ‚Ich' beschreibt (FGW XIII, 247–255).[8] Wegen des Bewusstseins unterscheidet sich der Geist im engeren und zugleich auch eigentlichen Sinne von jener Vorform, als die er im Gemüt auftritt. Im Gemüt

---

8 Nach Müller-Lüneschloß 2012, S. 266–269, ist der Sitz des Ich dagegen nicht eindeutig dem Geist zuzuordnen, sie erwägt, ob das Ich nicht auch einen Ort in der Seele haben könnte, lässt diese Frage zuletzt jedoch offen.

tritt Geist als bewusstlose Begierde auf, die sich auf der zweiten Stufe nun zu einer „*bewußte[n]* Begierde" wandle und als *Wille* erscheine, der „das eigentlich Innerste des Geistes" ausmache (AA II/8, 156; SW VII, 467). Schelling vertritt somit eine in der Begierde fundierte, willenstheoretische Auffassung des menschlichen Geistes. Wie in der Freiheitsschrift differenziert er auch hier zwischen dem individuellen Eigenwillen des Menschen und dem auf das Allgemeine bezogenen Verstand – eine Unterscheidung, die auf die Differenz von Grund und Existierendem in Gott zurückverweist. Nach Schelling verfügt auch der Geist wiederum über drei Seiten: Der individuelle, bis zum Egoismus steigerbare *Eigenwille* des Menschen ist die erste Seite, von der gilt, dass sie „blind wäre ohne den *Verstand*" (AA II/8, 158; SW VII, 467); der *Verstand* als zweite Seite des Geistes ist auf das Allgemeine gerichtet und insofern dem Eigenwillen entgegengesetzt. Beide werden drittens in der Instanz eines „eigentliche[n] Wille[ns]" zusammengeführt (AA II/8, 158; SW VII, 467), der zwischen den entgegengesetzten Prinzipien vermitteln soll und dabei im Idealfall auf die übergeordnete Instanz der Seele bezogen ist.

Die Seele als die dritte und höchste Instanz des psychischen Apparats ist laut Schelling „das eigentlich Göttliche *im Menschen*, also das *Unpersönliche*, das eigentlich Seyende, dem das Persönliche als ein Nichtseyendes unterworfen seyn soll" (AA II/8, 160; SW VII, 468). Sie sei der „innere Himmel des Menschen" und habe „eigentlich keine Stufen mehr in sich", sie sei jedoch „verschiedener Beziehungen mit dem Untergeordneten fähig" (AA II/8, 164; SW VII, 471). Schelling nennt sodann drei Beziehungen, die die Seele mit den Instanzen des Geistes und des Gemüts unterhält, sowie außerdem noch eine vierte Form, in der die Seele in völliger Selbstbezüglichkeit existiert.

Die Seele könne sich erstens auf Sehnsucht und Eigenwille beziehen, so entstünden Kunst und Poesie: „Ohne Eigenkraft von der einen und tiefe Sehnsucht von der andern Seite entstehen Werke ohne Realität; ohne die Seele Werke ohne alle Idealität." (AA II/8, 164; SW VII, 471)[9] Die Seele könne sich zweitens beziehen auf Gefühl und Verstand, so entstehe „Wissenschaft im höchsten Sinne, diejenige nämlich, die unmittelbar von der Seele eingegeben wird, – die *Philosophie*" (AA II/8, 164; SW VII, 471). Der passiv konnotierte Begriff der Eingebung ist hier zentral und steht im Hintergrund von Schellings Unterscheidung zwischen Verstand und Vernunft: Verstand ist für ihn „etwas mehr *Aktives*, Thätiges", Vernunft „mehr etwas Leidendes, sich Hingebendes" (AA II/8, 166; SW VII, 472). Als diese passive Instanz ist die Vernunft zugleich „nichts anderes als der Verstand in

---

9 S. hierzu auch Schellings Ausführungen in *Über das Verhältnis der bildenden Künste zur Natur* von 1807 (SW VII, insb. 292 u. 312–313).

seiner Submission unter das Höhere, die Seele" (AA II/8, 166; SW VII, 472). Philosophie im Sinne der Vernunft treiben, heißt demnach im Kern, auf intellektuelle Kreativität im emphatischen Sinne zu verzichten, indem man den eigenen Verstand der Seele unterordnet. Auf diese Weise ist Schelling zufolge Vernunft zu erreichen, die „nur das Aufnehmende der Wahrheit, das Buch, worein die Eingebungen der Seele geschrieben werden", sei, „aber zugleich auch ein[en] Probierstein der Wahrheit" abgebe (AA II/8, 166; SW VII, 472). Denn was die Vernunft nicht akzeptiere, „was sie zurückstößt, was sie nicht in sich verzeichnen läßt, das ist nicht von der Seele eingegeben, das kommt aus der Persönlichkeit" (AA II/8, 166; SW VII, 472). Es bleibt unklar, welchen Beitrag das Gefühl zur Philosophie genau zu leisten vermag. Schelling vermerkt lediglich, es sei das „dunkle Princip", das den „Stoff, woraus die Schöpfungen des höheren Wesens gezogen werden", enthalte (AA II/8, 166; SW VII, 472). Seiner Auffassung nach, die offensichtlich programmatisch bleibt, realisiert wahre Philosophie sich im Zusammenspiel eines dunklen Gefühls und einer passiven Vernunft, die sich in der Unterwerfung des individuellen Verstandes unter die Seele herausbildet. Drittens schließlich kann die Seele sich beziehen auf Wille und Begierde. Werden Wille und Begierde der Seele untergeordnet, sei „*Tugend* im höchsten Sinne" (AA II/8, 166; SW VII, 472) erreicht. Schellings moralischer Imperativ lautet: „Lasse die Seele in dir handeln, oder handle durchaus als ein heiliger Mann, dieß ist nach meiner Meinung das höchste Princip, [...] handle nicht als persönliches Wesen, sondern ganz unpersönlich, störe ihre Einflüsse in dir selbst nicht durch deine Persönlichkeit." (AA II/8, 166; SW VII, 473) Er sieht, wie in Abschnitt 1 bereits erwähnt wurde, die Seele nicht nur als gut, sondern als „die Güte selbst" an (AA II/8, 160; SW VII, 469).

Es ist leicht zu erkennen, wie sich in den drei Instanzen der Psyche das Spannungsverhältnis zwischen Geist und Natur niederschlägt. Zunächst spiegelt sich in der Mittelstellung, die der Geist im engeren Sinne innerhalb des psychischen Apparats einnimmt, eben jene Mittelstellung, die Schelling dem Menschen im Kosmos überhaupt zuerkennt. Wie der Mensch zwischen Realem/Natur und Idealem/Geist steht, so sieht er sich psychisch mit seinem geistigen Bewusstsein zwischen dem Gemüt, das das Natürlich-Reale vertritt, und der Seele, die für das voll verwirklichte Göttlich-Ideale steht, eingespannt. Innerhalb des Geistes wird die natürliche Seite vom Eigenwillen, die ideale vom Verstand vertreten. Die Spannung besteht somit nicht nur generell zwischen Natur und Geist, sondern spezifischer zwischen einem natur- und triebgebundenen Eigensinn einerseits und einem geistig-rationalen Allgemeinen andererseits. Wie Schellings Ausführungen zu Philosophie, Tugend und Kunst im Kontext der Seele zeigen, birgt dieses Spannungsverhältnis für ihn gleichsam eine theoretische, praktische und ästhetische Relevanz.

Schellings Schilderungen deuten bereits darauf hin, dass der menschliche Geist nur dann gesund sein kann, wenn er sich nicht dem Gemüt als dem Natürlich-Realen, sondern der Seele als dem Göttlich-Idealen unterwirft. Insbesondere die im Geist angesiedelte Persönlichkeit soll der göttlichen Seele als einem überpersönlichen, überindividuellen Prinzip unterworfen werden. Insofern vom menschlichen Geist stets eine Unterwerfung verlangt wird, argumentiert Schelling im Erkennen von Wahrheit, im guten Handeln sowie im Schaffen guter Kunst für eine passive Haltung des Geistes. Denn in allen diesen Fällen *empfängt* der menschliche Geist das Wahre, Gute und Schöne eher passiv vermittels der Seele von Gott als dass er es selbst im emphatischen Sinn aktiv hervorbringen würde. Schelling erklärt an einer besonders plastischen Stelle, dass im Idealfall zwischen Seele, Geist und Gemüt eine durchgängige Verbindung bestehen müsse:

> Vom Gemüth, und zwar von der tiefsten Sehnsucht an geht also eine stetige Folge bis zur Seele. Die *Gesundheit* des Gemüths und des Geistes beruht darauf, daß diese Folge ununterbrochen sey, daß gleichsam eine stetige Leitung von der Seele aus bis ins Tiefste des Gemüths stattfinde. Denn die Seele ist das, wodurch der Mensch in Rapport mit Gott ist, und ohne diesen Rapport mit Gott kann die Creatur, der Mensch aber insbesondere, keinen Augenblick existiren. (AA II/8, 160; SW VII, 469)

Das Bild der Leitung, die nach Schelling Seele, Geist und Gemüt verbindet, veranschaulicht jene Hierarchie, die er zwischen den psychischen Instanzen annimmt. Die gesamte psychische Konstitution des Menschen wird in Abhängigkeit von der Seele und darüber von Gott gebracht. Unsere geistige Gesundheit ist allein dadurch aufrecht zu erhalten, dass wir uns auf ein göttliches Prinzip stützen, zu dem wir über unsere Seele Zugang haben. Damit ist klar, dass der menschliche Geist für Schelling keine selbsttragende Instanz ist. Er ist Teil einer göttlichen Weltordnung, die sich in seiner Psyche spiegelt und in die er sich einzufügen hat.

Angesichts dieser Konsequenz führt der Vergleich mit Freud zuletzt auf eine erhebliche Differenz. Die entsprechende Stelle, die bei Schelling die Seele besetzt, hat in Freuds zweiter Topik das Über-Ich inne (FGW XIII, 256–267). Wie Freud das Über-Ich in der *Neuen Folge der Vorlesungen zur Einführung in die Psychoanalyse* von 1933 als „Vertretung aller moralischen Beschränkungen, [als] Anwalt des Strebens nach Vervollkommnung, kurz [als] das, was uns von dem sogenannt Höheren im Menschenleben psychologisch greifbar geworden ist" (FGW XV, 73), beschreibt, weist es zwar durchaus Berührungspunkte mit der Seelenkonzeption Schellings auf. Ein erster grundsätzlicher Unterschied besteht jedoch darin, dass das Freud'sche Über-Ich nicht mit dem Guten selbst identifiziert werden kann, sondern mit einer „beobachtende[n] und strafandrohende[n] Instanz im Ich", einer „richterlichen Tätigkeit des Gewissens" (FGW XV, 65). Das Über-Ich tritt bisweilen „überstreng" auf und „beschimpft, erniedrigt, mißhandelt das arme Ich, läßt es die schwersten Strafen erwarten, macht ihm Vorwürfe wegen längst vergangener Handlungen" (FGW XV, 66). Schelling spricht dagegen zwar von der Unterwerfung des Geistes unter die Seele, er hebt aber nirgends hervor, dass diese Unterwerfung aufgrund eines von der Seele ausgehenden Zwangs oder gar einer Strafandrohung geschehen würde. Die Autorität der Seele gründet bei ihm in nichts als ihrer Lauterkeit. Ein zweiter grundsätzlicher Unterschied zeigt sich darin, dass Freud auf Gott rekurrierende, religiöse Erklärungen von Moral und Gewissen, die im Über-Ich ihren Ort haben, nachdrücklich ablehnt. Stattdessen führt er die Genese des Über-Ich auf die Internalisierung der ursprünglichen Autorität der Eltern in der kindlichen Psyche und explizit nicht auf eine göttliche Autorität zurück (FGW XV, 67–69). Wenn Schelling dagegen erklärt, die Seele könne neben den drei genannten Formen in einer vierten „auch ganz rein, ohne alle Beziehung und völlig unbedingt wirken. Dieses unbedingte Walten der Seele ist *Religion* [...] als innere und höchste Seeligkeit des Gemüts und Geistes" (AA II/8, 168; SW VII, 473), vermag Freud ihm nicht zu folgen. Für Schelling ist es dagegen zentral, dass das „Wesen der Seele" in einer göttlichen Liebe besteht, die in der Folge auch alles prägt, „was aus der Seele entsteht"; so sei wahre Philosophie ein „Werk der Liebe", die vereint, was sonst getrennt betrachtet wird; die Philosophie hole dazu aus, „das ganze Universum zu Einem großen Werk der Liebe zu verschmelzen" (AA II/8, 168; SW VII, 474). Ein von göttlicher Liebe beseeltes Philosophieren beschreibe für den Menschen „den höchsten Gipfel [...], dessen er in diesem Leben fähig ist" (AA II/8, 168; SW VII, 474).

Die religiös konnotierte Emphase, mit der Schelling hier spricht, deutet darauf hin, dass er die Seele samt der zu ihr gehörenden Liebe nicht nur in einem übertragenen Sinn, sondern buchstäblich als etwas Göttliches betrachtet, das konstitutiv für die Gesundheit der menschlichen Psyche ist. Diese Sicht markiert einen schwerwiegenden Unterschied zum psychoanalytischen Ansatz Freuds und spricht überhaupt für eine begrenzte Aktualität der Schelling'schen Überlegungen im Kontext einer säkularen Psychologie. Wie sehr Schelling tatsächlich auf das Wirken der göttlichen Seele setzt, belegen auch seine Ausführungen zur Psychopathologie des Wahnsinns.

4 Der Wahnsinn als Basis und Wesen des menschlichen Geistes

Schellings Grundidee besagt, dass psychische Gesundheit allein dann herrscht, wenn die Seele als die göttliche Instanz innerhalb des psychischen Apparats die leitende Funktion innehat und in einer ununterbrochenen Verbindung mit dem

Geist und dem Gemüt steht. Entsprechend stellt Krankheit sich immer dann ein, wenn diese Verbindung auf irgendeine Weise unterbrochen ist: „Sowie die Leitung unterbrochen ist, ist *Krankheit* da" (AA II/8, 160; SW VII, 469). Die göttliche Seele selbst kann nach Schelling nicht erkranken – sie ist ein ausschließlich positives Prinzip, das Gesundheit verbürgt. Erkranken können allein Geist und Gemüt, wenn sie der Verbindung zur uneingeschränkten Positivität der Seele entbehren. Zu einer Unterbrechung der Leitung zwischen Seele und Gemüt kommt es etwa dann, „wenn die Sehnsucht über das Gefühl siegt" und dadurch das Gemüt erkrankt (AA II/8, 162; SW VII, 469). Wird die Leitung vom Verstand unterbrochen, kann nach Schelling einerseits der „*Blödsinn*" aufkommen, eine Geisteskrankheit, die er als typisch für eigensinnige Genussmenschen und einigermaßen „unschädlich" erachtet (AA II/8, 162; SW VII, 469). Die tiefgreifendste Form der Geisteskrankheit ist nach Schelling andererseits der Wahnsinn, der sich grundsätzlich ebenfalls dann einstellt, wenn der Verstand keine Bindung mehr mit der göttlichen Seele unterhält. Im Unterschied zum hedonistischen Blödsinn nennt er den Wahnsinn „das Schrecklichste" (AA II/8, 162; SW VII, 469) und lässt sich sogar zu der drastischen Aussage hinreißen: „Die Basis des Verstandes selbst also ist der Wahnsinn." (AA II/8, 162; SW VII, 470) Weiter erklärt er: „Das tiefste Wesen des menschlichen Geistes also, [...] wenn er in der Trennung von der Seele und also von Gott betrachtet wird, ist der *Wahnsinn*." (AA II/8, 162; SW VII, 470)

Die genauso radikale wie suggestive Behauptung, dass der Wahnsinn Basis und Wesen des menschlichen Geistes sei, lädt zu Missverständnissen ein und verlangt eine nuancierte Interpretation vor dem Hintergrund von Schellings Theorie der psychischen Instanzen.

Prinzipiell ist Schelling der Auffassung, dass der Wahnsinn eigentlich nicht entstehe, sondern vielmehr *hervortrete*, wenn innerhalb der Psyche der Verstand als das rationale Vermögen des Geistes keine Verbindung mehr mit der göttlichen Seele unterhält und stattdessen „die *Basis* des menschlichen Geistes" die Oberhand gewinnt, d. h. nicht mehr als Basis fungiert, sondern sich an die Spitze setzt (AA II/8, 162; SW VII, 470). Nun liegt die Basis des Geistes konkret in der psychischen Instanz des Gemüts. Insofern Schelling das Gemüt als naturgebunden, triebhaft, unbewusst und unpersönlich beschreibt, kann er sagen, dass es als Basis des Geistes zugleich „das Verstandlose", d. h. das Irrationale, sei und der Wahnsinn dann auftrete, „wenn das, was eigentlich Nichtseyendes, d. h. das Verstandlose ist, sich aktualisirt" (AA II/8, 162; SW VII, 470), d. h. zum dominanten Prinzip aufsteigt. Der Wahnsinn ist demnach ein Zustand der Irrationalität, der auf eine Dominanz des naturgebundenen Gemüts im psychischen Apparat zurückzuführen ist.

Wenn Schelling den Wahnsinn als Basis und Wesen des Geistes beschreibt, ihm zudem das ‚Entstehen' abspricht und stattdessen von seinem ‚Hervortreten' spricht, kann der fehlgeleitete Eindruck aufkommen, als wäre der Wahnsinn mit dem irrationalen Gemüt gleichzusetzen und selbst die basale Instanz der menschlichen Psyche. Schelling benutzt den Begriff ‚Wahnsinn' oft austauschbar mit dem der ‚Verstandlosigkeit' und damit direkt für die Irrationalität, durch die sich das naturgebundene Gemüt auszeichnet. Aber nach dem, was er der Sache nach nur meinen kann, bildet streng genommen allein das Gemüt mit seinen Gefühlen, Begierden und Sehnsüchten die irrationale Basis. Der Wahnsinn ist davon zu unterscheiden als ein psychischer Zustand des menschlichen Geistes, der von der Irrationalität des Gemüts zwar hervorgerufen, aber nicht einfach mit ihr identisch ist.

Dass es sich so verhält, macht Schelling zwar nicht in Bezug auf den Wahnsinn selbst hinreichend deutlich, es lässt sich aber ausgehend von den strukturanalogen Formen des Bösen und des Irrtums erschließen. So nennt er das mit dem Wahnsinn verwandte Böse „in gewissem Betracht das reinste Geistige", das „nicht aus dem Leib" als der natürlichen Verfassung des Menschen komme, „wie so viele noch jetzt meinen" (AA II/8, 160; SW VII, 468). Er betont, dass insbesondere auch der in der Natur gegründete egoistische Eigenwille keinesfalls „an sich selbst das Böse" sei, „sondern nur dann, wenn er herrschend wird" (AA II/8, 158; SW VII, 467). Das Böse tritt nach Schelling nicht etwa auf, wenn Geist durch Natur verdrängt wird, sondern wenn der menschliche Geist aktiv bleibt, sich dabei aber vom natur- und triebgebundenen Eigensinn und nicht von einem rationalen Allgemeinen leiten lässt, das mit der göttlichen Seele in Verbindung steht. Entsprechendes gilt für den Irrtum, der nicht Negation des Geistes oder auch nur „Mangel an Geist, sondern verkehrter Geist" sei (AA II/8, 160; SW VII, 468). Im Irrtum befindet sich nach Schelling stets ein aktiver Geist, der seinen Verstand eigensinnig gebraucht, ihn nicht dem höheren Prinzip ‚Seele' unterordnet und deshalb auch nicht über Vernunft verfügt. Zwar äußert Schelling sich nicht über schlechte Kunst. Wenn er aber über gelungene Kunstwerke sagt, sie seien „Werke, von denen man sagen möchte, die Seele habe sie allein ohne Zutun des Menschen vollendet" (AA II/8, 166; SW VII, 473), ist klar, dass schlechte Kunst auf ein geistig-ästhetisches Schaffen zurückzuführen sein muss, in dem das naturgebundene egoistische Gemüt der Künstlerin das ihren Geist leitende, aber keinesfalls verdrängende Prinzip ist.

Es ist offensichtlich, dass in diesen Formen stets der menschliche Geist im Mittelpunkt steht. Ob er böse ist, irrt oder schlechte Kunstwerke schafft, hängt davon ab, wovon er sich dominieren und leiten lässt: vom naturgebundenen Prinzip des Eigensinns oder aber vom Prinzip des an der göttlichen Seele orientierten Verstandes. Analog verhält es sich beim Wahnsinn: Er ist keine eigene, vermeintlich geistlose Instanz innerhalb der Psyche und kann auch nicht direkt mit dem naturgebundenen Prinzip identifiziert werden. Er ist vielmehr ein Fall ‚verkehrten Geistes', zu dem es genau dann kommt, wenn anstatt der göttlichen Seele das naturgebundene Gemüt Macht über den Geist gewinnt. Tritt dieser Fall ein, wird der menschliche Geist auf eine Weise von Irrationalität bestimmt, die differenziert zu betrachten ist.

Da Schelling den Wahnsinn häufig in Superlativen als *das Schrecklichste* und zugleich *Tiefste* bezeichnet, das gleichsam aus den dunkelsten Bereichen der menschlichen Psyche hervorbrechen soll, laden seine Ausführungen nicht nur dazu ein, den Wahnsinn zu hypostasieren und als eine vermeintlich eigenständige psychische Instanz aufzufassen. Schellings Ausdrucksweise erweckt ferner den Eindruck, als würde mit dem Auftreten des Wahnsinns stets eine völlige Überwältigung und Zerrüttung des Geistes durch das Irrationale einhergehen. An einem lebensweltlichen Beispiel, das er anführt, wird jedoch ersichtlich, dass er sich keineswegs nur für die Extremform interessiert: Dass der menschliche Geist wahnsinnig wird, weil er sich vom irrationalen Gemüt leiten lässt, sei nämlich auch schon „bei einem heftigen Schmerz" der Fall, bei dem der Verstand „keinen Trost mehr [zu] geben" vermag (AA II/8, 162; SW VII, 470). Zwei Punkte sind an diesem Beispiel aufschlussreich. Erstens belegt es, dass Schelling psychischen Zuständen, wie sie diesseits des Extrems im Leben vieler Menschen vorkommen können, die Kraft zugesteht, den Geist zu bestimmen. Unter dem ‚heftigen Schmerz', von dem er spricht, darf man sich starke negative Empfindungen und Stimmungen aller Art vorstellen. Es liegt nahe, dass letztlich alle Formen von Gefühlen, Begierden und Sehnsüchten, die Schellings Psychologie zufolge im Gemüt verortet sind, einen irrationalen Einfluss auf den Geist des Menschen ausüben können. Systematisch kommt es darauf an, dass diese Gemütszustände selbst zwar als irrational, aber nicht auch schon als wahnsinnig charakterisiert werden können. Zweitens betont Schelling nämlich, dass der Wahnsinn auftritt, wenn ‚der Verstand keinen Trost mehr geben kann', es ihm also nicht gelingt, die irrationalen Gemütszustände, mit denen er konfrontiert ist, *zu bewältigen*. Nicht die Irrationalität des Gemüts selbst ist pathologisch. Erst wenn sie auf das geistige Vermögen des Verstandes trifft und ihn überwältigt, stellt sich ein krankhafter Wahnsinn ein.

Rekonstruiert man Schellings Auffassung im Licht dieser beiden Punkte, tritt der Wahnsinn immer dann auf, wenn dem Geist die rationale Bewältigung irrationaler Gefühle, Begierden und Sehnsüchte nicht gelingt und er in der Folge von ihnen bestimmt wird. Das kann, aber muss nicht zur völligen psychischen Zerrüttung führen. Bereits ein einzelnes psychisches Leiden kann durchaus, wenn es sich nicht verarbeiten lässt, den Geist nachhaltig in Beschlag nehmen und für die Betroffenen mitunter jene ‚Schrecklichkeit' an sich haben, von der Schelling spricht. Wie zumal die Erfahrung lehrt, kann auch bereits der Ärger über eine Kleinigkeit den Geist emotional derart beeinflussen, dass er in seinem rationalen Funktionieren blockiert ist. Das Gemüt als Basis und Wesen des menschlichen Geistes zu begreifen, heißt vor diesem Hintergrund anzuerkennen, dass die Irrationalität von Gemütszuständen „ein nothwendiges Element" der Psyche ist und essentiell zu dem gehört, was es heißt, ein Mensch zu sein (AA II/8, 162; SW VII, 470). Dabei ist für Schelling zugleich klar, dass diese Zustände den Geist nicht dominieren sollen. In Anlehnung an Platon spricht er vom Verstand als einem „*geregelte[n]* [...] göttliche[n] Wahnsinn" (AA II/8, 162; SW VII, 470), in dem die irrationale Basis des Geistes als Quelle der Inspiration und intellektuellen Leidenschaft zwar hintergründig wirksam bleibt, aber vor allem gebändigt ist. In ihrer ungebändigten Form soll die Irrationalität des Gemüts ausdrücklich „nicht zum Vorschein kommen" (AA II/8, 162; SW VII, 470). Für Schelling bleibt der menschliche Geist der Ort des Verstandes und damit eine Instanz der Rationalität, die um die Bewältigung irrationaler Gemütszustände ringt.

Im Zentrum der Schelling'schen Psychologie steht die Überzeugung, dass diese Bewältigung ohne Rekurs auf die göttliche Seele nicht gelingen kann. Immer dann, „wenn Geist und Gemüth ohne den sanften Einfluß der Seele sind, bricht das anfängliche dunkle Wesen hervor, und reißt auch den Verstand [...] mit sich fort" (AA II/8, 162/164; SW VII, 470). Diese rigorose Überzeugung impliziert, dass der menschliche Geist nicht aus eigener Kraft dazu in der Lage ist, sich gegen die Irrationalität seines Gemüts zu behaupten. Schellings These, dass der Wahnsinn das Wesen des menschlichen Geistes sei, kann in dieser Perspektive zuletzt als Aussage darüber interpretiert werden, wodurch sich der Geist auszeichnet, sofern er allein im Zusammenhang mit seiner irrationalen Basis betrachtet wird. Der Wahnsinn ist dann immer noch nicht als Essenz des Geistes zu verstehen. Aber da der menschliche Geist auf sich allein gestellt den Wahnsinn niemals ganz von sich fernzuhalten vermag, kann Schelling mit einer gewissen Berechtigung sagen, dass der Wahnsinn in allen seinen Formen und verwandten Pathologien zumindest *als Zustand* quasiwesentlich mit ihm verbunden ist. Bleibt er auf sich allein gestellt, treibt der Geist für Schelling grundsätzlich mindestens ‚Blödsinn', wird von allerlei psychischen Leiden geplagt, agiert böse, befindet sich grundsätzlich im Irrtum und versagt außerdem ästhetisch. Im schlimmsten Fall wird er vom Wahnsinn völlig übermannt. Da sich all das nur vermeiden lässt, wenn der Geist sich ganz der lauteren Reinheit der göttlichen Seele anvertraut, ist seine Abhängigkeit von ihr fundamental. Eine therapeutische Lösung, die Abstufungen zulassen würde, gibt es bei Schelling nicht. Was er zur Bewältigung des irrationalen Gemüts verlangt, nimmt vielmehr die Dimension einer existentiellen Entscheidung an.

Nach allem, was Schelling darlegt, geht von der göttlichen Seele keinerlei Aktivität aus, in der sie sich den menschlichen Geist unterwerfen würde. Soll es zu einer Unterwerfung kommen, kann nur der Geist sie vollziehen. Für das strukturell ähnlich wie der Wahnsinn gelagerte Böse heißt es in der Georgii-Nachschrift zu den *Stuttgarter Privatvorlesungen* prägnant:

> Gerade darinnen besteht die Freyheit, daß der Mensch zwischen Gemüth und Seele im Indifferenz Punckt steht, daß er den Eingebungen der Seele, oder des Eigenwillens folgen kann. Folgt der Mensch der Seele, so ist er gut, folgt er blind dem Gemüthe [...], so wird er böse. (AA II/8, 167)

Überträgt man auf den Wahnsinn, was Schelling hier sagt, scheint auch er kraft einer Entscheidung überwindbar zu sein.[10] Sich für die Unterwerfung unter die göttliche Seele zu entscheiden, eröffnet die Perspektive auf eine vollkommene geistige Gesundheit – sich der Unterwerfung zu verweigern, lässt den Wahnsinn dagegen grundsätzlich unbewältigt. Dies birgt augenscheinlich eine drastische Konsequenz: Wenn beides letztlich auf eine Entscheidung zurückzuführen ist, gleichen die Wahnsinnigen bei Schelling zuletzt nicht nur Kranken, sondern auch Schuldigen, die ihr Schicksal hätten ändern können, aber ähnlich wie die Bösen eine falsche Wahl getroffen haben. Es liegt auf der Hand, dass das mit einer therapieorientierten Psychologie nichts mehr zu tun hat.

5 Zur kritischen Würdigung der Psychologie Schellings

Als eine Leistung Schellings ist zu würdigen, dass er den menschlichen Geist in einem vielschichtigen Gefüge psychischer Instanzen situiert, wo er mit einem irrationalen Trieb- und Gefühlsleben konfrontiert ist und sich anfällig für Pathologien erweist. Noch vor Schopenhauer, auf den Freud sich ausdrücklich bezieht, antizipiert Schelling damit durchaus die Einsicht der Psychoanalyse, dass der menschliche Geist „nicht Herr sei in seinem eigenen Haus" (FGW XII, 11). Zugleich ist jedoch Schellings Behauptung, dass eine mit dem Göttlichen in Verbindung stehende Seele unseren Geist von Pathologien zu kurieren vermag, eine problematische Annahme. Aus säkularer Perspektive muss sie mindestens als kontro-

---

10 In einer eigenen Rekonstruktion wäre zu untersuchen, inwiefern Schellings Überlegungen zur ‚intelligiblen Tat' in der Freiheitsschrift auch im Fall des Wahnsinns relevant sind (AA I/18, 151 ff.; SW VII, 383 ff.).

vers erscheinen, wenn nicht gar als schlicht unhaltbar. Woher rührt diese Annahme und inwieweit lässt sie sich rechtfertigen? Bei der Beantwortung dieser Frage lassen sich zwei Punkte explizit machen, auf die sich Schellings Position philosophisch stützt. Im Licht dieser Punkte kann anschließend das philosophische Profil von Schellings Psychologie im Kontrast zu Hegel noch einmal verdeutlicht werden.

Erstens hat Schellings Seelenauffassung aus den *Stuttgarter Privatvorlesungen* in dem, was die Freiheitsschrift über ‚Liebe‘ sagt, einen Vorläufer. Obwohl Schelling in den Vorlesungen die Liebe als Wesen der Seele bezeichnet (AA II/8, 166; SW VII, 473), muss dieser Zusammenhang nicht sofort auffallen, da der Seelenbegriff in der Freiheitsschrift keine prominente Rolle spielt. Bereits in der Freiheitsschrift spricht Schelling jedoch dem Geist ab, ‚das Höchste‘ zu sein, und zeichnet zwar nicht die Seele, aber die Liebe aus: „[D]er Geist ist noch nicht das Höchste; er ist nur der Geist, oder der Hauch der Liebe. Die Liebe aber ist das Höchste." (AA I/17, 170; SW VII, 405 – 406) Damit positioniert die Freiheitsschrift die Liebe bereits an genau der Stelle, wo in den *Stuttgarter Privatvorlesungen* ein Jahr später die Seele steht. Liebe ist definiert als Verbindung von Momenten, „deren jedes für sich seyn könnte und doch nicht ist, und nicht seyn kann ohne das andere" (AA I/17, 172; SW VII, 408). Schelling bezeichnet die Liebe in diesem Sinn als ein versöhnendes Band, das auch in der menschlichen Psyche wirksam wird: Wenn der Eigenwille des Menschen „ganz vom [göttlichen; J.S.] Licht durchdrungen und mit ihm Eins" sei, dann sei „Gott, als die ewige Liebe, oder als wirklich existirend, das Band der Kräfte in ihm" (AA I/17, 156; SW VII, 389 – 390). Im Rekurs auf Gott wird mithin schon in der Freiheitsschrift ein Band der Liebe zwischen Eigenwille und Verstand etabliert, das das Spannungsverhältnis zwischen diesen Polen zu überwinden erlaubt. Der christliche Hintergrund dieser Liebesauffassung ist nicht zu übersehen. So heißt es etwa im ersten Brief des Johannes: „Gott ist die Liebe; und wer in der Liebe bleibt, der bleibt in Gott und Gott in ihm." (1. Joh 4, 16b) Die Liebe und die Seele lassen sich somit im Kontext eines Versöhnungsideals begreifen, das in der Tradition des Christentums verwurzelt ist.[11]

Zweitens ist der Begriff ‚Seele‘ nicht nur im Sinne dieses christlich konnotierten Versöhnungsideals, sondern außerdem als ein Medium der Teilhabe zu verstehen, das im Zusammenhang mit der Annahme einer ‚Mitwissenschaft‘ des Menschen in der Schöpfung zu sehen ist.[12] Dieser Zusammenhang zeichnet sich in

---

11 S. zur grundlegenden Bedeutung der Liebe bei Schelling auch McGrath 2012, insb. S. 186 – 188.
12 Auf den Bezug zu Mitwissenschaft und Teilhabe weist auch Schmidt-Biggemann 2014, S. 76 ff., hin. S. auch Müller-Lüneschloß 2012, S. 276.

den *Stuttgarter Privatvorlesungen* ab, insofern Schelling bemerkt: „[D]ie Seele weiß nicht, sondern sie ist die Wissenschaft." (AA II/8, 160; SW VII, 469) In den Einleitungen zu den drei *Weltalter*-Entwürfen, an denen er ab 1811 arbeitet, wird er deutlicher: „Aus der Quelle der Dinge geschöpft und ihr gleich, hat die Seele des Menschen eine Mitwissenschaft der Schöpfung. In ihr liegt die höchste Klarheit aller Dinge und nicht sowohl wissend ist sie als selber die Wissenschaft" (WA I, 4; SW VIII, 200; vgl. WA II, 112). Schelling versucht damit eine Antwort auf die Frage zu geben, wie der Mensch Zugang zu jenem göttlichen Absoluten haben kann, das die Welt in umfassender Weise prägt und mit dem er nicht von vornherein einfach identisch ist. Wie dieser Zugang genau eröffnet wird, legt er am deutlichsten in seinen Erlanger Vorträgen von 1821 dar, wo er erneut auf die „Mitwissenschaft, conscientia" (SW IX, 221) zu sprechen kommt und betont, dass die Überwindung des subjektiven Standpunkts eine notwendige Voraussetzung sei: „[I]n der Philosophie gilt es, sich zu erheben über alles Wissen, das bloß *von mir* ausgeht." (SW IX, 228) Die Überschreitung dieses Standpunkts nennt der Erlanger Schelling „*Ekstase*" (SW IX, 229). Die Mitwissenschaft, die er der Seele zutraut, geht mit einer ekstatischen Auffassung des menschlichen Geistes einher, indem sie eine latente Präsenz des Absoluten im Menschen selbst annimmt, die verstellt bleibt, solange der Mensch sich als ein endliches Subjekt begreift. Überschreitet er den subjektiven Standpunkt, kann der menschliche Geist entdecken, dass er das Wahre, Gute und Schöne immer schon auf eine latente Weise so besitzt und präsent hat, wie es im Absoluten ist. Die Annahme einer solchen ekstatischen Mitwissenschaft trägt unverkennbar platonische Züge. Sie erinnert an die Anamnesis-Lehre, in der Platon eine vorgeburtliche Ideenschau der Seele behauptet, die mit dem Eintritt in das körperliche Leben in Vergessenheit gerät. Dass Schelling die Mitwissenschaft in den *Weltaltern* als ein „Princip" (WA I, 4; SW VIII, 200) und sogar als das „Wesen" des Menschen (WA II, 112) einführt, „das außer und über der Welt ist" (WA I, 4; WA II, 112; SW VIII, 200), erinnert an jenen „überhimmlischen Ort", von dem Platon im *Phaidros* (247c) spricht und an dem sich die Ideenschau der Seele ursprünglich ereignet haben soll. Schellings Psychologie kann vor diesem Hintergrund als ein Plädoyer dafür gedeutet werden, im Leben der Menschen einer göttlichen Liebe Geltung zu verschaffen, die in der menschlichen Seele latent vorhanden ist und an die wir uns gewissermaßen nur wiedererinnern müssen, um uns vom Wahnsinn zu kurieren.

Will man Schellings Psychologie verteidigen und dabei in ihrer philosophischen Anlage ernst nehmen, muss man die genannten Punkte akzeptieren. Freud würde das, wie wohl auch die meisten säkular gesinnten Leserinnen aus dem 20. und 21. Jahrhundert, nicht tun. Um Schellings Psychologie für die Gegenwart anschlussfähig zu halten, kann man sich, wie Marquard 1975, S. 22, es für die Naturphilosophie vorgeschlagen hat, an einer ‚Entzauberung' versuchen, um sie von ihren aus heutiger Sicht kontroversen religiösen und platonischen Implikationen zu entlasten. Verzichtet man darauf, nehmen zwar die Anschlussmöglichkeiten für einen säkulare Befassung mit der Psyche ab, es tritt aber zugleich deutlich hervor, inwiefern Schellings Psychologie sich von der geistphilosophischen Position unterscheidet, die sein Zeitgenosse Hegel vertritt. Die Pointe ist, dass der wesentliche Unterschied nicht einfach darin besteht, dass Schelling behauptet, der menschliche Geist sei anfällig für den Wahnsinn und daher nicht ‚das Höchste'. Der maßgebliche Unterschied liegt vielmehr darin, dass Schelling *anstelle* des Geistes die göttliche Seele als ‚das Höchste' betrachtet und im Rekurs auf sie eine Bewältigung des Wahnsinns für möglich erachtet.

Es lohnt sich in diesem Zusammenhang ein Blick in Hegels *Enzyklopädie der philosophischen Wissenschaften*, die 1817, 1827 und 1830 in drei Ausgaben erschienen ist. Hegels grundsätzliche Position zum Geist hat sich zwischen der *Phänomenologie*, gegen die Schellings Stuttgarter Vorlesungen sich implizit wenden, und der *Enzyklopädie* nicht verändert. Immer noch affirmiert Hegel das Gegenteil dessen, was Schelling sagt: „*Das Absolute ist der Geist:* diß ist die höchste Definition des Absoluten." (HGW 20, § 384) Bemerkenswert ist, dass auch Hegel im Kontext seines geistphilosophischen Projekts in der *Enzyklopädie* dem Begriff ‚Seele' eine zentrale Rolle zuweist. Im Gegensatz zu Schelling firmiert sie bei ihm jedoch nicht als höchste, sondern als basale erste Instanz der Geistphilosophie. Im Auftakt des geistphilosophischen Systemteils verwendet Hegel die paradoxe Formulierung, dass der Geist zu Anfang eine „*einfache* Allgemeinheit" sei, als die „er *Seele*, noch nicht Geist ist" (HGW 20, § 383). Das will sagen, dass die Seele sehr wohl schon eine Form von Geist ist, in der aber das, was den Geist insgesamt ausmacht, sich erst zu realisieren beginnt. In diesem Sinn bezeichnet Hegel die Seele auch als den „*Schlaf* des Geistes", der zugleich „der *Möglichkeit* nach Alles ist" (HGW 20, § 389). Was auf dem Niveau der Seele Möglichkeit bleibt, wird im weiteren Fortgang der *Enzyklopädie* vom subjektiven über den objektiven bis zum absoluten Geist sukzessive ausbestimmt. Worauf es im Verhältnis zu Schelling ankommt, ist, dass auch Hegel sich dabei der gesunden wie der kranken Psyche zuwendet. Er weiß ebenfalls vom Wahnsinn und nimmt ihn philosophisch ernst.

Grundsätzlich ist festzuhalten, dass Hegel in den Paragraphen zur Seele auf die Konstitution des menschlichen Selbstverhältnisses zielt.[13] Er betrachtet die Seele zuerst als etwas Allgemeines, nämlich als „die allgemeine Immateria-

---

13 Wie Sandkaulen überzeugend darlegt, geht es Hegel darum, „in Gestalt der Seele die *genuine Ausbildung unseres spezifisch menschlichen Selbstverhältnisses* geltend" zu machen (Sandkaulen 2011, S. 44). Über die Seele wird das menschliche Ich „in der Lebenswelt konkreter Subjektivität verankert" (Sandkaulen 2011, S. 47), die den weiteren Gestalten des Geistes vorgelagert ist.

lität der Natur" (HGW 20, § 389), die aber „ihre wirkliche Wahrheit nur als *Einzelnheit*, Subjectivität, hat" (HGW 20, § 391). Anders als bei Schelling ist die Seele bei Hegel somit nicht auf etwas Überindividuelles festgelegt, sondern gehört zuletzt einem „fühlende[n] Individuum" (HGW 20, § 403). In Bezug auf das Seelenleben eines Individuums, das Gefühle hat, wendet Hegel sich sodann psychischen Erkrankungen zu. Was er ‚Verrücktheit' nennt, kann ein „zum verständigen Bewußtseyn gebildete[s] Subject" befallen und zeigt sich konkret darin, dass dieses Subjekt „in einer Besonderheit seines Selbstgefühls beharren bleibt, welche es nicht [...] zu überwinden vermag" (HGW 20, § 408). Es vermag diesem besonderen Gefühl nicht mehr „die verständige Stelle und die Unterordnung" zuzuweisen, „die ihm in dem individuellen Weltsysteme, welches ein Subject ist, zugehört" (HGW 20, § 408). Psychische Gesundheit besteht demnach darin, dass es einem individuellen Subjekt gelingt, seine Gefühle zu meistern. Das verrückte Individuum ist dazu nicht in der Lage und deshalb für Hegel krank.

Hegels Auffassung der psychischen Krankheit ist mit derjenigen Schellings in mehreren Hinsichten verwandt. So behandelt auch Hegel in diesem Kontext ein Spannungsverhältnis zwischen Geist und Natur, das daher rührt, dass die Seele an der Scharnierstelle zwischen Natur- und Geistphilosophie steht und in sich einen Naturbezug birgt, mit dem sie als eine Figuration des Geistes umgehen muss. Dieser Naturbezug kommt vor allem darin zum Ausdruck, dass die Seele verleiblicht ist und nach Hegel gerade „um des Moments der Leiblichkeit willen", das in ihr „noch ungeschieden von der Geistigkeit ist", krank werden kann (HGW 20, § 408). Lässt die „Macht der Besonnenheit" – d. h. im weitesten Sinn: die Macht des menschlichen Geistes – „über das Natürliche" nach, können laut Hegel selbstsüchtige Triebe und Affekte die Oberhand gewinnen, „Eitelkeit, Stolz und die anderen Leidenschaften, und Einbildungen, Hoffnungen, Liebe und Haß", auch drohe „der böse Genius des Menschen" in der Verrücktheit herrschend zu werden (HGW 20, § 408 Anm.). Die Parallelen, die sich zwischen Hegel und Schelling abzeichnen, können hier nicht ausbuchstabiert werden. Für den abschließenden Punkt dieser Untersuchung ist lediglich ein grundsätzlicher Unterschied in den Blick zu nehmen, der in ihren gegensätzlichen Auffassungen von Heilung und Gesundheit der Psyche greifbar wird.

Während Schelling nicht müde wird, die Notwendigkeit einer Submission aller Instanzen der Psyche unter die göttliche Seele zu betonen, setzt Hegel ganz diesseitig auf die Konsultation eines Arztes und die habituelle Bewältigung unseres Gefühlslebens. Er knüpft an den Psychiater Philippe Pinel an und „setzt den Kranken als Vernünftiges voraus", der seine Gesundheit prinzipiell nicht vollständig, sondern nur zu einem gewissen Grad verloren hat (HGW 20, § 408 Anm.). Einem Zusatz zufolge spricht Hegel sich aufgrund der „noch nicht gänzlich zerstörten Vernünftigkeit" der Geisteskranken dafür aus, dass sie „eine rücksichtsvolle Behandlung verdienen" (HGW 25/2, 1052). Man müsse versuchen, sie „auf andere Gedanken zu bringen", etwa indem man sie dazu anhält, „sich geistig und vornehmlich körperlich zu beschäftigen", sie könnten etwa durch „*Arbeit* [...] aus ihrer kranken Subjectivität herausgerissen und zu dem Wirklichen hinge- trieben" werden (HGW 25/2, 1053). Der maßgebliche systematische Punkt hierbei ist, dass Hegel es offenbar der Vernünftigkeit des Menschen zutraut, mit ärztlicher Hilfe und aufgrund eines Tätigwerdens wie in der Arbeit, in jedem Fall aber ohne Unterwerfung unter eine göttliche Instanz wieder genesen zu können. Darin liegt ein erheblicher Unterschied zu Schelling, der sich weiter vertieft, wenn wir Hegels Sicht der gesunden Psyche einbeziehen.

Im Fall der Gesundheit gilt grundsätzlich, dass nicht etwa eine göttliche Seele, sondern das individuelle Subjekt „der *herrschende Genius*" ist, der jede mögliche „Empfindung, Vorstellung, Begierde, Neigung u. s. f.", mit der er nach- haltig zu tun hat, in das geordnete Ganze seines psychischen Haushalts einzu- gliedern versteht (HGW 20, § 408 Anm.). Nach Hegel gelingt das prinzipiell dann, wenn wir als Individuen einen habituellen Umgang mit unserem Gefühlsleben finden, kultivieren und uns dadurch von der potentiell verstörenden Macht der Gefühle und Triebe befreien. Damit redet Hegel keinem asketischen Ideal das Wort. Begierden und Triebe sind nicht etwa zu unterdrücken, sondern es kann ihnen oft gerade „durch die Gewohnheit ihrer Befriedigung" die Macht über un- sere Psyche genommen werden (HGW 20, § 410 Anm.). Das Ziel, das Hegel im Auge hat, ist letztlich eine Seele, die einen habituellen Umgang mit ihrem Ge- fühlsleben ausgebildet hat, sich in ihrem Leib wie in einem Kunstwerk auszu- drücken vermag und dabei zugleich frei für höherstufige geistige Aktivitäten ge- worden ist (HGW 20, § 411).

Die Möglichkeit, verrückt zu werden, bleibt bei Hegel auch in den an die Seele anschließenden Formen des Geistes hintergründig virulent. Immer dann, wenn der Geist mit einer ungewohnten Affektion, einem unassimilierbaren Umstand umzugehen hat, besteht die Gefahr, dass er darüber verrückt wird. Zweifellos ist Hegel zuversichtlich, dass das nicht besonders häufig geschieht. Aber da die Möglichkeit prinzipiell offenbleibt, muss er Schellings These, dass der Geist mit Gefühlen, Trieben und dergleichen konfrontiert ist, die ihn bisweilen in den Wahnsinn treiben können, nicht kritisch auf sich beziehen – er kann ihr sogar zustimmen. Kontrovers bleibt zwischen Schelling und Hegel jedoch die Frage, wie psychische Pathologien kuriert werden können. Während sich der menschliche Geist bei Schelling ganz der göttlichen Seele zu unterwerfen hat, muss er sich bei Hegel stets selbst als der herrschende Genius seines psychischen Lebens be- währen. Dabei ist der Mensch in gewisser Weise mit seinen Gewohnheiten allein. Die Gefahr einer Verrücktheit, die bei Hegel ohne göttliche Kur auskommen muss, ist am Ende vielleicht radikaler als der Schelling'sche Wahnsinn, obwohl sie sehr viel schlichter beschrieben wird.

Literaturverzeichnis

FGW | Freud, Sigmund. (1940 ff.). *Gesammelte Werke*. Chronologisch geordnet. Frankfurt a. M.: S. Fischer Verlag.

HGW | Hegel, Georg Wilhelm Friedrich. (1968 ff.). *Gesammelte Werke*. In Verbindung mit der Deutschen Forschungsgemeinschaft herausgegeben von der Rheinisch-Westfälischen Akademie der Wissenschaften. Hamburg: Felix Meiner Verlag.

AA | Schelling, Friedrich Wilhelm Joseph. (1976 ff.). *Historisch-kritische Ausgabe*. Im Auftrag der Bayerischen Akademie der Wissenschaften (Schelling – Edition und Archiv) herausgegeben von Thomas Buchheim, Jochem Hennigfeld, Wilhelm G. Jacobs, Jörg Jantzen und Siegbert Peetz. Stuttgart-Bad Cannstatt: Frommann-Holzboog.

SW | Schelling, Friedrich Wilhelm Joseph. (1856–1861). *Sämmtliche Werke*. Herausgegeben von Karl Friedrich August Schelling. Stuttgart/Augsburg: J. G. Cotta'scher Verlag.

WA | Schelling, Friedrich Wilhelm Joseph. (1946). *Die Weltalter. Fragmente*. In den Urfassungen von 1811 und 1813 herausgegeben von Manfred Schröter. München: Biederstein und Leibniz Verlag.

Die Bibel. (1985). Nach der Übersetzung Martin Luthers. Stuttgart: Deutsche Bibelgesellschaft.

Baumgartner, Hans Michael; Korten, Harald. (1996). *Friedrich Wilhelm Joseph Schelling*. München: C. H. Beck.

Bowie, Andrew. (2010). „The philosophical significance of Schelling's conception of the unconscious". In: Nicholls, Angus; Liebscher, Martin (Hrsg.). *Thinking the Unconscious: Nineteenth-Century German Thought*. Cambridge et al.: Cambridge University Press, S. 57–86.

Erhardt, Walter E. (1989). *Schellling Leonbergiensis und Maximilian II. von Bayern. Lehrstunden der Philosophie*. Stuttgart-Bad Cannstatt: Frommann-Holzboog.

Fyttche, Matt. (2012). *The Foundations of the Unconscious. Schelling, Freud and the Birth of the Modern Psyche*. Cambridge et al.: Cambridge University Press.

Hennigfeld, Jochem. (2002) „Der Mensch im absoluten System. Anthropologische Ansätze in der Philosophie Schellings". In: Jantzen, Jörg; Oesterreich, Peter L. (Hrsg.). *Schellings philosophische Anthropologie*. Stuttgart-Bad Cannstatt: Frommann-Holzboog, S. 1–22.

Marquard, Odo. (1975). „Schelling – Zeitgenosse inkognito". In: Baumgartner, Hans Michael (Hrsg.). *Schelling*. Freiburg: Karl Alber Verlag, S. 9–26.

Marquard, Odo. (1987). *Transzendentaler Idealismus, Romantische Naturphilosophie, Psychoanalyse*. Köln: Verlag für Philosophie Dinter.

McGrath, Sean J. (2012). *The Dark Ground of Spirit. Schelling and the Unconscious*. London et al.: Routledge.

Müller-Lüneschloß, Vicki. (2012). *Über das Verhältnis von Natur und Geisterwelt. Ihre Trennung, ihre Versöhnung, Gott und den Menschen. Eine Studie zu F. W. J. Schellings „Stuttgarter Privatvorlesungen" (1810) nebst Briefwechsel Wangenheim – Niederer – Schelling der Jahre 1809/1810*. Stuttgart-Bad Cannstatt: Frommann-Holzboog.

Oesterreich, Peter L. (2002). „Die Freiheit, der Irrtum, der Tod und die Geisterwelt. Schellings anthropologischer Übergang in die Metaphysik". In: Jantzen, Jörg; Oesterreich, Peter L.

(Hrsg.). *Schellings philosophische Anthropologie*. Stuttgart-Bad Cannstatt: Frommann-Holzboog, S. 23 – 50.

Sandkaulen, Birgit. (2004). „Dieser und kein anderer? Zur Individualität der Person in Schellings ‚Freiheitsschrift‘". In: Buchheim, Thomas; Hermanni, Friedrich (Hrsg.). *„Alle Persönlichkeit ruht auf einem dunkeln Grunde". Schellings Philosophie der Personalität*. Berlin: De Gruyter, S. 35 – 53.

Sandkaulen, Birgit. (2011). „‚Die Seele ist der existierende Begriff.‘ Herausforderungen philosophischer Anthropologie". In: *Hegel-Studien* 45, S. 37 – 52.

Schmidt-Biggemann, Wilhelm. (2014). „Die Theologie der Stuttgarter Privatvorlesungen". In: Hühn, Lore; Schwab, Philipp (Hrsg.). *System, Natur und Anthropologie. Zum 200. Jubiläum von Schellings Stuttgarter Privatvorlesungen*. Freiburg: Karl Alber, S. 159 – 182.

Sommer, Konstanze. (2015). *Zwischen Metaphysik und Metaphysikkritik. Heidegger, Schelling und Jacobi*. Paradeigmata 35. Hamburg: Felix Meiner Verlag.

Žižek, Slavoj. (1997). *The Abyss of Freedom/Ages of the World* by F. W. J. Schelling. Ann Arbor: The University of Michigan Press.

Daniel Whistler
Schelling's Politics of Sympathy: Reflections on *Clara* and Related Texts

Abstract. *In this essay, I read F. W. J. Schelling's* Clara *alongside a number of his other texts from 1804–1815 in terms of the* concept of sympathy. *In so doing, I illuminate the implicit role of this psychological concept in Schelling's metaphysics, epistemology, metaphilosophy and political philosophy of that period, and thereby suggest that the most fundamental consequence of its employment is a* populist reorientation *of philosophy. Philosophy is to be undertaken not just for the people, but by them too: Schelling identifies the activity of philosophising with the public action of a community bonded by sympathetic ties.*

In diesem Beitrag wird Schellings Clara *in Zusammenhang mit anderen Texten von Schelling aus den Jahren 1804–1815 unter der Perspektive des Begriffs der Sympathie gelesen. Auf diese Weise wird die implizite Rolle dieses psychologischen Begriffs in Schellings Metaphysik, Erkenntnistheorie, Metaphilosophie und politischer Philosophie dieser Zeit deutlich. Es wird damit auch der Vorschlag gemacht, dass die fundamentalste Konsequenz des Einsatzes von Sympathie eine populistische Reorientierung der Philosophie ist. Philosophie ist nicht nur für Menschen gemacht, sondern auch von ihnen. Schelling identifiziert die Aktivität der Philosophie mit einer öffentlichen Handlung einer Gemeinschaft, die durch Sympathie verbunden ist.*

1 Introduction: Visions of a Schellingian Community

Clara is F. W. J. Schelling's only work to make sustained conceptual use of the psychological affect of sympathy. It enumerates numerous sympathetic bonds that hold (i) between the various characters in the dialogue; (ii) between Clara and her deceased husband, Albert; (iii) between the living and the dead more generally; (iv) between these characters and a grocer's wife who appears in Part V; (v) between occult practitioners and their subjects; (vi) between natural phenomena; and, most abstractly, (vii) between the real and the ideal. Indeed, the very dialogue itself is a performance of sympathetic sociability—a return to symphilosophy or 'the Jena mode of discourse' (Ziolkowski 1990)—and it contains, as a brief *mise en abyme*, a set of guidelines for implementing such sym-

https://doi.org/10.1515/9783110673692-015

philosophising. Schelling's concept of sympathy is, nevertheless, not merely derivative of Romantic sources, but also influenced by seventeenth-century theories of universal sympathy found in Leibniz and the Cambridge Platonists, as well as mystic doctrines, like Swedenborg's. These different contexts result in a concept of sympathy in *Clara* that pertains to psychology, metaphysics, physics, mysticism, metaphilosophy—*and also politics*.[1]

Hence, I want to specifically argue that this focus on sympathetic sociability within *Clara* sheds light on a whole strand of Schellingian political thinking. That is, I maintain that, between (roughly) 1804 and 1815[2], Schelling was (at least, sometimes) committed to the following theses:

1. A group of religious believers bonded in sympathy is a condition of the possibility for political action;
2. Such communal political action is the correlate of genuine philosophical speculation (in Schelling's schematic terms: real : ideal = public action : philosophising);
3. Such speculation in turn fosters affects of sympathy that strengthen the community.

A mutually-reinforcing loop is thus generated between the elements of sympathy, belief, community and philosophy, and the overriding result of this feedback loop is, I suggest in what follows, a thoroughly *populist* philosophy, that is, a philosophising that comes from the people. In other words, in this strand of his philosophy, Schelling rejects any ideal of *Bildung* through philosophy: the philosopher does not rise above the masses, nor does her education conflict with the norms of public common sense; rather, she must become one with her public. What emerges here, I contend, is a thoroughgoing attempt to undertake *Volksphilosophie* or even *Populärphilosophie*, a philosophy that takes all its content, norms and modes of practice from 'the people'.[3] Philosophising is identified with the public action of a community bonded by sympathetic ties.

This vision of a politics of sympathy is, it must be admitted, a minoritarian tradition in Schelling's *opus*, and it has understandably been neglected in com-

---

1 I provide a synopsis of *Clara* in section three below.
2 Of course, Schelling's views on many topics change considerably between 1804 and 1815; my claim is merely that a number of his texts from the period make cumulative contributions to a broadly coherent account of the relation between philosophising, community and sympathy.
3 In what follows, I retain Schelling's indeterminate concept 'the people', which remains undefined throughout his writings (as in many *Volksphilosophien* of the period), and, indeed, is able to take on the many significant functions it does precisely, in part, because of such indeterminacy.

parison to the other naturalistic, Eleatic or proto-existentialist Schellings more familiar from the scholarship. For this very reason, however, the value of what follows lies in contesting stereotypical images of Schelling that have built up over recent decades—that is, its value lies in:

a. falsifying a traditional image of Schelling as aloof to political actuality (particularly in comparison to Hegel), since his vision of a politics of sympathy constitutes some of his most explicit attempts at political philosophy prior to the late 1840s.

b. illustrating the non-elitist character of some of Schelling's philosophy—that is, his vision of a politics of sympathy rubs against the post-Lukácian reading of Schelling as a philosopher of aristocratic hierarchy (Lukács 1980; Sandkühler 1998), as well as any tendency in Schelling's own earlier work to make philosophising 'not within everyone's reach' (SW 5, pp. 218–219).[4]

c. contesting a common perception of German Idealism generally—and Schelling's writing in particular—as obscure esotericism to be deciphered solely by adepts (as exemplified by Schelling and Hegel's early claim that 'in its relationship to common sense, the world of philosophy is in and for itself an inverted world' [Hegel/Schelling 1985, pp. 282–283]). Instead, *Clara* should be aligned with the many other examples of popular writing in Fichte, Jacobi, Solger, etc.[5] Schelling, too, calls for a kind of mutated continuation of *Populärphilosophie*.

d. highlighting Schelling's reflections on the proper genres of philosophical presentation. That is, in opposition to images of German Idealists practising 'a somewhat rigid and disciplined form of writing [...] [which] from the perspective of the modern reader, can look somewhat tedious or pedantic' (Stewart 2013, p. 81), Schelling's appeal to the popular illustrates his concern with the different genres in which philosophy can be written, and, particularly, with the idea of writing philosophy *into* life.

---

4 Although what follows contests this Lukácian charge of elitism, it does nothing to save Schelling from Lukács' more general critique of Schelling as 'reactionary'. A populist Schelling may not be a better Schelling politically, but he is certainly not aristocratic.

5 This comparison between *Clara* and other attempts at popular philosophy is briefly invoked by Grosos (2014, pp. 41–42); however, a fuller discussion of Schelling's contribution to this trend —something that stands outside the remit of this essay—is sorely needed. Likewise, a full treatment of the connections between *Clara* and Jena Romanticism's investment in 'new modes of participatory feeling' (Kneller 2014, p. 110) lies outside the scope of what follows. A complete discussion would need to refer to Schleiermacher's *Versuch einer Theorie des geselligen Betragens* and consequently also Schelling's review of Schleiermacher's *Weihnachtsfeier*. The influence of Herder's 1765 *Wie die Philosophie zum Besten des Volkes allgemeiner und nützlicher werden kann* would also be pertinent to such a project.

2 Schelling's Call for a Populist Insurrection

> What is this current separation of academics from the people supposed to bring? Truly, I can see the time come when the people, having had to become thereby more and more ignorant about the highest things, will rise up and make those philosophers account for themselves, saying: You should be the salt of your nation; so why don't you salt us? (SW 9, pp. 91–92; Schelling 2002, p. 66)

This passage is taken, not from a right-wing demagogue's tirade against expertise, nor from the resentful polemic of an outsider unable to access institutional structures, but from F. W. J. Schelling, formerly Extraordinary Professor of Philosophy at the University of Jena and Professor of Philosophy at the University of Würzburg, and, at the time when *Clara* was written[6], a leading member of the Bayerische Akademie der Wissenschaften. From the very heart of early nineteenth-century academia, Schelling calls for a populist uprising that will break down the cloistered walls of the university and transform philosophy into a thoroughly public enterprise.

In a similar vein, the closing paragraph to Schelling's all-encompassing *Würzburger System* reads as follows:

> Philosophy is the goal of the science of philosophy, even if—so long as it lacks the public life in which it can be intuited—philosophy can live only within the limits of science and only as science, not in itself. Philosophy—which is no longer science, but becomes life—is what Plato calls πολιτεύειν [the political], life with and within an ethical totality. (SW 6, p. 576)[7]

In the penultimate proposition, § 325, Schelling had argued that, 'In the state, science, religion and art become objective in a mutually penetrating one and all [...]. Neither true science, nor true religion, nor true art has another form of objectivity than the state.' In particular, Schelling goes on to specify that religion is made objective specifically through 'public ethics and the heroism of a nation' and art through 'the living rhythmic movement of public life' (SW 6, pp. 575–576). § 326 is, then, devoted to the formula, 'Reason : Cosmos = Philosophy : State' (SW 6, p. 576). In other words, philosophy does not have a localised polit-

---

6 When *exactly Clara* was written is famously a matter of some debate. The traditional attribution is 1810–1811 (e. g., Věto 2014, p. 21, Lindberg 2013, p. 235), but Scheerlinck (2019) has recently argued that 1807–1808 is more likely. For an English-language discussion of the dating controversy, see Steinkamp 2002, pp. xiii–xvii. My focus across the period 1804 to 1815 allows for either option.

7 Unless otherwise noted, translations are my own.

ical function, as religion and art do, but encompasses the whole realm of political action as such. Philosophy is the non-objectivised state—or politics insofar as it remains ideal. And yet, the closing sentences of the final paragraph reproduced above do not limit philosophy's political vocation to the legitimisation, creation or restitution of the state in particular; rather, philosophy is called on to become 'political *life*', to take on 'public life'. This is one example of Schelling's rare forays into political philosophy between the *Neue Deduktion des Naturrechts* and the *Stuttgarter Privatvorlesungen*, and he here argues that philosophy, freed from the constraints of science, becomes the very essence of life within a polis. Accordingly, the goal of philosophical activity becomes the liberation of thought, *bringing it back to life*—a resuscitation of thinking outside of any cloistered academy, an immersion of philosophy in community. The fulfilment of philosophy occurs, then, among the people. Once again, philosophy is to be a properly popular enterprise.

Populism is therefore an ideal to be found throughout much of Schelling's writing of the period—and *Clara* provides the most striking illustration of it. The quotation with which this section begins provides just one instance of a general trend in the work: to attack academic 'ivory-towerism' in the name of a 'turn towards the people' (Vëto 2014, p. 24). What is thereby instituted is a thinking that is meant not just *for* the people, but is also to emerge *from* the people and even *by* the people too.

3 All Saints' Day and the Grocer's Wife

It is, therefore, on the basis of such a pervasive populism—discernible in many of Schelling's writings of the period—that *Clara* can be interpreted. Hence, in this next section, I want to summarise the 'plot' of this novel, and, once again, two quotations will serve as illustrations. These two passages are taken, respectively, from the very opening and from towards the end of *Clara*; both are, I submit, intended to tell the reader something about what it looks like to sympathise properly—that is, to sympathise in a way that forms a community of believers that is the correlate to genuine philosophical speculation.

> We saw a crowd of people thronging toward a gentle incline [...]. We joined them so that for once we, too, could watch the moving festival dedicated to the dead that is celebrated this day in Catholic towns. We found the whole area full of people already. It was peculiar to see life on the graves, forebodingly illuminated by the dully shining autumn sun. As we left the trodden path, we soon saw pretty groups gathered around individual graves: here girls in their bloom, holding hands with their younger brothers and sisters, crowned their mother's grave; there at the grave of her children who were lost so young, a mother stood in silence

with no need for consecrated water to represent her tears [...]. Here all of life's severed relationships were revived for the spectators who were familiar with the people and the circumstances; brothers came again to brothers and children to parents; at this moment all were one family again. (SW 9, pp. 11–12; Schelling 2002, p. 9)

During this speech we'd noticed a woman below, walking around under the trees by the church [...]. I recognised her as the wife of a grocer from a small town three hours away from here. As she greeted us, I asked her what had brought her here; but she didn't want to say until I told her that I'd noticed her making an offering down there and that she must therefore have some matter of concern [...]. [After she finished telling her story,] I said to her: God has surely helped you, for He sees into the heart. Go home comforted and greet your husband and your children. The story had touched us all incredibly, so we remained in silence for a while before we set off again. (SW 9, pp. 102–104; Schelling 2002, pp. 73–74)

The first quotation sets the scene for *Clara*'s initial dialogue amidst the Catholic festivities of All Saints' Day[8], a festival that attempts to revive 'severed relationships' in order that all might be 'family again'. Indeed, Lindberg calls *Clara* as a whole 'a strange All-Saints'-Day novel of death and mourning' (Schelling 2013, p. 235). The first pages narrate how a 'crowd' of believers are intent on fortifying their sympathetic affinities with the dead by means of the festivities, such that the festival itself becomes a site for the renewal of bonds between this world and the next. *And yet*, exempted from the crowd, the protagonists of *Clara* themselves take no part in these festivities: they stand apart, unwilling and seemingly unable to participate in this celebration of sympathetic bonds with the departed. The priest and doctor merely watch, while Clara has shut herself away in 'solitude', in a 'secluded' Benedictine monastery (SW 9, p. 14; Schelling 2002, p. 11). Clara, in particular, practises an isolationist ascesis that impedes sympathetic bonds and so prevents any access to the spirit world. Moreover, the 'well-educated, young clergyman' (SW 9, p. 13; Schelling 2002, p. 10) who appears in this opening dialogue personifies such a failure of sympathy even more radically: his disconnection from the world and subsequent inability to recognise any positive connection between it and the next results in disparaging comments on the festival and ultimately to a sterile, pseudo-Kantian agnosticism (indeed, the part of town in which he resides is 'empty and deserted' [SW 9, p. 12; Schelling 2002, p. 10]). So, when the narrator comments, 'We should support all fes-

---

8 As a number of commentators note (Vëto 2014, p. 25; David 2014, p. 57), Schelling uses the antiquated 'Aller-Seelen-Tag' and not the more customary 'Allerheiligen' to designate this festival; he thus emphasises the significance of 'the soul' in its practices, as well as making conceptually productive use of anachronism.

tivals and customs in which we are reminded of a connection with the world beyond', the clergyman responds:

> Today's commemoration certainly has something moving about it; however, if its purpose is
> to support the thought that we can be connected to the inhabitants of that other world, then
> I would hold this commemoration to be one that is almost detrimental and I would submit
> that it be abolished in your church [...]. We must honour these old divisions. (SW 9,
> pp. 16–17; Schelling 2002, p. 12)

It is to such comments that Clara responds with a demand to return from intellectual isolation into the festive state: 'What do cold words and merely negative concepts have to do with ardent longing? Are we satisfied in this life with a bleak existence?' (SW 9, p. 18; Schelling 2002, p. 13). An alternative is required, and this alternative must provide a means to sympathise.

This is a question of building 'community' (SW 9, p. 16; Schelling 2002, p. 12) —both with the dead and with the festive crowd; it is a matter of managing—despite their intellectual isolation in the cloistered academy—to foster those 'higher relationships' of 'friendship and love' in which 'a quiet, unconscious, but thereby all the more compelling, necessity draws one soul to another' (SW 9, pp. 19–20; Schelling 2002, p. 14).

The dialogues that follow respond to Clara's provocation in a number of ways: (1) by imagining better models of intellectual sociability than those of the cloistered university—'a Platonic academy should gather [...] men from all of the arts and sciences should live a truly spiritual life here, in harmony and free from worry: they shouldn't be locked up in towns, in the constrictive conditions of society and far from nature' (SW 9, p. 24; Schelling 2002, p. 17); (2) by recognising that wisdom also resides outside the intellectual elite—'I have learned more about physics from the farmers than from the academics' lecture halls' (SW 9, p. 26; Schelling 2002, p. 19); and (3) by insisting on the universal sympathy that holds both within nature and between the natural and the supernatural. Indeed, much attention is paid by the characters to sympathies in nature as derivative of more mystic affinities: 'everything speaks to us and would so much like to make itself understood' (SW 9, p. 35; Schelling 2002, p. 26). The person who learns to recognise such sympathetic bonds in nature, it is implied, will come to recognise higher interconnections, i.e. that 'everything is of course contained in everything else: the lower level prophesies of the higher' (SW 9, pp. 52–53; Schelling 2002, p. 39). The role of the soul in Schelling's anthropology of the period is crucial here, for 'it is just [the soul] that we love above all; that draws us, as it were, in a magical way, so that we immediately give our trust to those of whom we say in this respect that they have soul' (SW 9, p. 45; Schelling 2002, p. 34). Mimicking the language of Bonnet's *palingen-*

esis, Schelling continues, the soul is 'the innermost germ of all', and so to 'transform that dark and obscure germ within [us] into clarity and light' is to intensify this 'magical' power of attraction and bonds of trust that make sympathy possible (SW 9, pp. 47, 69; Schelling 2002, pp. 35, 51). The soul acts as the condition of possibility for genuine community, the condition of returning to the festival and communing with the dead. We are already far from the clergyman's ascetic Kantianism.

It is at this point—the opening to Part V—that Schelling explicitly introduces the concept of sympathy, including the 'sensitivity' necessary for its correct employment and the 'wonderful entanglements of the internal and the external' it effects (SW 9, pp. 106, 110; Schelling 2002, pp. 76, 78). It occupies a crucial function in the philosophical architectonic there constructed: Schellingianism must be able to philosophise about everything, to become an absolute system that excludes nothing, and so it must *also* speak of the spirit world, life after death and the supernatural. To do so, the philosopher requires some access to these phenomena, some sympathy for them. Only through sympathetic description of the spirit world can Schelling's philosophy lay claim to the oneness, wholeness and absoluteness he craves. However, this recourse to sympathy still remains academic, part of an abstract discussion; the concept has not yet been 'brought to life' or 'become popular', as Schelling's ideal for philosophical practice at this period demands. And it is this demand for popularity that motivates the entry of the grocer's wife in the second passage reproduced above.

The narrator is in the middle of an extended theoretical speech on the mystic sympathies out of which language is constituted, when a woman (whom he recognises as the wife of a grocer from a nearby town) interrupts. She tells the story of an ill child and a neighbour's advice 'to make a vow to St. Walderich', for 'he has heard many vows already and has worked true miracles'. She continues,

> As the child was getting visibly worse and worse and there seemed to be no more help at all, I was overcome and inwardly I made a heartfelt, profound vow of a great offering to St. Walderich if he would help me in my need. And you see, she continued, hardly half an hour had passed when the child fell into a gentle sleep [...]. [The doctor] came and was completely astonished that the child was still alive, examined the child when he woke up, and said that the child had been saved; but it's truly a miracle, he said. (SW 9, pp. 102–104; Schelling 2002, p. 73–74)

The story evidently draws on themes present earlier in *Clara* including the value of popular religious practices, connections between the living and the dead and the causal effectiveness of the ideal. Nevertheless, what is most remarkable for my purposes is the other characters' reactions to this story. Rather than the disdain and condescension that characterised their response to the All Saints' Day festivities at the beginning of *Clara*, the characters now respond, in unison, with sympathy: 'The story had touched us all incredibly, so we remained in silence for a while before we set off again'. Clara continues—and one should note here the close proximity of concepts of belief, the people and being affected by others in the following: 'I, at least, am touched by the sight of a people who still have a protective spirit to which they can turn'. And it is at this very moment that she has the realisation towards which the whole series of dialogues had long been heading:

> 'Shouldn't we generally more often observe the same sensitivity to the departed that we believe we owe to the living? Who knows whether they partake more deeply with us than we think; whether the pain we feel so intensely, the excess of tears we weep for them, isn't capable of unsettling them?' At that moment we stepped out from the trees of the church and the whole area lay once more before us in a mild transfiguration. (SW 9, pp. 104–106; Schelling 2002, pp. 75–76)

This is Clara's *Aufklärung* and also her *Verklärung* (following David's conjecture that the name 'Clara' alludes to her role as *die Verklärte* [Schelling 2014, p. 52])[9]. Her transfiguration—along with that of the whole of the natural world[10]—is here accomplished by performance of and reflection on the power of sympathy engendered by the grocer's wife's story.

In other words, Clara and the others have learnt their lesson. The five dialogues chart a transition from a rejection of the popular, a rejection of supernatural beliefs and a rejection of sympathy towards a form of philosophical reflection that is achieved through a concrete instance of sympathising with a representative of 'the people'. The characters finally take the superstitions of popular belief seriously[11], and so the cloistered walls isolating academic discourse break down before the reader's eyes. It is a paradigmatic example of the Schellingian reunification of philosophy and life.

---

9 Many commentators note the narrative of transfiguration across the series of dialogues: *Clara* forms 'an itinerary of reconciliation' (Mabille 2014, p. 98), and what is at stake in the content of the conversations is 'the art and means of converting a soul without compulsion' (Roux 2014, p. 76).

10 This is but one more example of how in *Clara* 'the place, the landscape, the seasons, the annual festivals possess a certain significance for the conceptual development as well as also having literary value' (Věto 2014, p. 24).

11 As late as Part IV, one of the characters insists that some supernatural stories 'represent the very worst of society and were the real scum of mankind' (SW 9, p. 78; Schelling 2002, p. 56). On the contrary, as Marquet argues, the grocer's wife's story in Part V 'permits the recuperation of aspects of popular religion that had been most reviled by the Enlightenment' (1984, pp. 19–20).

4 Examples of Schelling's Own Practice of Sympathy

Schelling's most explicit allusions to the concept of sympathy are restricted to Part V of *Clara*, where, for example, he writes,

> Sympathy, which is a heavenly appearance here, only expressed much more dully and weakly, must reach a completely new degree of profundity there [in the ideal world]— just as we notice here that bodies transported into a more spiritual condition sense their relationships to each other more profoundly [...]. And I don't doubt concerning the expression of this sympathy that it's far more perfect than what's possible here. For even language contains a spiritual essence and a corporeal element. (SW 9, pp. 100–101; Schelling 2002, p. 72)

Nevertheless, sympathetic resonances are to be found throughout his writings of the period. Perhaps the most significant example is to be found at the very beginning of the *Freiheitsschrift*:

> Whoever takes the theory of physics as his point of departure and knows that the doctrine of 'like is recognised by like' is a very ancient one—such a one will understand that the philosopher maintains the existence of this knowledge, because he alone comprehends the god outside himself through the god within himself by keeping his mind pure and unclouded. (SW 7, p. 337; Schelling 1936, p. 8)

Here Schelling repeats a long-standing epistemic principle in his philosophy: the subject of knowing must maintain some kind of identity with the object of knowledge; there needs to be some bond between them for knowledge and therefore philosophising to be possible. 'Training in philosophy' (SW 7, p. 337; Schelling 1936, p. 8) consists in cultivating such bonds. In other words, the philosopher cultivates sympathy with the outside. Such calls to philosophical sympathy are to be implicitly found throughout Schelling's philosophical trajectory: whether in the description of the Spinozist immersing herself in the absolute in the *Philosophische Briefe über Dogmatismus und Kriticismus*, in the definition of heroic action in the *Würzburger System*, or—most significantly—in the appeal to *Mitwissenschaft* (a kind of participative intuition) in the introduction to the *Weltalter* drafts. Indeed, it is precisely this identification of knower and known that motivates Schelling's introduction of sympathy into *Clara:* in order for philosophy to become one absolute system, it must speak *even* of the supernatural and the spirit-world; hence, some bond of identity between the philosopher and these phenomena—some sympathetic affinity between them—needs to be cultivated. This is the topic of the latter pages of *Clara*—a response to the problem of 'recovering the *one* philosophy' across the seeming break between this world and the next. The text thereby forms part of 'the Schellingian attempt to maintain the unity of philosophy' (Marquet 1984, pp. 15–17). To put it more bluntly: what all these moments in the Schellingian corpus have in common is that they implicitly rehearse—in an academic register, to be sure—the very 'heavenly appearance' of sympathy between subject and object experienced by Clara herself at the grocer's wife's story.

Moreover, a glance at the various influences on Schelling's use of the concept of sympathy is also worthwhile at this juncture. Generally put, he taps into a tendency in the Western philosophical tradition in which the affect of sympathy holds a privileged philosophical place, not just as a concept within psychology, but as a constitutive principle in metaphysics, theology, erotics, political philosophy and of course ethics. Indeed, it should not be very surprising that Schelling makes recourse to the concept of sympathy, considering 'sympathy's eighteenth-century explosion' (Hanley 2015, p. 174), on the back of its 'increasingly important role in philosophy over the course of the seventeenth century' (Mercer 2015, p. 108). 'Cosmological, physical and psychological accounts of sympathy' (Schliesser 2015, p. 7) would have been familiar to Schelling not just from Stoic texts, but also from Newton's flirtation with the concept, from Leibniz's commitment to 'universal sympathy, according to which all creatures correspond sympathetically to all others' (Mercer 2015, p. 108), from Spinoza's 'implicit rehabilitation of the idea of cosmic sympathy' based on a 'vision of the fundamental unity of nature, and in particular his belief that all finite things are just modifications of one fundamental entity' (Hübner 2015, p. 151). And, of course, the concept would also have been very familiar to Schelling from late eighteenth-century discussions—in, for example, Kant's ethics—of the 'general duty' to sympathetic feeling (Ak. 4, pp. 456–457; Kant 2013, p. 250), i. e. of sympathy as 'an action-motivating sentiment capable of serving to establish social bonds between individuals' (Hanley 2015, p. 177).

What, first and foremost, connects Schelling to these precedents is his commitment to what Schliesser has dubbed 'the likeness principle [...] a metaphysical background commitment that is presupposed in nearly all applications of the concept [of sympathy]'—that is, 'that it takes place among things/events/features that are in one sense or another alike' (Schliesser 2015, p. 7). Whether or not Schelling's metaphysics is interpreted as changing drastically over time, some claim to ontological unity—and so an interest in the *connexio rerum* that results—seems a fairly constant feature from at least 1795 to 1815. Indeed, Véto argues, with respect to *Clara* in particular, that it 'conforms to the logic of his philosophy which professes the uninterrupted continuity between worlds and the mutual influence of all beings on each other' (Véto 2014, p. 26), and to this extent, Schelling 'posits a sympathy between beings, in a Leibnizian vein' (Vëto 2014, p. 29).

Moreover, just like the other philosophers enumerated above, Schelling draws on the ubiquity of modern uses of the concept of sympathy, the concept's 'vitality' and 'heterogeneity' (Bernier 2010, p. 4). That is, he taps into the metabatic tendency in philosophical treatments of sympathy—the tendency to proliferate sympathies across domains: 'like is known by like'[12] is not merely pertinent to his ethics, politics and religion, but stands as the key orienting principle of his overall methodology. Speculation itself is motivated by the affect of sympathy— an attractive bond which draws the philosopher and her subject matter together. The philosopher's 'training', as the *Freiheitsschrift* puts it, is in sympathy.

5 Schelling, Demagogue

Schelling's remarks on political philosophy during the years 1804 to 1815 are often overlooked, because they are scattered rather haphazardly within writings devoted to seemingly non-political topics, and, even then, occurr at the margins. However, my focus above on Schelling's use of the psychological concept of sympathy makes them far more visible. Multiple examples of Schelling's political reflections in *Clara* itself could be reproduced here, such as this one:

> I too, I said, prefer to see a philosopher with a sociable garland in his hair than with a scientific crown of thorns, through which he presents himself as the truly tormented *ecce homo* of the people [...]. Depth behaves like what appears to be its opposite, the sublime, in that it has all the greater effect if it is clothed in the simplest words that even working people and craftsmen can understand. The language of the people is as it were from eternity; the artificial language of the schools is that of yesterday. (SW 9, p. 87; Schelling 2002, p. 63)

Another example of this strain of Schellingian political reflection is to be found in the very final paragraph of his 1803–1804 lectures on the philosophy of art:

> Music, song, dance, as well as all the various types of drama, live only in public life, and form an alliance in such life. Wherever public life disappears, instead of that real, external drama in which, in all its forms, an entire people participates as a political or moral totality, only an inward, ideal drama can unite the people. This ideal drama is the worship service,

---

12 Empedocles, who Schelling names explicitly as his source for the maxim 'like is known by like', was a common reference-point in seventeenth-century discussions of universal sympathy. See Mercer 2015, pp. 119–120.

the only kind of truly public action that has remained for the contemporary age, and even so only in an extremely diminished and reduced form. (SW 5, p. 736; Schelling 1989, p. 280)

In line with much already described in this essay, Schelling here claims that the arts live 'only in public life', and that such public life is to be conceived as a 'real, external drama in which, in all its forms, an entire people participates as a political or moral totality'. He goes on to look to public organisations outside of the state (like the church) for a productive form of political life, and these alternative communities are understood as component parts of both a vital philosophising (as elucidated in section 2 above) and of participation in religious practices (as noted in section 3 above). Such communities are productive of speculation, belief and also the arts.[13]

The significance of Schelling's turn to community is even more striking in light of his critique of the state in the *Stuttgarter Privatvorlesungen* as 'an expression of failed freedom' (Zöller 2014, p. 209; see SW 7, pp. 460–465; Schelling 1994, pp. 226–229). While such a critique stands in continuity with some of Schelling's earlier political views (such as *Das älteste Systemprogramm*'s call for the state to be abolished), it still marks, as Zöller argues, a 'sharp turn' from many of his political remarks around 1800. In 1810, he sees only 'insufficiency and unfreedom in the realm of the state' (Zöller 2014, pp. 206, 213). My contention is that Schelling's more constructive comments on those alternative political communities that are more conducive to a productive 'political or moral totality' complement this religio-anarchic attack on the state in the *Stuttgarter Privatvorlesungen*. They form the basis of a positive vision of the type of society that ought to replace the state. The failure of established political institutions calls for alternatives, and the alternatives Schelling proposes are grounded on his sporadic recourse to the concepts of public action and sympathetic bonds.[14]

---

13 On the importance of the concept of public action in Schelling's philosophy around 1804, see Marquet 1973, pp. 275–276; Whistler 2013, p. 218.

14 McGrath (2017) argues for a very different relation between Schellingianism and populism in the post-1815 work, suggesting that Schelling's philosophy of revelation can form a bulwark against theological appropriations of populist rhetoric. Nevertheless, there is a sense in which the later philosophies of mythology and revelation continue the populist project of the years 1804 to 1815: they look to deposits of communal truth (e.g. Samothracian mythology) as moments of philosophical insight—deposits that are demonstrated to be *already* philosophical; the work of the philosopher is merely to identify them and analyse them, thereby making explicit the philosophical content they already contain. Speculation is anchored in a community of revelation and the philosopher must *tarry* with this community. Indeed, the more popular the language, it seems, the more revelatory of philosophical insight it is. The concept of tautegory

As I have argued above, this political vision of public action is developed by Schelling into a thoroughgoing populism—and the role of the philosopher is particular central to his account: she is to become 'one of the people', brought back into the community out of the cloistered academy. The first quotation in this section develops this vision. It comprises, once more, a critique of the philosopher who sets herself up as a messianic figure, 'as the truly tormented *ecce homo* of the people', writing the kind of artificial and esoteric prose only accessible to disciples; in contrast, the real task of the philosopher is the achievement of popularity. Simplicity becomes the ideal here—the ideal for a philosophy brought to life amidst the people. The passage ends with a reference to 'the language of the people', in contrast 'to the artificial language of the schools'. Philosophy must be reoriented towards the popular.

Such criticisms of the philosopher as tormented messiah recur in more well-known passages from the period too, such as the introduction to the *Weltalter*:

> Perhaps the one is still coming who will sing the greatest heroic poem, grasping in spirit something for which the seers of old were famous: what was, what is, what will be. But this time has not yet come. We must not misjudge our time. Heralds of this time, we do not want to pick its fruit before it is ripe nor do we want to misjudge what is ours. (SW 8, p. 206; Schelling 2000, p. xl)

The sentiments expressed here are not original to the *Weltalter*: invocations of the messianic occur frequently from *Das älteste Systemprogramm* onwards. In all such texts, Schelling characterises philosophy as 'at the end [becoming] what it was at the beginning—teacher of *mankind*' (Schelling 1995, p. 200).

And yet, what decisively distinguishes the *Weltalter* passage from such earlier invocations of an imminent philosophical poet-messiah is its *pessimism*. That is, in the 1810s, Schelling invokes the idea of a prophetic philosopher-poet only to hold it off, to postpone its coming indefinitely (see Lindberg 2013, pp. 238–239). Any suggestion in the earlier work that Schelling envisaged himself as the singer of the 'greatest heroic poem' is definitively laid to rest here. Schelling did of course write epic poetry, particularly during the late 1790s, and there is some evidence (see Whistler 2014) that these poems were envisaged as the speculative epic that would complete philosophy. Nevertheless, by 1811, he has offi-

---

employed in the lectures on the philosophy of mythology is particularly significant here: the task of tautegorical interpretation is not to interpret the popular languages of mythology, but to repeat them; myths are *not* basal units above which the *gebildete* philosopher ascends, but are themselves already sufficiently philosophical. Elsewhere, McGrath helpfully emphasises how central the connection between community and belief is to Schellingian philosophy (e.g. McGrath 2012, p. 163).

cially renounced this ambition: he envisions his role as something far more pre-liminary and preparatory—an explorer of the contemporary 'time of struggle', rather than the ultimate narrator of 'what was, what is, and what will be'.

The messianic position is one that is forever associated with the obscure, with the creation of new languages that at first appear cryptic to all but adepts. In 1811, Schelling insists that this messianic position should at present be kept empty. It is not just Schelling himself who vacates it; he insists that all philoso-phers ought to do so. The point is that Schelling's 1811 pessimism towards the philosopher as 'educator of mankind' is consonant with his *Clara*-critique of the tormented and isolated Christ-figure writing obscure jargon for a few. After 1804, Schelling continually rejects the idea of the philosopher as teaching the people anything, in favour of 'the language of the people' as itself constitutive of philosophy. He is thereby rejecting a whole tradition of *Bildung* through phi-losophy: philosophy is not there to better us or educate us; it should not try to somehow raise the non-philosophical up to its lofty heights, but rather it must itself leave behind its cloistered walls and abandon 'the artificial language of the schools'. Schelling's and Hegel's 1802 insistence that 'in its relationship to common sense, the world of philosophy is in and for itself an inverted world' is definitively rejected by Schelling after 1804.[15] The philosopher must not strike out alone, must not aim to improve or even change the world from a position of isolation. The philosopher must rather place 'a sociable garland in his hair'.

6 Guidelines for Symphilosophy

If philosophy is to become popular, what should it look like? Answering this question is the task undertaken by Part IV of *Clara*.[16] The previous section al-ready began to foreground the question of style at the heart of Schelling's populist reorientation of philosophising. A philosopher who places a 'sociable garland in his hair' writes in 'the language of the people', rather than the outdat-

---

15 This is not just a critique of Schelling's earlier self and of Hegel (as shown below), but also of Fichte, whom—as Schelling well knew—Jacobi described as 'the true Messiah of speculative rea-son' (Jacobi 1994, pp. 501–506).

16 Part IV functions then as kind of justification of Schelling's own writerly practices in *Clara*, 'a dialogue on the very nature of philosophical dialogue' (Marquet 1984, p. 5). Particularly im-portant is its emphasis on the need to combine dialogue and narrative (as *Clara* itself does), like a novel, such that unity of action is retained as something 'interior and spiritual' (Marquet 1984, pp. 9–10), i.e. 'a symbolic temporality of the interior path run by a soul in distress' (Roux 2014, p. 71).

ed 'language of the schools'. This is, Schelling goes on to elucidate, a language of simplicity—one that 'accesses the simple plenitude of human language' (Marquet 1984, p. 8)—through which the philosopher cultivates a social universality in her writings, such that conceptual content is as accessible to the 'craftsman' as it is to the academic.

Two additional quotations help further illustrate Schelling's engagement with this question:

> A few days or weeks or so later, a philosophy book arrived in which some of the excellent things it contained were written in a completely incomprehensible language and abounded, so to speak, with barbarism. Clara found it on my table and after she'd read it for a while, she said: Why do today's philosophers find it so impossible to write at least a little in the same way that they speak? Are these terribly artificial words absolutely necessary, can't the same thing be said in a more natural way, and does a book have to be quite unenjoyable for it to be philosophical? (SW 9, p. 86; Schelling 2002, p. 63)

> Germans have for so long philosophised among themselves alone that their speculations and their language has become further and further removed from what is universally intelligible [...]. After a few vain attempts to spread Kant's ideas beyond their borders, they have renounced the task of making themselves comprehensible to other nations and instead now regard themselves as the philosophical elect, forgetting that the original goal of all philosophy—a goal often forgotten but still necessary—is to obtain universal assent by making oneself universally intelligible. (SW 10, p. 204)

These quotations further develop the ideal of a simple, accessible philosophical style and its corollary, a critique of 'the philosophical elect'. Hence, the second quotation from Schelling's 1835 Preface to Victor Cousin's *Fragments philosophiques* takes up many of the themes at stake between 1804 and 1815 and redeploys them as part of his ongoing Hegel-critique. Schelling attacks the tendency to obscurity among post-Kantian philosopher-messiahs, and looks to France for part of the remedy: German philosophers must learn good style and analysis from the French, 'Who could not agree that for clarity and precision of style in scientific matters there is something to learn from our cousins in the west?' (SW 10, p. 204). Only through the absorption of French philosophical style into German systematising, Schelling argues, can a 'universally intelligible' philosophical style be attained.[17] A dose of clarity, precision and analytic thinking is required

---

17 A tension emerges here between the Cousin-preface's call for intelligibility that is *geographically* universal (i.e. a cosmopolitan account of stylistic accessibility) and the nationalist, even localist simplicity that Schelling advocates in *Clara* itself. In the latter text, he stresses the importance of idiom in the construction of a 'language of the people' (e.g. SW 9, p. 87; Schelling 2002, p. 63) and bemoans the fact that 'the Germans have to have foreign standards forced on them' (SW 9, p. 25; Schelling 2002, p. 18). This tension is perhaps explained by the later date

to cure philosophy of its Hegelian ills. This is Schelling as an ordinary-language philosopher *avant la lettre*.

Likewise the passage from *Clara* reproduced above. The literature typically identifies the unnamed 'philosophy book' which triggers Clara's critique of contemporary philosophy as the *Phänomenologie des Geistes*, and, whatever the exact volume Schelling had in mind, it is clear that he is thinking of the sorts of philosophical developments that Hegel's *Phänomenologie* exemplified for him. Again, there is an appeal to natural, not artificial style, to cultivated, rather than barbaric phrases, to a text that can be read with enjoyment at leisure, rather than slowly deciphered in an academic library. The rest of the fourth part of *Clara* is spent working out more concretely what such a philosophy of the people would look like—a dialogue drawn from contemporary life, full of the 'speech of the present', 'all the grace and tenderness of [the spoken word], all the charm of unexpected idioms' (SW 9, p. 90; Schelling 2002, p. 65). The populism implicit in all these guidelines is encapsulated in Clara's statement, 'I don't think much of a philosopher who can't make their basic view comprehensible to any educated human being; indeed, if necessary, to any intelligent and well-behaved child' (SW 9, p. 91; Schelling 2002, p. 66).

And what is more, the *concept of sympathy* is central to these guidelines on populist style. I have already noted that Schelling's explicit appeal to this concept in *Clara* occurs in a discussion of language—that is, in a discussion of the sympathetic affinities that hold between the physical and the spiritual. Language too, Schelling writes, possesses a bond with the spiritual, an 'essence' that manifests spirit through matter; hence, writing involves a kind of 'sensitivity' to the beyond, to the immaterial (SW 9, pp. 100–101; Schelling 2002, pp. 72–73). Language is a trace of the spirit world in our current condition, and so to understand language correctly is to become sympathetically aware of the beyond from within the here-and-now. Moreover, in addition to such mystical discourse on the sympathies inherent in language, Clara demands that philosophical style appropriate the properties of a sympathetic conversation between friends or lovers: 'Why can't he also speak about higher things to everyone with the same language he uses with the one he loves?' (SW 9, p. 88; Schelling 2002, p. 64). Sympathetic intimacy—affinity between author and reader or between characters in a

---

(1835) or unusual audience (those interested in French philosophy) of the Cousin-preface. More generally, nationalism seems a key component of Schelling's appeal to the people, as in any late romantic *Volksphilosophie*: just as Hegel had claimed in 1805 'that I want to teach philosophy to speak German' (Hegel 1984, p. 107), so too Schelling. Schelling merely adds that Hegel fails at this task, because he in fact asks the German people to speak his own obscure philosophical dialectic.

dialogue—thus becomes a key metaphilosophical criterion of good writing ('Why can't discussions such as we have between ourselves be written down?' [SW 9, pp. 89–90; Schelling 2002, p. 65]). And, as always in Schelling's populist reworking of philosophy, the notion of *revitalisation*, of bringing philosophy to life lies close to the surface: philosophers should 'erect small stages upon which they could summarize the lengthy debate, pull it into focus, as it were, and *make it live before our very eyes*' (SW 9, p. 88; Schelling 2002, p. 64; my emphasis).[18] It is through these means that philosophy becomes 'public'.

7 Conclusion: Mysticism, Populism, Philosophy

Clara is a text immersed in the mystic tradition. This is evident even from the subtitle attributed to it, *Über den Zusammenhang der Natur mit der Geisterwelt*, but it is also clear from the themes already resumed in this essay: the sympathy between the living and the dead, spiritual sympathies in language, 'magical connections' between man and nature, and the value of occult practices. This seems, on first blush, difficult to reconcile with Schelling's philosophical populism: the language of the mystic is typically seen as *just as* gnomic and inaccessible as the language of the academic metaphysician. And yet, Schelling resists any identification of mysticism with obscurity: in *Clara*, he instead allies mystic practices for attaining the beyond with universally accessible style, and so definitively rejects that tradition of philosophy for which the mystic is unable or unwilling to communicate clearly.

To conclude my reflections, I want to briefly consider this problem of the relation between *Clara*'s appeal to mysticism and its trenchant populism by means of a schematic comparison of Schelling and Kant on the relation between mysticism, populism and philosophy. The aim of such a coda is to better illuminate how the foregoing account of a politics of sympathy intervenes into debates within German Idealism more broadly. That is, it explores Schelling's vision of the philosophical enterprise and its role in public life from an alternative angle—interrogating what it does to religion, via a sustained comparison with

---

18 As Roux puts it, the aim is to give 'the illusion of a dialogue that unfolds under our eyes as in real life' (Roux 2014, p. 66). Emergent here is, as Grosos points out, an emphasis on *personality* in the philosophical text. He argues that such insistence on a character-centred presentation of philosophy is 'a response to the growing dissatisfaction Schelling himself experienced with the normative writing of philosophy as a *system* of knowledge' (Grosos 2014, p. 44). Or, in Schelling's own words, 'Philosophical discussions need certain types of people if they are not to be too dull' (SW 9, p. 88; Schelling 2002, p. 64).

Kant's influential template for the philosophy-popularity-mysticism triad. What I want to suggest is that, while Kant positions philosophy as a practice that is *neither* mystic *nor* popular, Schelling's *Clara* advocates a philosophising consonant with *both* mysticism *and* popular style. It describes the philosopher in an anti-Kantian manner. Schelling may follow Kant in linking mysticism to the problem of popularity, but instead of thereby shunning both, he considers the affirmation of both radical religious beliefs and popular style to be integral to the philosophical enterprise.

Kant's *Von einem neuerdings erhobenen vornehmen Ton in der Philosophie* provides a focused attack on recent 'philosophers of vision'—that is, the late Münster Circle of Stolberg and Schlosser which preached Catholic mysticism under the guise of exalted Platonism. In Kant's words,

> Things have lately gone so far that an alleged philosophy is openly proclaimed to the public, in which one does not have to *work* but need only hearken and attend to the oracle within, in order to gain complete possession of all the wisdom to which philosophy aspires. (Ak. 8, p. 390; Kant 2002, pp. 431–432)

The irony that Kant intends to trace through *Von einem neuerdings erhobenen vornehmen Ton* goes as follows: such a proclamation to the public is self-defeating, because the mystic—'brooding inwardly' (Ak. 8, p. 393; Kant 2002, p. 434)—is thereby attempting to communicate a private, ineffable feeling that by definition cannot be so communicated to a general public. Kant writes, these mystics make much of their possession of inner feelings, 'but are unfortunately unable to utter and disseminate [them] generally, by means of language' (Ak. 8, p. 389; Kant 2002, p. 431). Instead, only critical philosophy, founded as it is on 'the apodictic certainty which a *universally* binding law must possess', can be universally communicated (Ak. 8, p. 401; Kant 2002, p. 441). Only critical philosophy can be publicised, because it is founded on genuinely universal principles. Indeed, this is why the very test of good philosophy that Kant places at the heart of *Von einem neuerdings erhobenen vornehmen Ton* reads, 'As to how much sterling metal they contain at heart, who can offer a *publicly valid* testimony to this?' (Ak. 8, p. 402; Kant 2002, p. 442). Mysticism fails this test.[19]

---

19 In short, mysticism is esoteric. At best, as in Plato's letters, it can speak only to a few, to the initiated, and so it can never hope to gain the kind of universal acceptance that the critical philosophy will one day attain. Hence, Kant writes, 'Who can fail to see [in Plato's letters] the mystagogue, who not only raves on his own behalf, but is simultaneously the founder of a club, and in speaking to his adepts, rather than to the people (meaning all the uninitiated) plays the *superior* with his alleged philosophy!' (Ak. 8, p. 399; Kant 2002, p. 439).

On the basis of this fundamental opposition between mysticism as private-esoteric and criticism as public and universally-communicable, Kant goes on to set up a further opposition between poetry and prose. Kant writes at the very end of *Von einem neuerdings erhobenen vornehmen Ton*, 'At bottom, indeed, all philosophy is prosaic; and a proposal to now begin philosophising poetically again might well be received as one would a suggestion that the merchant should henceforth write his catalogues, not in prose, but in verse' (Ak. 8, p. 405; Kant 2002, p. 445). Such a claim draws on some earlier comments he had made associating mysticism with poetic talent and opposing such rhetorical ornamentation and showy ostentation to the plain simplicity of the moral law (Ak. 8, p. 393; Kant 2002, p. 434). The mystic writes beautifully, but such beauty necessarily falsifies and obscures the feelings that can never be clearly uttered. By rejecting mystic esotericism, the philosopher also rejects the poetic, and must instead act like a 'merchant' dully noting down the stocks of reason.

In fact, Kant slightly tempers this rejection of poetry elsewhere in *Von einem neuerdings erhobenen vornehmen Ton*. He distinguishes between his own style and an 'aesthetic way of presenting'. Here he does so not on the basis of an outright rejection of such aesthetic style, but because he considers it merely a *post factum* addition. It should only come after the fact of genuine philosophical labour, belatedly.[20] Kant writes of 'an aesthetic way of presenting [...] of which one can indeed *subsequently* make use, once the principles have been clarified by the first method' (Ak. 8, p. 405; Kant 2002, p. 444; my emphasis). There is a qualified acceptance here of the need to ornament philosophical prose in order, Kant continues, 'to vivify [pre-established] ideas by sensory, albeit merely analogical presentation' (Ak. 8, p. 405; Kant 2002, p. 444). Hence, another kind of popularity emerges here. There is the popularity of the universally-binding law, but also the popularity of a readable style. Kant may lay immediate claim to the first of these, but the second is always put off. Popular content is to be attained as quickly as possible, whereas popular style is a matter for a future date. From his early work onwards—but particularly in the wake of the Garve-Feder *Göttingische Anzeigen* review of 1782—Kant insists that he lacks 'the talent of a luminous, even graceful presentation'; it is, he emphasises throughout, 'something

---

20 Different models of temporality in the word/concept relation are notable here: whereas Kant insists that proper philosophical work—i.e. the labour of critique—always comes *before* its writing or communication, and one might conjecture that Hegel's 'owl of Minerva' signifies the belatedness of philosophical speculation, for Schelling, philosophy must exist as a component-part of public action—*present* in the very eruption of the event itself. As he puts it in *Clara*, 'speech [must] be *taken from the present*, or must once have been so taken, if it is to have a real effect on us' (SW 9, p. 89; Schelling 2002, p. 65; my emphasis).

I could not provide' (Ak. 8, p. 183; Kant 2007, pp. 217–218). In the Preface to the second edition of the *Kritik der reinen Vernunft*, this lack of stylistic talent is explicitly connected to the ideal of popularity: bemoaning his own lack of 'talent for lucid exposition', Kant goes on to anticipate the future perfection of the critical project by means of 'the requisite elegance' provided by 'men of impartiality, insight and true popularity' (Kant 1929, B xlii). Kant's continual deferral of popular style to the future or to others stems from a number of grounds, such as anxiety about philosophy's inability to present mathematically; an ascetic sacrifice of good writing in favour of getting at the truth in the simplest manner; and a recognition, once more, of the dangers of such popularity denigrating into visionary enthusiasm. Ultimately, in his late work, Kant is adamant that the philosopher must be resigned to unpopularity: 'This [i.e. the systematic critique of the capacity for reason itself] can never become popular [...]. Popularity (common language) is out of the question here; on the contrary, scholastic *precision* must be insisted upon' (Ak. 4, p. 206; Kant 2013, p. 36).

Kant, then, seems to crave the neutrality of a style without style. In Nancy's words, Kant aims to speak in a 'language as the zero degree of all language use, of all linguistic deviation and inflexion' (Nancy 2008, p. 78)—a neutral language that occurs as the 'neither ... nor' of popular ornament and mystic obscurity. Or, in the very language of the title of *Von einem neuerdings erhobenen vornehmen Ton*, 'Philosophy installs itself thus *not as merely another tone* [...] but as *the absence of tone* [...] and thus as an atonal exposition' (Nancy 2008, p. 78). Such style without style protects the philosophical enterprise from dangerous impurities, such as mysticism, poetry or even the popular form that Kant often craves but always denies himself.

While Kant associates mysticism with private language (in contrast to the universal communicability of the moral law), according to the Schelling of *Clara*[21], mystical content is properly articulated *in ordinary language*—and this is the very ordinary language that is proper to philosophical presentation as well. Again, the figure of the grocer's wife is exemplary: her story is meant as an expression of 'the language of the people', of supernatural intercession and piety outside the bounds of mere reason. And yet—rather than frustrating the philosophical endeavours of the characters, rather than impeding their construction of an abstract concept of sympathy—they admit that 'the story had touched us all incredibly'. The grocer's wife's story serves as a catalyst to their

---

21 By the 1830s, Schelling is far more critical of mysticism and his position has reverted to a more Kantian one: the mystic fails because she cannot publicly communicate her thoughts; see Whistler 2013a.

own transfiguration, their realisation that sympathetic affinities ground belief, community and good philosophising. Indeed, in order for philosophy to become whole, to encompass the world of the dead as well as of the living, it must cultivate the affect of sympathy. Philosophers are to form sympathetic bonds, leading to non-statist communities and public action. The sympathy being theorised in Part V of *Clara*, before the appearance of the grocer's wife, is performed in their reaction to her story: it occurs in response to the most exemplary instance in the dialogue of 'the language of the people'. *Sympathy binds together mysticism, popular style and philosophy.*

In contrast to Kant, therefore, Schelling is happy both to run the gauntlet of popularity and to ally philosophising with mystic practice. It is here, I think, that the significance of *Clara* lies in the context of German Idealism as a whole: the work sets out a resolutely anti-Kantian conception of the philosophical project— one that understands philosophising as an essentially mystic, popular and communal practice, a practice built on ties of sympathy.

Bibliography

Ak. | Kant, Immanuel (1900–68): *Gesammelte Schriften*. Königlich Preußische [now: Berlin-Brandenburgische] Akademie der Wissenschaften (ed.). Berlin: Reimer/De Gruyter 1900 ff.

SW | Schelling, F. W. J. (1856–61): *Sämmtliche Werke*. 14 vols. K. F. A. Schelling (ed.). Stuttgart: Cotta.

Bernier, Marc (2010): "Les metamorphoses de la sympathie au siècle des Lumières". In: Marc Bernier and D. Dawson (eds.): *Les lettres sur la sympathie (1798) de Sophie de Grouchy*. Oxford: Voltaire Foundation, pp. 1–17.

David, Pascal (2014): "*Clara*—ou la nuit transfigurée". In: Alexandra Roux (ed.): *Schelling: Philosophie de la mort et de l'immortalité—études sur Clara*. Rennes: Presses Universitaires de Rennes, pp. 48–62.

Grosos, Philippe (2014): "*Clara* ou le récit comme totalité intotalisable". In: Alexandra Roux (ed.): *Schelling: Philosophie de la mort et de l'immortalité—études sur Clara*. Rennes: Presses Universitaires de Rennes, pp. 39–47.

Hanley, Ryan Patrick (2015): "The Eighteenth-Century Context of Sympathy from Spinoza to Kant". In: Eric Schliesser (ed.): *Sympathy: A History*. Oxford: Oxford University Press, pp. 171–198.

Hegel, G. W. F. (1984): *The Letters*. Translated by Clark Butler and Christiane Seiler. Bloomington: Indiana University Press.

Hegel, G. W. F./Friedrich Hölderlin and F. W. J. Schelling [?] (1995): "The Oldest System Programme of German Idealism". Translated by Eckart Förster. In: *European Journal of Philosophy* 3. No. 2, pp. 199–200.

Hegel, G. W. F./F. W. J. Schelling (1985): "The Critical Journal of Philosophy: Introduction on the Essence of Philosophical Criticism Generally and its Relationship to the Present

State of Philosophy in Particular". In: G. di Giovanni/H. S. Harris (eds.): *Between Kant and Hegel: Texts in the Development of Post-Kantian Idealism*. Albany: SUNY Press, pp. 272–291.

Hübner, Karolina (2015): "Spinoza's Parallelism Doctrine and Metaphysical Sympathy". In: Eric Schliesser (ed.): *Sympathy: A History*. Oxford: Oxford University Press, pp. 146–170.

Jacobi, F. H. (1994): *The Main Philosophical Writings*. Edited and translated by George di Giovanni. Montreal: McGill-Queen's University Press.

Kant, Immanuel (1929): *Critique of Pure Reason*. Translated by Norman Kemp Smith. Basingstoke: Palgrave.

Kant, Immanuel (2002): "On a Recently Prominent Tone of Superiority in Philosophy". In: *Theoretical Philosophy after 1781*. Edited and translated by Henry Allison et al. Cambridge: Cambridge University Press, pp. 427–445.

Kant, Immanuel (2007): "On the Use of Teleological Principles in Philosophy". In: *Anthropology, History and Education*. Edited and translated by Robert Louden et al. Cambridge: Cambridge University Press, pp. 192–218.

Kant, Immanuel (2013): *The Metaphysics of Morals*. Edited and translated by Mary J. Gregor. Cambridge: Cambridge University Press.

Kneller, Jane (2014): "Sociability and the Conduct of Philosophy: What We Can Learn from Early German Romanticism". In: Dalia Nassar (ed.): *The Relevance of Romanticism: Essays on German Romantic Philosophy*. Oxford: Oxford University Press, pp. 110–126.

Lindberg, Susanna (2013): "Les hantises de Clara". In: *Revue germanique internationale* 18, pp. 235–253.

Lukács, Georg (1980): *The Destruction of Reason*. Translated by Peter Palmer. London: Merlin.

Mabille, Bernard (2014): "*Clara* et la quête du lien". In: Alexandra Roux (ed.): *Schelling: Philosophie de la mort et de l'immortalité—études sur Clara*. Rennes: Presses Universitaires de Rennes, pp. 95–115.

Marquet, Jean-François (1973): *Liberté et existence: Étude sur la formation de la philosophie de Schelling*. Paris: Gallimard.

Marquet, Jean-François (1984): "Avant-Propos". In: F. W. J. Schelling: *Clara ou Du lien de la nature au monde des esprits*. Translated by Élisabeth Kessler. Paris: L'Herne, pp. 5–30.

McGrath, Sean (2012): *The Dark Ground of Spirit: Schelling and the Unconscious*. London: Routledge.

McGrath, Sean. (2017): "Populism and the late Schelling on Mythology, Ideology and Revelation". In: *Analecta Hermeneutica* 9, pp. 2–20.

Mercer, Christia (2015): "Seventeenth-Century Universal Sympathy: Stoicism, Platonism, Leibniz and Conway". In: Eric Schliesser (ed.): *Sympathy: A History*. Oxford: Oxford University Press, pp. 107–138.

Nancy, Jean-Luc (2008): *The Discourse of the Syncope: Logodaedalus*. Translated by Saul Anton. Stanford: Stanford University Press.

Roux, Alexandra (2014): "*Clara* ou le récit d'un retour à la vie". In: Alexandra Roux (ed.): *Schelling: Philosophie de la mort et de l'immortalité—études sur Clara*. Rennes: Presses Universitaires de Rennes, pp. 63–87.

Sandkühler, H. J. (1998): *F. W. J. Schelling*. Dordrecht: Springer.

Scheerlinck, Ryan (2019): *Gedanken über die Religion: Der ,stille Krieg' zwischen Schelling und Schleiermacher*. Stuttgart: Frommen-Holzboog.

Schelling, F. W. J. (1936): *Philosophical Inquiries into the Nature of Human Freedom.* Translated by James Gutmann. La Salle: Open Court

Schelling, F. W. J. (1989): *Philosophy of Art.* Translated by Douglas W. Stott. Minneapolis: Minnesota University Press.

Schelling, F. W. J. (1994): "Stuttgart Seminars". In: *Idealism and the Endgame of Theory: Three Esssays.* Edited and translated by Thomas Pfau. Albany: SUNY Press, pp. 195 – 243.

Schelling, F. W. J. (2000): *The Ages of the World (3ʳᵈ Draft).* Translated by Jason M. Wirth. Albany: SUNY Press.

Schelling, F. W. J. (2002): *Clara or, On Nature's Connection to the Spirit World.* Translated by Fiona Steinkamp. Albany: SUNY Press.

Schliesser, Eric (2015): "On Sympathy". In: Eric Schliesser (ed.): *Sympathy: A History.* Oxford: Oxford University Press, pp. 3 – 14.

Steinkamp, Fiona. (2002): "Editor's Introduction". In: F. W. J. Schelling: *Clara or, On Nature's Connection to the Spirit World.* Albany: SUNY Press, pp. vii – vl.

Stewart, Jon (2013): *The Unity of Content and Form in Philosophical Writing: The Perils of Conformity.* London: Bloomsbury.

Vëto, Miklos (2014): "*Clara:* les thèmes majeurs d'un dialogue philosophique". In: Alexandra Roux (ed.): *Schelling: Philosophie de la mort et de l'immortalité—études sur Clara.* Rennes: Presses Universitaires de Rennes, pp. 21 – 38.

Whistler Daniel (2013a): "Silvering, or the Role of Mysticism in German Idealism". In: *Glossator 7,* pp. 151 – 186.

Whistler, Daniel (2013b): *Schelling's Theory of Symbolic Language: Forming the System of Identity.* Oxford: Oxford University Press.

Whistler, Daniel (2014): "Schelling's Poetry". In: *Clio* 43. No. 2, pp. 143 – 176.

Ziolkowski, Theodore (1990): *German Romanticism and its Institutions.* Princeton: Princeton University Press.

Zöller, Günther (2014): "Church and State: Schelling's Political Philosophy of Religion". In: Lara Ostaric (ed.): *Interpreting Schelling: Critical Essays.* Cambridge University Press, pp. 200 – 215.

Jeffrey Reid
Friedrich Schlegel and Romantic Psychology: The Fragmentary Self as Ironic System

"By their fruits ye shall know them."

Abstract. *This paper first specifies Romantic psychology in counter-distinction to Enlightenment-informed faculty-psychology, whose scientific paradigm is fundamentally materialistic and mechanistic. Romantic psychology is then presented through Friedrich Schlegel's theory and practice of the literary fragment. In the fragment, we discover selfhood that is self-positing, powered by electrochemical wit (Witz) and animated by stimulating otherness. Romantic psychology determines the self as an ironic system, complete and yet organically open. The paper shows that the fragmentary self is phenomenological in nature. Romantic psychology's contemporary legacy can be found in psychoanalysis and psychoanalytical hermeneutics.*

In diesem Aufsatz wird zunächst romantische Psychologie im Unterschied zur aufklärungsnahen Vermögenspsychologie charakterisiert, deren wissenschaftliches Paradigma fundamental materialistisch und mechanisch ist. Romantische Psychologie wird dann durch Friedrich Schlegels Theorie und Praxis des literarischen Fragments vorgestellt. Im Fragment entdecken wir ein Selbstsein, das selbstsetzend ist, angetrieben durch elektrochemischen „Witz" und angeregt durch stimulierende Andersheit. Romantische Psychologie bestimmt das Selbst als ein ironisches System, es ist vollständig und doch organisch offen. Als Fragment ist es phänomenologischer Natur. Sein heutiges Erbe kann in der Psychoanalyse und in psychoanalytischer Hermeneutik gefunden werden.

In this article, I attempt to establish the specificity of Romantic psychology. I do so, first of all, by distinguishing it from psychological science as it is conceived in the Enlightenment, in what might be broadly defined as faculty-psychology. To provide an idea of such Enlightenment-informed faculty-psychology, I examine the content of a college-level course in psychology as it was taught at the Tübingen *Stift* (Seminary) in 1789. I will then juxtapose this view with what I believe is the specificity of Romantic psychology, which I discover by examining the work of Early German Romanticism's main protagonist, Friedrich Schlegel, from around his *Athenaeum* period writings (1797–1800). My contention is that

https://doi.org/10.1515/9783110673692-016

if indeed a psychology is to be found in Schlegel, it takes place in his theory and practice of the literary fragment.

In Schlegel's Romantic fragment, we discover a notion of selfhood as essentially self-positing, an interpretive instantiation of the Fichtean "I". Besides this well-established element of Schlegel's work, I bring to light the dynamic ontology of creative wit (*Witz*) as an expression of electrochemical force. Finally, I show how Schlegel's science of the literary fragment relies on the organic biology of "stimulation" that he discovers in John Brown's popular theory of medicine. The stimulating Other is thus shown to be an essential element of Romantic psychology.

If Schlegel's theory and practice of the literary fragment are indeed revelatory of a psychology specific to Romanticism generally, we should be able to observe its key elements in other Romantic players. I illustrate how this might be tested with cursory sketches of how my findings might apply to Novalis and Schleiermacher. Finally, I conclude with a brief remark on Romantic psychology's contemporary legacy, again in its contrast from the faculty-based science of the psyche tributary to Enlightenment thought. Is it possible to find in today's experimental, empirical and neurologically-centered practice of psychology the descendance of the Enlightenment's faculty-psychology and its attempt to locate and categorize different mental functions in such a way as to colonize even the most apparently irrational provinces of the mind? Conversely, are more act and language-centered, phenomenological and psychoanalytical approaches to the mind not based on notions of creative self-expression that can be found in Schlegel's view of the fragmentary self?

1 Enlightenment Psychology

According to the account that I am putting forward, early articulations of modern faculty-psychology can be situated in the late 18th century. I would like to present this scientific approach to the mind by evoking a source that I am familiar with: the material from a college-level course that was taught at the Tübingen Seminary (*Stift*), in 1789, by Johann Friedrich Flatt, entitled "Empirical Psychology", which presents its object, the human psyche, in terms of distinct faculties (*Vermögen*), which are derived, at least in part, from psychological interpretations of Kant's first *Critique*.

Of course, I am not presenting Flatt's course or even the German Enlightenment as the exclusive and actual beginning of psychology. Reflections on *Seelenkunde* and *Seelenlehre* (theory or doctrine of the soul), as the discipline of *Psychologie* was also referred to in the late *Aufklärung*, are, of course, present in

Aristotle, Aquinas, and again in the classical thought of Hobbes, Descartes, Leibniz etc. However, by the mid-18th century, thinkers associated with the Enlightenment were putting forward a new vision for the scientific study of the "soul", one that promoted "psychology" as distinctly non-metaphysical, i. e. divorced from both its theological dimensions and the early Modern emphasis on *a priori* enquiry into the self. The self-consciously anti-metaphysical efforts of late-Enlightenment psychology explain one sense of the term "empirical" that was then attached to the proposed method. The other sense refers to the "empirical" aesthetic mental faculties taken from Kant's first *Critique* as the basis for faculty-psychology. Nonetheless, since the Enlightenment's empirical conception of the mind rested on materialistic principles of causation that are universally attributed to both mind and nature, its foundation was "metaphysical", as is the case with Romantic psychology's reliance on the universal ontology of "forces". In fact, it may well be the case that any general conception of the mind involves metaphysical principles, and the attempt to thoroughly define psychological science in opposition to metaphysics is misguided. Rather, one might more productively work to show how the metaphysical principles underlying Enlightenment and Romantic psychologies are different from each other and yet share a mutual opposition of Cartesian metaphysics, where the laws of the mind are *a priori* and thus exclusive of natural determination.

We have access to J. F. Flatt's course content through Hegel's notes, from when he was a student at Tübingen, notes that he conserved and later used in developing his own material on Subjective Spirit (Mind), in the later elaborations of that section of his *Encyclopedia of Philosophical Sciences*.[1] I am not here concerned with Hegel nor how he later used this material. I am simply taking Flatt's course as a fulsome expression of what university-level, faculty-psychology generally looked like in the late *Aufklärung* of 1780's Germany. Since Flatt himself seems to have developed his course material by drawing from a number of contemporary sources on psychology, notes from his course are particularly pertinent.[2]

---

1 See Reid 2013.

2 Hegel, GW 1, pp. 483–487. A word about the provenance of Hegel's notes from the Flatt's course. The editors of the critical Hegel *Gesammelte Werke*, having analyzed the manuscript's handwriting and the paper's watermark, conclude it was penned while Hegel was in Bern, probably in 1794. However, referring to the testimonial of Hegel's fellow student Betzendörfer, Johannes Hoffmeister attributes the source of the Hegel manuscript to J. F. Flatt, whose course in empirical psychology Hegel had indeed taken, in 1789/90. The course was officially listed listed as either *"empiricam psychologicam"* or *"Psych. empiricam"* in the Tübingen course calendar (GW 1, pp. 484–485). Hegel's 1794 manuscript on psychology therefore seems to be the later

Johannes Hoffmeister's remarkable analysis of the central portion of the 1794 manuscript further establishes that its content represents Flatt's compilation taken from a number of sources, in preparation for his 1789 course: the *Critique of Pure Reason*, but also secondary literature, such as works by J. F. Abel, C. C. E. Schmid, Johann Schultz and Karl L. Reinhold. As we will see, it is the latter's reading of Kant's transcendental aesthetic and its faculties as principally productive of representations that is particularly determinant in Flatt's conception of "Empirical Psychology".

Who was J. F. Flatt and can we establish his Enlightenment *bona fides?* Flatt has been referred to disparagingly by Frederick Beiser as the "Scrooge of Tübingen".[3] Certainly, he was the assistant of the dogmatic theology professor G. C. Storr, himself famous for his anachronistic and quixotic defense of orthodox religion and the literal truth (i.e. revelation) of the Bible, the Trinity and miracles, in the face of the Kantian *Critiques*. However, as Beiser himself points out, there are, in fact, two Flatts, the "reactionary" professor of theology, defender of supernaturalism[4] and the earlier version, a champion of Leibnizian/Wolffian late Enlightenment reason, against Kant's critique of metaphysical thought. In his respected polemical reviews of Kant's work (1788 and 1789),[5] Flatt is arguing for the objective reality of transcendent causation and the consequent possibility for a cosmological proof of the existence of God. In other words, Flatt defends the Enlightenment reason of Leibniz, Wolff and Mendelssohn against the limitations imposed by Kant's first *Critique*. It is this J. F. Flatt who put together the lecture notes on empirical psychology, wherein Kant's contribution is restricted to a psychological reading of the Transcendental Aesthetic.

That Flatt's course reflects an early example of faculty-psychology (*Vermögenspsychologie* or *Seelenvermögen*) is evident from the omnipresence of the term "*Vermögen*" throughout the Hegel transcription of his course notes, a use

---

transcription of the course notes that he took while attending Flatt's lecture four or five years earlier. This supposition seems confirmed by Dieter Henrich, who in 1964 discovered the course notes of Friedrich Klüpfel, another fellow Tübingen student of Hegel's who also took Flatt's course in 1790. The content of the Klüpfel course notes is virtually identical to most of Hegel's 1794 psychology manuscript.

3 Beiser 1987, p. 210.

4 "Reactionary" is from Beiser 1987, p. 11. The supernaturalism of Storr/Flatt used Kant's first *Critique* in a tendentious way: Because the noumenal realm is beyond empirical knowledge, its content must be known by revelation.

5 In other words, while he was preparing his lectures on empirical psychology, he wrote his *Fragmentarische Beyträge zur Bestimmung und Deduktion des Begriffs und Grundsatzes der Caussalität* and the *Briefe über den moralischen Erkenntnissgrund der Religion*. See Beiser 1987, pp. 211–214.

inspired, no doubt, by Kant's own establishment of mental *Grundvermögen* in the Transcendental Aesthetic: sensibility, imagination, representation, understanding and reason. Among other faculties, Flatt's course refers to *Anschauungssvermögen, praktische Vermögen, Vermögen der Vernunft, Empindungsvermögen, Begehrensvermögen, Erkenntnisvermögen and Gefühlsvermögen.*[6]

Flatt's course was entitled "Empirical Psychology" not because it espoused an experiment-based methodology as we might understand it today, but rather because it referred to the empirical aspects of the soul, as presented in Kant's Transcendental Aesthetic and in his theory of knowledge generally. Following Reinhold's popular presentation of Kant, in his *Versuch einer neuen Theorie des menschlichen Vorstellungsvermögens* (1789), Flatt considered the material production of consciousness to be principally representational. Indeed, as we find in the course notes, *"der Seele Grundkraft [ist] vorstellende Kraft"* (the soul is a representing power) (Hoffmeister 1974, p. 199), and from those representations the *Verstand* is meant to produce judgments or knowledge statements. While reason remains detached from the content of experience (*"kommt nicht über die Erfahrung hinaus"*), as the faculty of the unconditioned, reason nonetheless "grounds" the entire process of representation: *"Ein Schein ist in dem Vermögen der Vernunft selbst gegründet"* (an appearance grounded in the faculty of reason itself) (Hoffmeister 1974, p. 196). In other words, the various mental faculties are arranged in a hierarchical fashion, in a way that points to their ultimate use by reason in its unconditioned, legislative vocation, making "synthetic *a priori* judgments" (Hoffmeister 1974, p. 196), including practical or moral ones.

Thus, Flatt's topology of the mind is divided into the "lower" faculties of sensibility (*Empfindungsvermögen* and *Phantasie*) and the "higher" faculties of *Verstand* and *Vernunft*. The latter is what makes (universal) laws, under which the lower faculties must fall. In other words, the very possibility of psychology as a science of the psyche rests on the legislative abilities of the highest mental faculty, reason, in establishing the laws of the psyche generally. This legislative activity of reason is particularly crucial when faced with the unruly aspects of feeling and fantasy.

---

6 It is true that the manuscript also employs the term "Kraft", which can likewise be translated as "faculty", as we see from the usual translation of Kant's *Critique* of "*Urteilskraft*". However, "*Kraft*" retains a dynamic dimension of "force" and "power" which should be distinguished from the more passive, mechanical, representational operation of the *Vermögen*. Indeed, to the extent that Kant's notion of "*Urteil*" is thoroughly positive, "faculty" is perhaps not the best translation for its "power". The same is perhaps the case with Kant's conception of the power of the imagination.

The first lower faculty is sensibility. Its representations are divided in two: those produced by the outer senses and those produced from inner sense. In both cases, the aim of psychology, as presented in Flatt's course, is to establish "laws, conditions or causes" governing the production of representations. Regarding the outer senses, this is fairly straightforward and involves the interplay between the sense organs and the strength of the sensation felt. In the course material manuscript, the representations which are drawn from the outer senses, through the sense faculties (*Gefühlsvermögen*) of touch, taste, smell, hearing and sight, all depend on the "concept" (rather than the Kantian "form") of space (Hoffmeister 1974, pp. 197–198).

Of greater interest to Enlightenment psychology is the second group of representations, the ones derived from the faculty of inner feeling (*Empfindungsvorstellungen*). Such inner representations are generated through the concept of time rather than through that of space. While some of these are consciously evoked through the power of conscious thought and will, what seems to provide a real challenge for the "empirical" psychology of the Enlightenment are those inner representations that are produced "from the soul without being produced by consciousness" (Hoffmeister 1974, p. 199). In more contemporary terms, the fundamental psychological question addressed in this part of the notes from Flatt's course concerns the ability of rational science to explain the irrational representations of the unconsciousness mind.

This task clearly stretches beyond Kant's project in the Transcendental Aesthetic where the material of sensibility is worked on by the imagination in order that the understanding (*Verstand*) may produce representations for the purpose of judgment and knowledge. Here, in Flatt's course on "Empirical psychology", the inner soul itself is observed to produce representations unbidden, without any claim to the production of empirical knowledge (Hoffmeister 1974, p. 199). The scientific question therefore becomes: what laws, conditions or causes govern the composition of unconscious representations? How do they arise, "without remembering, without consciousness" as in cases of sleepwalking, dreaming or clairvoyance?

Significantly, it is not the provenance of the inner representations that determines their degree of clarity. The "laws of clarity" that the manuscript evokes have nothing to do with whether representations are derived from conscious remembering of outer sensations through the will or whether they arise unbidden from the inner soul. In fact, the problem is that clarity is completely unrelated to truth, either as an *a priori* Cartesian criterion or as the reliable trace of a recent empirical impression (Hobbes, Hume). Rather, the undeniable clarity of certain inner representations is governed by such factors as physiological conditions, strong emotions like grief or the desire to escape a new and unpleasant condition that breaks our habitual existence (Hoffmeister 1974, p. 200).

Of the "lower faculties" of sensibility and "*Phantasie*", the notes spend significantly more time on the latter. While *Phantasie* seems to fulfill some of the synthesizing role that Kant assigns to the imagination (as *Einbildung*) in the production of representational material upon which the *Verstand* will operate, *Phantasie* is much more creative and unruly. While it contributes to artistic production through the *Dichtungsvermögen* (artistic faculty) and to knowledge through its role in the conservation (*Aufbehalten*) or the recalling (*Gedächtnis*) of representations, as well as through its agency in recognition and remembering (*Rekognition, Erinnerung*) (Hoffmeister 1974, p. 200), *Phantasie*'s representations are most significantly analysed with respect to their unbidden, pathological and unruly character. It is the uncontrolled "reawakening" (*Wiedererweckung*) of the *Phantasievorstellungen* (imaginary representations) that Flatt's course on empirical psychology seems especially concerned to describe. Given that such pathological phenomena occur, the notes are particularly interested in determining the "laws" and "causes" that govern their appearance. "*Nach welchen Gesetzen*" (according to which laws)? Flatt asks (Hoffmeister 1974, p. 201). What are the "*Ursachen der Wiedererweckung der Vorstellungen?*" (causes of the reawakening of representations?) (Hoffmeister 1974, p. 202), "*Was veranlasst die Seele, bestimmte Ideen oder Ideenreihen zu erwecken?*" (What causes the soul to reawaken certain ideas or trains of thought?) (Hoffmeister 1974, p. 203).

The central idea of Flatt's course is that the "lower" faculties of the mind produce representations; in certain cases, these arise unbidden but nonetheless vivid (*klar*). These unbidden representations explain the existence of pathological, paranormal and sometimes artistic phenomena, which can all be traced back to the spontaneous production of representations by the faculties of sensibility and *Phantasie*. We may thus "explain" such phenomena by tying them to the faculties involved in representation. And we can "use" this theory to "explain" "certain conditions" (Hoffmeister 1974, p. 205) (dreaming, sleepwalking, madness, premonitions, visions). Some of these conditions may be explained with "general laws" (Hoffmeister 1974, p. 202), which seem to pertain to a causality among the representations themselves (e. g. similarity between representations and their proximity, obeying "laws of association" (Hoffmeister 1974, p. 206) and thus function like Hume's general principles of the imagination. However, most of the re-awakened, unbidden representations occur as a result of "special laws", which refer to material or physiological causes: fever, sickness, headaches, dispositions of the brain, the weather, light and darkness, bodily conditions like "*Blut nach der Brust, Angst*" (blood to the chest, fear) as well as drunkenness and hypochondria (Hoffmeister 1974, p. 203).

There is thus a marked materialism involved in the new science of Enlightenment psychology as presented in Flatt's course. First and most obviously, there is materialism in its physiological account of mental states, which are caused either by bodily conditions or through neurological "mechanical causes [where] one fiber stirs another" thus creating an unbidden "representation" (Hoffmeister 1974, p. 202). More subtly perhaps, Flatt's Enlightenment account supposes a material causality between representations (or ideas) themselves. The "general laws" of their association (e. g. similarity, contiguity) imply a corporeal ontology that is just as material as that found in the Newtonian configuration of Hume's principles of the imagination or even in Hobbes' presentation, in his *Leviathan*, of ideas joining together to form trains of thought.

Configuring ideas as material entities is the hallmark of materialism and its fondest project. Significantly, the materialistic, empirical slant of Enlightenment psychology allows it to overcome the crucial metaphysical hurdle subsidiary to Cartesian "psychology" of the self: the fact that for Descartes, there can be no interaction between the two substances of extension and thought (between body and mind). In such *a priori* psychology, there can be no reference to physical causality, and even the empirical observation of mental pathologies remains as dubious as the phenomena Descartes observes in his experiment with candle wax.[7]

Particularly noteworthy, with respect to the more active, creative notion of selfhood that we will observe in Romanticism, in Flatt's course the material agency of unbidden representations goes as far as to explain the "*Dichtungsvermögen*" (artistic faculty). On the Enlightenment psychological reading, the creative faculty does indeed "produce representations" (Hoffmeister 1974, p. 205) but it does so through the workings of the (Kantian) categories of the understanding: quantity, quality, relation. What the artist does, in producing "new" representations, is reduced to the re-working of received material, for example, in rearranging the order, proportion, size or producing representations that are "general abstractions", which may be taken, I believe, as symbols. Such mechanical production, where artistic representations are run through the faculties of the understanding, stands in opposition to the dynamic conception of self-creation that I will present through an examination of Schlegel's theory and practice of the literary fragment.

---

7 All mental phenomena must be explained in terms of rational thinking, which explains, *pace* Foucault and Derrida, why Descartes so summarily dismisses the madness hypothesis in the first Meditation. A thoroughly rational self cannot brook conditions of "*déraison*", which must be ascribed to a hypothetical "*malin génie.*" Leibnizian metaphysical psychology is equally confined. The soul as a monad that is ultimately reducible to perception and appetite, and which has no window onto other souls, cannot provide a rich explanation for a variety of "irrational" states.

Perhaps the most recognizably modern aspect of Enlightenment psychology, with its empirical, material presuppositions, is the "applicable" nature of its findings. In other words, because the material of faculty psychology is actually *material*, it can be materially applied to certain "conditions where *Phantasie* plays a part" (Hoffmeister 1974, p. 205). Such conditions are empirically observed manifestations of the inner workings of unbidden representations, which are generally conceived as pathological, to the extent that they do not fall under the mechanisms of knowledge production and reason. Enlightenment psychology does make "clinical" psychology possible. For in order to conceive of such states, they must be empirically observable (through the body), and for them to be treatable they must be made accessible through the body, involving such "*Körperliche Heilart*" as changes of diet and the removal of "*Krankheitsmaterie*" from the brain (Hoffmeister 1974, p. 207).

Flatt's course is particularly interested in this applicable aspect, reflecting a timely interest in the diagnosis of "paranormal" or irrational states, their explanation in terms of a theory of the representation arising from the *Phantasievermögen* and their eventual treatment.[8] In explaining paranormal manifestations like dreams, sleepwalking, madness, premonitions, visions etc. (Hoffmeister 1974, p. 205), Enlightenment psychology not only hopes to "reason the unreasonable" but to debunk any Pietist, sentimentalist and, let it be said,

---

8 I have shown, in Reid 2013, that at least some of the material that Flatt draws upon is from C. P. Moritz's *Magazin zur Erfahrungsseelenkunde*, a popular review published in Berlin between 1783 and 1793. Although the *Magazin* regularly presents speculations on the nature of the soul, most of the volumes are dedicated to recounting testimonials of dreams, nightmares, somnambulism, as well as what we might call parapsychological or even paranormal experiences. Most significantly, the *Magazin* then brings these cases into the realm of scientific explanation, debunking them, one might say, by presenting them in terms of pathology, in order that we may reasonably know those aspects of the self that seem to lie beyond reason. The often colorful, highly subjective anecdotes and accounts are the stuff of empirical psychology or empirical anthropology, in the sense of the journal's scientific concept of *Erfahrungsseelenkunde*. Flatt's 1789/90 lectures on empirical psychology were certainly inspired by the *Magazin*'s late Enlightenment mission of using "modern" anthropology to show that the excess of *Phantasie*, and particularly, the manifestations of *Schwärmerei* (fanaticism) are pathological conditions of the soul. In this light, it should be no surprise that Moses Mendelssohn served as an early advisor to the review. The full title of the *Magazin* is actually, *Gnothi sauton* (in Greek letters = know yourself) *oder Magazin zur ...* etc. See the informative doctoral thesis on the *Magazin* by Kim, Soo-Jung (2001). On Mendelssohn, see p. 15. Another late Enlightenment figure is pivotal in the understanding of mental illness as a struggle between reason and unreason: Kant's well-read "*Von der Macht des Gemüts durch den blossen Vorsatz seiner krankhaften Gefühle Meister zu sein*", published in periodicals in 1796, and again in his *Conflict of the Faculties*. One might also refer to Kant's pre-critical (1770) essay "*Versuch über die Krankeiten des Kopfes*" in this light.

(pre)romantic interpretation of such supposedly "supernatural" (Hoffmeister 1974, p. 210) phenomena. It is significant that the final pathological state on which the faculty-psychology of representations can be applied is religious enthusiasm and fanaticism, which are explained in terms of a morbid *"Reizbarkeit der Organe"* (Hoffmeister 1974, p. 210).

In the same way that today's neuropsychology tends to limit its explanations of mental events and pathologies to observable phenomena within the brain, through neurological imaging, Enlightenment psychology seemed quite content to ground its explanations in the newly discovered "science" of representation. In other words, Reinhold's interpretation of Kant's Transcendental Aesthetic allowed the new, empirical psychology to reduce psychic activity to the mental faculties (*Vermögen*) associated with producing representations. The material nature of these faculties (and of both the outer and inner sense material from which they derive their equally material representations) implies a causal and thus explanatory complicity between body and mind. Such a vision takes the mind as a fundamentally passive apparatus that processes the content of sentiments and feelings in its faculties, according to prescribed causal laws. Against this view, I would like to present a specifically Romantic psychology, where the psyche is construed primarily as a self-positing activity, where the dominant scientific paradigm relies on natural forces and where the mind is essentially intersubjective.[9] Briefly, to be a self is to posit oneself into and for otherness. Consequently, by examining the posited "fruits" of the self, we are given access to its psychology. I will explore this idea through Friedrich Schlegel's theory and practice of the literary fragment. This choice is justified by Schlegel's foundational role in German romanticism, in his pioneering definition of Romantic poetry in terms of what might best be called "spirit" or "mind" (*Geist*) and by the fact that his actual fragments carry philosophical weight: their theory and practice are conjoined.[10]

---

9 It is not sufficient to specify Romantic psychology as unique and original based solely on the fact that it postulates the inter-penetration of mind and nature, where "the manifestations of the natural world and the structures and concepts of the human mind correspond harmoniously" (Barkhoff 2009, p. 210). For the same interpenetration and harmony between psyche and nature can be observed in the Enlightenment view where both are conceived as thoroughly materialistic and mechanical.

10 In the history of ideas, it is tempting to locate one source of Romantic psychology in Herder, specifically in his theory of artistic genius as articulated in his essay, "The Causes of Sunken Taste Among those Peoples Where it had Once Blossomed" (1773). In its opening discussion of *Seelenlehre*, the essay puts forward a notion of the self whose genius is animated by "a mass of powers [*Kräfte*]", thus distinguishing his vision from the mechanistic Enlightenment view. It is significant that Herder's essay won the Academy of Berlin prize, the institution

2 Friedrich Schlegel's Fragments

Schlegel's theory of the fragment is found, first and foremost, in his fragments themselves, as they appear around the *Athenäum* period, between 1797 and 1800. Broader, less lapidary forms of expression, such as his essay "On Incomprehensibility," which appeared in the final issue of that journal, and his novel *Lucinde* (1799), do not represent an abandonment of the fragmentary project. Rather, they are themselves further fragmentary expressions, presupposed by the project's ultimate articulation as universal progressive poetry (*Geist*), which also remains fragmentary. As I have written elsewhere, it is not because we are dealing with a theory of the fragment and irony that Schlegel's theory itself should be viewed as unsystematic and incoherent. Nor does it mean that our understanding of it must be fragmentary and ironic.

Schlegel's theory and practice of the fragment presents a *phenomenon (Erscheinung)* of his *Seelenkunde*, of his psychology. They can be comprehended according to three participating currents of contemporaneous scientific thought.[11] Together, these collaborate in the organic architecture of Romantic selfhood and its fragmentary expression. These are: Fichte's fundamental principle of the self as essentially self-positing; J. W. Ritter's explorations into the chemical nature of galvanic electricity; John Brown's medical theory of organic irritability. These currents are present in Schlegel's conception of the Romantic self to the extent that they are presented in his fragmentary works.

2.1 Fichte's Self-positing I

Schlegel, like many German intellectuals in the final five years of the 18th century, was inspired by J. G. Fichte's revolutionary grasp of selfhood. According to Fichte's 1794 *Wissenschaftslehre*, the Absolute I is the self-positing activity of conscious mind in general. This activity implies an oppositional Not-I, an objective otherness that it seeks to overcome in a process of endless, willful striving. The debt Schlegel's aesthetic ideas owe to Fichte's seminal work is noted by al-

---

where, several decades earlier, thinkers like Louis de Beausobre and Johann Heinrich Formey had enjoyed success for their arch-Enlightenment work in materialistic "Empirical Psychology". Cf. Herder, SW 5, pp. 600 – 601. I owe the reference to Beausobre and Formey to Daniel Dumouchel's presentation at the *Canadian Philosophical Association* (2018) in Montreal, at a workshop (with Christian Leduc) on philosophy at the Academy of Berlin. The reference to Herder's essay also came from the same workshop, thanks to a presentation by Nigel de Souza.

11 For a more detailed account, s. Reid 2008, pp. 1–16.

most every commentator, beginning with G. W. F. Hegel, who sees Schlegel as the individual personification of the self's absolute pretensions.[12] More positively, the Schlegel-Fichte relationship has been explored by more recent commentators. As Schlegel himself acknowledges in *Athenäum* Fragment 216: "The French Revolution, Fichte's *Doctrine of Science* and Goethe's *Meister* are the great trends of our time".[13]

While Fichte's dialectical grasp of subjectivity is hardly the sole source of Schlegel's inspiration in the *Athenäum* period, it is certainly crucial to his theory of the literary fragment and thus, as I am arguing, to his presentation of Romantic psychology. What Schlegel adopts from Fichte's notion of selfhood is first and foremost the notion that the I is essentially an act of free self-positing. Mind or spirit (qua *Geist*) is a manifestation of such action: Thus, "*Geist* partakes in an eternal self-demonstration" (AF 284). The self is essentially self-creative, in the broadest sense of the word. Nonetheless, of key importance in the development of Schlegel's theory of the fragment is the idea that such positing only takes place against the background of the Not-I, which in Fichte is at least initially a thoroughly abstract resistance that the I must encounter, both theoretically, as the condition of possibility for any object of knowledge, and practically, as the possibility of any object of the will.

In Schlegel, the abstraction of the Not-I is first encountered as a limiting factor, against which self-positing expansion must exert itself. Self-creation is equally a self-limiting, a necessary conditioning through which finite objects are determined (*bedingt*). According to Schlegel's theory of the fragment, the creative self reproduces the interaction between the I and the Not-I in such a way that the expansive self-positing and self-limiting produce real individual objects which are, in essence, fragmentary articulations of the (fragmentary) self. Consequently, self-limitation becomes "the highest duty" of the always-creative self, and furthermore, "one can only limit oneself at those places where one possesses infinite power, infinite self-creation" (CF 37).[14]

While adopting the fundamental Fichtean structure of an interaction (*Wechselwirkung*) between the self-positing I and the self-limiting resistance that it en-

---

12 Hegel reduces the Fichtean aspect of Schlegel's thought to individualistic solipsism. See Reid 2014, pp. 8–49. Cf. Norman 2000 and 2007.

13 Schlegel's fragments occur in three different sets: the *Critical Fragments* (CF), published in the journal *Lyceum* in 1797; the *Athenäum Fragments* (AF), published in *Athenäum* in 1798; and *the Ideas* (I), appearing in the same journal in 1800. The translated fragments can be found in Firchow 1971. The translations in this article are my own, although they are informed by Firchow's. For the German s. KA 17.

14 "A poem is just an object of nature that seeks to become a work of art" (CF 21).

counters in the Not-I, Schlegel releases the movement from its transcendental confines, within individual conscious mind, and ascribes it to nature itself, where, perhaps inspired by F. W. J. Schelling's nascent *Naturphilosophie*,[15] the free self-positing of the I takes place in nature's infinite creativity. The Not-I can therefore occur in Schlegel as the conditioning self-limitation or resistance that the creative impulse of selfhood encounters in order to actually produce its profusion of finite, diverse objects, just as nature does. Of course, as Schelling's philosophy of nature teaches, natural objects are themselves informed with a degree of subjectivity. The same is true of the literary fragments produced in Schlegel. They, like the artist that produces them, participate in "nature's art" (CF 1). However, breaking with Fichte's foundational scientific project, Schlegel writes in AF 290:

> There is a spiritual (psychical) richness wherever *Geist* manifests itself incessantly or at least makes frequent and new appearances under diverse figures, and not just once, at the beginning, as with many philosophical systems.

In releasing the I from its transcendental confines, Schlegel reciprocally releases the corresponding Not-I from its Fichtean abstraction. Now, the Not-I is free to represent any object "of nature", first, the literary fragment but ultimately that most privileged of "objects", the other self. In other words, Schlegel's appropriation of the Fichtean model anticipates the intersubjectivity that I will further develop below and which I believe is an essential feature of Romantic psychology. As Schlegel writes in AF 328, "Only one who posits himself may posit others". Significantly, this statement illustrates the psychological generality of Schlegel's Romantic selfhood, whose creativity is not the sole purview of that distinct category of individuals we refer to as "artists" but rather is a general feature of selfhood in its natural expressiveness. The specific human spiritual endeavors of art and science simply participate in the general act of "self-limiting [that is] the result of self-creation and self-negation" (CF 28).[16]

---

15 Schelling taught at Jena until 1800 and was involved with the *Athenäum circle*, contributing his polemical poem (against Schleiermacher) "The Epicurean Confession of Heinz Widerporst" and marrying August Wilhelm Schlegel's ex-wife, Caroline. Schelling's *First Outline of a System of the Philosophy of Nature* was published in Jena in 1799.
16 The question of negativity as it relates to selfhood in German Idealism and Romanticism certainly merits its own study. Here, I believe we can take it as derived from the Spinozistic idea that relates negation to determination. If every determination is a negation, then self-determination is a self-limiting self-negating. Briefly, to be something is not to be something else.

2.2 The Electro-chemical Dynamics of Selfhood

It is true that both Enlightenment faculty-psychology and Romantic psychology conceive of selfhood within general ontologies of nature. They are thus distinguished from Cartesian psychology in that they are tied into and determined by principles acknowledged in the natural sciences. Nonetheless, they are distinguished from each other by the views of nature to which each is beholden. Faculty-psychology is tributary to a mechanistic, materialistic view of nature, as found, for example, in the "anti-metaphysical" ontologies of such Enlightenment figures as Fontenelle, Diderot and the lesser known but psychologically significant Louis de Beausobre and J. H. Formey,[17] while romantic psychology is tributary to a dynamic view of nature, where "force" rather than "matter" provides the fundamental *archè* of the cosmos.

Nonetheless, "force" remains a highly ambiguous term, found in natural sciences as diverse as those of Newtonian physics and mesmerism. The Romantic view of nature and psychology certainly partakes of such ambiguity. My point is not to resolve the ambiguity but simply to emphasize that Romantic psychology relies on conceptions of force just as today's phenomenological psychology relies on forms of intentionality or care (*Sorge*). The error is to simply qualify the underlying forces at play in Romantic conceptions of nature and the psyche as "occult" and to thereby imply that they are somehow supernatural. While the forces underlying the Romantic conceptions of nature and the psyche may be hidden or invisible, they are very much anchored in the natural sciences of the time. This point is hard for us to grasp today, mainly because our own experimental-empirical-materialistic view of "science" makes it difficult to take seriously the scientific pretentions of galvanic animal magnetism or centrifugal and centripetal forces. In Schlegel, the natural dynamics at work in creative selfhood are predominantly electrochemical.

Chemistry is essential to understanding Schlegel's theory of the fragment, to his idea of *Geist* and to his science of selfhood. As he puts it, in characteristically hyperbolic fashion, "the chemical nature of the *Roman* (novel), of criticism, of wit (*Witz*), of sociality, of modern rhetoric and of history up to now is evident" (AF 426). Rather than seeing chemistry as a mere metaphor for literary creativity, Schlegel sees it as actually and metonymically present in the dynamic of the literary fragment itself, informing it with its own creative selfhood. However, the dynamic nature of the chemical reactions that power the literary fragment makes sense only if we are sensitive to a crucial aspect of late 18th century

---

17 See note 10 above.

chemistry: the galvanic notions of electricity and their relation to organic medicine.

Although it is true that 18th century chemistry was fascinated by the combinations and elective affinities between chemical elements, it was also "mesmerized" by the contemporary discovery that chemical reactions could produce electrical energy, whose effects could be empirically witnessed in the dissected nervous and muscular fibers of animal organisms. Recognizing the importance of such galvanic notions allows us see how, for Schlegel, the "universal, progressive poetry" he calls Romantic (AF 116) and which I believe is best understood as an expression of *Geist* (spirit/mind), is actually powered by electrochemical forces. Further, the galvanic (electrical) aspect of chemical reactions allows the fragment to transcend chemistry and attain the organic. If "the chemical epoch should be followed by an organic epoch" and if history has been chemical in nature only "up to now" (AF 426), it is because chemical reactions are now known to produce the forces unleashed by electrical power. Of course, chemical galvanism is aesthetically and psychologically importable for Schlegel because it corresponds to the fundamental Fichtean paradigm of self-expansion and limitation that I outlined above, while further cohering with the popular theory of organic medicine put forward by John Brown, which I will discuss below.

The self-positing creative force and its corollary resistance from the Not-I informs the literary fragment and is more generally a feature of Romantic natural science, where expansion and limitation are omnipresent. In astronomy, the interplay of expansive centrifugal and limiting centripetal forces maintains planetary movement in constant orbits. In chemistry, acids and bases interact, creating new elements. Similarly, both magnetism and electricity are dynamic phenomena implying the existence of two opposing poles. At the organic level, the one Schlegel sees as animating the Romantic epoch (AF 426) and its productions of genius (AF 366), the lively nature of self-position and determinant limitation is manifest in the discovery of chemically produced electricity and the production of *"Witz"*.

The insight into electrochemistry and its enigmatic relation to organic life, stemming from the work of Luigi Galvani, was conveyed to Schlegel by the brilliant, self-taught apothecary Johann Wilhelm Ritter. Ritter published his book *Proof That, in the Animal Kingdom, a Constant Galvanism Accompanies the Life Process,* in 1798, at 22 years of age. The book reprised his lecture at the Natural History Society in Jena, the year before, which had created such a stir that Ritter was offered a professorship at the university. Schlegel was so taken with the young physicist, introduced to the *Athenäum* circle by Novalis, that he intended to invite him to formally collaborate on the journal.

Briefly, Ritter produced a new theory that the electricity observed in Galvani's animal experiments was actually chemical in nature, produced through chemical reactions created by the differences in the types of metal brought into contact with the muscles or nerves. Ritter presented these findings to the Jena scientific community in the above-mentioned lecture (1797, the year Schlegel produced his first series of fragments), drawing further conclusions in his 1799 article "Some Observations on Galvanism in Inorganic Nature and the Relationship between Electricity and the Chemical Quality of Bodies." Here, Ritter helps liberate chemical electricity from its animal embodiment and shows how it is generated through a chemical process of oxidation and reduction, involving two polarized metals in a confined space, paving the way for his invention of the dry-cell battery in 1800.

Happily, Ritter's ideas on the chemical nature of electricity can be considered complementary to the Fichtean paradigm described above. Like other natural phenomena, chemically generated electricity follows the same logic that Schlegel had found in the interaction between the I and the Not-I. The juxtaposition of two different metals can be considered a case of self-positing and self-limitation through opposition, bringing about a conditioned, real result: electrical energy. Ritter's electrochemical theory, however, adds another significant element to the theory of the production of electricity, beyond the fact of productive opposition. The heterogeneous elements (metals) are necessarily brought together in a discrete, enclosed space (eventually, the battery), in a state of conductive compression where chemical reactions take place in a spontaneous manner. Electrical sparks fly as the result of the fortuitous, internal chemical interactions that the compression produces. The natural rhythm of expansion and conditioning resistance, together with discrete compression, the interaction of different self-positing/self-limiting elements and the resultant electrical discharge are the fundamental markers of Schlegel's theory and practice of the literary fragment, and consequently, of his psychology. Wit and irony are operational concepts in both.

Of course, neither the molecular nor indeed the atomic nature of these interactions was understood at the time. Electricity could not yet be grasped as the flow of charged electrons or ions, interactions which indeed remained, at the time, occult or hidden. Rather, the productive chemical combinations that Ritter and others saw as a source of electrical current were conceived according to the reigning model of the day: static electricity produced by the rubbing together of individual objects. In other words, the interactions that take place through the chemical combinations were understood as producing electrical energy through friction. However, such molecular misunderstanding of the actual nature of the electrical force produced makes it particularly pertinent in its psychological application. The chemistry of Schlegel's early Romantic period relied on the combinatory nature of diverse elements, where the "friction" of their chemical encounters, brought about by their "free sociality" (CF 34) within an enclosed space, produced an electrical outcome, the spontaneous production of electrical force in the form of *Witz*.

The difficulty readers have in defining what exactly Schlegel means by the crucial concept of *Ironie* makes it tempting to blur its definition with that of wit, which tends to be seen simply as an expression or type of the former. In fact, the two terms refer to concepts with distinct technical meanings that become clearer in light of the electrochemical framework discussed above.[18] Accordingly, irony should be understood as the created, one might say engineered, compressive encounter between the self and its self-differenced Other. It is a "form" that is inherently "paradoxical" (CF 48), and as such, it "contains and excites the feeling of the insoluble conflict between the unconditioned and the conditioned [...]" (CF 108). Or again, "[irony is] an absolute synthesis of absolute antitheses, the constant self-engendering exchange between two conflicting thoughts" (AF 121).

If we are attentive to Schlegel's definitions, we see that wit is distinctly presented as an electrical "explosion" that results from ironic compression (CF 90). Thus, the forced friction of heterogeneous elements that takes place in irony fills the imagination "with all sorts of life before the electrifying moment can happen" and gives forth "brilliant sparks, lustrous rays or thunderbolts" (CF 34). Drawing on the Fichtean and galvanic structures of Romantic selfhood outlined above reveals how Schlegel understands irony in its relation to wit. Irony can be defined as a process of compression, where opposing chemical elements are put in contact in such a way that they interact and spontaneously generate wit, which occurs as an electrical discharge. The dynamic production of electrical wit takes place within the formal limitations of the written fragment, which is, ironically, both the condition for the production of wit and the conditioned product of the process. Simply put, fragmentary wit produces new (witty) fragments.

Of course, this is also how wit is produced in society, in the interaction between "fragmentary" selves, and Schlegel understands wit as inherently sociable, not in a vertical, hierarchical fashion but rather "horizontally," as Gilles Deleuze and Félix Guattari use the term in their *Anti-Oedipus*. Salon society, like irony, is a compression of intersubjectivity, bringing together and combining di-

---

18 For example, Steven E. Alford writes, "Critics have despaired of finding a single meaning to Schlegel's term 'irony.'" (Alford 1984, p. 17) Alford quotes Walter Benjamin, who makes the same assertion.

verse elements in a confined space; one thinks of the Berlin salon culture of Henriette Herz and Rahel Levin, where, in that propitious year of 1797, Schlegel met his future wife, Dorothea Veit, encountered Ritter, developed his cherished ideal of *Symphilosophie*, and began writing fragments! Practically, the symphilosophical ideal involved the combining of different selves in the relatively confined space of the *Athenäum* circle, stirring together Schelling, Schleiermacher, August Ludwig Hülsen, Franz Xavier von Baader, Johann Ludwig Tieck, Novalis, and others. This is the dynamism of the "combinatory art" Schlegel refers to in some of his fragments, a literal social alchemy, ironically combining diverse elements of selfhood which then interact in a frictional, fortuitous way, producing sparks of wit.[19] The collaborative journal *Athenäum* is the fragmentary manifestation of this social chemistry, and the soul of the journal is, of course, the fragment.

The fragment is both the self-limiting figure implied by free, creative expansion and the privileged space of ironic compression for the production of electrochemical wit. The duality of this role, as both product and productive, as both a result and a condition, means that the fragment participates in the universal progression of *Geist*. The fragment is thus a "world" in itself (I 213), or as Schlegel writes in AF 383 (ironically echoing Kant's systematic aspirations in the *Critique of Pure Reason*) wit should be "architectonic". Schlegel's comment is ironic, because his fragmentary system is not likened to universal science but rather to the prickly hedgehog (AF 206), a singular organism that rolls itself into a ball, inviting the caress while never allowing itself to be fully grasped. Indeed, we can say that as both self-positing and self-limiting, as both fragmentary and systematic, the fragment is an ironic system. As such, it is alive on an organic level, one that incorporates and goes beyond the internal electrochemical forces of its constituents (AF 426) to form a living, engendering organism. It is an individual form of "nature's art" (CF 1). Schlegel's fragment should not therefore be seen as the savant construction of the artistic genius but rather as the creative, productive embodiment of the I. In observing or "reading" the fragment, we gain phenomenological knowledge of the Romantic self and its psychology as an ironic system.

To understand the organic quality of selfhood as an ironic system, we must take a brief look at how the electrochemical dimension of Schlegel's theory and practice of the fragment draws from a theory of medicine that was popular at the time. More precisely, reference to John Brown's theory of organic life allows us to

---

19 In fact, Schlegel seems to have delighted in engineering possibilities of personal opposition within the group, for example, he attempts to confront Schleiermacher's religiosity with Schelling's Epicurean confessions.

see how fragmentary psychology involves the full determination of the once abstract Not-I, not only as an instance of ironic self-limitation but as a stimulating other self.

2.3 The Stimulating Not-I

Endlessly dynamic, the universal, progressive Romantic poem (*Geist*) is, of course, itself self-contradictory, alive in the ironic compression of system and fragment. The living, organic nature of such systematic incompleteness implies a particular relation to the otherness that lies outside itself, to a Not-I that is more than a self-imposed limitation. In fact, otherness actually participates in the organic constitution of the system as a form of stimulation that solicits the essential positing of the self. The relation between an (always incomplete) organic system and the otherness of its environment is, generally speaking, the subject matter of medicine. In Schlegel's Romantic psychology, otherness takes the form of other people, and in the self-creative context of the literary fragment, it is associated hermeneutically with the critical reader.[20] To understand stimulating otherness, I want to look briefly at John Brown's theory of organic life and medicine, and its notion of stimulation. The reference shows how the electrochemical nature of wit, drawing upon the dialectic of the Fichtean self and its Other, fuels a process of *Geist* that is alive and reproductive.

Scottish physician John Brown's theory was much in vogue in Germany following the translation of his work in 1795. Brown's ideas responded to a general requirement of the time: the need to find a unique principle of organic medicine that was as universal as Newton's laws of force. Although its applications and diagnostics were doubtlessly arcane and often dangerous—for example, Schelling's "Brunonian" treatment of the young Augusta Böhmer in Jena seems to have led to her death—Brown's theory itself was painfully simple. Animal vitality (health) is seen as dependent on a level of organic excitability. Excitability represents the degree to which an organism can react to external stimulus. Highly excitable states bring about sthenic pathologies, while asthenic conditions are characterized by weakness and lethargy. Most diseases are considered asthenic, and consequently, treatment involves increased levels of stimulation, for example through such external agents as red meat, alcohol, and laudanum. These external stimuli are meant to solicit a response from the patient. In some cases, indirect asthenic pathologies may arise as a result of over-stimulation. Such con-

---

20 See note 22.

ditions require what may be described as a homeopathic treatment where depressants are administered to the depressed (asthenic) patient in order to solicit the contrary response and provoke vital excitability. Brown's theory sees life as a fragile, ephemeral state of excitation, only temporarily and uncertainly held from stillness and dissolution through the imperfect intervention of external, stimulating agents.[21]

When applied to the Fichtean conceptual structure, Brown's idea of organic vitality as the capacity for external stimulation adds a new distinguishing characteristic to the increasingly determinate Not-I, and therefore to the Romantic psychology of selfhood. Rather than being seen as a general limiting condition through which a specific self-positing I becomes effective or the further condition of ironic compression necessary for the production of electrical wit, the Not-I now plays the active, determined role of a particular stimulus that actually solicits and excites the self-positing of the I. Applied to the organic, living entity that characterizes both the fragment and the self that produces it, Brown's paradigm leads to the recognition that otherness has an actual role in creative self-expression, adding the real quality of reciprocal selfhood to Schlegel's appropriation of the hitherto faceless Not-I. Such stimulating otherness can now be seen as a "sense of chaos outside the system" (I 55), "from which a world may spring" (I 213), where "the excitation of the smallest contact, friend or enemy" draws forth "brilliant sparks, lustrous rays or thunderbolts" (CF 34). The Not-I is now the exciting other, the "thou" for whom s/he lives and self-creates, and who can never fully comprehend or grasp the ironic system of selfhood.[22]

When superimposed on Ritter's electrochemical discoveries, Brown's idea that life results from external solicitation adds a rich, intersubjective dimension to the concept of limiting ironic compression, which can now be seen as a form of otherness that stimulates the psychological vitality of the always self-creative self. Together, these elements underlie Schlegel's symphilosophical *Athenäum*

---

21 See Neubauer 1967, pp. 367–382. As Neubauer shows, both Schelling and Novalis were also fascinated and influenced by Brown's ideas, but only because the philosophers were able to interpret the material relation between excitability (life) and foreign stimulation as a Fichtean relation between the I and the Not-I (cf. Neubauer 1967, pp. 375–376). In fact, as Neubauer also points out, both philosophers react strongly against the perceived mechanical nature of Brown's theory of medicine when left on its own.

22 See Schlegel's essay "On Incomprehensibility" in which he writes: "I wanted to show that the purest incomprehension emanates precisely from science and the arts—which by their very nature aim at comprehension and at making comprehensible—and from philosophy and philology". Further on: "Everything is going to become more and more critical, and artists can already begin to cherish the just hope that humanity will at last rise up in a mass and learn to read" (Firchow 1971, pp. 260–261).

project and constitute his theory and practice of the literary fragment.[23] Given these elements, Schlegel's conception of Romantic selfhood is perhaps best summarized in ironic, existentialist terms: it is a living, systematic fragment, transcendently universal and yet solicited by an irreconcilable otherness.

3 Conclusion: The Specificity of Romantic Psychology

In attempting to specify Romantic psychology through its actualized embodiment in Schlegel's literary fragment, here, in summary, is what we have discovered:

A. Romantic psychology relies on the Fichtean paradigm of the self-positing I, along with the acknowledgement of a self-limiting Not-I.
B. Romantic psychology conceives of the self-positing I in terms of natural forces, which are universal in scope and application. In Schlegel, these forces are electrochemical, productive of *Witz*.
C. Romantic psychology conceives of the limiting Not-I as organically related to the self-positing I. For Schlegel, the Not-I is the stimulating Other, the "chaos outside the system", without which the system is impossible.

Having thus specified Romantic psychology, the question arises as to whether our findings can be generalized, i.e. discovered in other contemporaneous Romantic figures. While I do not have the time nor space to explore this adequately, here are a few potential lineaments for Romantic psychologies that might be investigated in Schlegel's principle collaborators at the *Athenäum* journal: Novalis and Schleiermacher.

3.1 Novalis

The self-positing I is an obvious feature of Novalis' thought. In his "Logological Fragments", for example, he clearly puts forward a view where *Poesie* appears as

---

23 Perhaps the most poignant expression of this dialectic is found in Lucinde, in the section, "A Dithyrambic Fantasy on the Loveliest Situation in the World", in which Julius evokes for Lucinde their "wittiest and most beautiful" moment, when, in their love-making, they exchange roles, thus creating "a wonderful, deeply meaningful allegory of the development of man and woman to full and complete humanity" (Firchow 1971, p. 49).

the result of the I's initial voyage of compressive inner discovery (philosophy), in an expansive, externalized verb by which the things of nature are poeticized. Such essential, poetical self-positing allows us to view the self as it is read in the marvelous phenomena of nature. The dynamic aspect that we discovered in Schlegel's view of electrochemical *Witz* may be more difficult to identify in Novalis, although he clearly sees nature as inscribed with vital forces, which extend beyond the organic realm into the very heart of geological "life", as we see in his novel, *Heinrich von Ofterdingen*. Clearly, his vision of the psyche and nature is dynamic, driven by forces, and opposed to the mechanical, deterministic Enlightenment psychology that we observed in Flatt's course. In fact, the enchanted visions of Novalis's writings, perhaps best witnessed in his *Hymns to the Night*, where, prostrated on Sophie's tomb, he experiences the vision of her resurrection, are just the sort of unbidden representations that Enlightenment psychology seeks to explain and treat. Finally, the Brunonian aspect that we identified in Schlegel as the enlivening solicitation of other selves may be fruitfully explored in Novalis's idea of the mediator, which may take the form of the Christ, of Sophie or of any natural object capable of soliciting the poetical verb. The mediator stimulates the self to embark on its own voyage of inner discovery, realized in the poeticization of nature.

3.2 Schleiermacher

In the first edition (1799) of Schleiermacher's *Discourses on Religion to its Cultured Despisers*, *Anschauung* (intuition) might certainly be grasped, according to his definition of religion as an individual "intuition of the universe", as an active self-positing that embraces the entirety of nature. The ambiguous treatment given to corresponding *Gefühl*, defined in more passive, intimate terms, may be viewed as a form of self-limitation: the reciprocal agency of the universe impressing itself on the individual, sensitive self. Intuition and feeling share a clearly dynamic character, partaking of universal force and eschewing the mechanistic Enlightenment paradigm. As well, Schleiermacher's intuition self-limits itself in specific, finite forms: natural science, art, morality and metaphysical philosophy are all fragmentary expressions of religion qua intuition of the universe. In Schleiermacher, the stimulating Not-I can either be ascribed to his theory of mediators as stimulating human guides who have experienced and recognized the true nature of religion or, perhaps better still, witnessed in his second-person evocation of religion's "cultured despisers" to whom the *Discourses* are addressed.

3.3 Romantic Psychology's Legacy

Taken together, the above-mentioned criteria outlined in A, B and C, imply that Romantic psychology actually takes place in and through the "fruits" of the self. In other words, just as Schlegel's *Seelenkunde* is discoverable in his theory and practice of the literary fragment, as a self-creative ironic system in living relation to other selves, other examples of Romantic psychology are observable in and through their productions. Romantic psychology can therefore faithfully be described as phenomenological, a psychology in which the science of the self is, above all, descriptive of human behaviors. As such, it is not reliant upon the elaboration of inner mechanisms, which today often take the form of neuroscientific explanations, where certain, loosely defined neuropathways, regions and "hardwirings" are meant to explain the production of pathologies (unbidden representations). In the broadest, historical sense, Romantic psychology opened the door to modern psychoanalysis, through the pioneering work of such practitioners as Philippe Pinel (1745 – 1826), whose nosography of mental pathologies is descriptive and who initiated the ground-breaking psychological approach that involved actually talking to and listening to "alienated" patients.

Pinel's humanistic methods can be juxtaposed with the Enlightenment's more mechanical approach, which often involved cruel manipulations of the body in order to bring about "cures" to mental pathologies, an approach that perhaps may be the ancestor of today's overly pharmaceutical trends in psychotherapy. Conversely, the talking cure became possible when the patient's pronouncements were taken as more than senseless ravings. They are meaningful to the extent that they are expressions of the self, solicited by the "stimulating Other", here, the psychoanalyst. Today, we seem caught between the two paradigms. Defining pathological states through their specific behaviors and discourses is the approach favored by today's principal handbook of psychiatry, the famous *Diagnostic and Statistical Manual of Mental Disorders*. However, the treatments proposed there generally rely on drugs rather than the talking cure.

Perhaps most obviously, we can say that psychoanalytical hermeneutics (Freudian, Jungian, Lacanian ...) is inspired by Romantic psychology. As we have hopefully seen through our discussion of Schlegel's theory and practice of the literary fragment, the Other's interpretation of the "work" is always psycho-analytical, and psychoanalysis is necessarily and endlessly hermeneutical. Indeed, one of Freud's early writings on interpretation (1905) is entitled, "*Witz* and its relations with the unconscious".

Bibliography

GW | Hegel, G. W. F. (1968 –): *Gesammelte Werke*. In Verbindung mit der Deutschen Forschungsgemeinschaft herausgegeben von der Nordrhein-Westfälischen Akademie der Wissenschaften und der Künste. Hamburg: Meiner.

KA | Schlegel, Friedrich (1991): *Kritische Friedrich-Schlegel-Ausgabe*. E. Behler with J. J. Anstett and H. Eichner (eds.). Munich: F. Schöningh. [*The Critical Fragments* (CF), the *Athenäum Fragments* (AF), and the *Ideas* (I) can be found in KA vol. 17.]

SW | Herder, J. G. (1967): *Sämtliche Werke* [Berlin: 1891]. Hildesheim: Georg Olms Verlagsbuchhandlung.

Alford, Steven E. (1984): *Irony and the Logic of the Romantic Imagination*. New York: Peter Lang.

Barkhoff, Jürgen (2009): "Romantic Science and Psychology". In: Nicholas Saul (ed.): *The Cambridge Companion to German Romanticism*. Cambridge: Cambridge University Press.

Beiser, Frederick C. (1987): *The Fate of Reason*. Cambridge Mass.: Harvard University Press.

Deleuze, Gilles/Guattari, Félix (1972): *L'anti-Oedipe*. Paris: Les Editions de Minuit.

Hoffmeister, J. (ed.) (1974): *Dokumente zu Hegels Entwicklung* [1936]. Stuttgart-Bad Canstatt: Frommann-Holzboog.

Kim, Soo-Jung (2001): *Vorhersehungsvermögen und Taubstummheit: Zwei Aspekte der Leib/Seele-Problematik in Karl Philipp Moritz' "Magazin zur Erfahrungsseelenkunde"*. Kiel: Christian-Albrechts-Universität.

Neubauer, John (1967): "Dr. John Brown and Early German Romanticism". In: *Journal of the History of Ideas* 28. No. 3, pp. 367–382.

Norman, Judith (2000): "Squaring the Circle: Hegel's Critique of Schlegel's Theories of Art". In: William Maker (ed.): *Hegel and Aesthetics*. Albany: SUNY Press, pp. 131–144.

Norman, Judith (2007): "Hegel and German Romanticism". In: Stephen Houlgate (ed.): *Hegel and the Arts*. Evanston: Northwestern University Press, pp. 310–336.

Novalis (1965): *Heinrich von Ofterdingen*. Stuttgart: Reclam.

Novalis (1977): *Schriften*. Paul Kluckhohn and Richard Samuel with Hans-Joachim Mähl and Gerhard Schulz (eds.). Darmstadt: Wissenschaftliche Buchgesellschaft.

Reid, Jeffrey (2008): "Galvanism and Excitability in Friedrich Schlegel's Theory of the Fragment". In: *Clio* 38. No. 1 (Fall 2008), pp. 1–16.

Reid, Jeffrey (2013): "How the Dreaming Soul Became the Feeling Soul, Between the 1827 and 1830 Editions of Hegel's Philosophy of Subjective Spirit". In: David Stern (ed.): *Essays on Hegel's Philosophy of Subjective Spirit*. Albany: SUNY Press, pp. 37–54.

Reid, Jeffrey (2014): *The Anti-Romantique: Hegel Against Ironic Romanticism*. London: Bloomsbury.

Schlegel, Friedrich (1971): *Friedrich Schlegel's Lucinde and the Fragments*. Peter Firchow (ed., trans., intro.). Minneapolis: University of Minnesota Press.

Schleiermacher, Friedrich (1967): *Über die Religion. Reden an die Gebildeten unter ihren Verächtern*. Göttingen: Vandenhoeck und Ruprecht.

II. Rezensionen/Reviews

Daniel M. Feige

Rachel Zuckert und James Kreines (Hrsg.): *Hegel on Philosophy in History.* Cambridge: Cambridge University Press 2017. 260 S. ISBN: 9781316145012

Mit der von Paul Redding diagnostizierten Rückkehr des hegelschen Denkens in der analytischen Philosophie,[1] die mit ihren Gründungsfiguren wie Bertrand Russell ursprünglich angetreten war, dem hegelschen Denken den Garaus zu machen, sind nicht allein prägnante Appropriationen von Motiven der hegelschen Philosophie entstanden. Vielmehr sind dabei bislang ganze Kontinente der hegelschen Philosophie unentdeckt geblieben. Neben der Ästhetik ist hier vor allem die Geschichtsphilosophie zu nennen. Der vorliegende Band, der zugleich eine Festschrift für Robert Pippin darstellt, gilt dem Thema der Geschichtlichkeit der Philosophie und der Philosophie der Geschichte. Die dreizehn Beiträge arbeiten sich in mehr oder weniger intensiver, mitunter affirmativer, häufig aber kritischer Weise an Pippins Arbeiten ab. Zu den Stärken des Bandes gehört nicht allein, dass alle Beiträge ausnahmslos lesenswert sind, sondern auch, dass er einschlägige Autoren*innen ganz unterschiedlicher philosophischer Traditionen versammelt; neben der deutschen und amerikanischen Hegelforschung ist die kritische Theorie vertreten und selbst die Ljubljana Schule. Diese Breite trägt Pippins Wirksamkeit Rechnung: Nicht allein ist Pippin maßgeblich daran beteiligt gewesen, dass die Hegellektüre auch für strikter analytisch geprägte Philosophen*innen wieder salonfähig wurde, sondern seine Forschungen haben in ganz unterschiedlichen philosophischen Traditionen Wirksamkeit entfaltet.

Die Beiträge des Bandes sind in drei Sektionen gegliedert: McDowells, Sedgwicks und Sieps Artikel sind der ersten Sektion (I) und damit dem Thema zugeordnet, welche systematische Rolle Geschichtlichkeit in Hegels eigener Philosophie spielt. Die Beiträge von Redding, Stern, Pinkard, Horstmann und Ameriks stellen in der zweiten Sektion (II) die Frage, wie Hegels Philosophie sich zu jeweils bestimmten ihrer Vorgänger verhält. Die Artikel des dritten Teils (III) von Menke, Honneth, Bernstein, Žižek und Lear hingegen loten die Aktualität Hegels im Lichte seiner Rezeption aus.

Die erste Sektion (I) eröffnet mit einem Paukenschlag: John McDowells und Sally Sedgwicks Beiträge sind gleichermaßen auf höchstem Niveau und gehen doch in diametral entgegengesetzte Richtungen. McDowells Aufsatz kann als jüngste Iteration des viele Aufsätze umspannenden Streits mit Robert Pippin über

---

1 Paul Redding: *Analytic Philosophy and the Return of Hegelian Thought.* Cambridge: Cambridge University Press 2007.

die richtigen Lesarten Kants und Hegels gelten. In negativer Weise entwickelt McDowell eine letztlich stark aristotelisch geprägte Zurückweisung von Pippins sozialtheoretischer und geschichtsphilosophischer These, dass unsere Rationalität und Freiheit auch geschichtliche Errungenschaften sind. In positiver Weise schlägt er vor, den formalen Begriff einer Freiheit, der „part of being a rational subject" (31) ist, von einem inhaltlichen Begriff der Freiheit derart zu unterscheiden, dass ersterer eine Tatsache über uns als Lebewesen ausdrückt, während letzterer dahingehend geschichtlich ist, dass Gründe für unser Handeln und Denken auch schlechte Gründe sein können und wir ihnen nur fälschlicherweise eine entsprechende rationale Kraft zugestehen. An McDowells exzellentem wie problematischem Artikel werden zentrale Potentiale wie Einseitigkeiten jüngerer Beiträge zu Hegel deutlich: Hegels Philosophie gewinnt allein Kontur als Erweiterung von aristotelischen und kantischen Überlegungen. Von Aristoteles soll sie unterscheiden, dass in ihr anders als bei Aristoteles „self-consciousness and freedom" (18) thematisch werden, von Kant letztlich, dass die Kategorien und Anschauungsformen um eine historisch-genetische Perspektive erweitert werden. Angesichts der Tatsache, dass die zentrale Rolle, die Hegel der Dialektik in seinem Denken zugesteht und dass auch sein Denken der Geschichte mit seinem Verständnis von Dialektik eng verbunden ist, sollte man nicht nur skeptisch sein angesichts McDowells schlichter Lesart des Geistbegriffs, die besagt, dass die Philosophie des Geistes „the philosophy of the human soul in an Aristotelian mode" (15) sei. Vielmehr sollte man darauf hinweisen, dass die Unterscheidung von Form und Inhalt unserer Freiheit kolossal undialektisch ist. Hegel taucht einmal mehr in Form einer aristotelischen oder kantischen Scharade auf.

Als Gegenposition muss deshalb der exzellente Aufsatz von Sally Sedgwick gewürdigt werden. Sie geht hier dem ambitionierten Projekt nach, von dem Systemteil Hegels, der auf den ersten Blick wenig mit Geschichte zu tun hat, nämlich der *Logik*, nachzuweisen, dass Geschichtlichkeit, verstanden als Kontingenz und Endlichkeit, durchaus in die *Logik* hineinragt. Dazu zeigt sie überzeugend, dass gilt: „[B]y Hegels own lights, the Science of Logic is not presuppositionless[; it] rests on a particular set of substantive philosophical assumptions" (37), die genauer die besondere Art von Einheit betreffen, durch die die entsprechenden Begriffe der Logik gekennzeichnet sind. Zugleich gelte: „[T]he Science of Logic is contingent in that Hegel does not take himself to have established [...] that its thought-forms and the system to which they belong are valid once and for all" (48). Kritisch könnte gleichwohl angemerkt werden, dass zu den besonders instruktiven Aspekten von Hegels *Logik* gehört, dass die Art von Einheit, die ihre Überlegungen zeitigen, gerade nicht schon *vor* ihrer dialektischen Entwicklung gegeben ist. Und mit Blick auf die Frage der Kontingenz könnte man geneigt sein, diese weniger extern, als vielmehr derart intern zu begreifen, dass Hegel in der

Logik vielleicht selbst Ressourcen dafür bereitstellt, Entwicklungen, die nach ihr kamen, noch in den Sinn ihrer eigenen Begriffe einzutragen. Diese Rückfragen schmälern aber keineswegs die wichtigen Überlegungen Sedgwicks.

Wollte man die erste Sektion des Bandes als abstrakte Variante dialektischen Denkens verstehen, so könnte man Ludwig Sieps Aufsatz als Aufhebung der von McDowell und Sedgwick präsentierten Alternative verstehen. Das ist natürlich nicht sein Anspruch – und das leistet er auch nicht. Vielmehr diskutiert er in kenntnisreichem Bezug auf die Kritik an der Geschichtsphilosophie des 20. Jahrhunderts und auf jüngere sozialontologische und handlungstheoretische Fragestellungen die für die Münsteraner Hegelrezeption insgesamt charakteristische Frage, ob und inwieweit es bei Hegel nicht doch eines Standpunktes außerhalb des historischen Prozesses und kollektiver Aushandlungen um die Frage bedarf, wie wir uns verstehen sollten, um sein Projekt insgesamt zu rechtfertigen. Auch wenn Siep in erhellender Weise am Ende seines Beitrags drei denkbare Positionen einer Geschichtsphilosophie nach Hegel vorstellt und diskutiert, so scheint mir keineswegs so klar zu sein, dass eine retroaktiv-teleologische Position, wie Hegel sie entwickelt, heute aus prinzipiellen Gründen schon vom Tisch ist. Dass das teleologische Denken insgesamt eine irreduzible Dimension in den Blick nimmt, haben nicht zuletzt jüngere, an Anscombe orientierte Beiträge gezeigt. Wenn man Hegels geschichtsphilosophische Überlegungen richtig versteht, könnte es durchaus so sein, dass sie mit jüngeren geschichtstheoretischen Debatten in Einklang zu bringen sind.

Der eröffnende Beitrag der zweiten Sektion (II) von Paul Redding entwickelt eine heterodoxe Lesart der systematischen Rolle der Stoa für Hegels Denken: In ihr taucht eine Art von Allgemeinheit auf, die Platon und Aristoteles noch nicht denken konnten und die letztlich ein Scharnier zur abstrakt-formellen römischen Lebensform darstellt und die dennoch ein wesentlicher dialektischer Schritt für ein angemessenes, nicht länger abstraktes Denken des Allgemeinen darstellt. Robert Sterns Beitrag unterbreitet vor dem Hintergrund der Frage, inwieweit Hegel sich auf den modernistischen Gedanken der Selbstgesetzgebung oder auf den antiken Gedanken der Selbsrealisierung bezieht, im Rahmen einer ebenso klaren wie erhellenden Rekonstruktion des Streits zwischen McDowell und Pippin den Vorschlag, dass es sich hier um eine falsche Alternative handelt: Wir können Hegels Philosophie nur um den Preis einer Ausblendung zentraler Dimensionen mit Pippin so denken, dass es sich hier um ein modernistisches Projekt der Selbstgesetzgebung, verstanden als Selbsthervorbringung, handelt. Was Stern gleichwohl nicht hinreichend thematisiert, ist, dass es eine Alternative zu der Alternative von McDowell und Pippin geben könnte, in der sich der Gedanke des Historischen und der Gedanke einer basalen Normativität nicht derart unversöhnt einander gegenüberstehen, wie es letztlich in Sterns Ausführungen durchscheint.

Überraschend ist der dritte Beitrag von Terry Pinkard: Er entwickelt instruktive Überlegungen zu einer an Hegel orientierten Handlungstheorie und zeigt überzeugend, dass Hegels Theorie nicht als Vorläuferin einer Wunsch-Überzeugungs-Theorie erläutert werden kann. Überraschend ist der Beitrag deshalb, weil er das Thema der Geschichte nur am Rande streift – wo der Autor doch jüngst eine der wichtigsten Monographien zu Hegels Geschichtsphilosophie vorgelegt hat.[2] Der Beitrag von Rolf-Peter Horstmann dreht daraufhin die Frage nach dem Geschichtsverständnis Hegels um, wenn er mit der Diagnose beginnt, dass Hegel im 20. Jahrhundert eine weniger wohlwollende Rezeption zuteil geworden ist als Kant, der auf den ersten Blick viel seltsamere Thesen zu vertreten scheint. Er führt das darauf zurück, dass die Art und Weise, wie Hegel zu ihnen gelangt, kontroverser sei als die Art und Weise, wie Kant zu seinen Thesen gelangt – und bleibt skeptisch, was die Aktualität von Hegels Begriff des Begriffs angeht, den er letztlich im Sinne von in den Objekten selbst wirksamen Normen ihrer Realisierung erläutert. Abgeschlossen wird die zweite Sektion durch einen Text von Karl Ameriks, der größere historische Linien nachzeichnet und letztlich gegen Hegels Geschichtsphilosophie für eine Reanimation der Frühromantiker plädiert.

Die Beiträge der dritten Sektion (III) loten in unterschiedlicher Weise das Erbe Hegels im Lichte seiner späteren Rezeption und Kritik aus. Zu den stärksten Beiträgen des Bandes gehört der die dritte Sektion eröffnende Beitrag von Christoph Menke. In begrifflich prägnanter Form rekonstruiert er Pippins Projekt und weist nach, dass ihm in einer sozial- und praxistheoretischen Lesart, die die Geschichtlichkeit des Geistes als sein Gewordensein wie sein Werden begreift, eine entscheidende Dimension des hegelschen Denkens entgleitet, dass nämlich gilt: „[T]he formation of the autonomous shape of Spirit is not the autonomous deed of Spirit" (168). Dazu rekonstruiert er Hegels Anthropologie und macht geltend, dass in kalkulierter Weise das Paradox der Freiheit – entweder Willkür oder externer Zwang – hier wiederkehre: Gegen den Gedanken des ganz bei sich selbst seienden Geistes klagt Menke ein, dass der Geist sich beständig an etwas abarbeitet, was nicht in ihm aufgeht – ohne dass dieses deshalb außerhalb des Geistes wäre. Macht Pippins Lesart „freedom into the formal determination of the social" (175), so klagt Menke zu Recht ein, dass „the social is [...] at the same time the medium and the other of freedom. In participation in the social, the subject wins and loses freedom" (175). Unklar bleibt für mich aber, ob Menke damit tatsächlich dem geschichtsphilosophischen Erbe Hegels gerecht wird: Sein Ergebnis liest sich weniger wie eine dialektische Lektion, als vielmehr wie ein dekon-

---

2 Terry Pinkard: *Does History Make Sense? Hegel on the Historical Shapes of Justice.* Cambridge/ Mass.: Harvard University Press 2017.

struktives Manöver, bei dem die Bedingung der Möglichkeit von Freiheit zugleich die Bedingung ihrer Unmöglichkeit ist. Allerdings kann man diesen Gedanken auch so verstehen, dass das, was im Geist gerade nicht positiv aufgeht, im Zuge der Selbstthematisierungen des Geistes zugleich als sein Anderes mitverhandelt wird – und damit im Sinne einer *negativen* Dialektik, die sich durchaus auf das Erbe Hegels berufen kann. Der Beitrag von Axel Honneth, dem zweiten Vertreter der kritischen Theorie im Band, klagt gegenüber Isaiah Berlins klassischer Unterscheidung zwischen positiver und negativer Freiheit die soziale Freiheit als dritte Form der Freiheit ein – als paradigmatische Beispiele werden dabei kollektive Prozesse der politischen Willensbildung sowie Freundschaft und Liebe erwähnt. Gerade wenn Honneth sagt, „that we are not able to assess the value of solidary relationships without reference to the positive experience of social freedom" (192), geht aber eine der wesentlichen und zentralen Ressourcen der kritischen Theorie verloren bzw. wird so heruntergekocht, dass sie impotent zu werden droht: die Ideologiekritik. Pointierter ist in dieser Hinsicht der Beitrag Jay M. Bernsteins, der letztlich Adornos Hegel gegen Pippins Hegel ausspielt. Man muss den Schlussfolgerungen dieses Beitrags gar nicht zur Gänze zustimmen, um zu sehen, dass Bernsteins Kritik an Pippin schlagend ist: Pippin bezeichnet in *After the Beautiful* das Problem der Freiheit in argumentativ ungedeckter Weise als unendliches und unlösbares und übergeht damit seine manifesten sozialpolitischen Ursachen. Nicht zuletzt zeigt Bernstein überzeugend, dass Pippin, um sich nicht mit Adornos Kritik identifizieren zu müssen, diese letztlich karikaturhaft verkürzt (was nebenbei bemerkt aus anderen Gründen auch für Pippins Heideggerlektüre gilt). Einen etwas versöhnlicheren Ton schlägt erstaunlicherweise der Beitrag von Slavoj Žižek an, der wie Bernsteins Beitrag seinen Ausgangspunkt bei Pippins *After the Beautiful* nimmt und damit wie dieser Ästhetik und Geschichtsphilosophie zusammen diskutiert. Anders als in seinem Hegelbuch lässt sich Žižek aber in seinem gerade in den Passagen zu Manet starken Beitrag nicht auf Bodengefechte um Hegels Geschichtsbegriff ein. Abgeschlossen wird der Band von Jonathan Lear, der in anderer Weise als Žižek das psychoanalytische Erbe mit und gegen Hegel ausspielt – der Beitrag mutet nicht allein wegen der ersten Fußnote wie ein lesbarer Festvortrag für Pippin an und beschließt den Band damit in gelungener Weise.

Ich hoffe zweierlei deutlich gemacht zu haben: Erstens kommt niemand, der sich ernsthaft für Hegels Verständnis des Verhältnisses von Philosophie und Geschichte interessiert, um einen Blick in die Beiträge dieses ausgezeichneten Bandes herum. Zweitens gelingt der Band symptomatologisch auch in dem, was den meisten seiner Beiträge noch nicht gelingt: Hegels Begriff der Geschichtlichkeit der Philosophie und seine Philosophie der Geschichte in einer Weise zu explizieren, die diesen nicht vorschnell einer neoaristotelischen und/oder neo-kantianischen Agenda zuschlägt.

Desmond Hogan

Courtney D. Fugate and John Hymers (eds.): *Baumgarten and Kant on Metaphysics.* Oxford: Oxford University Press 2018. xv + 235 pp. ISBN: 9780198783886.

Many of the papers collected in this fine volume were presented at a 2014 conference on Alexander Gottlieb Baumgarten's *Metaphysica* held at La Salle University in celebration of the publication of Fugate and Hymers' splendid 2013 English translation of that work. The present volume includes contributions on Baumgarten's rationalism (Brandon Look), his rational psychology and theory of freedom (Clemens Schwaiger, Corey Dyck, Henry Allison), his doctrine of existence (Courtney Fugate, Jeffrey Edwards), his place in the emergence of psychology as an independent discipline between Descartes and Kant (Gary Hatfield), and his theory of determination (Angelica Nuzzo). It also includes discussions of Baumgarten's influence on Kant's concept and refutation of idealism (Paul Guyer), his theory of contradiction and privation (John Hymers), and his account of representational clarity and distinctness (Rudolf Makkreel).

As the editors' introduction reminds us, the *Metaphysics* played an outsized role in Kant's academic activity and intellectual development. He taught from the text nearly fifty times between 1756 and 1796, while his anthropology lectures grew in part out of its treatment of empirical psychology. Kant employed the book as the basis for lectures even after the publication of his own magnum opus, the *Critique of Pure Reason*. Handwritten notes densely blanketed his own copy of its 4th edition, providing what Adickes described as the richest yield of the reflexions on metaphysics collected in volumes 17 & 18 of the Academy edition. Kant refers to Baumgarten as 'the Coryphaeus of metaphysics,' and makes clear his regard for him as a practitioner of sharp-sighted analysis (Academy edition [Ak.], vol. 1, p. 408). Enduring engagement with the *Metaphysics* provided inspiration and an important foil for the development of the critical philosophy. On the other hand, Kant acknowledges 'the darkness that appears to surround this most useful and foundational of all textbooks' (Ak. 1, p. 503). Baumgarten's preface describes the *Metaphysics* as a 'desiccated skeleton of metaphysics,' whose analyses are to be fleshed out in lectures. The terseness of its arguments makes sometimes for a difficult read, and the present volume is a welcome contribution to a remarkably small critical literature on Baumgarten's views, his influence on Kant, and his intellectual debts to Leibniz, Wolff, and Pietist contemporaries.

A common theme of several contributions is that we should modify a view influentially promulgated by Max Wundt according to which Baumgarten as metaphysician was an unimaginative disciple of Christian Wolff. (Baumgarten's innovative contributions in aesthetics, broached here only by Makkreel, have long been recognized.) A famous drama of the eighteenth century German academy was Wolff's 1723 banishment from Halle at the instigation of Pietist theologians led by Joachim Lange—described as an 'enemy of philosophy' in Herder's notes on Kant's lectures (Ak. 28, p. 944). Brandon Look, Corey Dyck, and Clemens Schwaiger argue that Baumgarten's early education in Halle in fact left him with considerable sympathy for Pietist preoccupations surrounding the doctrine of the will and the relation of faith and reason. According to Dyck and Look, this residual sympathy for Pietism expresses itself in what Dyck calls 'subtle but meaningful revisions' to Wolff's doctrines (p. 78). These include a shift of focus in rational psychology to the soul's temporal as opposed to merely spatial perspective on the world, and an original analysis of some mental powers pertinent to moral psychology, including foresight and anticipation. This 'crypto-Pietist' reading echoes a central theme of Schwaiger's 2011 Baumgarten monograph, though Look and Dyck both keep Baumgarten more firmly in the Wolffian camp.

Schwaiger's essay is a translation of a central section of his 2011 book and focuses on the freedom of the will. Baumgarten presents freedom as a power of willing according to a rational preference. Schwaiger sees in this a response to Lange's critique of Wolff, one amending the latter's 'flat equation' of freedom and spontaneity by renewing Leibniz's insistence on intelligence as requisite of freedom (p. 49). While Lange may have interpreted Wolff as Schwaiger proposes, it is undoubtedly a caricature. The reading may be suggested by § 518 of Wolff's *German Metaphysics* taken in isolation, as Schwaiger points out. However Wolff, who was also intimately familiar with Leibniz's *Theodicy*, has just explained that free action is contingent (§ 515), and he immediately adds that it involves suitably distinct representations, so that 'reason is the ground of freedom' (§ 520). At the heart of Schwaiger's argument is an analysis of Baumgarten's moral psychology arguing that this 'decisively weakens' Wolff's principle of volition according to which 'whatever we represent as good to us, we desire' (p. 45). He draws on a dissertation by Baumgarten's student S. W. Spalding affirming the existence of *peccata proaeretica* or deliberately committed sins. Schwaiger summarizes Spalding's thesis, imputed also to Baumgarten, as follows: 'Someone can desire something that he distinctly recognizes as evil, and while he recognizes it as such' (p. 45). This is an accurate if potentially misleading summary, insofar as it suggests that Spalding envisages immoral desires grounded in distinct knowledge of evil. Neither Spalding nor Baumgarten is proposing action *sub ratione mali*. Baumgarten affirms that, 'what I desire, pleases' (*Metaphysica* § 664), and, 'what pleases me, I intuit as good, under the aspect of the good' (*Metaphysica* § 651). Spalding's claim is just that we may desire what is distinctly known as bad if our recognition is outweighed by enough confused representations of the bad thing as good—thus if the distinct knowledge is swamped by motives of the lower faculty of desire. It may be that Wolff failed to give due consideration to such motivational conflict. I don't think it follows that Baumgarten 'decisively weakened' Wolff's rule that 'whatever we represent as good to us, we desire.' In the case considered, there is no representing as good that isn't accompanied by desire, furthermore the bad act is desired at all only insofar as it is confusedly represented as good. Insofar as it is distinctly known as bad, Baumgarten agrees with Wolff that we have an aversion to it. As Schwaiger concedes, Leibniz seems to have intended a similar analysis of Medea's famous *video meliora proboque, deteriora sequor*. In the early dialogue *Confessio Philosophi*, and again in the *Theodicy*, Leibniz presents the Medea case as one in which 'the morally good is mastered by the agreeably good, which makes more impression on souls when they are disturbed by the passions' (*Theodicy* § 154).

Remaining on the topic of free will, Henry Allison's essay compares Baumgarten's Leibnizian analysis of freedom to the so-called ML_1 transcript of Kant's metaphysics lectures, dated to the mid- to late-1770s. Allison makes an important point also noted by Hatfield and Dyck, namely that Baumgarten conceives all powers of the mind through the one faculty of representing the universe (*Metaphysica* § 744). This psychological monism is crucial to his overarching project of explaining in conceptual terms the commerce between mental faculties. (It also provides a reason to resist Schwaiger's formulation (p. 50) according to which Baumgarten differs from Wolff in presenting the will (*arbitrium*) as a 'completely separate [*ganz eigenständiges*] faculty of the soul.') Allison points out that ML_1 departs dramatically from Leibniz, Wolff and Baumgarten in its account of human freedom. It attributes to us a faculty of 'transcendental freedom' defined as involving an absolute or unconditioned spontaneity, and illustrated in 'an almost Sartrean manner' with the claim that we can in principle freely resist compulsion of choice even by torture (p. 177). Transcendental freedom *qua* unconditioned spontaneity remains central to the critical philosophy, as Allison emphasizes, though in keeping with the deflationary interpretation he has long championed he believes it is reconceived there as a 'mere idea,' one retaining a merely 'subjective necessity' as the condition 'on which I can alone conceive of myself as an agent' (p. 180). His essay concludes with an imagined dialogue in which Kant suggests that his sharp separation of understanding and sensibility following the 'Great Light' epiphany of 1769 first allowed him to entertain an unconditioned spontaneity of thought, and subsequently of agency. The suggestion that Kant's theory of agency is intimately related to the *Inaugural Dissertation*'s new theory of sensibility is, I think, correct, though it seems to me the order of explanation runs mainly in the other direction. A difficulty for Allison's proposal, at any rate, is that Kant's shift to a libertarian account of human agency takes place much earlier. It is visible already in the *Only Possible Argument* essay of 1763 (Ak. 2, p. 110), and firmly established in reflections dated by Adickes to before 1769 (e.g. Reflection 3855, 1764–1768).

Paul Guyer's contribution reexamines Kant's Refutation of Idealism in light of the doctrines and categories of Baumgarten's work. It makes the important observation that Baumgarten's version of Leibniz's pre-established harmony upholds a universal 'ideal influence' between non-spatial finite substances, which Kant may reasonably have regarded as a precedent for his own mature doctrine of affection by non-spatiotemporal things in themselves. Guyer argues that the idealism targeted by Kant's Refutation is best understood in terms of Baumgarten's definition as the doctrine that only minds exist. On this reading, the entities whose existence the Refutation is concerned to prove need not be spatial, since what counts is just that they are not minds. Guyer's interpretation of the Refutation as an ambitious attempt to prove the existence of transsubjective or wholly mind-independent entities ultimately leads him back to old complaints about its strategy and persuasiveness. He finds a basic tension between the Refutation's aims and Kant's insistence in the Paralogisms chapter that we cannot know whether things in themselves are intrinsically different from minds. Kant's admission that, 'maybe there are only thinking things after all,' implies, according to Guyer, that 'the Refutation collapses' (p. 169). Such open inconsistency might also be taken as evidence for another popular reading of the Refutation, namely as arguing only that complete time-determination requires an objective if still transcendentally ideal empirical order alongside merely subjective perspectives on the world. An apparently formidable objection to this weaker reading is Kant's famous description of his Refutation as responding to a 'scandal' that philosophy has been forced to take the existence of 'things outside us' 'merely on *faith*' (B xxxixn). As Ameriks and others have argued, however, this formulation can be viewed in the context of Kant's resounding rejection of Jacobi's early attempt to co-opt the *Critique of Pure Reason* in support of his own fideist epistemology by highlighting allegedly unargued presuppositions of Kant's epistemological framework.

A review of this scope can only give a taste of the volume, which includes much of value besides. Courtney Fugate's essay offers a careful analysis of Baumgarten's neglected distinction between existence as the complement of essence, and actuality as full determination with respect to compossible affections. He suggests that this distinction provides Baumgarten with resources to resist Kant's famous critique of the ontological argument. Jeffrey Edwards asks whether Kant's *Opus Postumum* envisages an *a priori* existence proof that abandons his critical doctrine of existence as absolute or unanalyzable positing. Rudolf Makkreel's very useful essay offers an analysis of kinds of representational distinctness in Baumgarten and Kant. John Hymers examines Baumgarten's treatment of contradiction and its relation to Kant's fourfold 'table of nothings' in the *Critique of Pure Reason*. Angelica Nuzzo considers the meaning of 'determination' in Baumgarten's ontology, and traces its fate in Abbt, Maimon, and Hegel. A dazzling essay by Gary Hatfield compares the psychology of Descartes to that of Wolff and Baumgarten. Hatfield argues that Descartes 'in effect instigated a distinction between the mental and the psychological,' insofar his project included a 'machine psychology' that 'spreads its explanations for the functioning of the sensory and rational powers across mind and body' (pp. 62, 74). While Wolff and Baumgarten emerge in his history as important figures in the development of a psychology focused on analysis of conscious mental states, we must abandon a prevalent picture of Descartes as similarly separating psychology from physiological processes: Descartes is in fact the instigator of psychophysiological functional psychology.

This volume is an excellent companion to Fugate and Hymers' recent translation of Baumgarten's *Metaphysics*. English-speaking scholars of Kant and of eighteenth century German philosophy owe both of them a substantial debt.

Lore Hühn/Philipp Höfele/Jan Kerkmann

Fred Rush: *Irony and Idealism. Rereading Schlegel, Hegel, and Kierkegaard*. Oxford: Oxford University Press 2016. XVI + 312 S. ISBN: 978-0-19-968822-7

Dass ein poststrukturalistisches Denken, das jedes unmittelbar zugängliche Signifikat durchstreicht und jegliche systematische Schließung zurückweist, eine natürliche Affinität zur Reflexionsform der romantischen Ironie aufweist, ist seit Ernst Behler und Winfried Menninghaus ein offenes Geheimnis. Fred Rush hebt in seiner Monographie *Irony and Idealism. Rereading Schlegel, Hegel, and Kierkegaard* indessen hervor, dass bei allen Affinitäten der romantischen Philosophie und des Poststrukturalismus Vorsicht angesagt ist, nicht beides zu schnell über einen Leisten zu schlagen und der Romantik pauschal zu unterstellen, ihr ginge es um eine generelle konzeptuelle Destabilisierung und Abweisung überkommener Absolutheits- und Rationalitätsansprüche. Gegen die Schwarz-Weiß-Malerei und das Schubladendenken ‚romantisches Denken hier und idealistische Systemkonzeption dort' schreibt Rush mit jeder Zeile seiner Arbeit an und hebt vor allem mit Violetta Waibel darauf ab, dass sich das romantische Denken und die Ironie als dessen Reflexionsform zwar an den idealistischen Systemgebäuden insbesondere eines Fichte und Hegel abarbeiten, ohne aber deshalb als gänzlich ‚antisystematische' Denkform interpretiert werden zu müssen.

Vor dem Hintergrund dieses systematischen Anliegens unternimmt Rushs Werk *Irony and Idealism* den breit angelegten Versuch, eine Funktionsbestimmung und kritische Reflexion der Ironie anhand von drei zentralen philosophiegeschichtlichen Knotenpunkten der Neuzeit zu leisten. Unter dem Titel „Jena Romanticism and the Philosophical Significance of Irony" (vgl. S. 13–100) wendet sich der erste der drei Teile der Untersuchung der ‚Herausbildung' der Jenenser Romantik aus der fichteschen Subjektivitätsphilosophie zu. Obgleich auch Friedrich von Hardenbergs *alias* Novalis' Akzentuierung der diskursiven Uneinholbarkeit des Absoluten in dessen *Fichte-Studien* (vgl. S. 27–38) eine explizite Berücksichtigung erfährt, bilden doch den thematischen Schwerpunkt des ersten Teils Friedrich Schlegels Konzeption des Wechselgrundsatzes, die Rechtfertigung der ‚unendlichen Annäherung' sowie die Darlegung der Aussagekraft des Fragments (vgl. S. 39–89). Der „Irony Discplaced, or Hegel" überschriebene zweite Teil (vgl. S. 101–210) arbeitet anschließend Hegels ambivalente Beurteilung der frühromantischen Konstellation im Allgemeinen und die dort verhandelte Bestimmung der Ironie im Besonderen heraus. Dabei rekurriert Rush auf die historischen und begrifflichen Horizonte für Hegels Verständnis der Jenenser Romantik (vgl. S. 122–127), um jene Elemente verorten zu können, die Hegel im Moralitätskapitel der *Phänomenologie des Geistes* für seine Kritik an dem kraftloseitlen Attentismus der ‚schönen Seele' heranzieht. Zugleich hebt Rush hervor, dass Hegels dialektische Ontologie im Hinblick auf die Theorie des Widerspruchs und auf die sich durch fortwährende Selbstentzweiung bewährende Bewusstseinskonstitution gravierende Überschneidungen mit frühromantischen Auffassungen besitzt und nicht allein als deren unvermittelbarer Gegensatz aufzufassen ist (vgl. S. 155–168). Der dritte und letzte Teil der Untersuchung „Irony Redivivus, or Kierkegaard" (vgl. S. 212–284) konzentriert sich schließlich mit Søren Kierkegaard auf jenen Autor, der neben Friedrich Schlegel die wohl ambitioniertesten und philosophisch bedeutsamsten Überlegungen zur Ironie vorgelegt hat. Hierzu verfolgt Rush die Wandlung in Kierkegaards Betrachtung der Ironie von der Dissertationsschrift *Über den Begriff der Ironie mit ständiger Rücksicht auf Sokrates* bis hin zu ihrer Erhebung zum *confinium* zwischen den Existenzsphären des Ästhetischen und des Ethischen. Als zweiter Hauptstrang des dritten Teils kann die detaillierte Analyse der für die Ironie wesentlichen Momente der Unmittelbarkeit, der Distanz und der Möglichkeit in Kierkegaards Werk *Entweder – Oder* markiert werden. Neben dem hedonistischen Existenzentwurf reiner Unmittelbarkeit, der sich paradigmatisch im Typus des Don Giovanni (vgl. S. 218–221) verdichtet, beleuchtet Rush die Ironiedisposition der ‚reflektierten Ästhetiker' Faust und Johannes aus dem *Tagebuch des Verführers*, wozu ihm Kierkegaards Theorie der *Wechselwirkung* als aufschlussgebendes Interpretationsinstrument dient (vgl. S. 230 ff.).

Die drei Teile der Monographie suchen dabei vier in dem einleitenden Abschnitt „Introductory Remarks" vorab entwickelte Leitthesen zu plausibilisieren, die sowohl zur Strukturierung der einzelnen Kapitel beitragen als auch tradierte, etwa durch den Poststrukturalismus inspirierte Forschungsansichten in Frage stellen sollen. Die erste These wird von Rush unter dem Gesichtspunkt eines „Regulative Romanticism" (S. 7) vorgetragen. Während zumeist Fichtes Wissenschaftslehre und dessen Lehrtätigkeit in Jena als „strongest proximate impetus to their [der Frühromantiker] initial philosophical activity" (S. 7) exponiert werden, betont Rush den grundlegenden Einfluss von „Kant's account of regulative principles and reflective judgement" (S. 7). Vor diesem Hintergrund deutet er Schlegels Kritik an der fichteschen Grundsatzprogrammatik als Geltungsradikalisierung des regulativen Vernunftgebrauchs. Die Destabilisierung eines suisuffizienten ersten Prinzips der Philosophie werde im Falle Schlegels durch Einsichten in den kontingent-historischen und tendenziell unabschließbaren Auffassungssinn des Absoluten angereichert. Rush veranschaulicht diese hermeneutisch-pragmatische Dimension in seiner Diskussion des Wechselgrundsatzes. Mit diesem 1796 (im Rahmen der Rezension von Jacobis *Woldemar*) eingeführten Topos optiert Schlegel für eine dyadische Systembegründung (vgl. S. 43 f.). Fichtes thetisch-unbedingter Satz ‚Das Ich setzt sich selbst' müsse durch das ebenbürtige, praktische Postulat ‚Das Ich soll sich setzen‘ ergänzt werden, wobei keiner der Sätze eine für sich stehende Evidenz fordern könne. Der zweite Satz beschreibt die Operation, die zur Annahme des ersten Satzes immer schon vollendet sein muss. Umgekehrt bedingt der erste Satz den zweiten, weil das Ich sich bereits zu etwas bestimmt haben muss, um zum Empfänger einer Forderung avancieren zu können. Da das Ich den Akt der bewussten und beschränkenden Bestimmung aufgrund seiner unbegrenzten Tätigkeit nicht selbst initiieren kann, ist es auf den „Anstoß *[check]*“ (S. 21) einer limitierenden Gegenwirkung ange-wiesen. Als externe (obzwar durch das Ich auf das Ich zurückbezogene (vgl. S. 21) Instanz verwehrt diese Anstoßkraft die vollständige Selbstdurchsichtigkeit des Ich, weswegen sich das entäußerte Postulat des umfassenden Seinsollens aus-gerechnet in dem iterierten Streben nach seiner Aufhebung ununterbrochen fortproduziert. In diesem Zuge richtet Rush den Fokus auf Schlegels Differenzie-rung zwischen dem ‚Prinzip‘ (welches mit dem ersten Relat des Wechselgrund-satzes identifiziert wird, vgl. S. 45) und der ‚Idee‘ (die dem zweiten Relat ent-spricht). Der Anfangspunkt kann nach Schlegel nicht als unverrückbare ἀρχή oder als „ontological ground from which the very possibility of subjectivity springs“ (S. 45) erschlossen werden. Die Wahl des Beginns verdankt sich keiner Deduktion aus der Unbezweifelbarkeit des ‚Ich bin‘, sondern beruht auf dem ursprünglichen „Gefühl eines Mangels *[a feeling of lack]*“ (S. 46), das sich als Sehnsucht nach dem Unendlichen enthüllt. Der Aufforderungscharakter der Selbstsetzung manifestiert sich unter anderem darin, dass zwar ein provisorisches Prinzip installiert werden muss, dieses jedoch von vornherein nur als „first ex-periential point in an infinite series of such points that stem from it“ (S. 45) be-trachtet werden kann. Die Idee, wonach das Ich sein soll, kann also nicht in der ersten Setzung verwirklicht worden sein, weil diese eine ultimative Kontingenz darstellt. Dergestalt entfaltet sich die Figur eines universalen Progresses, der durch eine doppelte Unendlichkeit in Gang gehalten wird: Das Gefühl der sub-jektiven Insuffizienz setzt die Ahnung frei, dass das Absolute „as a totality complete in itself“ (S. 46) keiner vereinzelten Erfahrung zugänglich sein kann. Deswegen muss die Annäherung an das Absolute selbst eine unendliche Bewe-gung exemplifizieren, deren „constant constructive activity“ (S. 46) sich in der Kreation einer „plenitude of different structures that find their roots in the ab-solute“ (S. 46) artikuliert. Es ist das Fragment, das Rush zufolge diesen asym-ptotischen Prozess inmitten des perspektivischen Wechselgeflechts der Gegen-satzpaare von Begrenzung und Unendlichkeit sowie von Einzelheit und Ganzheit versinnbildlicht:

> Any whole of which an individual fragment is a fragment is 'infinite', accordingly, in the
> two senses always pertinent for Schlegel: (A) 'infinite' because it is in principle beyond

statement from a finite point of view and (B) 'infinite' because its surpassing of definitive statement within the system, coupled with the inherent human propensity to attempt to grasp the absolute, means that it will generate more and more interpretations of the absolute, thereby increasing the components, and therefore the density, of the system. [...]

Any fragment, taken by itself, is both a system and not a system. It is 'not a system' in the sense that it is presented as a fragment, as a part of some greater whole that can, because of its status as a part, only obliquely give an indication of the whole. A fragment is 'a system' in the sense that it also presents itself as a complete entity because of the way it focuses thought. (S. 84 f.)

Der Ironie kommt die ebenfalls unerschöpfliche Aufgabe zu, diesen produktiven Widerspruch innerhalb des Kosmos der Fragmente hervorzubringen, anzusteuern, festzustellen, auszubalancieren und erneut zu umreißen. Die affirmative Ausrichtung der Ironie parallelisiert Rush mit dem Totalitätsanspruch des in sich abgerundeten Fragments, das sich nach Schlegel wie ein „Igel *[hedgehog]*" (S. 84) nach außen abschirmt und auf diese Weise sich selbst bestimmt. Indem die Aussage eines Fragments affirmiert wird, wird dieses situativ als vollendete Wesenserfassung der Welt, als kristallisierte Monade verstanden, wodurch die Suggestion der „definitive nature of 'complete' utterances" (S. 84) entsteht. Demgegenüber korrespondiert die distanzierende Komponente der Ironie der „incompleteness" (S. 84) des Fragments. Jedes Fragment ist durch eine sich selbst transzendierende Semantik und durch eine produktive Bedeutungsirritation gekennzeichnet. Das Fragment indiziert Rush zufolge ein „missing piece" (S. 84), das es selbst zwar nicht direkt thematisiert, auf das sich jedoch jeder Interpretationsansatz verwiesen sieht.

Die zweite, „*The Precedence of Schlegel*" überschriebene These (vgl. S. 8 f.) baut insofern auf der erstgenannten auf, als sie Friedrich Schlegel zur Schlüsselfigur der Frühromantik erhebt und damit die geläufige Priorisierung Novalis' bestreitet. Diese Bedeutungsverschiebung begründet Rush mit der ‚Relevanzvertiefung' der schlegelschen Ironiekonzeption. Ironie erfülle nicht allein die systemerodierende Funktion einer Einklammerung philosophischer Absolutheitsansprüche und dürfe daher nicht in erster Linie als Vehikel eines unverbindlichen Relativismus aufgerufen werden. Darüber hinaus erschöpfe sie sich auch nicht darin, das ausgezeichnete Reflexionsmedium der ‚Unverständlichkeit' (d.h. der unermesslichen Perspektivenvielfalt respektive der unlimitierten Interpretationsmöglichkeiten) des Kunstproduktes zu repräsentieren. Vielmehr könne Schlegels Begriff der Ironie, wie er sich besonders in der Werkphase von 1796–1801 widerspiegle, als Ausdrucksmittel der „relation between self-consciousness and belief" (S. 8) gefasst werden. Da die Ironie als ‚*epideixis* der Unendlichkeit' die jeweilige Positionierung des sich als wesentlich begrenzt erfahrenden Bewusstseins zum sich permanent entziehenden Absoluten explizieren kann und diese temporäre Standpunktfixierung zugleich aufzulösen imstande ist, wird ihr der eminente Praxisbezug einer „existential orientation" (S. 8) zugesprochen.

Unter dem Titel *„Hegel's Irresolute Romanticism"* (vgl. S. 10 f.) führt des Weiteren die dritte These die bis in die Gegenwart hineinreichende Marginalisierung der philosophischen Dignität der Frühromantik zuvorderst auf die wirkmächtige Ausstrahlung des hegelschen Verdikts zurück. So werden gerade im zweiten Teil des Buches die Gründe für Hegels „misunderstanding" (S. 10) der Romantik transparent gemacht. Als bemerkenswerte Gemeinsamkeit profiliert Rush dabei, dass sowohl Hegel als auch Friedrich Schlegel die unhintergehbare, dialektische Struktur der Vernunft konstatieren. Doch während Hegels Dialektik die Bedingungen für die Schließung des Systems diktiere und ihren Erfolg anhand der Einbettungsfähigkeit des Wahrheitsgehalts anderer Theorien bemesse (vgl. S. 10), leiste Schlegels dialektische Ironie das Gegenteil, indem sie ein System von Fragmenten generiere, das „inherently prospective and tentative" (S. 10) verfasst sei. In dieser provokanten Offenheit entdeckt Rush ein hervorstechendes Motiv für Hegels Ablehnung der Romantik: Hegel konzediere Schlegel durchaus, zur Wesensstellung dialektischen Denkens vorgedrungen zu sein. Der zentrale Vorwurf Hegels lautet, dass Schlegel inkonsequent bleibe, weil er nicht in der Lage sei, ebenjene Bedingungen für die Selbstvermittlung des Systems anzugeben und dessen Autotelie methodisch zu begleiten. In dem verborgenen Dissens über die ‚wahre' Dialektik wurzelt denn auch Rush zufolge Hegels Präsentation der Romantik in der Gestalt der ‚schönen Seele', die in der scheinbaren Integrität der reinen Innenwelt kreist, weil sie die Befleckung des wahren Motivationskerns ihres Handelns durch den verändernden Einbruch der Wirklichkeit fürchtet („the conatus of the Beautiful Soul is to seek refuge from the world of action and judgement in a community", S. 130). An dieser Stelle zeichnet sich für Rush allerdings das Potenzial einer Re-Adressierung des Inkonsequenz-Vorwurfes ab. Eine resolute und redliche Dialektik wäre demzufolge gerade dadurch charakterisiert, innerhalb der von Kant gezogenen Grenzlinien zu agieren.

Der dritte Teil profiliert schließlich die vierte *„Kierkegaard the Ironist"* betitelte These (S. 12), bei der Rush von einer „evolution" (S. 12) in Kierkegaards Gewichtung der Ironie ausgeht. Kierkegaards Beurteilung der romantischen Ironie verhält sich Rush zufolge durchaus proportional zu seiner Emphase für die Philosophie Hegels. So übernehme Kierkegaard in seiner Dissertation nicht nur die Dialektik Hegels, sondern referiere in seiner Klassifizierung der romantischen Ironie als ‚unendliche absolute Negativität' auf hegelsche Interpretationsvorgaben (vgl. den Abschnitt „Irony: Kierkegaard's Initial View", S. 237 ff.). Damit konvergiert das in der Dissertation gezeichnete Eigenschaftsbild des Sokrates. Nach Kierkegaard begibt sich Sokrates mit Hilfe einer habitualisierten Ironieausübung in eine sich selbst immunisierende, verantwortungsentbundene Schwebehaltung und evoziert durch den verborgenen, der Dechiffrierung bedürftigen Hintersinn seiner Aussagen einen esoterischen Kreis der Zugehörigen. Die Distinktionsstiftung zwischen dem externen, verbalen Akt und dem impliziten Bedeutungsgehalt ist folglich nur ein vordergründiger Aspekt der sokratischen Ironie. Im Hinblick auf das Gefüge der Polis wirkt Sokrates' ironische Praxis als sozialer und politischer Bifurkationsfaktor. Für die Eingeweihten, die aufgrund ihrer „mental quickness" (S. 239) die verlautbarte Sinnverkehrung intuitiv revidieren, äußert der Ironiker Sokrates keineswegs das Gegenteil des eigentlich Gemeinten. Demgegenüber kann der überwiegende Teil des Publikums niemals eine Gewissheit darüber erlangen, ob und wann Sokrates' Fragen und Argumente einem kalkulierten Täuschungsmanöver zuzurechnen sind. Wenn den Hörern *ex post* erläutert und offenbart wird, was ihnen in Sokrates' Rede zunächst enigmatisch erschien, potenziert sich die herabmindernde Erfahrung „to feel inferior in intellect und social status" (S. 238).

Gleichwohl darf Rush zufolge nicht übersehen werden, dass Kierkegaard bereits in der Dissertation eine Relativierung der kritischen Bestandsaufnahme der Ironie zulässt, indem er diese als subversives Mittel und als „skeptical impulse" (S. 244) instantiiere, um politische Systeme und dominierende Ideologeme in indirekter Weise angreifen zu können. Im Spätwerk Kierkegaards diagnostiziert Rush eine gewichtige Aufwertung der Ironie, die nicht mehr als Flucht in die folgenlose Poetisierung der Wirklichkeit oder als Inbegriff der Absenz des für die adäquate Verhältnisbildung zu Gott erforderlichen Ernstes problematisiert wird. Stattdessen gestattet die Ironie, die Rush als Weiterentwicklung der letzten Station des reflektierten Ästhetikers deutet (vgl. S. 255), eine existenzielle Befreiung. Die Ironie bildet das primäre Imaginationsvermögen, um von sich selbst (und damit auch von dem rastlos-unentschiedenen Oszillieren zwischen den Möglichkeiten) Abstand zu nehmen und sich die eigene Lebensform – nach Maßgabe des Entwurfs der *Wechselwirtschaft* – unter der Bindung an das Allgemein-Ethische *vor*zustellen, ohne sich dieser Existenzsphäre schon faktisch *unter*stellt zu haben. Dergestalt öffne die Ironie „the door to being ethical" (S. 255).

Nicht allein im Blick auf Kierkegaard unternimmt Rush so den Versuch, die Ironie nicht ausschließlich dem Bereich des Ästhetischen zu überantworten. Vielmehr zeigt die von ihm vorgelegte Monographie einmal mehr, dass die Reflexionsform der Ironie nicht nur ein literaturtheoretisch interessantes Paradigma darstellt. Auch wenn gerade Experten auf diesem Gebiet wie etwa Behler, Bohrer und Wellek maßgebliche Arbeiten zur Romantik und deren Reflexionsformen vorgelegt haben, ist die Ironie doch zugleich ein Thema, das ins Zentrum der Philosophie reicht, ohne dass diese mit deren Integration in den postmodernen Strom einer generellen Leugnung alles Systematisch-Rationalen einmünden müsste. Bei allem Respekt vor der interpretatorischen Leistung ist jedoch kritisch anzumerken, dass Rush die Forschungsliteratur seines Themas höchst selektiv aufgenommen und verarbeitet hat. Die Nähe von Hegels und Kierke-gaards Negativitätstheorien, insbesondere deren Figur einer ‚unendlichen abso-luten Negativität', zur romantischen Reflexionsform ist in der deutschen und dänischen Forschung breit diskutiert,[1] ohne dass diese kontroverse Debatte Ein-gang in die Überlegungen Rushs gefunden hätte. Seine Arbeit hätte deutlich an philosophischer Tiefe gewonnen, wenn sie sich hinsichtlich der europäischen Idealismus- und Romantik-Forschung weniger Zurückhaltung auferlegt hätte und etwa auch die Arbeiten von Bernhard Lypp, Winfried Menninghaus und Philipp Schwab näher zur Kenntnis genommen hätte.[2]

---

1 Cappelørn, Niels J./Deuser, Hermann/Söderquist, K. Brian (Hrsg.) (2009): *Kierkegaard Studies. Yearbook 2009 (Kierkegaard's Concept of Irony)*, Berlin/New York: De Gruyter.
2 Lypp, Bernhard (1972): *Ästhetischer Absolutismus und politische Vernunft. Zum Widerstreit von Reflexion und Sittlichkeit im deutschen Idealismus*, Frankfurt am Main; Menninghaus, Winfried (1987): *Unendliche Verdopplung. Die frühromantische Grundlegung der Kunsttheorie im Begriff absoluter Selbstreflexion*, Frankfurt am Main; Schwab, Philipp (2008): „Innen und Außen. Zu Kierkegaards Auseinandersetzung mit der romantischen Ironie vor dem Hintergrund der Mittei-lungsform von *Entweder/Oder*", in: *Kierkegaard Studies. Yearbook 2008*, S. 38–52; ders.: „Zwi-schen Sokrates und Hegel. Der Einzelne, die Weltgeschichte und die Form der Mitteilung in Kierkegaards *Über den Begriff der Ironie*", in: *Kierkegaard Studies. Yearbook 2009 (The Concept of Irony)*, S. 127–152; ders.: „Der ‚ganze Kierkegaard im Keim' und die Tradition der Ironie. Grund-linien der deutschsprachigen Rezeptionsgeschichte von Kierkegaards *Über den Begriff der Ironie*", in: *Kierkegaard Studies. Yearbook 2009 (The Concept of Irony)*, S. 373–492.

Stefan Lang

David James and Günter Zöller (eds.): *The Cambridge Companion to Fichte*. Cambridge: Cambridge University Press 2016. xx, 419 pp. ISBN: 978-0-521-47226-5 Hardcover. ISBN 978-0-521-47805-2 Paperback.

Seit einigen Jahren ist in der englischsprachigen Philosophie ein zunehmendes Interesse an Fichte deutlich bemerkbar. Der von David James und Günter Zöller herausgegebene Sammelband reagiert auf diese erfreuliche Entwicklung und wird sie verstärken. Das Ziel der Herausgeber ist es, die englischsprachigen Leserinnen und Leser in Fichtes Philosophie einzuführen und Fichte als gegenüber Schelling und Hegel gleichwertigen systematischen Denker der philosophischen Entwicklung nach Kant auszuweisen (S. 1–2). Sie haben dieses Ziel erreicht. Der Sammelband bewältigt souverän die anspruchsvolle Aufgabe, in Fichtes vielschichtiges Werk einzuführen und Schlüsselthesen, zentrale Begriffe sowie die Beziehungen zwischen Fichte und seinen Zeitgenossen zu erläutern. Zudem enthält er starke Thesen, die Anlass zu wichtigen Debatten geben. Es steht außer Frage, dass der Band zu den Referenzwerken der Fichte-Forschung zu zählen ist und Eingang in die Forschung und Lehre finden wird.

Zu den Beiträgen des Bandes: Wayne Martin und Frederick Beiser untersuchen Fichtes frühe Schriften. Martin gibt einen instruktiven Überblick über die Entwicklung von Kant zu Fichte und stellt zentrale Einflüsse auf Fichtes Philosophie dar wie Jacobis Kantkritik, Reinholds Elementarphilosophie, Schulzes skeptische Einwände und Creuzers *Skeptische Betrachtungen über die Freiheit des Willens*. Zudem erläutert er wichtige Aspekte von Fichtes Kritik an Reinhold und Schulze sowie von einem Schlüsselbegriff von Fichtes Philosophie, dem Begriff der Freiheit. Beiser legt die enge Beziehung dar, die zwischen Fichtes Wissenschaftslehre und seinen frühen politischen Ansichten, insbesondere über die Französische Revolution besteht. Er verteidigt den Standpunkt, „that his [Fichtes] political aims could not be achieved without his epistemology, and that his epistemological ends could not be accomplished without his politics." (S. 40) Beisers zentrale These lautet, dass allererst durch moralische und politische Handlungen das Skeptizismus-Problem gelöst werden könne, mit dem Fichtes Philosophie ringe (S. 52).

Christian Klotz, Daniel Breazeale und Günter Zöller untersuchen Fichtes Darstellungen der Wissenschaftslehre. Ihre Beiträge sind allen, die sich mit Fichtes Wissenschaftslehre auseinandersetzen (möchten), zu empfehlen. Klotz stellt gut fasslich zentrale Anliegen, Aussagen, aber auch systematische Spannungen innerhalb der *Grundlage der gesamten Wissenschaftslehre von 1794/95* („Grundlage") dar. Er erläutert nicht nur die drei Grundsätze und die zentralen

Thesen des theoretischen und des praktischen Teils, sondern auch den Einfluss Kants, Reinholds und Schulzes. Von seinen insgesamt überzeugenden Ausführungen kann an dieser Stelle nur eine Überlegung erwähnt werden. Nach Klotz ist es u. a. Fichtes Ziel, anhand von Tätigkeiten des Subjekts die repräsentationale Struktur des Bewusstseins zu begründen (S. 68). Zu diesen Tätigkeiten zählt die berühmte Tathandlung, die Klotz als einen performativen Akt deutet.[1]

Breazeale untersucht Fichtes *Wissenschaftslehre nova methodo* (Wlnm). Er erläutert wichtige Unterschiede zwischen Fichtes und Kants Theorien sowie zwischen der „Grundlage" und der Wlnm. Breazeale skizziert die Struktur und Bestandteile von Fichtes Jenaer System sowie die Zielsetzungen, Inhalte und den Aufbau der Wlnm. Abschließend diskutiert er offene Fragen der Fichte-Forschung (S. 127). Angesichts dieser großen Anzahl an Themen verwundert es nicht, dass Breazeale starke Behauptungen aufstellt, die nicht näher begründet werden, obgleich sie diskussionswürdig sind. Breazeale behauptet beispielsweise, dass der Ausdruck ‚intellektuelle Anschauung', der in der Wlnm verwendet wird, (in einer Hinsicht) „a synonym for the pure I, qua *Tathandlung*" (S. 107) sei, die Fichte in der „Grundlage" darstellt. Diese These ist nicht unumstritten.[2]

Zöller untersucht Fichtes spätere Darstellungen der Wissenschaftslehre. Er erläutert den Einfluss Jacobis, Platons, Spinozas und insbesondere Schellings auf den mittleren und späten Fichte. Seine These lautet, dass Fichte zentrale Begriffe der Theorien dieser Philosophen übernimmt (wie beispielsweise Jacobis Begriff des Lebens), sie jedoch aus der Perspektive der Wissenschaftslehre interpretiert und in seine Theorie integriert. Zöller weist überzeugend die Annahme zurück, Fichte habe in seinen späteren Darstellungen der Wissenschaftslehre seinen Standpunkt grundsätzlich geändert und Anschluss an die vorkritische metaphysische bzw. theologische Tradition gesucht. Dementgegen betont er die „Identität" (S. 144) von Fichtes früherem Projekt und seinen späteren Darstellungen der Wissenschaftslehre. Hervorzuheben ist seine glasklare Erläuterung von Fichtes Verständnis des Absoluten. Zöllers These besagt, das Absolute sei auch beim späten Fichte keine eigenständige ontologische oder theologische Entität, sondern die grundlegende logisch-epistemische Eigenschaft unbedingter Gültigkeit, die mit der Funktion des absoluten Ichs der „Grundlage" durchaus kompatibel sei (S. 154).

---

1 Werner Stelzner hat m. W. als Erster eine performative Interpretation der Tathandlung entwickelt. Vgl. Werner Stelzner: „Selbstzuschreibung und Identität". In: W. Hogrebe (Hg.): *Fichtes Wissenschaftslehre 1794. Philosophische Resonanzen*. Frankfurt/M.: Suhrkamp 1995.
2 Vgl. beispielsweise Dieter Henrich: „Fichtes ursprüngliche Einsicht". In: D. Henrich/H. Wagner (Hg.): *Subjektivität und Metaphysik*. Frankfurt/M.: Vittorio Klostermann 1966.

Zu den Stärken des Bandes zählt, dass zentrale Schriften Fichtes und Bestandteile seines Systems in mehreren Beiträgen aus unterschiedlichen Perspektiven untersucht werden. Dadurch wird ihr systematischer Zusammenhang deutlich erkennbar. Beispielsweise erläutern Allen W. Wood und Jean-Christophe Merle von jeweils unterschiedlichen Schwerpunktsetzungen ausgehend u. a. Fichtes Vertragstheorie oder auch seinen Eigentumsbegriff (S. 178, 203–204), und mehrere Autoren, insbesondere Alexander Aichele, behandeln Fichtes berühmt-berüchtigte *Reden an die deutsche Nation*, die teilweise unterschiedlich bewertet werden. Wood erörtert Fichtes Vertragstheorie und Eigentumsbegriff im Rahmen seiner klaren und inhaltsreichen Einführung in Fichtes Politische Philosophie, Rechtsphilosophie und Ethik. Im Zentrum seines Beitrags steht die Darstellung der *Grundlage des Naturrechts* (1796/97) und des *Systems der Sittenlehre* (1798). Er erläutert jedoch auch ihre Beziehung zur „Grundlage" und Unterschiede gegenüber Fichtes späteren Schriften wie beispielsweise seiner *Rechtslehre* (1812). Instruktiv ist seine bündige Erörterung von Schlüsselbegriffen wie der Anerkennung, Pflicht, Rechtsbeziehung oder des Strebens und des Triebs, die im Zentrum der deutschen Philosophie um 1800 standen.

Merle analysiert Fichtes Modell einer politischen Ökonomie in *Der geschlossene Handelsstaat*. Eine wichtige These lautet, Fichtes ökonomische Theorie sei nicht primär von der politischen Ökonomie seiner Zeit beeinflusst, sondern gründe auf seiner Rechtstheorie, d. h. dem Begriff des Eigentums (S. 200). Merle erläutert ausführlich Fichtes Auffassung dieses Begriffs und Unterschiede gegenüber Kants Definition. Zudem begründet er, warum Fichtes ökonomisches Modell keine Utopie ist, und er erläutert, wie Fichte sich die Organisation und die Einführung eines geschlossenen Handelsstaats vorstellt. Bemerkenswert ist seine These, Fichtes Theorie sei weder kommunistisch noch kapitalistisch, sondern mit beiden Modellen inkompatibel (S. 209).

Ein weiterer Vorzug des Bandes besteht darin, dass Fichtes Beiträge zu wichtigen Themen erläutert werden, die in der Forschung vergleichsweise wenig untersucht werden. Beispielsweise stellt Wood Fichtes Beurteilung des Selbstmordes dar und Ives Radrizzani Fichtes Philosophie der Geschichte. Radrizzani untersucht die Fragen, ob eine Philosophie der Geschichte auf der Grundlage der Wissenschaftslehre überhaupt möglich ist und welchen Ort die Geschichte und insbesondere die Zukunft innerhalb von Fichtes philosophischem System einnehmen (S. 222). Eine Philosophie der Geschichte habe eine Deduktion der transzendentalen Struktur der Geschichte zu enthalten. Da Fichte sie nicht in systematischer Form ausgeführt habe, stellt Radrizzani sich die Aufgabe, zu rekonstruieren, wie sie aussehen könnte. Zudem erläutert er ausführlich die zeit-diagnostische Funktion dieser Theorie und ihre Bedeutung für ein zentrales An-

liegen von Fichte, nämlich zur Realisierung von Freiheit und Vernunft aktiv bei-
zutragen.

Auch Hansjürgen Verweyen berücksichtigt bei seiner Darstellung von Fichtes
Philosophie der Religion seine Interpretation der Geschichte, und zwar inso-
fern sie der Ort göttlicher Offenbarung ist. Verweyen stellt zudem anhand einer
Untersuchung von Fichtes *Versuch einer Kritik aller Offenbarung*, des berühmten
Atheismusstreits und der *Anweisung zum seligen Leben* die Entwicklung von
Fichtes Gedanken zur Religion dar und er erläutert die ihr zugrunde liegenden
Problemstellungen sowie Unterschiede gegenüber Kants Standpunkt. Eine zen-
trale These von Verweyen lautet, dass für Fichte die Religion nicht eine Vorstufe
gegenüber dem absoluten Wissen darstelle, vielmehr sei sie dieses absolute
Wissen selbst. Für Fichte bestehe dem Gehalt nach kein Unterschied zwischen der
Offenbarung und der Philosophie (S. 288, 298).

Die Beiträge von Elizabeth Millán, Sebastian Gardner und David James erläutern die Beziehungen zwischen Fichte und der Frühromantik, Schelling sowie
Hegel. Millán stellt Fichtes Einfluss auf die Frühromantik dar. Sie berücksichtigt Hölderlin, Novalis und Schlegel. Während einerseits Fichtes Betonung der
menschlichen Freiheit begrüßt werde, sei andererseits sein Einfluss v. a. anhand
der frühromantischen Kritik an seiner Philosophie erkennbar. Millán referiert
daher zentrale Einwände von Hardenberg, Hölderlin und Schlegel. Dazu zählen
u. a. Hölderlins berühmte Kritik in „Urteil und Seyn" an Fichtes These, das absolute Ich sei das erste Prinzip der Philosophie, und Novalis' sowie Schlegels
Kritik an Fichtes Entwicklung eines philosophischen Systems von einem obersten
Prinzip ausgehend (S. 310, 318–319), die, wie Millán zeigt, von Carl Christian
Erhard Schmid beeinflusst ist. Die Frage, ob diese Einwände gegen Fichtes Philosophie überzeugen, wird von Millán nicht diskutiert.[3]

Gardners Beitrag ist der Debatte zwischen Fichte und Schelling gewidmet.
Er untersucht v. a. ihren Briefwechsel und ihre frühen Schriften. Schwerpunkte
seines Aufsatzes bilden die kursorische Darstellung von Schellings Schriften bis
1801, Schellings Kritik an Fichte sowie von Unterschieden zwischen Fichte und
Schelling, die bereits mit ihren frühen Schriften vorliegen und den im Jahr 1802
erfolgten Abbruch ihrer Beziehung vorbereiten. Gardners Eingangsthese lautet,
dass Fichte und Schelling in dem Punkt übereinstimmen, dass sich ihre Theorien
insbesondere durch ihre unterschiedlichen Antworten auf die Frage nach der
Realität der Natur in Opposition befinden (S. 326). Abschließend beantwortet er

---

3 Eine solche Diskussion von Hölderlins Kritik an Fichte findet sich bei Jürgen Stolzenberg:
„Selbstbewusstsein ein Problem der Philosophie nach Kant. Zum Verhältnis von Reinhold –
Hölderlin – Fichte". In: K. Viertbauer (Hg.): *Präreflexives Selbstbewusstsein im Diskurs*. Freiburg/
München: Karl Alber 2018.

eine Fragestellung, die auch Beiser (S. 39) diskutiert, nämlich ob das absolute Ich der „Grundlage" existiert. Gardner entwickelt eine Interpretation, der es gelingt, Fichtes Aussagen, dass das absolute Ich einerseits existiert und andererseits eine Idee darstellt, die durch die praktische Vernunft realisiert werden soll, zu vereinbaren.

James untersucht die Beziehung zwischen Fichte und Hegel insbesondere mit Blick auf ihre berühmten Theorien der Anerkennung. James erläutert Fichtes Begriffe der Aufforderung und der wechselseitigen Anerkennung, ihren Einfluss auf Hegel in der *Phänomenologie des Geistes* (1807) und Hegels Bemühen, Probleme von Fichtes Theorie mit seiner eigenen Konzeption zu lösen. In James' Rekonstruktion spielt eine Aussage von Fichte aus der *Grundlage des Naturrechts* eine wichtige Rolle, deren Bedeutung in der Forschung umstritten ist. In einem Korollar untersucht Fichte die Frage „Wer erzog denn das erste Menschenpaar"? Seine Antwort lautet: „Ein Geist nahm sich ihrer an, ganz so, wie es eine alte ehrwürdige Urkunde vorstellt" (*Gesamtausgabe* I/3, S. 347–348). Nach James enthält Hegels Theorie des Kampfes um Anerkennung eine alternative genetische Erklärung der Anerkennungsbeziehung. Hervorzuheben ist James Untersuchung der Frage, wie Fichte und Hegel die Sklaverei beurteilen, die ein eindeutiges Beispiel für eine intersubjektive „Beziehung" darstellt, die kein Fall von wechselseitiger Anerkennung ist. James zeigt, dass ihre Einschätzungen der Sklaverei vielschichtig und durchaus problematisch sind (S. 368, 370).

Paul Franks Verteidigung von Fichtes Philosophie gegenüber klassischen Einwänden wie etwa von B. Russell bildet den gelungenen Abschluss des Bandes. Franks diskutiert den wirkmächtigen Einwand, der besagt, Fichte entwickle eine subjektivistische Theorie. Eine Theorie ist subjektivistisch, „if it regards every possible thing as capable of existence only within a mental realm, to which philosophy has a privileged access akin to the privileged access we are said to have to our own minds" (S. 374). Franks widerlegt diesen Einwand, indem er zeigt, dass Fichte weder die kreativistische Position vertritt, dass der Geist seine bewussten Objekte erzeugt, noch den konflationistischen Standpunkt, gemäß dem Bewusstsein stets Selbstbewusstsein darstellt, noch die internalistische Überzeugung vertritt, dass mentale Gehalte unabhängig von der Bestimmung extramentaler Realität bestimmt bzw. individuiert werden können. Franks leistet durch seine klare Argumentation einen wichtigen Beitrag zu Fichtes „Revival" in der Gegenwartsphilosophie, indem er ungerechtfertigte Vorurteile pointiert widerlegt.

Abschließend ist eine kritische Anmerkung zu formulieren. Der Verlag *Cambridge University Press* verspricht der Leserin/dem Leser, dass „all the major aspects of Fichte's philosophy" berücksichtigt werden. Dieses anspruchsvolle Versprechen kann in *einem* Band nicht eingelöst werden. Ich erwähne ein Thema und zwei Autoren, die in dem Band nicht hinreichend behandelt werden. Es handelt sich zum einen um Fichtes Auffassung des methodischen Verfahrens der Philosophie, das mit dem Programm einer Geschichte des Selbstbewusstseins sowie den Begriffen der Deduktion und der Konstruktion in der Anschauung verbunden ist, zum anderen handelt es sich um Salomon Maimon und Ernst Platner, deren Einfluss auf Fichte nicht übersehen werden darf (vgl. S. 105). Auch in der schmalen Bibliographie werden Schlüsselwerke der Forschung nicht erwähnt. Angesichts der ausgezeichneten Qualität der meisten Beiträge und der Vielfalt an Themen und Autoren, die berücksichtigt werden, schmälern diese Anmerkungen jedoch nicht die Bedeutung des Sammelbandes, der allen an Fichte Interessierten mit Nachdruck zu empfehlen ist.

Charles Larmore

Béatrice Longuenesse: *I, Me, Mine. Back to Kant, and Back Again.* Oxford University Press 2017. ISBN: 978-0-19-966576-1.

In his lectures on the history of philosophy, Hegel remarked that when we come to Descartes, we feel like sailors who after a long voyage on stormy seas can finally cry out, "Land ahoy!" Descartes, he declared, was the first to articulate the modern principle that self-consciousness is an essential element of our relation to the world. Yet how much can our awareness of ourselves as thinking beings, however indubitable it may be, tell us about what we are really like? On this matter, Kant held a more modest view than Descartes. Béatrice Longuenesse's new book is a closely argued and engaging study of his theory of self-consciousness. She aims to show what we can still learn from Kant in this area – both from his insights and from his failings. Her book falls into three parts, mirrored in its subtitle, "Back to Kant, and Back Again". In the first, she surveys the contributions of several 20th century philosophers – Wittgenstein, Sartre, Anscombe, and Evans – to an understanding of the uses of "I" in expressing awareness of our own thinking. The second part is devoted to examining Kant's account of the nature of self-consciousness along with his corresponding criticisms of his predecessors, particularly in the sections of the *First Critique* on the "paralogisms of pure reason". With one notable exception, having to do with our sense of ourselves as moral beings, Longuenesse largely endorses Kant's views. It is in order to propose a remedy to what she considers his chief mistake that she returns in the third part to another 20th century figure, namely Freud. His theory of the *ego* and the *id*, while coinciding with Kant's position in important respects, also provides in her opinion the resources to improve it. Kant may be Longuenesse's philosophical hero. But he too comes in for critique.

Descartes held famously that in perceiving that I am thinking this or that, I can be certain of my own existence as a being who thinks. But he then went on to use this certainty as a basis for establishing what as a thinking being my nature essentially is. This, as Longuenesse explains, was in Kant's view the fatal error committed not just by Descartes, but by the many rationalist metaphysicians, in particular Leibniz, who followed his lead. I am not really in a position to conclude, given the indubitability of my existence as a thinking being, that I am a single substance – as opposed to a composite of different substances – or that I remain the same being over time – as opposed to a series of distinct entities each able to communicate its consciousness to the next. Such is the core of Kant's argument in his sections on the paralogisms. Certainly I cannot avoid attributing the thinking of which I am reflectively aware, at a given time or over an extended period, to a single thinking being who is myself. But this fact, as Longuenesse puts it in contemporary terms, only expresses how I view myself from a first-person standpoint. To know, she claims, whether I am in fact a single substance enduring over time, I must look at myself from a third-person standpoint, acquiring evidence as to whether I am indeed one substance or instead a composite and locating myself spatially as one body among others in order to be able to re-identify myself as the same body over time. When Kant distinguished between consciousness of myself "as subject" and consciousness of myself "as object", he meant this difference between first-person and third-person perspectives on myself, the latter being necessary if I am to determine, so far as experience can say, what sort of being I fundamentally am. (What I am like "noumenally", apart from being an object of experience, was for Kant of course unknowable.)

Now what I am aware of, according to Kant, in reflecting on myself is not just my various mental states, but also my very activity of thinking. In particular, I can then become conscious of what he called the syntheses of apprehension, reproduction, and recognition by which I combine various representations in order to arrive at concepts and judgments. One of Longuenesse's central concerns is to underscore how I can exercise this first-person awareness of my synthetic activity as a thinking being without having to regard myself, from a third-person standpoint, as an embodied entity occupying some position in space along with other objects. In practice, I move easily back and forth between the two perspectives. And, as noted, I cannot grasp my fundamental nature except from the third-person point of view. But I need not rely on knowledge of the particular empirical person I am, in order to be able to refer, without risk of misidentification, the mental states and thinking activity of which I am aware to myself as a thinking being. As she states on the first page of this book (p. xi), Kant's insight into the independence of these two kinds of self-consciousness – as subject and as object – is what started her on its writing. And near the end (p. 231), she declares it to be his "groundbreaking legacy" to "have identified a type of self-consciousness that is distinct from bodily self-consciousness although intimately connected with it". This is "the consciousness of being engaged in bringing rational unity into the contents of one's mental states".

There is, however, some unclarity about just what sort of knowledge, if any, Longuenesse believes our consciousness of ourselves as subjects gives us of the beings who we are. That for Kant it does not give us knowledge of what we are fundamentally like is clear. But does it give us no self-knowledge at all? Longuenesse allows that the "I" in "I think" does indeed "refer to" (p. 146), "attest" to (p. 118), give us "access to" (p. 87), or "represent" (pp. 107, 131) an "existing" thing or entity that thinks. If "we don't thereby know what kind of entity the self is" (p. 112), this must mean that our self-consciousness as subjects does not disclose to us what kind of entity we fundamentally are, what our "essence" is (p. 87). For it certainly – at least according to Kant – shows us something true about ourselves, namely, that as thinking beings we "synthesize" what is given to us in experience in order to arrive at concepts and judgments (p. 86). Yet Longuenesse also asserts that it does not allow us to derive "any knowledge of the nature of the referent of 'I'" (p. 6), that on its basis "we have no knowledge at all about the kind of entity we are" and that "the entity represented by 'I' remains thereby unknown" (p. 132). Such denials appear over-stated since, again, our self-consciousness as subjects purportedly informs us correctly that as thinking beings we "synthesize the manifold". It would seem more sensible to say, as she does at one point, that "in the context of the prop-osition 'I think', the predicate 'think' adds *nothing further* to our knowledge of the nature of the referent of 'I'" (p. 102, my emphasis). That is, "it tells us neither that the referent of 'I' is *only* a thinking thing, nor that it is anything besides a thinking thing" (her emphasis).

In short, our first-person perspective on ourselves as thinking beings does give us some knowledge of what we are like. It simply falls short of giving us knowledge of our fundamental nature. True, we cannot help but attribute the mental life of which we are reflectively aware, both at the moment and over time, to a single thinking being that is ourselves. But it is also true that we would be wrong to conclude that each of us is therefore a single enduring sub-stance. Drawing that conclusion is falling prey to the paralogisms Kant diag-nosed. What we are fundamentally like can be fully known only from the out-side, by examining from a third-person standpoint how we are related to other entities in the world. At times Longuenesse acknowledges that our knowledge of ourselves depends on a combination of first-person and third-person perspec-tives (pp. 150–151). But this means it is wrong for her to say that how I must re-flectively think of myself, as the single subject of all my mental states and activ-ity, "tells me nothing about what I *am*" (p. 119). It seems wrong to dismiss this self-conception, as she does twice on that page, on the grounds that "thinking doesn't make it so" (see also p. 164). This notion of ourselves is not unfounded. Whatever may be my ultimate constitution, insofar at least as I am a thinking being the mental life of which I am reflectively aware must all count as be-longing to the single thinking being I am. If this were not so, if our first-person perspective did not give us this knowledge of ourselves considered just as think-ing beings, then by the same token it could not also be said to apprise us, as Lon-guenesse believes it does, of the mental activity by which we synthesize various elements of our experience in order to "come up with concepts, combined in judgments, connected in inferential patterns" – precisely what she calls

"Kant's groundbreaking thesis in the Transcendental Deduction of the Categories" (pp. 4, 231).

In the *First Critique* (A 365–366, quoted on p. 152), Kant asserted that our first-person conception of ourselves as the single, enduring subject of our mental life, even though it is insufficient to settle what at bottom our nature really is, has nonetheless an essential practical function. It sustains our understanding of ourselves as moral beings. For we cannot regard ourselves as subject to the moral law unless, according to Kant, we suppose we are free, and free in the radical sense of being responsible for initiating by our actions a series of events without being determined by antecedent conditions. Any empirical, third-person knowledge we acquire about our nature would, by contrast, involve situating us in the causal order and thus cancel out this supposed freedom of self-determination. Such is the point on which Longuenesse takes Kant to task. She even accuses him of "a paralogism of pure practical reason" (p. 152). We need, she holds, to base even our self-understanding as moral beings ultimately on what we can learn about ourselves empirically. In other words, we have to recognize how our sense of moral right and wrong and our capacity to act accordingly are the result of our interactions with others, particularly those involving the childhood internalization of authority figures in our environment. It is on this score that in the third part of her book she turns to Freud.

I think Longuenesse is right to criticize Kant on these grounds. But I have some reservations about the way she goes about it. First, the choice of Freud seems to me arbitrary, since richer and more plausible accounts of how our moral consciousness develops through internalizing the perspectives of others are to be found, I believe, in Adam Smith and George Herbert Mead. Second, she characterizes her approach as "naturalizing" Kant's conception of moral personhood (pp. 166, 173, 176). "Naturalism" is these days all the rage. But the notion has difficulties, not the least of them being how it can make sense of such basic things as reasons, which are objective yet normative and thus not identifiable with the physical and psychological phenomena that are the objects of the natural sciences. All that she may mean by the term, as she suggests in one passage (p. 227), is seeing moral personhood as part of the causal order. That is better. But it brings me to a third point. She claims that we can dispense with Kant's belief that our moral self-understanding requires a radical idea of freedom if we find "a way to account for the notion of self-determination [...] without appealing to Kant's notion of absolute spontaneity" (p. 156, also p. 165). Yet she never says what this more modest idea of moral freedom would be. And how it could count as an idea of "self-determination" seems puzzling, if it is to consist in a freedom that involves being determined by antecedent causes.

III. Anhang/Appendix

Autoren/Authors

Prof. Willem deVries
University of New Hampshire
Philosophy Department
95 Main St
Durham, NH 03824
USA
willem.devries@unh.edu

Prof. Dr. Dina Emundts
Freie Universität Berlin
Institut für Philosophie
Habelschwerdter Allee 30
14195 Berlin
Germany
dina.emundts@fu-berlin.de

Prof. Dr. Daniel Feige
Akademie der Bildenden Kunst Stuttgart
Campus Weißenhof: Neubau 2
Raum 0.13
Am Weißenhof 1
70191 Stuttgart
Germany
daniel.feige@abk-stuttgart.de

Prof. Gary Hatfield
University of Pennsylvania
Department of Philosophy
Cohen Hall 433
Philadelphia, PA 19104 – 6304
USA
hatfield@sas.upenn.edu

Prof. Desmond Hogan
Princeton University
Department of Philosophy
206 Marx Hall
Princeton, NJ 08544
USA
deshogan@princeton.edu

Dr. Philipp Höfele
Albert-Ludwigs-Universität Freiburg
Philosophisches Seminar
Platz der Universität 3
79085 Freiburg
Germany
Philipp.hoefele@philosophie.uni-freiburg.de

Prof. Dr. Lore Hühn
Albert-Ludwigs-Universität Freiburg
Philosophisches Seminar
Platz der Universität 3
79085 Freiburg
Germany
Lore.huehn@philosophie.uni-freiburg.de

Jan Kerkmann
Albert-Ludwigs-Universität Freiburg
Philosophisches Seminar
Platz der Universität 3
79085 Freiburg
Germany
Jan.kerkmann@philosophie.uni-freiburg.de

Dr. Manja Kisner
Ludwig-Maximilians-Universität München
Fakultät für Philosophie, Wissenschaftstheorie und Religionswissenschaft
Geschwister-Scholl-Platz 1
80539 München
Germany
Manja.Kisner@lmu.de

Prof. Patricia Kitcher
Professor of Philosophy
Columbia University
708 Philosophy Hall
1150 Amsterdam Avenue
New York, NY 10027
USA
pk206@columbia.edu

Prof. Katharina T. Kraus
University of Notre Dame
Department of Philosophy
309 Malloy Hall
Notre Dame, IN 46556
USA
Kkraus2@nd.edu

PD Dr. Stefan Lang
Martin-Luther-Universität Halle-Wittenberg
Seminar für Philosophie
Emil-Abderhalden-Str. 26a
06108 Halle/Saale
Germany
Stefan.lang@phil.uni-halle.de

Prof. Charles Larmore
Brown University
Department of Philosophy
Corliss Bracket 218
45 Prospect St.
Providence, RI 02912
USA
Charles_larmore@brown.edu

Prof. Andreja Novakovic
University of California, Berkeley
Philosophy Department
314 Moses Hall, MC 2390
Berkeley, CA 94720 – 2390
USA
andreja@berkeley.edu

Dr. Julia Peters
Eberhard Karls Universität Tübingen
Philosophisches Seminar
Bursagasse 1, Zi. 216
72070 Tübingen
Germany
Julia.peters@uni-tuebingen.de

Prof. Jeffrey Reid
University of Ottawa
Department of Philosophy
Desmarais Building, room 8101
55 Laurier Ave. East
Ottawa, ON Ontario, K1N 6N5
Canada
jreid@uOttawa.ca

Prof. Dr. Georg Sans SJ
Hochschule für Philosophie München
Kaulbachstraße 31a
80539 München
Germany
georg.sans@hfph.de

Dr. Johannes-Georg Schülein
Ruhr-Universität Bochum
Institut für Philosophie I (Raum GA 3/54)
Universitätsstraße 150
44801 Bochum
Germany
johannes-georg.schuelein@rub.de

Prof. Sally Sedgwick
Boston University
Department of Philosophy
745 Commonwealth Avenue, Room 516
Boston, MA 02215
USA
ssedgw@bu.edu

Prof. Dr. Dieter Sturma
Rheinische Friedrich-Wilhelms-Universität Bonn
Institut für Wissenschaft unbd Ethik (IWE)
Bonner Talweg 57
53113 Bonn
Germany
dieter.sturma@uni-bonn.de

Prof. Daniel Whistler
Department of Philosophy
Royal Holloway, University of London
Egham, Surrey
TW20 0EX
GB
Daniel.Whistler@rhul.ac.uk

Hinweis an die Verlage/Letter to Publishers

Wir möchten alle Verlage bitten, uns auf Neuerscheinungen aufmerksam zu machen, in denen der Deutsche Idealismus Thema ist.

We request publishing houses to inform us of new materials related to the theme of German Idealism.

https://doi.org/10.1515/9783110673692-023